This book brings together contributions from researchers in anthropology, psychology, communications, sociology, and cognitive science who are interested in redefining the methods and topics that constitute the study of work. They investigate work activity in ways that do not reduce it to a "psychology" of individual cognition or a "sociology" of societal structures and communication (whether "micro" or "macro").

A key theme in the material is the relationship between theory and practice. This is not treated as an abstract problem of interest merely to social scientists. Instead, it is discussed as an issue that working people address when they attempt to understand a task and communicate its demands. Mindful practices and communicative interaction are examined as situated issues at work in the reproduction of communities of practice in a variety of work settings including courts of law, computer software design, scientific laboratories, health care repair and maintenance of advanced manufacturing systems, the piloting of airliners, the coordination of air traffic control, baggage handling, and traffic management in underground railway systems.

Cognition and communication at work

# Cognition and communication at work

*Edited by*
YRJÖ ENGESTRÖM
DAVID MIDDLETON

CAMBRIDGE
UNIVERSITY PRESS

Published by the Press Syndicate of the University of Cambridge
The Pitt Building, Trumpington Street, Cambridge CB2 1RP
40 West 20th Street, New York, NY 10011-4211, USA
10 Stamford Road, Oakleigh, Melbourne 3166, Australia

First published 1996

Printed in the United States of America

*Library of Congress Cataloging-in-Publication Data*

Cognition and communication at work / edited by Yrjö Engeström, David
  Middleton.
      p.   cm.
    ISBN (invalid) 0-521-44104-8
    1. Communication in organizations.   2. Interpersonal
communication.   3. Symbolic interactionism.   I. Engestrom, Yrjö,
1948–    .   II. Middleton, David.
    HD30.3.C56   1996
    658.4'5—dc20                                                95-25574
                                                                   CIP

A catalog record for this book is available from the British Library

ISBN 0-521-44109-6 Hardback

# Contents

# Contributors

**Susanne Bødker**
Department of Computer Science
Aarhus University
Aarhus, Denmark

**Yrjö Engeström**
Department of Communication and
 Laboratory of Comparitive Human
 Cognition
University of California, San Diego
La Jolla, California

**Joseph Glick**
Graduate School and University
 Center
City University of New York
New York, New York

**Charles Goodwin**
Department of TESL and
 Applied Linguistics
University of California, Los Angeles
Los Angeles, California

**Marjorie Harness Goodwin**
Department of Anthropology
University of California, Los Angeles
Los Angeles, California

**Kaj Grønbæk**
Department of Computer Science
Aarhus University
Aarhus, Denmark

**Christian Heath**
School of Social Studies
University of Nottingham
Nottingham, England

**Edwin Hutchins**
Department of Cognitive Science
University of California, San Diego
La Jolla, California

**Tove Klausen**
Centre for Cognitive Informatics
Roskilde University
Roskilde, Denmark

**Edith A. Laufer**
Laboratory of Cognitive Studies of
 Activity
City University of New York
New York, New York

**Paul Luff**
School of Social Studies
University of Nottingham
Nottingham, England

**David Middleton**
Department of Human Sciences
Loughborough University
Loughborough, England

**Chandra Mukerji**
Department of Communication
University of California, San
   Diego
La Jolla, California


**Leena Norros**
State Technical Research Centre
Espoo, Finland


**Arne Raeithel**
Department of Psychology
Hamburg University
Hamburg, Germany

**Harley Shaiken**
Department of Education
University of California, Berkeley
Berkeley, California

**Susan Leigh Star**
Department of Sociology and
   Program in Women's Studies
University of Illinois,
   Urbana–Champaign
Urbana, Illinois

**Lucy Suchman**
Xerox Palo Alto Research Center
Palo Alto, California

# Acknowledgments

We gratefully acknowledge and thank all those persons who have patiently contributed to the preparation of this volume, especially the authors for their generous cooperation, and all our colleagues at the following academic departments and research groups: the Department of Communication and the Laboratory of Comparative Human Cognition at the University of California, San Diego; the Department of Education and the Centre for Activity Theory and Developmental Work Research at the University of Helsinki; and the Developmental Studies Group at Loughborough University. We are also most grateful for the interest and effort of Julia Hough at Cambridge University Press and Paul Schwartz of Ampersand Graphics in the production of this volume. Finally, we thank Georg Engeström for permission to reproduce his work on the book cover.

# 1  Introduction: Studying work as mindful practice

*Yrjö Engeström and David Middleton*

The authors contributing to this volume represent a growing concern within anthropology, psychology, communications, sociology, sociology of science, and cognitive science for redefining the methods and topics that constitute the study of work. They investigate work activity in ways that do not reduce it to a "psychology" of individual cognition or a "sociology" of communication (whether "micro" or "macro") and societal structures. The chapters aim to demonstrate approaches that have moved beyond such Cartesian orthodoxies. Mindful practices and communicative interaction are examined as situated issues at work in the reproduction of communities of practice in a wide variety of work settings including courts of law, health care, computer software design, scientific laboratories, telephone sales, control, repair, and maintenance of advanced manufacturing systems, the piloting of airliners, air traffic control, baggage handling, traffic management in underground railway systems, and auto-engine assembly plants.

## Sociology of work

In sociological studies of work, two broad traditions may be identified: macrolevel discussions of the impact of technological development on the skills and organization of work and microsociological analysis of locally constructed and negotiated work activities. The macrosociological discussions [sometimes dubbed the labor-process debate (Wood, 1982; 1989)] have moved from general assessments of automation to more differentiated analyses of "post-Fordism," flexible production, and "lean production" (e.g., Warner, Wobbe, & Brodner, 1990; Womack, Jones, & Roos, 1991; Berggren, 1992).

There is also continuing sociological analysis and debate concerning historical changes in the patterning and social positioning of work (see, for example, Adler, 1992). However, important issues appear to remain outside the conceptual and analytical terms of reference of such discussion. What is missing are issues of human agency embedded in the everyday actions and interactions of people doing work in various organizational positions and settings.

## Human agency and interaction

Largely independent of the macrodebate on technology and the labor process, a microsociological discourse on work evolved. Central to this development is the work Everett Hughes (1958, 1971) and other sociologists of the "Chicago" school. They approached work and occupations as locally constructed and negotiated activities. Rooted in the common philosophical foundation of Dewey's and Mead's pragmatist theory of action (Strauss, 1991, 1993), this perspective provided the theoretical impetus for a number of detailed ethnographies of work based on participant observation in a range of settings (e.g., Becker et al., 1961; Glaser, 1976; Strauss et al., 1985; Harper, 1987).

The developing ethnomethodological discussion also made work an important focus of microsociological debate and empirical study. Garfinkel (1986, p. vii) wrote that "there exists a locally produced order of work's things; that they make up a massive domain of organizational phenomena; that classic studies of work, without remedy or alternative, depend upon the existence of these phenomena, make use of the domain, and ignore it." In exploring the "locally produced order of work's things," ethnomethodological debate shifted the focus onto detailed analyses of the use of language and representational practices in interaction (e.g., Lynch, Livingston, & Garfinkel, 1983; Lynch, 1985; Pollner, 1987).

From the general theoretical assumptions of ethnomethodology, conversation analysis (CA) emerged as a rigorous perspective for the study of talk in interaction. Recent CA publications have tackled varieties of talk in institutional settings. Talk-in-interaction is analyzed as "the central medium through which the daily working activities of many professionals and organizational representatives are conducted" (Drew & Heritage, 1992, p. 3).

In these microsociological approaches, contexts and structures of work are regarded as outcomes of local interactions and negotiations. Claiming that social action and interaction are formative of social structure inverts the relationship between interaction and social structures compared to those found in macrosociological arguments (Strauss, 1993, p. xii). However, within the rich texture and detail of microsociological historical issues – constantly addressed in the macrosociological literature on technological development and skills – are very often absent. This is manifested in the absence of studies on major technological and organizational transformations in workplaces. Contrasting the studies of human agency in work with those primarily concerned with transformations of work over time can be characterized as a comparison between agency-driven microsociology-without-history and historically relevant macrosociology-without-agency.

## Rejoining agency and history

The chapters in this book signal a change in this regard. Many are certainly rooted in microsociological traditions. They emphasize local interaction, negotiation, and talk. Yet, they are also representative of an emerging sensitivity to incorporate analysis of transitions and changes in work. They also represent a concern to examine reflexive relationships between situated research practices and transitions and changes attendant upon rapidly evolving new technologies and organizational forms. This new concern is manifest in many studies concerned with "computer-supported cooperative work" (CSCW) (Greif, 1988; Bowers & Benford, 1991; Schmidt & Bannon, 1992; see also Button, 1993).

This volume also highlights that interest in such issues extends beyond debates exclusively focused within various aspects of the sociological literature. Situated studies of work practices in transformation has become the focus of research across a range of literatures including psychology, communication, cognitive science, computer science, linguistics, anthropology, and education. Discipline boundaries cease to contain the areas of research when the concern is not so much in "doing" a discipline but with the way human practices emerge as work: as societally located and socially intelligible actions of reasoning and communication. In exploring issues that transcend disciplinary orthodoxies, previously underrepresented theoretical traditions, such as activity theory (Engeström, Miettinen, & Punamäki, in press), become topical and new theoretical approaches, such as distributed cognition (Hutchins, 1994), are articulated and examined.

**Practice**

"'Practice! Practice! More practice!' Such is the inscription on the flag of the new battalion of students coming from the sociology, philosophy, and history of science" (Latour, 1993, p. 487). It is no accident that the notion of "practice" has become central in such related fields of inquiry as social studies of science and technology (Pickering, 1992) and culturally oriented studies of learning and cognition (Lave, 1988; Lave & Wenger, 1991; Chaiklin & Lave, 1993). Analyzing culturally mediated work practices does not accommodate directly issues of agency and history within the same analytical stance. Rather, it is a beginning of a search for more integrative and boundary-crossing units of analysis, conceptual tools, research methods, and alliances. As Pickering (1992, pp. 6–7) points out, what is needed are "new conceptual frameworks, frameworks built out of concepts that speak directly to practice." The search leads to questioning such basic dichotomies as subject:object and nature:society.

**Mindfulness**

Various aspects of analyzing work as culturally mediated practice may be distinguished. First, taking local human agency into account requires a consideration of the "mindfulness" of human action (remembering, reasoning, seeing, learning, inventing, etc.). The human practices of work are analyzable in terms of the social intelligibilities of mindful practices.

However, "mind" enters work in a very different manner than within Cartesian and "cognitivist" notions of rational planning and goal-oriented action. Cartesian rationalism breaks down with the recognition that the "cognitive" does not reside inside the heads of individuals. "Cognition" is analyzable as distributed between individuals and between humans and their artifacts (Cole & Engeström, 1993; Hutchins, 1994; Latour, 1987; Middleton & Edwards, 1990; Resnick, Levine, & Teasley, 1991). Cognitive action incorporates the manipulation of artifacts and representational media in the communicative construction of socially intelligible meanings. Work practices are ineluctably communicative practices (Weick & Roberts, 1993). The extent to which such action is termed private and "internal" mental process is a function of the manner in which individuals are located as participants in culturally mediated practices.

## Artifacts

Dichotomies between instrumental and communicative actions are not very useful in this perspective. Work practices are mediated by technological artifacts. Artifacts range from notational systems and special vocabularies to machines and buildings (Gagliardi, 1990). Many of them have the potential of "making people smart" (Norman, 1988); none of them guarantee it. Information technologies provide a crucial demonstration of these two aspects of artifacts – the semiotic and the instrumental forming layers of mediation in new and complex ways.

Artifacts can come to embody the stable and structural in work practices. In Leont'ev's (1978) terms, they may be seen as "crystallized operations." However, artifacts are not just there. They are invented, purchased and put in use, they wear out, they are discarded and replaced by new ones. Thus, there is an ongoing dialectic between what is taken to be structural or processual, stable or dynamic, representational or discursive forms in work practices. The authors represented in this volume variously address these dilemmas of work action: of stabilization in routine or skilled performance on the one hand and disruption, innovation, and change on the other.

## Expertise

The notions of expertise and skill are put in a radically new light in the chapters of this volume. Cognitivist accounts of expertise as stable individual mastery of well-defined tasks (Chi, Glaser, & Farr, 1988; Ericsson & Smith, 1991) give way to a view of expertise as ongoing collaborative and discursive construction of tasks, solutions, visions, breakdowns, and innovations.

## Continuity and change

Both continuity and change can be analyzed within a single work practice, as internal systemic achievements. However, an analysis of a local practice often leads to the discovery of "a whole social network of resources beyond the confines of the . . . setting" (Laufer, this volume). It becomes necessary to trace the connections of the work practice to other practices and thus to discover and construct networks of practices. While challenging both theoretically and empirically, such a move does not have to lead to an abandonment of the principle of local agency. In social studies of science and technology, the actor network theory of Callon (1992) and Latour (1992; see also Grint, 1991) represents an attempt in this direction.

## Data sources

Many of the chapters in this volume use transcripts of conversations from work practices as their primary data. These strips of discourse are regularly embedded in thick ethnographic descriptions of the institutional setting and flow of work actions. Several chapters focus on the dilemmatic, argumentative, and contradictory aspects of talk at work, pointing to the nature of work practices as continuous problem solving and resolution of local crises. The transcripts also bring out multiple voices from the communities of work practice. Many of the papers exemplify an effort to conduct what Clifford (1988) termed "dialogical" and "polyphonic" ethnography, "surrendering large spaces of the ethnographic text to direct . . . transcriptions of the informants' voices" (Hess, 1992, p. 9). In some of the chapters, the multivoicedness of work practices is highlighted by means of systematic comparisons. These include analytic contrasts between the viewpoints of workers situated in different locales and roles, between novices and experts, between two plants, and between cultural setting.

## Modalities in presentation

Throughout the chapters, transcripts of talk are complemented and enriched by visual representations of work settings and specific sequences of interaction. This complementarity of textual and graphic modes of representation is a distinctive expansion of the more traditional models of discourse and conversation analysis. The visual representations employed by the various authors range from straightforward use of photographs to diagrammatic conceptual models. It seems that focusing on the mediational roles of artifacts clearly calls for multiple modalities, for "thinking with eyes and hands" (Latour, 1986). Visual representations serve a reflexive function in that they break down the tight flow of written argument, forcing both the writer and the reader to stop and look, and then to realign the two modalities.

## Doing work and research

The chapters illustrate the study of work as produced in the local pragmatics of communication concerning "what it is to know what to do" as distributed within the reproduction and continuing creation of communities of practice. In doing this, the chapters demonstrate an integration of previously separated domains: work as a topic for members of communities of practice and as a topic of study. Thus, a particular concern of the volume is to examine the reflexive relationship between research methodologies that analyze work as situated practice and their impact on that practice.

## Settings

The empirical chapters in this volume explore "the doing" of thinking, learning, and communicating in a variety of work settings. Two theoretical chapters (by Susan Leigh Star and Arne Raeithel) provide concluding theoretical commentaries on the issues raised and findings presented in the empirical chapters.

"Distributed Cognition in an Airline Cockpit" by Edwin Hutchins and Tove Klausen (Chapter 2) is a case study that illuminates the analytic possibilities of a new approach in cognitive science. In his earlier research on the organization of work, Hutchins developed a theory of distributed cognition that takes as its unit of analysis a culturally constituted functional group rather than an individual mind. This theory reconceptualizes "information" as the propagation of representational states of mediating structures that make up the dynamic and substance of any complex system. These structures include internal as well as external knowledge representations, (knowledge, skills, tools, etc.). This approach permits descriptions of knowledge generation by tracing the movement of representations of states of affairs through a system and characterizes the organization of the system that affords performance, as individual members and as a functioning group.

In previous work Hutchins (1990, 1995) examined the distributed nature of navigation procedures on a large ship. In the study presented here, the focus shifts to another complex work setting, that of flying an aircraft. Again, the emphasis is on the way members of the air crew and ground staff handle uncertainty in the coordination of their actions in safely flying the aircraft. The functional group of the cockpit crew exercises its expertise in flexible ways within conventionalized patterns of command and division of labor. Hutchins and Klausen argue that to understand the flexible expertise within a cockpit system involves more than an account of any putative cognitive properties of the individual pilots, second officers, and air traffic controllers. The cognitive properties of the functional group that makes up the cockpit system "are also determined by the physical properties of the representational media across which the task-relevant representational state is propagated, by specific organization of the representations supported in those media, by the interactions of metarepresentations held by the members of the crew, and by the distributional characteristics of knowledge, and access to task relevant information across the members of the crew." Crucial, then, to such an analysis is a consideration of the technological artifacts that afford varieties of representations concerning the current state of the plane over the duration of any particular journey.

Lucy Suchman's pathfinding book, *Plans and Situated Actions* (1987), adopted an ethnographic analysis based on insights drawn from ethnomethodology in the analysis of human–machine communication. The overall conclusion of her analysis of our interactions with complex technologies was that the structure of action could not be explained either in terms of existing cognitive schema or as determined by institutionalized social norms. The work Suchman reports here (Chapter 3) adopts this perspective in an analysis of the way shared work spaces are interactionally produced in the service of joint work. The airline industry once again comes under close scrutiny, but this time it is work activity of the ground-operations room of a mid-sized metropolitan airport in the United States. Handling the vagaries of schedule changes and breakdowns cannot be predetermined or dealt with in a random manner. Suchman's aim is to examine the accomplishment of order within episodes of routine trouble through a detailed analysis of a particular episode of a plane arriving at a gate and the routine difficulties encountered in coordinating deplaning the passengers. She examines how participants formulate an awareness of the problem from their own particular organizational and physical locales, and then develop a shared orientation to the situation and establish places for the achievement of coordinated work necessary to overcome those routine problems. She reveals how the centers of coordination cannot be conceived of as preestablished but are continually reconstituted within the complex dynamic of relations of technology, persons, and space.

Charles Goodwin and Marjorie Harness Goodwin (Chapter 4) analyze the relations between skilled work and the material environments within which it occurs. Their data is drawn from a parallel study of the same work situation examined by Suchman. They share a concern to understand the ordered accomplishment of resources that are deployed in the coordination of jointly realized work. Their extension of conversation analytic insights to the taken-for-granted assumptions of how the objects of working practice (planes) are actually "seen" by ground-control operatives challenges the preconceptions of studies that assume those objects to have a nonproblematic status, either as objects of working concern or as a priori analytical categories. They approach seeing as an activity constructed within the complex dynamic of the operations room. In doing so they demonstrate that it is analyzable as an emergent property of the ordering of communicative interactions rather than dependent upon preexisting cognitive schema or cultural categories. In examining how airport personnel look at planes, behavior as minute as a momentary glance becomes significantly structured by organizational practices, by the tools mediating their contact with the working environment, and by the local community that sustains their working practice. Practitioners must learn to see in organizationally appropriate ways the routine scenes of their work. Goodwin and Goodwin argue that formulating task-relevant views is crucial to the accomplishment of collaborative work.

These authors apply conversation analytic techniques to human interactions while acknowledging their being situated within a material world shaped by the historical activities of others. In doing this they explore links between conversation analysis (CA), activity-theoretical concepts drawn from the writings of Vygotsky and Leont'ev, and the growing discussions on distributed cognition.

Two chapters (5 and 6) are also concerned with technological mediation of collaborative work. However, they address their discussions of empirical findings directly to implications for the design and development of technologies to support complex cooperative work activities.

Christian Heath and Paul Luff (Chapter 5) share the analytical approach of the previous two chapters in being concerned with ethnomethodologically oriented investigations of work practices and conversational interactions. They argue that despite technical advances in the area of system support for cooperative work, over the past few years there still has been relatively little understanding of the organization of collaborative activity in real-world, technologically supported work environments. They discuss the possibility of applying recent developments within sociology, and, in particular, the naturalistic analysis of organizational conduct and social interaction, as a basis for the design and development of tools and technologies to support collaborative work. Focusing on the Line Control Rooms of London Underground, a complex multimedia environment in transition, they begin to explicate the informal work practices and procedures whereby personnel systematically communicate information and coordinate a disparate collection of tasks and operations. Their investigations form the basis for the design of new tools to support collaborative work in the Line Control Rooms, technologies that are intended to be sensitive to the ordinary conduct and practical skills of London Underground personnel. This emphasis on ordinary work practices and situated conduct is argued to be the key to successful technological reform that has in the past been insensitive to such local and apparently mundane issues.

Susanne Bødker and Kaj Grønbæk (Chapter 6) are also concerned with tools for cooperative work. However, their direct concern is with development of computer software that is capable of supporting complex cooperative work situations. The chapter illustrates their approach by examining the design of computer support for casework in a technical department of a Danish municipality. Their analysis is doubly reflexive. They are embedded as researchers within the cooperative processes they are both designing, researching, and producing tools for.

In addition, the very activity of prototyping is used as a way of exploring and developing the work situation it is being formulated to support. Bødker and Grønbæk analyze cooperative prototyping wherein users are involved actively and creatively in design of the computer applications they might subsequently employ and in a reflexive analysis of the work situation they are involved with. The chapter examines situations that occur where openings for learning are created during the design process. The research methodology is based on a view of learning that is principally concerned with identifying innovations in practice in order to expand the range of application of that community of practice (Engeström, 1987). The authors deploy concepts derived from Activity Theory in order to discuss transformations of working practice. This activity-theoretic discussion is elaborated further in the next three chapters (7, 8 and 9) by Leena Norros, Edith Laufer and Yrjö Engeström.

Leena Norros's analysis (Chapter 7) concentrates on the disturbances to practice that occur as a result of the implementation of new technologies in industrial work processes. She argues that no matter how good the design of complex processes is, unpredictable future demands and potential design faults create uncertainty in the functioning of any system. It inevitably falls to the operators of any system to cope with the consequences of that uncertainty. The discussion is based on analysis of the way operators handle disturbances in the flexible manufacture of machine gears. Rather than viewing system disturbances as inevitably detrimental to plant functioning, the analysis demonstrates that they provide a basic resource for transforming both the flexible skills of the operator and the refinement of the production process itself. The analysis provides a basis for developing a model of system disturbance that can be used as a framework for developing operator expertise as part of collaborative working practices. In addition this model highlights that situated practice is enlivened by operator concerns that extend beyond the immediate demands of skilled performance. Operators' accountabilities to others, as employees and breadwinners, colleagues and citizens are also sources of practical uncertainty. The tension between these local and general concerns is examined in the mapping out of a model that both accounts for and can be used as a springboard for the development of operator expertise.

Edith Laufer's and Joseph Glick's contribution (Chapter 8) is also concerned with transformations in working practice from an activity-theoretic perspective. They focus on what is involved in "being" an expert in a community of practice. They provide a detailed comparison of novice and expert functioning in the production of cost estimates for customers seeking to purchase a complex range of manufactured fasteners (e.g., nuts, bolts, screws, washers, etc.). Through detailed ethnography, experimental modeling of the work setting, and interviews, they identify both what it is to do cost estimations on customer's orders and what it is to be an expert cost estimator in comparison to being a novice in this business setting. Their work challenges orthodox cognitive models of novice–expert differences as residing primarily in the quality and sophistication of their problem representation. Expert estimation is revealed as involving serendipity and guess-work. If the analytic focus remains on individual actions of what it is to do esti-mating, then the actions of expert estimators are not socially intelligible, they flout basic information requirements for producing an "accurate costing." The critical contribution of such guesswork can only be understood within an analy-sis of what it is to be an estimator within a culture of business practice. Laufer and Glick demonstrate how the analytic concepts developed within the frame-work of activity theory afford an analysis of work practices that bridges individ-ual–societal dualisms.

Yrjö Engeström's (Chapter 9) continues the analysis of expertise as realized in joint rather than individual activity. This comparative study of courts of law in Finland and California examines the range and variability of participants' (both the judiciary and the defendants) orientation or voice in formulating the issues and procedure in drunk-driving cases. Engeström identifies and compares the varieties of voices these two judicial locations generate in dealing with their work loads. Differing deployment of voices and the handling of mismatches be-tween unpredictable features of a case and inflexible procedural rules, judicial instruments, and divisions of labor provide both an analytical framework and participants' resources for working out what collective procedures might be available to resolve dilemmas within particular cases and current practice. The analysis of disturbances within the flow of routine procedure is again seen to be the key to understanding human expertise as ordered within the contingencies of local rather than general circumstances. Expertise is argued to be understood as formulable as part of ordered social interactions rather than preexisting cognitive schema and as containing the basis for the creative generation of new ways of doing things rather than depending upon the orthodoxy of received wisdom.

The final three empirical chapters deal directly with accomplishment of col-lectivity in work settings.

David Middleton's chapter (Chapter 10) examines examples of unscheduled conversations about team work recorded in a multidisciplinary Child Develop-ment Centre (CDC) at a British National Health Service (NHS) hospital. The analysis examines the construction of collectivity in team practice that occurs through the argumentative structure and content of team conversations. Two spe-cific issues are discussed. First, an analysis is made of the consequences of con-versationally realized argumentation for the way team members generated and maintained common knowledge for current cases and procedures. The analysis then focuses on the rhetorical resources available to team members in improvis-ing interim solutions to unexpected problems. The analytic perspective adopted examines "team practice" as a topic of concern within teams. This involves tak-ing account of the way members formulate what is to do the teamwork. In deal-ing with uncertainties in the representation of practice, team members' talk gives voice to contradictory and dilemmatic aspects of team practice. Attempting to evade or resolve such contrary themes involves argumentation in the way speakers account for their practice and are able to distance themselves from the contradictory consequences of those accounts. The overall conclusion is that teams should be understood performatively as constructed in and through the multiple occasions on which members define them and debate their definitions.

Chandra Mukerji's chapter (Chapter 11) focuses on dilemmas of collectivity and individualization of practice in scientific laboratories. She reports on a detailed ethnographic study examining work within scientific research laboratories. Such collaborative work has been the focus of much research energy in the recent past, especially within the sociology of scientific knowledge (SSK). Those studies have examined the production of "scientific knowledge" as a social object that develops collectively from group relations and patterns of communication. Her analysis recognizes the value of this work but argues that focusing on the local production of knowledge leads to ignoring the larger cultural meaning of science and the social meanings of scientists who enter into everyday interaction and communication. She argues that scientific findings only make sense and have authority within particular cultural frames. Scientists are argued to make sense of what they do using cultural assumptions about the importance of science, scientific method, and scientific thought. How they do this and its consequences are the focus of analytical attention. Through observations and interview data on oceanographers, an examination is made of the convergence of the production of knowledge and the culture of science in everyday activities of laboratory workers. The attribution of the collective thinking undertaken in laboratories to the "chief assistant" is discussed as one means of reproducing the notion of "scientific genius" as a "cultural type." Central to the discussion is the notion of "laboratory signatures." These identify the way different laboratories develop and use idiosyncratic combinations of research techniques, theoretical allegiances, and empirical goals. This notion provides a way of linking the practices by which labs "think" about their topics to the cultural work that reproduces cultural images of science.

Harley Shaiken's contribution also explores the collective nature of skill in the automobile industry (Chapter 12). His discussion combines the concern of macrosociological studies of work organization and change with microsociological concerns to examine the local accomplishment and organization of work in the interactions of participants. He centers his analysis on a comparative study of two high-technology production plants established in the 1980's in Mexico by US car manufacturers. His long-term study tracks the way these plants achieved remarkable standards of output and quality and developed the collective skills base to support such output. Effective working of high-technology production facilities cannot be understood in terms of the Tayloristic separation of planning from doing. Interdependencies between advanced automated processes and distributed understandings of how to maintain those processes is a feature of the collective repertoire of operator skills. Shaiken analyzes the human agency that maintains and repairs the cultures of practice that is the key to the way advanced manufacturing facilities evolve into effective systems. He demonstrates that skill formation is located by participants as a collective concern, wherein communities of memory for know-how have to be actively worked on as participant concerns.

The theoretical chapter by Susan Leigh Star (Chapter 13) contrasts a range of theoretical concerns that have already been introduced in earlier chapters (the collective nature of "thinking" considered as "distributed cognition" and the material basis of social action and thought discussed in sociohistorical discussions of activity theory) with the perspective of American symbolic interactionism. The concern of the chapter is to create a dialogue between these orientations that can be seen as supporting movements that seek to establish a scientific coherence that is antideterministic, communitarian, and based in a situated pragmatic theory of action wherein behavior is only meaningful as situated. The main voice of the discussion is declared as coming from the perspective of American symbolic interactionism. For activity theory, American symbolic interactionism is rich in understanding the subtle differences between types of work and practice. Reciprocally, activity theory offers in its own right an approach that represents a sophisticated understanding of the historical and material specificity of cognition and a way to do away with arguments about perception and cognition that are either idealist or deterministic. The whole discussion is illustrated with reference to several classic interactionist studies of work and workplace culture from the 1950s. The often fragmented and multivocal resistances to rationalism and monovocalism are seen as already offering solid ground for a new coherence that transcends the dichotomies of organism/environment, individuality/collectivity, mind/body, and formal learning/everyday learning. The chapter explores the various ways in which these multiple voices both resonate and interfere with one another.

Arne Raeithel's concern (Chapter 14) is to examine the implications of ethnographic studies of cooperative work. In doing this, he too draws on the recent discussions of distributed cognition in addition to examining examples from the ethnomethodologically related field of science studies. The implications for developing ethnographies of work that analyze work as a topic of concern for participants lies at the center of his discussion. The overall concern is twofold. First, to highlight some of the characteristic features of semiotic cooperation in cooperative work. Second, to examine the application of methods widely used in ethnology and cultural anthropology to studies of the semiotic regulation of work practices. Raeithel demonstrates that such techniques afford a sounder methodological footing for investigating salient aspects of the semiotic regulation of cooperative work.

The last two chapters draw together a number of the main theoretical issues that were raised in the earlier empirical chapters. At the same time, the two theoretical chapters develop their own particular perspectives for further conceptualizations of work as practice. They sum up the challenges outlined in the volume and provide the basis for extending the range and application of the work presented.

## References

Adler, P. S. (Ed.) (1992). *Technology and The Future of Work.* New York: Oxford University Press.

Becker, H. S., Greer, B., Hughes, E. C., & Strauss, A. (1961). *Boys in White.* Chicago: University of Chicago Press.

Berggren, C. (1992). *Alternatives to lean production: Work Organization in the Swedish Auto Industry.* Ithaca, NY: ILR Press.

Bowers, J. M. & Benford, S. D. (Eds.) (1991). *Studies in Computer Supported Cooperative Work: Theory, Practice and Design.* Amsterdam: North-Holland.

Button, G. (Ed.) (1993). *Technology in Working Order: Studies of Work, Interaction, and Technology.* London: Routledge.

Callon, M. (1992). The dynamics of techno-economic networks. In R. Coombs, P. Saviotti, & V. Walsh (Eds.), *Technological Change and Company Strategies.* London: Academic Press.

Chaiklin, S. & Lave, J. (Eds.) (1993). *Understanding Practice: Perspectives on Activity and Context.* Cambridge: Cambridge University Press.

Chi, M. T. H., Glaser, R., & Farr, M. J. (Eds.) (1988). *The Nature of Expertise.* Hillsdale, NJ: Lawrence Erlbaum.

Clifford, J. (1988). *The Predicament of Culture.* Cambridge, MA: Harvard University Press.

Cole, M. & Engeström, Y. (1993). A cultural-historical approach to distributed cognition. In G. Salomon (Ed.), *Distributed Cognitions: Psychological and Educational Considerations.* Cambridge: Cambridge University Press.

Drew, P. & Heritage, J. (Eds.) (1992). *Talk at Work: Interaction in Institutional Settings.* Cambridge: Cambridge University Press.

Engeström, Y. (1987). *Learning by expanding: An Activity-Theoretical Approach to Developmental Research.* Helsinki: Orienta-Konsultit.

Engeström, Y., Miettinen, R., & Punamäki, R-L. (Eds.) (in press). *Perspectives on Activity Theory.* Cambridge: Cambridge University Press.

Ericsson, K. A. & Smith, J. (Eds.) (1991). *Toward a General Theory of Expertise: Prospects and Limits.* Cambridge: Cambridge University Press.

Gagliardi, P. (Ed.) (1990). *Symbols and Artifacts: Views of the Corporate Landscape.* New York: Aldine de Gruyter.

Garfinkel, H. (1986). Introduction. In H. Garfinkel (Ed.), *Ethnomethodological Studies of Work.* London: Routledge & Kegan Paul.

Glaser, B. (1976). *Experts Versus Laymen: A Study of the Patsy and the Subcontractor.* New Brunswick: Transaction Publishers.

Greif, I. (Ed.) (1988). *Computer Supported Cooperative Work: A Book of Readings.* San Mateo: Morgan Kaufman.

Grint, K. (1991). *The Sociology of Work: An Introduction.* Cambridge, UK: Polity Press.

Harper, D. (1987). *Working Knowledge: Skill and Community in a Small Shop.* Chicago: University of Chicago Press.

Hess, D. J. (1992). Introduction: The new ethnography and the anthropology of science and technology. In A. Rip, D. J. Hess, & L. L. Layne (Eds.), *Knowledge and Society: The Anthropology of Science and Technology.* Vol. 9. Greenwich, CT: JAI Press.

Hughes, E. C. (1958). Men and their work. Glencoe, IL: The Free Press.

Hughes, E. C. (1971). *The Sociological Eye: Selected Papers.* Chicago: Aldine-Atherton.

Hutchins, E. (1990). The technology of team navigation. In J. Galegher, R. E. Kraut & C. Egido

(Eds.), *Intellectual Teamwork: Social and technological foundations of cooperative work.* Hillsdale, NJ: Erlbaum.

Hutchins, E. (1995). *Cognition in the Wild.* Cambridge, MA: The MIT Press.

Latour, B. (1986). Visualization and cognition: Thinking with eyes and hands. In H. Kuklick & E. Long (Eds.), *Knowledge and Society: Studies in the Sociology of Science, Past and Present.* Vol. 6. Greenwich: JAI Press.

Latour, B. (1987). *Science in Action.* Cambridge, MA: Harvard University Press.

Latour, B. (1992). Where are the missing masses? Sociology of a few mundane artifacts. In W. E. Bijker & J. Law (Eds.), *Shaping Technology/Building Society: Studies in Sociotechnical Change.* Cambridge, MA: The MIT Press.

Latour, B. (1993). Some scholars' babies are other scholars' bathwater. Contemporary Sociology: *A Journal of Reviews, 22,* 487–489.

Lave, J. (1988). *Cognition in Practice: Mind, Mathematics and Culture in Everyday Life.* Cambridge: Cambridge University Press.

Lave, J. & Wenger, E. (1991). *Situated Learning: Legitimate Peripheral Participation.* Cambridge, UK: Cambridge University Press.

Leont'ev, A. N. (1978). *Activity, Consciousness, and Personality.* Englewood Cliffs, NJ: Prentice-Hall.

Lynch, M. (1985). *Art and Artifact in Laboratory Science: A Study of Shop Work and Shop Talk in a Research Laboratory.* London: Routledge & Kegan Paul.

Lynch, M., Livingston, E., & Garfinkel, H. (1983). Temporal order in laboratory work. In K. Knorr-Cetina & M. Mulkay (Eds.), *Science Observed: Perspectives on the Social Study of Science.* London: Sage.

Middleton, D. & Edwards, D. (Eds.) (1990). *Collective Remembering.* London: Sage.

Norman, D. (1988). *The Psychology of Everyday Things.* New York: Basic Books.

Pickering, A. (Ed.) (1992). *Science as Practice and Culture.* Chicago: University of Chicago Press.

Pollner, M. (1987). *Mundane Reason: Reality in Everyday and Sociological Discourse.* Cambridge: Cambridge University Press.

Resnick, L. B., Levine, J. M., & Teasley, S. D. (Eds.) (1991). Perspectives on socially shared cognition. Washington, DC: A.P.A.

Schmidt, K. & Bannon, L. (1992). Taking CSCW seriously: Supporting articulation work. *Computer Supported Cooperative Work: An International Journal, 1,* 7–40.

Strauss, A. (1991). *Creating Sociological Awareness: Collective Images and Symbolic Representations.* New Brunswick, NJ: Transaction Publishers.

Strauss, A. (1993). *Continual Permutations of Action.* New York: Aldine de Gruyter.

Strauss, A., Fagerhaugh, S., Suczek, B., & Wiener, C. (1985). *The Social Organization of Medical Work.* Chicago: University of Chicago Press.

Suchman, L. (1987). *Plans and situated actions: The Problem of Human-Machine Communication.* Cambridge: Cambridge University Press.

Warner, M., Wobbe, W., & Brodner, P. (Eds.) (1990). *New Technology and Manufacturing Management: Strategic Choices for Flexible Production Systems.* Chichester, UK: Wiley.

Weick, K. E. & Roberts, K. H. (1993). Collective mind in organizations: Heedful interrelating on flight decks. *Administrative Science Quarterly, 38,* 357–381.

Womack, J. P., Jones, D. T., & Roos, D. (1991). *The Machine that changed the World: The Story of Lean Production.* New York: Harper Perennial.

Wood, S. (Ed.) (1982). *The Degradation of Work? Skill, Deskilling, and the Labour Process.* London: Hutchinson.

Wood, S. (Ed.) (1989). *The Transformation of Work? Skill, Flexibility, and the Labour Process.* London: Unwin Hyman.

# 2    Distributed cognition in an airline cockpit

*Edwin Hutchins and Tove Klausen*

Most people who travel frequently by air occasionally find themselves sitting in the passenger cabin wondering what is happening on the other side of the cockpit door. What are the pilots doing, and whatever it is they are doing, are they doing it well?

Although we cannot present data from an actual flight, we can provide the next best thing: data from an actual airline flight crew performing in a very high fidelity flight simulator.[1] Consider the transcript below, taken from a full-mission simulation of a flight from Sacramento to Los Angeles. It is the second flight of the day for this particular crew. They are about 8 minutes out of Sacramento and are climbing through 19,000 feet toward their cruise altitude of 33,000 feet. The simulated aircraft is a Boeing 727-200, which requires a crew of three: Captain (Capt), First Officer (F/O) and Second Officer (S/O).

We open the cockpit door and peek inside. The Captain has just removed a departure chart[2] from the control yoke and is replacing it in his airway manual. The first officer is flying the plane, monitoring the flight instruments and handling the controls. The second officer has completed his departure paperwork and begins a departure report by radio to the company offices on the ground.

## Transcript

| 0216 | S/O | xxx NASA nine hundred. |
|---|---|---|
| 0224 | S/O | Departure report. |
| | S/O | NASA nine hundred from Sacramento to Los Angeles International we have . . . fuel on board twenty seven point eight fuel boarded is not available out time is one six four five up time is one six five five. |
| 0247 | Capt | Oakland center NASA nine hundred request higher. {F/O reaches to vicinity of altitude alert setting knob when ATC begins transmission.} |

0254    OAK24L    NASA nine hundred . . . roger contact Oakland center one
                  thirty two point eight.
                  {F/O pulls his hand back from the altitude alert knob when
                  ATC says "contact Oakland center." 2.5 seconds after the end
                  of ATC transmission, F/O looks at Capt}
                  {Capt looks at F/O.}
0300    F/O       Thirty two eight.
        Capt      Thirty two eight?
        F/O       Yeah.
        Capt      OK
0303    S/O       That's correct, NASA nine hundred.
        Capt      One three two eight, NASA nine hundred.
                  {Capt twists knob on radio console.}
                  {F/O looks in direction of Capt}
0315    Capt      Center NASA nine hundred twenty one point seven for two
                  three zero requesting higher.
0323              {S/O turns towards front of cockpit.}
0325              {F/O looks at Capt}
0325    OAK15H    NASA nine hundred . . . Oakland center climb and maintain
                  flight level three three zero and expedite your climb please.
0327              {F/O reaches the altitude alert as ATC says "climb and main-
                  tain."}
0330              {When ATC says "expedite your climb" S/O turns to the per-
                  formance tables on the S/O work surface.}
0331    F/O       OK.
0333    Capt      Three three zero NASA nine hundred.
                  {Capt leans toward and looks at F/O.}
                  I didn't catch the last part.
0336    F/O       Expedite your climb.
        Capt      OK.
0339              {S/O reaches thrust levers and pushes them forward.}
0341    Capt      That's firewall thrust {Capt looks at F/O.}
        All       (Laugh).

Unless you know quite a lot about aviation, reading this transcript probably
did not help you much in deciding what the pilots are doing and whether or not
they are doing it well. Of course, in a very important sense, the question of interest to you as a passenger should not be whether a particular pilot is performing
well, but whether or not the system that is composed of the pilots and the technology of the cockpit environment is performing well. It is the performance of
that system, not the skills of any individual pilot, that determines whether you
live or die. In order to understand the performance of the cockpit as a system we

need, of course, to refer to the cognitive properties of the individual pilots, but we also need a new, larger, unit of cognitive analysis. This unit of analysis must permit us to describe and explain the cognitive properties of the cockpit system that is composed of the pilots and their informational environment. We call this unit of analysis a system of *distributed cognition.*

The excerpt of cockpit activity presented above is only approximately 1½ minutes in duration, yet it is very rich. It contains within it illustrations of many of the central concepts of a theory of distributed cognition. We will present and discuss these concepts by going through the elements of the example in chronological order and noting what the events in this example tell us about the nature of this particular system and about systems of distributed cognition in general.

This is a descriptive use of the theory. We will attempt to show that certain observed behaviors are instances of certain theoretical concepts. It is only by mapping from the data to a theory that we can generalize beyond the specifics of these observations. Establishing such a mapping from the data to the theory is itself a problematic cognitive activity. A short digression on method is in order.

**The method of analysis**

In some kinds of behavioral research, the mappings from observed events to the terms of a theory are taken to be obvious. In others these mappings are justified by "operational" definitions. In our case, however, the theoretical interpretation of some events may depend on the meanings that the participants themselves attach to those events. Because the setting is not familiar to most readers, the mappings from events to theory are unlikely to seem obvious. Because of the complexity of the setting, it cannot readily be made familiar. And since the sort of thing an event is in the theory may depend on meanings that the participants attach to the event, there are no simple operational definitions of many of our terms. Instead, we must rely on an ethnography of the setting to provide the interpretive bridge from the structure of the recordings of activity to the terms of the theory of distributed cognition.

We have pursued a strategy of analysis in which we insist that the connections between the data and the theory must be established explicitly. Our analysis begins with video and audio recordings of the events in the cockpit environment. We take the video and audio records to be a first-generation representation of what happened in the cockpit. Some aspects of the setting are already lost in the video and audio. The camera angle leaves some parts of the environment obscured, for example. The camera mounted in the flight simulator records a black and white image from infrared sensors, so color is lost. Odors are not recorded by video. Although they are incomplete, the video and audio recordings are rich sources of data.[3]

From the video and audio recordings we create another representation of what happened in the cockpit, this time in the medium of print. We create a *transcript* of the verbal and other behavior, in the cockpit. This representation leaves out even more than the video and audio representations, but it is still rich, and for some analytic tasks, it is far superior to the raw recordings. Both the translation from real events to video and audio recordings and the translation from video and audio to written transcript is heavily theory laden (Ochs, 1979). The actual recorded acoustic signals are meaningless in themselves. It is only in interaction with the knowledge of a listener who understands the language that the acoustic signals become segmented into words. The role of transcriber knowledge becomes even more apparent where specialized vocabularies are employed. Most people in our culture do not speak "aviationese" and just as it is impossible to transcribe recordings in a language one does not speak, it is impossible to transcribe discourse from technical domains without knowing something about the domain of discourse. As analysts, we know well that what people hear depends on what they expect to hear, and in a noisy technical environment very little can be heard at all without some expectations. This raises an important concern. If even the transcription process involves the tacit knowledge of the researcher, might the analysis be covertly shaped by the analyst's expectations?

One way to protect oneself from the possibility of unexamined assumptions driving the work is to attempt a form of "objectivity" in which all assumptions are hopefully banished. Such approaches cling to a "coding scheme," a set of "objective criteria" for the existence of instances of various classes of events. Every coding scheme, however, ultimately depends on the skills of coders to assign complex real events as instances of the coded categories. This in itself is a complex cognitive activity that is far from objective (Goodwin, 1994). We opt for another possibility, that is, making sure the assumptions do not remain unexamined (Moreman, 1969; Duranti, 1985). With this in mind, we ground the translation from video and audio record to transcription in an explicit set of propositions that are independently verifiable in the ethnography of the setting (Agar, 1986).

Consider a simple example from the excerpt above. The transcript indicates that at time 0327 the first officer reached the altitude alerter. We know this is the correct description of this event because we have access to other resources. A diagram of instrument layout shows that the altitude alerter is located just where the first officer reached. But there is more to it than that. Setting the altitude alerter is a meaningful action for the pilots at this point in time. Company procedures require that the altitude alerter be set whenever a new altitude is assigned to the aircraft.

From the transcripts we generate yet another representation of the events that were recorded. This is a description of the *actions* that took place. The stream of behavior in the transcript is segmented into culturally meaningful chunks and is related to an ethnographically grounded system of goals and expectations in which the actions achieve their meaning for the participants. Again, we attempt to be completely explicit about the grounds for the composition of every action. The development of ethnographic grounding leads us to many sources of cultural knowledge. These include operational manuals for the aircraft, the layout of the cockpit instrumentation and controls, crew training materials, published navigation procedures (commonly known "rules of thumb" in aviation), interviews with pilots, and observations of pilots in actual flights, to mention only a few.[4]

A fourth representation of the events gives *interpretations* to the actions that were identified in the previous stage. Again, the translation from the action representation to that of interpretations is given an explicit grounding in an independently verifiable ethnography of the setting. Furthermore, even the richest ethnography may not uniquely constrain interpretations. Any particular identified action may have many meanings.

Finally, we draw on all of these representations to create the mapping from data to the theory. As the theory of distributed cognition unfolds in this paper, the reader will recognize that this analytic device is modeled on the notion of the propagation of a representational state across a series of representational media. Each representation brings a different sort of information into the foreground. This is one of the central concepts of the theory. Unfortunately, we do not have the space here to give a complete explication of the process of analysis for even this brief excerpt. What we will do instead is weave together the data, the actions, the interpretations, and the ethnographic grounding as they are needed in a narrative that seeks to present a theoretical account of the observed events.

## Analysis of the event

Let's begin with a brief summary of what we saw. This is the sort of description that a pilot would give.

*As the crew approached the altitude to which they were cleared, the Captain called Air Traffic Control and asked for a clearance to a higher altitude. The controller handed them off to a high-altitude controller who gave them a clearance to their cruising altitude and instructed them to expedite the climb. The Second Officer increased the thrust and they continued their climb.*

This is an entirely normal event. But now let us look much more closely and examine the cognitive properties of this system.

### *Cognitive labor is socially distributed*

Flying a modern jet airliner is a job that cannot (at least not in current practice) be done by an individual acting alone. This is why your safety as a passenger depends on the properties of the crew/aircraft system rather than on the skills of any individual. The excerpt we have presented begins with the crew operating in a fairly autonomous mode. They are in a relatively light workload phase of flight; the stresses of the takeoff are behind them and they have now established a climb on a constant heading. The First Officer, who is actually flying the airplane, is the only crew member involved in time-critical performance at this point. The Captain is dividing his attention between housekeeping tasks (putting away a navigation chart) and monitoring aircraft and crew performance. In his role as "pilot not flying," he is also responsible for communications with the Air Traffic Control system (ATC), but there are no communication demands at the beginning of this example. Simultaneously, and quite independently, the Second Officer is involved in another kind of housekeeping task, making a report to the company of the condition of the flight. At this instant there is little explicit interaction among the members of the crew. Although no member of the crew is taxed by these circumstances, the system as a whole may still be doing more cognitive work than could be done by any individual alone. The fact that such systems proceed with several individuals working autonomously in parallel is well known and, from a theoretical point of view, easy to understand. Things become much more interesting when the members of the crew are required to coordinate their activities with each other.

*Planning*

At time 10:02:47, the Captain calls the Oakland, California Air Route Traffic Control Center (abbreviated to "Oakland Center") low-altitude controller and requests a clearance to a higher altitude.[5] This is an important piece of evidence about planning in the cockpit. The aircraft is currently climbing through an altitude of about 19,000 feet. It is currently cleared to an altitude of 23,000 feet. This means that without a clearance to a higher altitude, it cannot legally climb above 23,000 feet. However, the flight plan[6] filed for this flight calls for a cruise altitude of Flight Level 330 (33,000 feet).

In this context, we can attribute to the Captain the goal of climbing to the filed cruise altitude of FL330 and, furthermore, we can attribute to him the goal of making the climb uninterrupted by leveling off at an intermediate altitude.[7] In order to realize these goals, the aircraft will need to have a clearance to climb to a higher altitude. The Captain's request is part of a plan to achieve the subgoal of getting the required clearance. In order to have this plan now, he must have been monitoring the progress of the flight. That is his job as Captain and as the pilot not flying.[8] He used the information available – present altitude, cleared altitude, cruise altitude, plus his knowledge of the legal status of cleared altitude and the role of ATC – to construct a plan. It's a tiny bit of action in the cockpit, but is is the tip of a large iceberg of information and knowledge.

*Distribution of access to information*

Up to now we have been primarily concerned with relatively autonomous activities of the crew. That changes when the Captain speaks. All members of the crew normally monitor the ATC frequency unless they need to be on another frequency for some reason.[9] The Captain's radio transmission can be heard by the First Officer. The distribution of access to information is an important property of systems of distributed cognition. The properties of the larger system emerge from the interactions among the interpretations formed by the members of the crew and the contents of those interpretations are determined in part by the access to information.

*The trajectories of information*

It is important to note that we cannot predict in advance where the information will actually go. For example, we do not know that the First Officer will actually attend to and hear the Captain's radio call. We do know from the structure of the setting and a knowledge of how the radios are operated that the First Officer could have attended to and heard any communication with ATC. This sort of knowledge permits us to establish a set of possible pathways or trajectories for information. Occasionally, the observation of particular pilot techniques may demonstrate possible pathways that have not been anticipated on the basis of the normal operation in the setting. Once the possible pathways have been identified, it is possible to examine the data for evidence concerning where the information actually went. It is often possible, after the fact, to unambiguously determine that information has followed some particular trajectories in the system.

*Formation of expectations*

Given the content of the Captain's plan, we attribute to him an expectation concerning the reply from Oakland Center. His radio call is the opening turn in a conversation with a highly predictable structure. The expectation is that ATC will answer, saying something like, "NASA nine hundred, climb and maintain flight level three three zero." If the First Officer was attending to the Captain's request, he may also have formed this expectation. Note that at this point in the analysis we cannot confidently attribute this expectation to the First Officer. As was the case with the potential trajectories for information structure in the system, we cannot always know what cognitive consequences follow from the arrival of a particular piece of information. Thus, even if the information reached the First Officer, the development of an expectation about ATC's response is only a possibility. Additional evidence from the transcript would be required to support this interpretation.

In this case, more evidence is available in the form of the First Officer's reaching toward the altitude-alert setting knob as the ATC controller begins his reply to the request for a higher altitude clearance. The altitude-alert system is required by federal aviation regulations. The crew must set the cleared altitude into the window. The system sounds an alarm warning of approach within 750 feet of the assigned altitude. Altitude busts (flying through the assigned altitude) were a frequent and serious problem prior to the introduction of these systems. We believe the First Officer's reaching behavior is evidence of a plan to change the setting of the altitude-alert system in response to the expected clearance to a higher altitude. The currently cleared altitude (23,000 feet) is displayed. The First Officer intends to change the setting to whatever altitude ATC specifies. He expects the filed cruise altitude of 33,000 feet. The reaching behavior gives us an additional constraint on the ascription of an expectation to the First Officer.

This sequence shows how the distribution of access to information and a shared body of knowledge about the operation of the system permits the formation of shared expectations that are then the basis of coordinated actions by the crew. This is one of many events in this excerpt that highlight the cultural nature of this task performance and its reliance on shared knowledge. To the extent that coordinated actions of the crew are grounded in mental representations of possible but not yet realized states of affairs, we say that shared expectations are real.

*Violations of expectations*

As it turns out, the expectation is violated by the response of ATC. The expected clearance to a higher altitude is not forthcoming. Instead, the crew is instructed to contact another controller at Oakland Center – this time a high-altitude controller. This is a violation of the crew's expectations. Unable to carry out the planned change in the altitude-alert system, the First Officer withdraws his hand from the altitude-alert setting knob.

The frequency change instruction gives rise to a new expectation. All information from ATC is supposed to be acknowledged.[10] Both the Captain and the First Officer expect the Captain to acknowledge the instruction. But the Captain does not acknowledge the instruction immediately. Two and a half seconds after the end of the ATC transmission, the First Officer looks at the Captain. The First Officer's expectation of a timely acknowledgment has now been violated.

*Intersubjectivity as a basis for communication*

The next several actions are interesting because they establish one another's meanings. The Captain looks at the First Officer and says nothing. The First Officer says "thirty two eight" to the Captain. Then the Captain asks, "thirty two eight?" What is going on in this interaction?

It is useful to consider this interaction in terms of speech act theory (Austin, 1960; Searle, 1969). Speech act theory considers utterances as simultaneously being several kinds of acts at once. What a speaker actually says is called the locutionary act. The force of what is said is the illocutionary act, and the intended effect is the perlocutionary act. For example, saying "Can you pass the salt?" at the dinner table has the locutionary force of a question: is the addressee capable of passing the salt? Of course, the speaker doesn't really want an answer to that question. The illocutionary force of the utterance is an indirect request for the salt to be passed. The perlocutionary act is an enticement to lead the addressee to pass the salt.

The First Officer's response to the Captain's glance is an elliptical version of the frequency that is to be acknowledged to ATC.[11] The locutionary aspect of this utterance is the specification of the frequency to be used.

That seems appropriate in context. But, what would have to be true of the world in order for that to be an appropriate thing to say? The illocutionary force is "I am answering the question you posed by looking at me without saying anything." That is, the First Officer's utterance assigns a meaning to the Captain's blank stare to which it is a response. It classifies the Captain's action of looking at the First Officer as a question about the frequency to be used. Once made, this assignment of meaning to the Captain's look is available for negotiation. The Captain could, for example, dispute the classification and claim that he knew the frequency. But he does not. The Captain's next utterance, repeating the frequency back with rising intonation, has an illocutionary force that concurs with the First Officer's classification of the looking behavior.

There is one more level of meaning in the First Officer's response to the Captain's look. The perlocutionary force or intended effect of the First Officer's utterance is to enable the Captain to continue with his job.

This interaction is evidence for the notion of interaction as the construction of a shared understanding of the situation in which the interactants find themselves. Certainly, the pilots entered this situation with a considerable amount of shared prior knowledge about how things are supposed to go or how they typically go. As they are members of a community of practice, we may expect that to be the case. In the course of their interaction, they use that shared knowledge as a resource to negotiate or construct a shared understanding of their particular situation. This constructed shared understanding of the situation is known as an intersubjective understanding (Rommetveit & Blakar, 1979; Wertsch, 1985). As D'Andrade (1980) points out, what each participant in the situation knows is itself part of the situation being jointly understood. Following this notion of intersubjectivity, we would say that the First Officer's original looking at the Captain is evidence that he knows that the Captain is supposed to respond to the ATC call. The Captain's look at the First Officer is evidence that he knows that the First Officer knows that the Captain is supposed to respond to the ATC call. Finally, the First Officer's utterance is evidence that he knows that the Captain knows that the First Officer knows that the Captain is supposed to respond to the ATC call. It says, "I know that you know that I know that you should respond."

Intersubjectivity supports efficient kinds of communication. It is what permits human actors to intend and find meanings in many nonverbal behaviors and in the aspects of verbal behaviors that go beyond the literal locutionary force of the utterance. It was not just something in the Captain that made his glance at the First Officer so eloquent. Rather, it was the fact that this glance occurred in a context of intersubjectively shared understandings about the nature of the current situation that permitted it to so smoothly and successfully communicate the Captain's need. Again, the shared expectations become real in the sense that they organize the behavior that determines the properties of the larger cognitive system.

It is important to note that this interaction depends on the intersubjective sharing of representations of aspects of the situation that were never made explicit by either of the interactants. There was no conversation about what each knew about what the other knew. The fact that these crew members can do this is all the more surprising when one considers that these pilots had never flown together before the day of the simulated flight. Prior to the reported excerpt they had flown one flight segment and had spent only about two hours together. Clearly, the grounds for the construction of intersubjectively shared understandings depends on a very special distribution of knowledge in the pilot community.

Intersubjectivity is important for the functioning of the system of distributed cognition because the trajectory of information in the system depended on the intersubjectivity of the crew. Norman (1990), in a paper on aviation automation, has pointed out that the communication between the current generation of automatic devices in the cockpit and the crew is primitive and leaves much room for improvement, especially with regard to providing the crew feedback about the condition of automated systems. Norman compares the case of a copilot flying an airplane with the case of an autopilot flying. He points out that if a copilot encounters a situation that requires unusual control inputs in order to maintain the desired flight path, the copilot is likely to say something about it to other crew members. An autopilot of the current generation, however, will simply make whatever control inputs are required without notifying the crew. This has led to some near disasters. Some readers of Norman's paper have responded by saying that the state of the art in artificial intelligence would permit the automated system to represent the information that the pilot needs.[12] This may well be so, but the issue is not simply whether the automation could represent its own state. The issue is whether or not the system could interact with the pilots in the way that they interact with each other. With human interactants, we have seen that intersubjectively shared representations permit a silent look in a particular context to have the meaning of a request for specific information. This sort of phenomenon is a reminder of the complexity and subtlety of human interaction. It is difficult to imagine what sort of machine could engage in this kind of interaction.

## Distribution of information storage

The fact that the Captain succeeds in getting the required frequency from the First Officer illustrates another aspect of this system of socially distributed cognition. The distribution of access to information is such that the First Officer also hears the communications with ATC, even though he is not responsible for radio communications. This permits the formation in the crew system of a redundant storage of information. Under ideal conditions, both the Captain and the First Officer (and the Second Officer if he is not otherwise engaged) will hear all ATC clearances. This means that if, for any reason, one of the members of the crew fails to attend to, store, or retrieve the information, it may be available from one of the other members of the crew. Such a redundant information-storage system is robust in the fact of local failures as long as there is a way to move information around inside the system. As we saw above, the communication of information inside the system can be quite efficient.

## Redundant readbacks for error checking

Having gotten the frequency from the First Officer, the Captain reads the frequency back to the ATC controller. The expectations of the crew members are now met. Furthermore, the readback of the elements of any ATC clearance provides an opportunity for redundant error checking (Palmer et al., 1993). While there is no legal requirement to read back clearances, it is considered good practice in the aviation community and is the express policy of most airlines. It is normally thought that the error checking is to be provided by the ATC controller, but we can see that there is also a possibility of error checking of the readback by other members of the crew. Since both the original clearance and the readback are available not only to ATC, but to all members of the crew, including the Captain himself, every member of the crew has an opportunity to detect an error in the readback.

In the most general case, we can say that redundant error checking depends on a redundant distribution of access to information about the performance of the members of the crew. This is supported in other ways in the airplane cockpit. For example, civil transport aircraft provide duplicate flight instruments for the two pilots. There are several frequently cited functions served by these duplicate instruments. First, they permit either pilot to fly the airplane. Second, they provide a measure of redundancy in the event that the instruments on one side fail. Third, by cross-checking instruments, failures that might otherwise be difficult to detect can be discovered. Seen from the perspective of distributed cognition, these duplicate instruments serve yet another important function. They provide a redundant distribution of access to information that supports mutual monitoring between the crew members and is essential in the maintenance of intersubjectively shared understandings of and expectations about the situation of the aircraft. A similar argument can be made for the prominent position of the control "yokes." With the two yokes mechanically linked, it is easy for one pilot to monitor the flying style of the other without having to turn to watch.

There is a trend in current cockpit design to build two separate crew work stations for the two pilots. Mechanically linked control yokes are being replaced in some cockpits by side-stick controllers that are mounted outboard of the pilot's seats and are not mechanically linked to each other. From the perspective of individual pilot performance, side-stick controllers are functionally equivalent to (or perhaps superior to) control yokes. From the distributed cognition perspective, however, the side-stick equipped cockpit has a different distribution of access to information and this may affect the cognitive properties of the cockpit system. A similar situation is created by current implementations of the Flight Management Computer System (FMCS). Duplicate computer interfaces to the FMCS are provided to the two pilots. This appears on the surface to have the same desirable properties as duplicate flight instruments. This would be the case if they were in fact directly linked to each other. However, for perfectly good operational reasons, the actions taken on one interface are not necessarily reflected on the other. This results in a common complaint among pilots that unless extraordinary measures are taken to communicate intentions, one pilot may not know what the other is doing. And even if extra measures are taken, they often result in both pilots going "head down," one leaning across the center console to monitor a programming task as it is performed by the other.

The problems of restricted or nonoverlapping distribution of access to information have the potential to create difficulties in normal operations and may interfere more severely with training. Although, as one pilot remarked, "the cockpit is a poor classroom," a considerable amount of training takes place there.[13] Implicit learning through shared activity is an important component of learning a complex job like flying an airplane. It is possible to design computer systems with open interfaces (Hutchins, 1990) that support learning in joint action but this can only be done when the designer goes beyond the conception of the isolated individual user.

*Propagation of representational state through the system.*

After reading back the frequency, the Captain tunes the number one communication radio to the specified frequency. This sets the radio to transmit and receive on the specified frequency. At this time, the First Officer glances at the Captain and at the frequency window of the radio. The First Officer has an expectation that the Captain will tune the radio to 132.80 MHz.

Notice the trajectory of the radio frequency information. It arrived in the cockpit as a string of spoken words. It went by way of the First Officer's memory to spoken words exchanged between the First Officer and the Captain, then by way of the Captain's memory to the readback and then on to the setting of the radio. Each appearance was slightly different from the one before it:

| | |
|---|---|
| ATC: | "One thirty two point eight." |
| F/O ↔ Capt: | "Thirty two eight." |
| Read back: | "One three two eight." |
| Radio: | 132.80 MHz |

We can see that the information moved through the system as a sequence of representational states in representational media. From speech channels to internal memories, back to speech channels, to the physical setting of a device. Its representation in each medium is a transformation of the representation in other media. Notice also that the various media in which the information is represented have different properties (Norman, 1993). Speech is ephemeral. It requires one to attend to information at the time it is delivered. Representations in the memories of individuals endure longer than those in speech. This is what permits the Captain to retrieve the information that was in the ATC instruction without having to ask the controller for it again. Although the ATC transmission had ended and was no longer available, the information in it was still represented in the memory of the First Officer. Finally, a portion of the information in the ATC instruction was imposed on the airplane itself, in the tuning of the radio. This is the same information that had been represented verbally, but now it is in a relatively durable representation, because the setting of the radio is continuously available and will not change until the next frequency is tuned.

This movement of information structure across various representational media and ultimately to the controls of the airplane itself is the essence of control of the aircraft and the way that coordination among aircraft is maintained. That is, if we step back and look at the entire aviation system and ask how it is that aircraft are kept separated from each other, we see that it is through the propagation of the representational state of descriptions of flight paths into the state of the aircraft controls themselves.

*Distribution of labor again*

With the radio now set to the appropriate frequency, the Captain contacts the Oakland Center high-altitude controller at 10:03:15. He is back to the point in his plan where he was with his original request for a higher altitude. That plan is still pending and is in fact somewhat more urgent now, as the plane is closing rapidly on its currently cleared altitude. In this case, he gives the current altitude of the plane and the altitude to which they have been cleared, then adds the request for a higher altitude.[14]

The Captain's radio call contains the current altitude and the altitude to which the aircraft has been cleared. We may ask where these values come from. The current altitude of the aircraft must come from the airplane's altimeter. Since the plane is climbing, this value is continually changing. Altitude is represented on the altimeter by the positions of two hands and a bar on the clock-like face of the gauge and also by a digital readout window. The Captain must transform this representation of altitude information into a spoken one. There are at least two possibilities for the source of the information about the altitude to which the plane is currently cleared. One is the Captain's memory. The airplane was cleared to flight level 230 about four minutes before the Captain's radio call and he may simply remember that altitude. The other is the altitude-alert system. Since the altitude to which the plane is cleared should always be shown in the window of the altitude-alert system, it is an alternate source of this information. In this case, it does not appear that the Captain consults the altitude-alert system, but we have seen many cases in which a crewman making initial contact with an ATC center will give the current altitude, pause, look at the altitude-alert system, and then give the altitude to which the aircraft has been cleared.

By this time, the Second Officer has completed his departure report and is again attending to the actions of the other crewmen. The captain's request is available to all members of the crew and leads them all to a shared expectation concerning the response from ATC.

Again, all members of the crew have the expectation that ATC will answer back with something like "Climb and maintain flight level three three zero." This expectation is partially met and partially violated. ATC responds to the request by saying "NASA nine hundred . . . Oakland Center climb and maintain flight level three three zero and expedite your climb please." As we shall see in a moment, the additional information "expedite your climb" seems to be heard by the First Officer and the Second Officer, but not by the Captain. This bit of structure evokes in the First Officer and the Second Officer a model of the expedited climb while the Captain seems to still be thinking standard climb.

This ATC clearance spawns more work to be conducted more or less autonomously by the members of the crew.

*Memory in the state of artifacts: The altitude-alert system*

The First Officer now has the information he needs to set the altitude-alert system. As soon as ATC says, "Climb and maintain" he knows an altitude is coming next and he reaches forward to the altitude-alert setting knob. The setting of the altitude in the window of the altitude alert system is similar to the setting of the radio frequency in that in both cases information that had verbal representation comes to be represented in the state of a device in the cockpit. In both cases, the representation in the medium of the device is much more durable than the representation in speech, and it is much less vulnerable to interruption or displacement by other information than the same information represented in individual internal memory.

The strategy of using physical state as a form of memory is widespread. Unfortunately, its very ubiquity may lead us to overlook its importance and miss its theoretical significance. Writing something down to remember it is a common example with which we are all familiar. This happens in the cockpit too. Each pilot has a small clipboard near at hand with slips of paper on which clearances and other information may be written. But in the cockpit there are also other sets of devices that both remember the information and act on it autonomously. The altitude-alert system is a simple example.

## Computation by propagation and transformation of representational state: Computing and using the maximum EPRs

The portion of the clearance that said "expedite the climb" spawned some autonomous action on the part of the Second Officer as well. The expedited climb requires maximum thrust from the engines. The concept of the expedited climb leads, for the Second Officer, to the notion of setting the engines to maximum thrust. This is done by pushing the thrust levers forward until the engine pressure ratio (EPR) gauges read the maximum permissible values given the current air temperature and altitude. We attribute to the Second Officer the goal of setting maximum engine thrust. In order to achieve this goal, the Second Officer needs to know what the maximum EPR settings are.

When ATC says "expedite your climb," the Second Officer turns to the engine performance tables that are printed on the work surface below his instrument panel and finds the appropriate EPR values. With the EPR values in memory, the Second Officer turns to the thrust levers and pushes them forward while monitoring the readings on the EPR gauges for a match to the remembered values. Thus, having satisfied the subgoal of finding the EPR values, the Second Officer returns to the top-level goal of setting the engines for maximum thrust.

Here again, we see the propagation and transformation of representational state across a number of media. The Second Officer's model of the expedited climb included an implication of maximum thrust. He propagated that information (plus altitude and total air temperature) into the climb EPR table. That transformed the inputs into outputs of EPR settings for the engines, which he then propagated to the EPR gauges by manipulating the thrust levels. Some of the media across which this information was propagated are internal to the Second Officer, others, like the EPR table, thrust levers, and the gauges, are external.

The table that the Second Officer uses to compute the appropriate maximum climb engine pressure ratios is a mediating artifact of a special sort. Originally, the values in the table were determined by the engineers who built the engines. This involves both empirical testing and theoretical calculations. The knowledge that was gained through that process is now crystallized as a hard artifact: the EPR table. In the EPR table, the information is represented in such a way that the task of extracting the appropriate values is very simple.

*Intersubjectivity and distribution of storage again*

While the Second Officer was computing the maximum climb EPRs, and the First Officer was setting the altitude-alert system, the Captain also had a job to do. He was supposed to read the clearance back to ATC. At 10:03:33 he read back, "three three zero NASA nine hundred." This is just the part of the clearance that matched the Captain's expectations about what sort of clearance he was to receive. Since, as we noted above, the Captain's readback is also available to the First Officer, it is possible that the Captain's readback violated the First Officer's expectation that the readback would contain mention of the "expedite your climb" portion of the clearance.

After his incomplete readback (which was not challenged by ATC) the Captain turned to the First Officer and said, "I didn't catch the last part." The locutionary force of this statement is simply that the Captain did not hear something. The illocutionary force is an indirect request for the First Officer to tell the Captain whatever the "last part" was. An interesting question at this point is: How can the First Officer know what the Captain means by the phrase "the last part"? The First Officer answers "expedite your climb," which is both a response to the illocutionary force of the Captain's statement and a claim about what the Captain meant by "the last part." The Captain immediately says, "OK," which indicates that the First Officer did know what the Captain meant.

One conjecture is that the First Officer could establish the meaning of "the last part" on purely syntactic grounds. The instruction portion of the clearance consisted of two main clauses: "climb and maintain flight level three three zero" and "expedite your climb please." Perhaps the "last part" simply refers to the second main clause. We believe that such an interpretation is implausible because there are no pragmatic conventions for referring to grammatical structures in this way. More likely, the First Officer, on the basis of what he has heard from the Captain's readback, may already suspect that the Captain did not hear the instruction to expedite the climb. Or, even without forming this expectation, when the Captain says he didn't catch the last part, the First Officer may ask himself what the "last part" could mean and may remember that just one second earlier the Captain left "expedite the climb" out of his readback. In either case, the intersubjectively shared expectations about the Captain's responsibilities in this situation form the basis for effective communication.

*Firewall thrust!*

Having learned that the clearance was to expedite the climb, the Captain now shares the image of the expedited climb with the other two members of the crew. As the Second Officer reaches for the thrust levers and begins pushing them forward to the maximum-climb thrust position, the Captain turns to the First Officer and Second Officer and says, "That's firewall thrust." Notice that no command is given to the Second Officer to increase engine thrust. He performs his role here without explicit verbal interaction with the other members of the crew. This action is interesting in two ways. First, it is another example of a sort of seamless joint performance constructed by a team whose members met for the first time only a few hours before takeoff. It suggests a kind of interchangeability of human parts that is a striking cultural and social organizational accomplishment. Second, one has to wonder whether any crew member would do something as consequential as this without verbally interacting with other crew members if the action were not completely visible to the other members of the crew. Given the location of the thrust levers, any manipulation of them is quite accessible to both the Captain and First Officer. In other portions of the flight, especially when the crew is faced with an equipment failure, the Second Officer takes other actions that are not visible to the pilots and notifies them of what he has done. This is only to say that the Second Officer makes decisions about the distribution of access to information and organizes his verbal behavior to compensate for the fact that some of his actions are not available to the other members of the crew.

The Captain's comment "That's firewall thrust!" and the reaction of other members of the crew establishes the distribution of awareness of the Second Officer's action. The phrase itself is a figure of speech. It is a form of trope known as a synecdoche. Its interpretation requires a bit of history. In the old days, when single-engine planes had an engine in the front and the pilot's cockpit directly behind the engine, there was a hopefully fireproof wall between the cockpit and the engine. In case the engine caught fire, this wall (the "firewall") was supposed to protect the crew from the fire. Throttles (the piston engine equivalent of jet thrust levers) were pushed forward for increased thrust. Maximum thrust was achieved by pushing the throttle levers right up to the firewall, hence the expression "firewall thrust."[15] This colorful expression brings to mind an image of pushing the thrust levers all the way forward to the stops.

The locutionary aspect of this comment is inaccurate (it is not firewall thrust) and the illocutionary force of this statement is inappropriate (one would not push the thrust levers forward to the stops in this airplane except in an emergency because doing so would most likely damage the engines). The perlocutionary aspect of the statement, however, is an assertion by the Captain that he now knows what is going on. He understands that the aircraft is cleared to climb at its maximum rate and that such a climb will require increased thrust.

## Discussion

In this chapter, we have considered only a tiny fraction of one simulated airline flight. Yet, a close examination of even this one excerpt illustrates a number of features of the cockpit as a cognitive system. Information processing in the distributed system can be characterized as a propagation of a representational state across representational media. In the cockpit, some of the relevant representational media are located within the individual plots. Others, such as speech, are located between the pilots, and still others are in the physical structure of the cockpit. Every representational medium has physical properties that determine the availability of representations through space and time and constrain the sorts of cognitive processes required to propagate the representational state into or out of that medium. Changes in the medium of representation of task-relevant information or in the structure of representations within a particular medium can therefore have important consequences for the cognitive conduct of the cockpit system.

The movement of information through the system has consequences for the formation of expectations and models of the situation of the aircraft. These expectations and models organize the behavior of the crew and, when shared, permit the crew members to coordinate their actions with each other. Furthermore, the movement of information among members of the crew sometimes depends on the crew members' assessments of their own states of knowledge and those of the others. The relationship between the cognitive properties of the cockpit system, as determined by the movement of representations, and the cognitive properties of the individual pilots is therefore very complex.

The analysis identifies a set of possible pathways for information through the cockpit system during ATC clearance-handling events. Some of the pathways observed are those that are anticipated by the design of the system. Others, which were perhaps not intended in the design of the system, nevertheless contribute to its performance characteristics. Although we can never know in advance which particular pathways for information will actually be used, the analysis of this event establishes a sort of existence proof for the observed pathways. As we have seen, there are many possible pathways for information in this system. In some cases the pathways are redundant so that if one is blocked, task-relevant information can still proceed via another. This redundancy appears to contribute to the robustness of the system in the face of local failures.

Certainly, the cognitive properties of the cockpit system are determined in part by the cognitive properties of the individual pilots. They are also determined by the physical properties of the representational media across which a task-relevant representational state is propagated, by the specific organization of the representations supported in those media, by the interactions of metarepresentations held by the members of the crew, and by the distributional characteristics of knowledge and access to task-relevant information across the members of the crew. Understanding the properties of individual cognition is therefore only a first step in an effort to understand how these more complex human cognitive systems operate.

## Acknowledgments

Research support was provided by grant NCC 2-591 to Donald Norman and Edwin Hutchins from the Ames Research Center of the National Aeronautics and Space Administration in the Aviation Safety/Automation Program. Everett Palmer served as technical monitor. Additional support for Tove Klausen was provided by the Danish government.

## Notes

1 The simulator is part of the NASA–AMES research facility at Moffett Field, California. It is a very high fidelity simulation. The cockpit simulator interior is a real airline cockpit with all the appropriate instruments and controls. The "box" is mounted on hydraulic rams that give it six degrees of freedom motion. High-resolution television monitors are mounted over the windows of the cockpit to provide complete computer-generated night and dusk visuals.

2 A Standard Instrument Department (SID) for Sacramento. This is a published procedure for departing the airport area. The aircraft has completed the departure segment and is in the enroute climb segment of the leg, so this chart will not be needed again.

3 Our data stream is actually richer than this indicates. Because these are flights in a computer-controlled simulator, we also have data on the readings of all of the primary cockpit instruments and the settings of all of the controls for the duration of the flight. This data is very useful in reconstructing the description of the events as they occurred.

4 The highly rationalized nature of this domain makes this sort of documentation possible. It may be that this sort of analysis would be much more difficult to conduct in a domain that lacks the long history and explicit representations of procedures and concepts that is available for aviation.

5 This action-level description of the observed verbal behavior, "Oakland Center United nine hundred request higher," is based on ethnographic constructs involving the syntax (who is being called, who is calling, nature of request) and semantics of communications with ATC.

6 The flight plan is actually developed by company dispatchers rather than by the pilots themselves. The planning activity here does not concern the development of the flight plan itself, but what is required in order to fly the flight as planned.

7 The latter part of this claim depends on company policy with respect to procedures that maximize fuel economy.

8 On every flight segment one of the pilots is designated "pilot flying" and the other "pilot not flying." This distinction marks a high-level division of labor. The pilot flying is responsible for the control of the aircraft, whereas the pilot not flying is responsible for communications. Flight crews usually alternate in these roles from one flight segment to another.

9 In this instance, the Second Officer is on another channel making his departure report. Among the crew up front, it is important to know who is listening to what and when. Normal procedures require a crew member to notify the other members of the crew when he is not monitoring the primary ATC frequency.

10 The Airman's Information Manual says, "Acknowledgement of frequency changes: When advised by ATC to change frequencies, acknowledge the instruction. If you select the new frequency without acknowledgement, the controller's workload is increased because he has no way of

knowing whether you received the instruction or have had a radio communications failure"
(FAR-AIM, 1989, Chapter 4, Paragraph 193, Section d).

11  The format of the numbers and the knowledge of the frequencies allotted to VHF radio communications for ATC (from 118.0 to 135.95 MHz) make this an abbreviated but unambiguous statement of the frequency, 132.8 MHz.

12  D. A. Norman, personal communication.

13  This is in part because training is expensive and does not generate any revenue. Operators thus
have a strong economic incentive to get pilots out of the training system and into revenue operations as soon as is legally possible. Several months of actual flying experience seem to lie between legal qualification and real mastery of the cockpit.

14  The syntax of the initial contact with a controller is spelled out in the Airman's Information Manual, Chapter 4, Section 7, Paragraph 340: ARTCC communications.

15  Because the throttle levers are normally capped with balls, an alternate expression was "balls to
the wall." In American automotive parlance, the equivalent expression is "pedal to the metal."

# References

Agar, M. H. (1986). *Speaking of Ethnography*. London: Sage Publications.

Austin, J. L. (1960). *How to Do Things with Words*. Oxford: Clarendon Press.

D'Andrade, R. G. (1980). The cultural part of cognition. *Cognitive Science 5,* 179–195.

Duranti, A. (1985). Sociocultural dimensions of discourse. In T. van Dijk (Ed.) *Handbook of Discourse Analysis*. Vol. 1. New York: Academic Press.

Goodwin, C. (1994). Professional vision. *American Anthropologist 96*(3), 606–633.

Hutchins, E. (1990). The technology of team navigation. In J. Galegher, R. Kraut, & C. Egido (Eds.)
*Intellectual Teamwork: Social and Technical Bases of Collaborative Work*. Hillsdale, NJ:
Lawrence Erlbaum Assoc.

Moerman, M. (1969). A little knowledge. In S. Tyler (Ed.) *Cognitive Anthropology*. New York: Holt,
Rinehart & Winston.

Norman, D. A. (1990). The "problem" with automation: Inappropriate feedback and interaction, not
"over-automation." *Philosophical Transactions of the Royal Society of London, B, 327.*

Norman, D. A. (1993). *Things That Make Us Smart*. Reading, MA: Addison-Wesley.

Ochs, E. (1979). Transcription as theory. In E. Ochs & B. Schieffelin (Eds.) *Developmental Pragmatics*. New York: Academic Press.

Palmer, E. A., E. L. Hutchins, R. A. Ritter, & I. van Cleemput. (1993, October). Altitude deviations:
Breakdowns of an error tolerant system. *NASA Technical Memorandum 108788*. National Aeronautics and Space Administration, Ames Research Center, Moffett Field, CA.

Rommetveit, R. & Blakar, R. M. (Eds.) (1979). *Studies of Language, Thought and Verbal Communication*. London: Academic Press.

Searle, J. R. (1969). *Speech Acts*. London: Cambridge University Press.

Wertsch, J. V. (1985). *Vygotsky and the Social Formation of Mind*. Cambridge, MA: Harvard University Press.

# 3    Constituting shared workspaces

*Lucy Suchman*

This chapter takes up the problem of relations between lived work practices and the material environments they inhabit, animate, provide for the significance of, and rely upon (see also Goodwin & Goodwin, this volume). More particularly, the goal is to come to terms with a single case of the moment-to-moment, inter-actionally achieved production of shared workspaces in the service of joint work. The starting premise is that work activities and workspaces are mutually consti-tuted, in ways that are structured and available for detailed understanding. At the same time, there is an ordering between the two, in that parties engaged in work are not concerned equally with the constitution of the place of their work and with its objects and outcomes. Rather, when all goes well, the former is taken by participants to be a previously given, largely transparent background for the work at hand. To gain insight into the material basis of the structuring of work practices and the practical bases for the structuring of work materials, therefore, requires a closer look.

Lynch has argued (1991) that the physical place of a worksite comprises a complex of equipment and action, of spatial orders produced in and informed by the knowledgeable practices of setting members. Taking up from Shapin the question of the "siting of knowledge production," he urges an inquiry into the scientific laboratory as "an ecology of local spaces integrated within disciplinary practices" (ibid., p. 74). Although defined by physical boundaries, points of ac-cess and lines of site, he proposes that the place of the laboratory for those who inhabit it is organized not by spatial coordinates but rather as *topical contextures* associated with indigenous orders of equipment and practice. On this view, place is constituted by, rather than the container for, culturally, historically, and locally meaningful forms of lived activity.

Ethnomethodological studies of the discovering sciences have made evident the contingent spatiotemporal ordering of disciplinary practices, while at the same time noting members' disinterest in that order as other than a transparent means to the accomplishment of ends taken, at least in the successful case, to be independent of it (see for example Lynch et al., 1983). This study takes up another form of work, which for members includes the successful reproduction of a local spatiotemporal ordering as among the work's central concerns (see also Filippi & Thereau, 1993; Harper & Hughes, 1993; Heath, 1992; Hutchins, 1990; Whalen, 1993). The setting for this case is the operations room of an airline (hereinafter called Atlantic) at a mid-size metropolitan airport in the United States.[1] The operations room is the communications center for the coordination of ground activities involved in servicing arriving and departing airplanes.[2] The latter include other sites for the airline's operations at this same airport (its gates, baggage ramps, and the like), other airlines' territories at the airport, other airports with which members of the operations room interact, and other locations of the national organization of which this operation is a part. The room in this sense is both a workplace in its own right and part of a larger network of activities and associated locales. The aim here is to discover how operations personnel actually inhabit these spaces as local environments for their work.

One logical conception of a center of coordination like the operations room would view it as a singular, unitary locus for the assembly of disparate activities into a coherent network or whole. The goal of this analysis is to contribute to a respecification of the center of coordination in general, and the operations room in particular, as an achieved product of the continuous (re)constitution of the room's centrality by airlines personnel.[3] At the same time, I hope to show something of how the room's location in an organizational, spatial, and temporal field sets up the conditions within which the work of operations gets done. The strategy is to investigate the operations room as a site of differentially situated perception and action, uncovering just what work is involved in maintaining this site both as coherent and as a center vis à vis other sites with which operations room personnel interact and whose activities they are charged to coordinate. The identification of the center with a singular locale or site belies the extent to which operations is constituted through interactions distributed across space and time. The operations room on this view is not so much a locale as a complex but habitual field of equipment and action, involving intimate relations of technology and practice, body and person, place and activity.

**The episode**

The case that we are considering affords a simple story as a starting place. An airplane pulls into a gate and, as is routinely done, gate agents wheel out onto the ramp a set of stairs to be aligned with the door so that the passengers can disembark. But in this case, for a reason that is not immediately clear, the stairs cannot be raised up high enough to meet the level of the plane.[4] As a consequence, the passengers are left waiting in the plane while workers on the ground mobilize themselves to resolve the problem.

Told in this way, of course, the story constitutes a post hoc account of the episode from an omniscient observer's point of view—a kind of view from nowhere. What we will be interested in, in contrast, is how this course of events emerged as the specifically situated focus of participants differently located in relation to the scene. In reconstructing the event, we will be interested in how participants came to an awareness of the problem from their particular organizational and physical locales, developed a shared orientation to the situation, and established places for their joint work.

The episode can be viewed as an occasion of routine trouble. That is, it represents the kind of contingency to which the normal order of operations is perpetually subject. As such, it discloses the accomplished nature of that order: that each time a plane arrives at the gate a collaborative production of activities must be pulled off if passengers are to get up out of their seats, wait for a period that is perhaps noticeable but not unacceptable for the doors to be opened, and exit the plane in an orderly way. We can think of the problem for members of the operations room faced with trouble such as this one as the assembly of the various resources at hand into an ad hoc system dedicated to the trouble's resolution. For this assembly to happen there are three requirements. First, that the trouble be noticed, formulated and brought to the attention of relevant others; second, that whatever human and technological resources might contribute to its resolution be mobilized; and third, that the consequences of those mobilizations be monitored and assessed for the resolution that could occur at any time, rendering further mobilization and coordination unnecessary. A precondition for and product of this activity is the constitution, out of distributed and discontinuous locales of differential attention, of shared workspaces in which the joint work can get done.

### The operations room as situational territory

The operations room is what Goffman (1971) has called a *situational territory*; that is, fixed space and equipment "made available to the populace in the form of claimed goods while in use" (p. 29). Like most workplaces in modern capitalist economies, the operations room is not the legal property of any of its inhabitants. Rather, the room is owned by the city in which the airport operates and leased to the airline for which operations room members work. Complex contractual arrangements govern rights to access for the room and its environs, access being restricted to those who are credentialled members of the organizational community or who have some specific grounds for being there (e.g., as researchers). Rules of entry are not simply stated and administered, but rather each entrance into the room is subject to assessment, and to different assessment depending upon the circumstances of the moment (e.g., how crowded is the room already, what order of business is in progress there, and how does one's own relate to it), for its occasioned, situational warrant.

At first glance, the operations room is most obviously a communal, public space. The absence of interior walls or other fixed boundaries within the room maximizes mutual access and defines this as a space designed not for private reflection or confidential conversation, but rather for the joint work of the company. Within the room, boundary markers, or objects that mark the line between two adjacent territories, are notable for their absence, boundaries being defined more by the placement of persons and equipment, and by the dynamic structuring of activity, than by the presence of explicit designators of ownership.

Despite the absence of walls, however, members of operations establish spaces within the room that are in a sense personal and private, delineated into what Goffman terms *use space*; that is, "the territory immediately around or in front of an individual, his claim to which is respected because of apparent instrumental needs" (p. 35). Roughly, each role in the division of labor within operations is mapped to a specific location in the room—what are called "positions" capture very nicely this double sense of location in the organization of the work and in the arrangement of space. The stable assignment of positions to members of an ongoing operation makes it possible for participants to categorize each other with reference both to characteristic activities and to place, organizing their own activity and placement in relation to the projectable location of relevant others.

We will mark the opening of the sequence we are interested in with a call that comes into operations over the radio one evening at 8:44 PM. At the start of this episode we find the operations room inhabited by five coworkers, each of whose presence is warranted in virtue of taking up some role in the division of labor.[5]

The Passenger Service Planner (PP) (seated front left in Fig. 1) is responsible for monitoring the booking, connections and, when necessary, rebooking of passengers. Operations A (Ops A) (seated beside PP) has responsibility for monitoring incoming flights and communicating with pilots via radio and an onboard computer system. The Baggage Planner (BP) (seated front right) advises the ramp crew of the arrival of incoming flights, the readiness for "push back" of outbound flights, and in general coordinates the loading, unloading, and transfer of bags. Operations B (Ops B) (seated beside BP) coordinates the servicing of an affiliated commuter airline. Finally the Supervisor of Ramp Services (Sup) has overall responsibility for the work of operations.[6]

When the radio call comes in, each member of the workgroup is engaged in their own activities, oriented away from the center of the room and toward their respective workspaces. Ops B is engaged with the computer system, BP is on the phone, and Ops A and PP are similarly oriented:[7]

| 1. | Radio: | Operations::ah (.) | |
|---|---|---|---|
| 2. | (pilot) | Four seventy one? | |
| 3. | Ops A: | (4.0) Rrahhh. | *struggling with radio* |
| 4. | | (.2) Four seventy one. | |
| 5. | Radio: | Yessir would you send. | |
| 6. | | somebody out here the::ah (.) | *Ops A looks to video* |
| 7. | | agent working the *jet*way here | *monitor* |

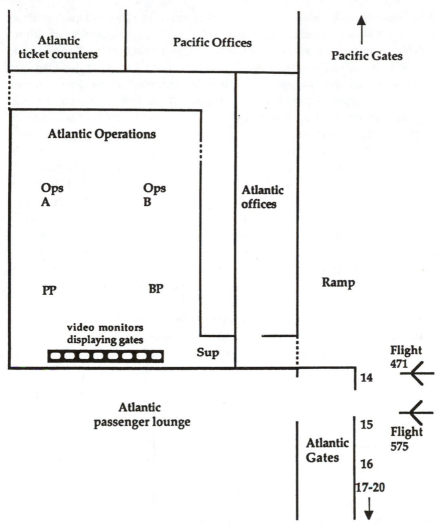

Figure 1.

| 8. | | is running around with their |
|---|---|---|
| 9. | | *hands* up in the air (.2) |
| 10. | Ops A: | //(laugh) |
| 11. | Radio | //obviously |
| 12. | | doesn't know how to work |
| 13. | | //the uh: (.8) stairways or |
| 14. | | can't get it to work (one). |
| 15. | | We need some help. |
| 16. | Ops B: | //Must be Sarducci.        *looks to monitor* |
| 17. | Ops A: | Will advise.              *looks to PP* |
| 18. | | (1.0) |

When the call comes into the room it seems to be marked only by Ops A, who selects himself as its intended recipient (see Fig. 2).[8] His self-selection is predictable insofar as this is "his" radio; that is, it goes with the Ops A position and thus with the person who inhabits it at any given time. We note, however, that whereas individuals in the operations room lay temporary claim to a workspace in virtue of their assignment to a position in the division of labor, their claims to that space are practical and contingent ones. That is to say, rights of access to the use spaces of the operations room are responsive to requirements of the moment, being subject to replacement (if the assigned occupant is out of the room or otherwise engaged) or displacement (if the space holds a technology to which another needs temporary access). If Ops A were out of the room, it would be the responsibility of his coworkers to fill in. So we can assume that while there is no visible reorientation to the call on the part of Ops A's coworkers, they are aware, or at least are assuming in the absence of evidence to the contrary, that Ops A is present there to take the call. Given that, and given its unavailability to the caller, Ops A's vocalization as he struggles with the radio can be understood to display to his coworkers that he is there, has heard the call and is responsive, despite the time that it takes him successfully to respond.

The pilot's use of "here" employs what Hanks (1990) terms the "body as indexical ground" (p. 14). That is, in locating the trouble relative to himself, the pilot simultaneously provides instructions for its location by operations. As the pi-

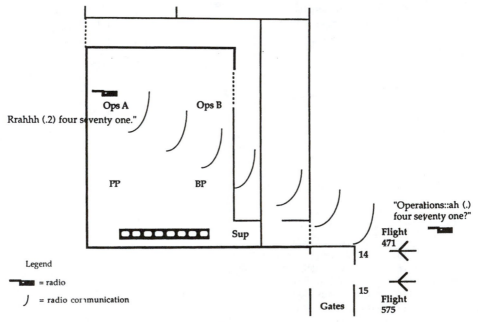

Figure 2.

lot locates the trouble, and by implication his request "out here," Ops A shifts his gaze to the video monitor by which his own environment is aligned with the gate that he takes that "out here" to index (see Fig. 3).[9]

His re-orientation is done in the course of the pilot's emerging report, putting him in alignment with the locale in advance of his having learned just what's going on out there, but in a state of readiness for it (see Goodwin & Goodwin, this volume). At the same time, he maintains a bodily orientation toward his own workspace, displaying an aspect of spatial-orientational positioning identified by Kendon (1985) and developed extensively by Schegloff (1990); that is, through the segmentation of the body's orientation displaying his only temporarily or partially redirected focus of attention.

Ops B's comment regarding "Sarducci," similarly, is directed to the monitor/gate at which he presumably locates the scene that the pilot reports. At the same time, in turning his gaze to the monitor, Ops B also directs his comment out into the room, disengaging momentarily from his own work and workspace to align himself to the now public business of Ops A, the pilot, and their developing situation. While Ops B's comment is addressed to his coworkers in the operations room, it implicitly references the scene out at the gate. The gaze to the monitor, then, not only indexes what he takes to be the pilot's locale (and, if his conjecture

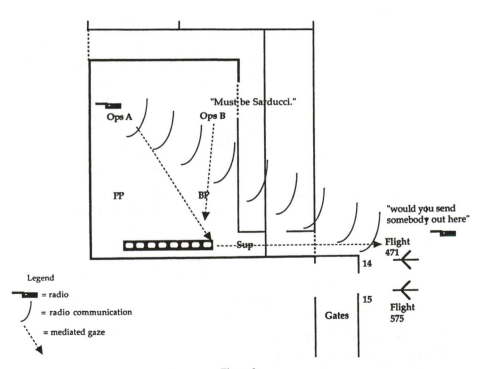

Figure 3.

were correct, that of Sarducci), it also indicates to those present that his comment is a comment on the scene that the pilot reports. Like Ops A, however, his body remains primarily oriented to his own terminal, his hands not leaving the keyboard, and he returns to the typing, his comment having been made. In this way he constitutes his workstation as a "home position" and the work he is doing there as ongoing, thereby displaying what Schegloff terms "the embodied articulation of multiple courses of action" (1990, p. 6). More specifically, in establishing his work at the keyboard as a primary course of action, he accords his comment the status of "crossplay," and maintains his footing as a bystander rather than a participant in the emerging situation (Goffman, 1981, p. 134). As Schegloff points out, this is itself a form of action; one that in this case is central to the simultaneous maintenance of both shared and differential workspaces within the room.

### Spatial orientational positioning for joint action

Following Goffman, Kendon (1985) argues that a characteristic of joint activity is the requirement that persons who would act in concert maintain a shared "definition of the situation," a congruent analysis of what is relevant and irrelevant to their common purposes at hand. He provides a rich set of concepts for analyzing in detail the resources available to interactants for the achievement of this interpretive work, one of the most powerful being his analysis of the structure of spatial-orientational positioning.

Kendon takes off from the observation that "a person's activity is always located somewhere. Any line of action that a person is pursuing is always carried out in a specific relation to a specific environment" (1985, p. 237). Starting with the individual, Kendon proposes the notion of *transactional segment*:

> The transactional segment is the space into which the individual addresses his gaze as he carries out his line of activity, whatever it may be; it is the space from which he immediately and readily reaches for whatever objects his current project may require he manipulate; it is the space immediately in front of him that the individual projects forward and keeps clear if he is moving. In short, it is the space that the individual seeks to maintain clear for his own purposes (p. 237).

With respect to shared workspace, this observation underscores that the systematic organization of work is a systematic organization of space as well:

> The establishment and maintenance of spatial-orientational arrangements, it seems, is one way that participants can provide one another with evidence that they are prepared to sustain a common orientational perspective. By arranging themselves into a particular spatial-orientational pattern they thereby display to each other that they are governed by the same set of general considerations. By co-operating with one another to sustain a given spatial-orientational arrangement, they can display a common state of readiness (p. 237).

On this view, it is the constitution of joint transactional segments through material and interactional means that makes up the more and less shifting boundaries of a shared workspace. Within the operations room, there is both a differentiated and an incipiently shared orientation. Seated at their respective workstations, members in one sense would appear to be arranged in a spatial-orientational pattern that indicates their *lack* of common orientational perspective. Each maintains a different perspective on the ongoing operations. Yet, given the shared orientation to timely operations that the division of labor and the arrangement of space is meant to sustain, their very presence at their workstations displays a certain "common state of readiness." From that state they are able to conjoin transactional segments dynamically and in ways responsive to contingencies of the moment, through partial shifts in gaze, changes in body position and the like.

In this case, following the call, Ops A and PP exchange glances, while maintaining their primary bodily orientations to their respective workstations (Fig. 4):

```
17. Ops A:  Will advise.              looks toward PP
18.         (1.0)
19. PP:     What gate was that?    looks to Ops A
20. Ops A:  Four//teen.
21. PP:     //four seventy one?
22. Ops A:  Yeah.
23. PP:     Operations to Alex?
24.         (.8)
```

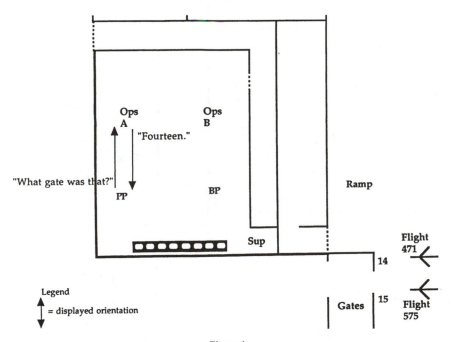

Figure 4.

Ops A's look to PP, and the latter's request for clarification of the location of the pilot-reported trouble, constitutes Ops A's glance as a "silent hand-off" of the call to the gate from Ops A to PP. In this moment, the respective transactional segments of Ops A and PP are partially conjointed, creating a common space between them, and through that bodily alignment an alignment of their respective actions.

PP's radio call to Alex initiates the opening of another, technology-mediated workspace between himself and the "lead" of the crew out on the ramp. Coincidently, however, and in place of a response from Alex, comes another, alternative summons from another gate (see also Brun-Cottan, 1991) (Fig. 5):

    25. Radio:   Gate ah fifteen operations?
    26. PP:       Go ahead.
    27. Radio:   Stairs don't work
    28.           on five seventy fi::ve
    29.           (.5)
    30. Radio:   Pump's (outXoff).
    31.           (4.0)
    32. PP:       D'you say the pump'so:ff?
    33. Radio:   (It) *do*sn't *work.*

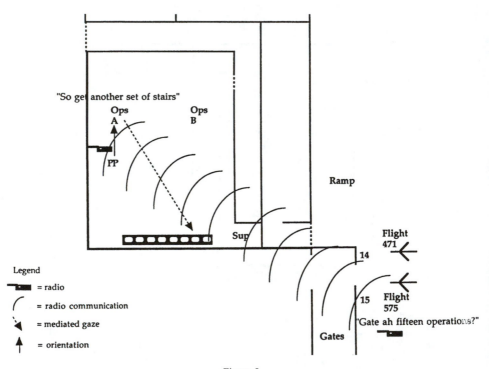

Figure 5.

```
34. Ops A:  So get another set of stairs
35.            off of sixteen or something.=
36. PP:      =Off the five seventy five?
37. Ops A:  //(yeah) (head shake)
38.            sixteen.
```

This call provides a second report of trouble, again seeking to direct attention in the operations room to a locale at which a situation is developing for which, the claim is implicitly made, operations has some responsibility and to which it should be orienting. At this point there is reason to believe that there are now two locations of trouble, one at 471/gate 14, this other at 575/gate 15, though there is no obvious orientation to that duplication by the participants themselves.[10]

Ops A's suggestion regarding "another set of stairs," made over his shoulder with a glance to the monitor, is structurally responsive to the trouble report and addressed to the caller at the gate, but insofar as he shares no interactive space with the caller, the remark is rhetorical, available only to his coworkers within the room. The remark is taken up by PP, as "overhearer," as a genuine proposal for what should be done. In that spirit, PP requests clarification.

## Power as bodily re-placements

Kendon (1985) observes that a distinction is routinely made by interactants between those actions taken to be part of a main line of activity and those viewed as merely instrumental or even irrelevant to the business at hand. To a large extent talk, vocalization and a subset of specific nonvocal activities are assigned to the first category, while replacements in space are assigned to the second or third. Kendon proposes that it is precisely because of their allocation to the "unofficial" line of action that spatial orientation and positioning are effective devices for the management of attention to activities proposed or underway:

> Thus what is required for focussed interaction to get underway is that there be (1) aspects of behaviour that serve in the process of providing spatial and temporal locus to the activity of the interaction, and (2) that these aspects of behaviour be different from those aspects constituted as the main-track activity (p. 236).

In the case at hand, the conjoined orientation established by PP and Ops A is broken by their supervisor, who walks over and places himself in between them, facing PP (Fig. 6):

```
39. S:   //(inaudible)                         walking over
40.        We need to go to Pacific.
41.        We need to get Pacific's stairs=
42.        call: Pacific. They got lon—
43.        they got high stairs don't they?
44. PP:  U::m.                                  picks up phone, dials
45.        (8.0)
```

With this move S enters the line of action set up by the call from the pilot and redirects the joint activity underway between Ops A and PP, instructing PP to ini-

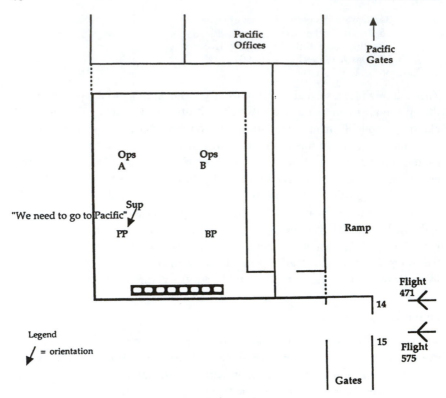

Figure 6.

tiate a phone call to another airline, Pacific, in order to enlist them into the activity as well.[11] Having done that, S uses the video monitors to align himself with the gate and, having inspected the gate, reaches for the phone. He interrupts his own trajectory to recruit BP into the action as well, instructing her to initiate a call to ground maintenance via another medium (Fig. 7):

| 46. | S: | | *working camera,* |
|---|---|---|---|
| 47. | | | *reaches for phone,* |
| 48. | | | *then turns to BP,* |
| 49. | S: | Call groun- | *taps BP on shoulder* |
| 50. | | Call ground maintenance at | |
| 51. | | (.) gate fifteen (im) real. | |
| 52. | | quick (.) as fast as they can | |
| 53. | | (.2) on the radio | |
| 54. | | I got (th)em on the phone. | *picking up phone* |
| 55. | | (1.0) | |
| 56. | BP: | Call them on the radio? | |
| 57. | S: | Yeah, I got//them on the | |
| 58. | | phone. | |

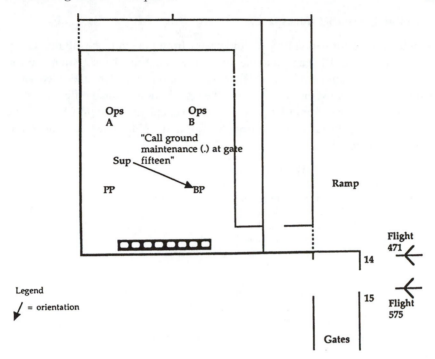

Figure 7.

BP's disattention to the situation requires S to recycle his instruction and intensi-fy his implicit summons to an explicit one. Specifically, he reaches across the room to tap her on the shoulder, bringing her out of the separate space she occu-pies on the phone and with a visiting coworker from the ramp, and into the in-creasingly joint activity addressed to the trouble.

From BP's point of view, of course, it is not so much that she is specifically disattending to the trouble situation as that she is attending to other things: first, a phone call and later an interaction with her coworker from the ramp. And yet, to maintain her differential attention, given the escalating level of activity in the room behind her, requires some special work. Specifically, if we watch BP up to this point we can see how she uses her whole body to maintain her separate ori-entation, first encompassing the phone call in which she's engaged when the sit-uation arises, then an interaction with the coworker. Even with respect to the lat-ter, she maintains her primary orientation toward her separate workspace, still holding onto the phone if not actually talking into it, rather than opening up fully to face him. In this way she maintains the boundary between her own position and the rest of the room. In reaching across that boundary, S interrupts her sepa-rate engagement and brings her into the joint activity, thereby making a claim for its priority.[12]

### Assembling a shared workspace

As S breaks the formation between the visitor from the ramp and BP the former disengages, and as BP leans in to the radio in response to S's instruction, the visitor departs. PP summons Pacific, BP and S summon ground maintenance, and a period of mobilization ensues involving the constitution of three different but related orientations: 1) from PP to Pacific via the telephone, 2) from BP to ground maintenance via the radio, and 3) from S to ground maintenance via another line of the telephone (Fig. 8):

| | | | |
|---|---|---|---|
| 59. | PP: | Hi Dan at//Atlantic | *on phone* |
| 60. | | again. | |
| 61. | BP: | //Ground maintenance | *on radio* |
| 62. | | come in please? | |
| 63. | PP: | Do you folks have | |
| 64. | | high stairs that go up to uh: (.) | |
| 65. | | as high as our seven sixty | |
| 66. | | seven? | |
| 67. | Radio: | //(inaudible) | |
| 68. | S: | //Fred, Victor in Ops. | *on phone* |

While the different locations of callers and those called preclude the kind of spatial orientational positioning between them described by Kendon for face-to-face interaction, each of the callers displays in their respective summons their own spatial location vis à vis those called. Most literally, S positions himself, telephone at his ear, so as to be able while he is talking on the telephone to monitor the video feed into operations and thereby, indirectly, the activity at the gate. In that way he simultaneously juxtaposes his own location with that of his collaborator at ground maintenance (via the telephone) and both of their locations to the site of the trouble (via the video monitor).

In the construction of their summons as well, callers differentially display their relations to their interlocutors (see Schegloff, 1972). PP's identification of himself to Pacific by means of first name and organizational affiliation locates him as an outsider to, but personally recognizable by, someone in the other organizational venue. BP's unmarked summons to ground maintenance via the radio relies upon the identifying character of the radio frequency itself, as something to which only those located within the organization, and particular positions within it, have access. Finally S's telephone summons is answered by Fred, who presumably self-identifies and is recognized by S, who in turn implicitly locates himself as a comember by reference to a place, "in Ops," without any further organizational affiliation. The form of the reference proposes operations as a place recognizable to Fred, and implicitly locates S within the same organizational territory. In these ways, participants locate themselves at the "intersection between physical locales and social distinctions" (Lynch, 1991, p. 51).

The multifocussed participation framework set up by these summonses is fur-

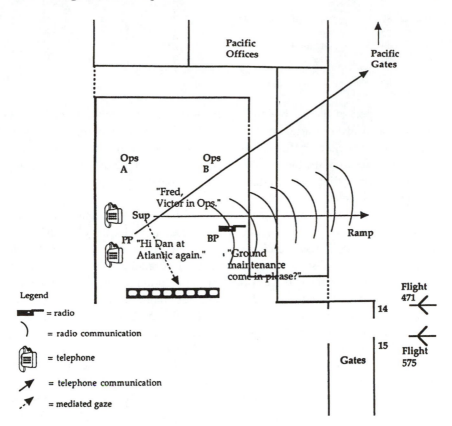

Figure 8.

ther complicated by a call *into* the room that comes between BP's call to ground maintenance and its awaited answer:[13]

| | | | |
|---|---|---|---|
| 67. | Radio: | //(inaudible) | |
| 68. | S: | //Fred, Victor in Ops. | *on phone* |
| 69. | | Ah the sixty seven | |
| 70. | | //just pulled in and the | |
| 71. | BP: | //(Aright, go ahead Carl.) | *into radio* |
| 72. | S: | stairs just took a crap= | |
| 73. | | //can you guys get up here? | |
| 74. | | (2.0) | |
| 75. | S: | Thank you sir= bye (.2) | *hangs up* |
| 76. | | okay. | |
| 77. | Radio: | //(inaudible) | |
| 78. | | down here the uh (.) | |
| 79. | | stair's won't pull up or work | |
| 80. | | for the (.) six seven so | |
| 81. | | we're in trouble and | |

| 82. | we need them down there | |
| 83. | now. | |
| 84. S: | Maintenance is on their | *to BP* |
| 85. | way up. | |
| 86. BP: | //Okay, they're (on their | *into radio* |
| 87. | way up) right now. | |

This third report of the trouble into operations, from the ramp, interrupts BP's call to ground maintenance. At the same time, her radio summons to ground maintenance is obviated by the progress of S's telephone call to them. In particular, we can infer from the fact that S goes ahead to report the trouble to Fred and request assistance (lines 68–75) that his call to ground maintenance has reached its intended recipient.

Note that at the outset of this sequence, S and BP are both issuing summonses to the same location—ground maintenance. The alternate technologies they employ, however, require them to disengage from their primary orientation to each other for the duration of their respective calls. The radio call in from the ramp further differentiates their focus in that for the duration of her interaction with the ramp BP is no longer engaged with S in the joint attempt to reach ground maintenance. Yet, the space and trajectory of their work reconverges. The radio call from the ramp informs BP of the trouble, to which up to this point she has not been visibly orienting, other than indirectly, through her taking up of S's instruction to call ground maintenance. As she receives the report, overhearable by anyone in the room due to the radio technology used, S completes his telephone call to ground maintenance. He then turns to BP and provides her with the answer to the ramp's implicit request ("Maintenance is on their way up"), which he has just obtained, and which she then smoothly passes along to the ramp:

BP:    Okay, they're (on their way up) right now.

PP, meanwhile, is pursuing the alternate path of attempting to persuade a neighboring airline to transfer equipment from their workspace into his own. S turns to that ongoing situation at the completion of his work with ground maintenance and BP, by initiating another summons to the ramp (line 94 below; see Fig. 10):

| 88. PP | //Hi Dan at Atlantic (.) | *on phone* |
| 89. | Do you folks have a: | |
| 90. | set of stairs that go up pretty | |
| 91. | high that we could use | |
| 92. | on a seven sixt(y)- | |
| 93. | (4.0) | |
| 94. S: | Ops to Alex? | *into radio* |
| 95. | (5.0) | |
| 96. Radio: | Go ahead Ops. | |

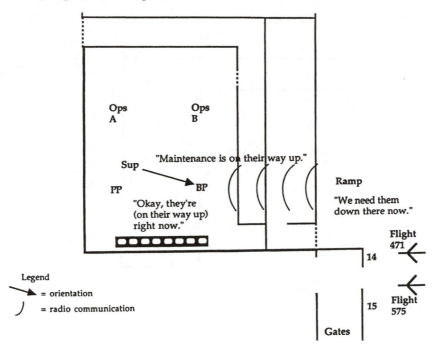

Figure 9.

```
 97. S:       Alex you near gate fifteen?
 98. Radio:   (in the main office)
 99. S:       'kay I need you at fifteen
100.          the stairs took a crap=
101.          we can't get anybody off the
102.          sixty seven (.) probably
103.          going to have to run
104.          somebody over to Pacific to
105.          use theirs.
106. Radio:   Okay I'll c- take care of it
107.          thank you.
```

In his call to Alex, S effectively orients Alex to the developing trajectory of PP's call to Pacific. First, S locates Alex in relation to the trouble ("you near gate fifteen?"), then recruits him to the site ("I need you at fifteen"). S then provides an account of the trouble there, its "probably" solution, and Alex's projected role in that solution, as a course of action taking up from where PP's phone call will leave off. As in the coordination of his actions with BP's, S here takes up a line of action parallel to PP's that is differently focussed, but nonetheless aligned with and responsive to the unfolding course of PP's call.

At the close of his call to Pacific, PP "returns" to operations to report back.

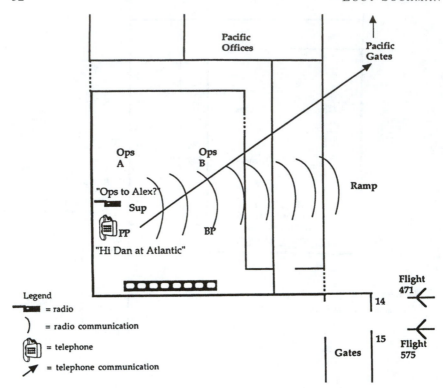

Figure 10.

The problem appears to be that Pacific claims not to have an appropriate set of stairs to loan:

| | | |
|---|---|---|
| 119. PP: | Pacific's reluctant, they | *to the room* |
| 120. | don't think it'll go up that | |
| 121. | high and they don't really | |
| 122. | *want* it to go up that high. | |
| 123. Ramper: | What about tee du:b. | |
| 124. Ops A: | They've had a seven-fifty- | |
| 125. | seven here before that | |
| 126. | they've used their stairs on. | |
| 127. PP: | What about B S B don't | |
| 128. | they have something here? | |
| 129. | (1.0) | |
| 130. | And where are they. | |
| 131. Ops A: | ((inaudible)) Don't they | |
| 132. | //work uh: (.) Alaska? | |

This discussion of who might have the set of stairs to loan is constructed in terms of the availability of the necessary object "here," presumably meaning in this case "on the premises," or "here at the airport." PP's question statement regarding one of the candidates, "And where are they," shifts more specifically to just where the potential providers are located within the larger territory of "here," as a prerequisite to being able actually to contact them. PP's query is a situated inquiry into a spatial order of social relations, motivated by the practical requirements of projected action.

## A common focussed gathering

Much of the work of the operations room is structured as activities distributed over time and space and interspersed with other, more or less related, interactions. The result is an interorganization of activities, each one of which may be just a fragment of some larger course of events. This spatiotemporal fragmentation combines with the division of labor to produce a differentiated structure of attention among operations room members and their affiliated locations. That is to say, for much of the time, participants are attending to different events, in separate locations. Even those occupying the same physical space, insofar as their orientations are different, may be inhabiting separate attentional and interactional workspaces.

The episode in question, in contrast, has the shape of what Goffman (1982) has named a focussed encounter, which he describes in the following way:

> The opening will typically be marked by the participants turning from their several disjointed orientations, moving together and bodily addressing one another; then closing by their departing in some physical way from the prior immediacy of correspondence (p. 130).

At this point in the day's work, inhabitants of the operations room are all oriented, via the video monitor, to the scene at gate 15. They thereby constitute what Goffman calls "a common, focussed gathering," becoming an audience to the scene at the gate as well as participants in it. A radio call into operations from the gate reveals the disjuncture between physical colocation with the trouble site and interactional access to the scene (Fig. 11):

| | | | |
|---|---|---|---|
| 133. | Radio: | //radio check ops | |
| 134. | | radio check. | |
| 135. | | (.8) | |
| 136. | PP: | Loud and clear. | *into radio* |
| 137. | Radio: | Thank you. | |
| 138. | Ops A: | They work Alaska. | |
| 139. | PP: | Is ground equipment | *reaching for camera* |
| 140. | | down there? | *controls* |
| 141. | | (.8) | |
| 142. | PP: | Did we get a hold of them? | |
| 143. | S: | We've used Pacific's before | |
| 144. | | they're not going to let us | |
| 145. | | use them? | |

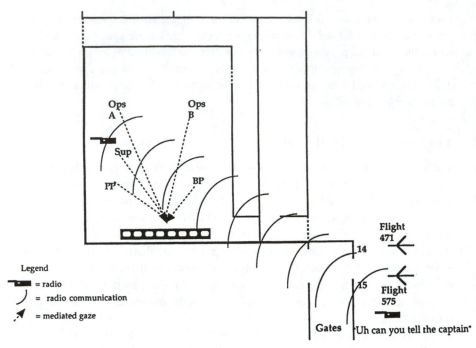

Figure 11.

146. PP:      We have?
147. S:       //Yeah.
148. Radio:   //Gate fifteen Operations?
149. PP:      Their lead is not here
150.          that's why uh (1.0)
151. S:       Go ahead.                        *into radio*
152. Radio:   Uh can you tell the captain
153.          on five-seventy-five that
154.          it'll be a couple more
155.          minutes (to) replace that
              belt?
156.          (1.0)
157. S:       Okay thanks.
158.          (.8)

The radio call from the gate requests that operations act as relay to the captain on the plane, providing him with an update on the situation. Parties in the room maintain an orientation to the gate via the monitor as the caller makes his report, juxtaposing the auditory space in the room with their visual access to the place from which the call comes and to which it refers. The call makes clear that whereas the captain is in some sense more directly present at the scene than operations is, he is a less direct participant in the relevant interactional workspace.

It is the centralization of such informings about ongoing events that constitutes and maintains operations as the center of coordination for work across multiple worksites and participation frameworks. And it is the equipment through which those informings are mediated that makes the centralization possible.

## Problem dissolution

At the close of the radio call, and in spite of the report that ground maintenance's effort to repair the stairs is underway and is projected to be complete in only "a couple more minutes," S resumes the discussion into which the call broke with a direct proposal that they revisit Pacific and try again to enlist their assistance:

```
159.  S:    U::m (.) let's call them back      to PP
160.        we've used them before (.)
161.        who—who'd you talk to at
162.        Pacific?
163.  PP:   Uh somebody at their Ops
164.        (.) I was transferred there and
165.        he didn't think they would
166.        go up but he said I don't
167.        have a lead here tonight
168.        and I don't want them to go
169.        up that high (.2)
170.        So (.5)
171.  PP:   I'll be glad to call them
172.        back (.) um
173.        (.8)
174.  PP:   They were truck stairs
175.        is that what we used?
176.        (1.0)
177.  S:    Looks like they might have       gaze to monitor
178.        got it started.
179.        (1.0)
180.  S:    They got it.
181.        (5.0)
```

S at this point has walked over to answer the radio call from the gate and is therefore standing just behind PP, or at least PP's sustained orientation toward the monitors places his back to S. In discussing the call to Pacific with S, PP addresses him over his shoulder, with glances as well toward the phone that indexes the previous and the prospective call. His body orientation remains toward the monitor, however, and possibly toward the work of ground maintenance that could at any moment obviate the need for another appeal to Pacific. In the course of PP's story about his call to Pacific, S's gaze is also on the monitors. And in lieu of a response to PP's query regarding the type of stairs they've borrowed from Pacific before, S offers the observation that the trouble appears to have been remedied by a repair. From that point the scene is progressively reconstituted into multiple, differently focussed activities.

Lave (1988) argues that the classical notion of problem solving misconceives and mislocates processes of practical reasoning, being blind to their social and material grounds and assigning to them a primarily mental locus within the heads of individuals. In opposition to that tradition she poses an inquiry into what she calls *structuring resources*; that is, culturally/historically constituted relations of persons, settings, and activity. Problem solving on this view "is part of an articulatory phenomenon constituted between persons-acting and the settings of activity" (p. 159). Dilemmas are not so much solved as they are "dissolved" through structuring resources inventively employed. For the operations room as a center of coordination, those resources appear as a heterogeneous environment of persons and equipment, distributed across physical locales and social relationships, assembled into a working system for the reproduction and restoration of a normal order.

## Conclusion

The occasion of work reconstructed here took place over a period of roughly five minutes of clock time, during which a routine breakdown in the reproduction of a normal order was observed, reported, and resolved. For the participants, this incident was an unremarkable one, requiring a momentary mobilization of available resources into a concerted course of action, quickly forgotten once the moment had passed.[14] These processes of observation, reportage, and repair turn out to comprise a complex round of activities, however, involving persons distributed in space, each with different preoccupations at the outset of the event. Participants become engaged through partial, continuously changing awareness to a shared situation, and establish their own relationship to it or are enlisted in it by others, as practical actors and as contributors to its resolution.

In considering the course of this event as the emergent structuring of a shared spatial order, I have foregrounded the following thematic interests:

*The worksite as situational territory*—the predominance in the modern workplace of familiar habitats that are anonymously owned and temporarily appropriated by workers. In the case of the operations room, the place of work is maintained simultaneously as a restricted area and as a public space, as the ground for social distinctions, and as a site for joint activity. The territory comprises stable positions reproduced across changes in occupants, at the same time that persons occupying those positions establish for themselves a local order of familiar equipment and practice, specifically constituted for the work at hand.

*Local orders of spatial-orientational positioning*—how bodies are engaged in the work of maintaining and transforming attention and participation, including partial and discontinuous engagement in multiple trajectories of orientation and interaction.

*Replacements in space*—unremarkable resources for the redirection of orientation and interaction.

*Multiple, interacting participation frameworks,* and the artful accomplishment of a shared situation through the discrimination and recognition of mutual relevances.

*A focussed gathering*—the contingent assembly of multiple lines of activity into a shared focus of attention.

*Problem dissolution*—the ad hoc engagement of heterogeneous human and technological resources in the restoration of a working order.

The workspace afforded by the operations room is not simply given by the room's interior design, but is a collaborative achievement involving the continuous production and transformation of personal space, of spaces jointly held, and of the boundaries between them. As a center of coordination for activities distributed in space and time, the operations room displays in its design the competing requirements of joint work and of a division of labor; of a single, common focus and a discontinuous ordering of differentiated workspaces. As colleagues copresent to each other, inhabitants of the operations room structure their cooperative activity in concert, whereas in their assignment to the monitoring and direction of activities at other relevant locations, each is differentially oriented. Within the room the absence of walls or other barriers to mutual monitoring makes possible a continuous state of incipient interaction: the possibility that, at any moment, workspaces constituted in the service of one line of activity may be redefined by or for another. At the same time, the spatial-orientational positioning of operations room members away from each other, toward the equipment that constitutes the enabling technologies for their respective tasks, supports the systematic disattention to each others' activities that the division of labor requires. Members' places in a complex system of activities distributed across ramps, gates, and the like makes them differentially available to involvement in the work of distant others, effected by means of technologies that extend their reach beyond the confines of the room itself. Through their interactions with each other and with their environment, members of the operations room create the space for their joint and individual activities at the same time that those activities are structured by the spaces in which they occur.

Through recent cultural/historical studies we have acquired a programmatic discourse with which to locate stabilities of social order in the reproduction of specific arrangements of persons, technologies, and disciplinary practices. Ethnomethodological studies provide the possibility of access to the lived work through which such arrangements are produced and reproduced as local orders of culturally constituted ordinary activities. In doing so, moreover, these studies contribute to the displacement of a view of local orders as the manifestations of a master plan, as small reflections of a "larger" organization, proposing instead "a

discontinuous ecology that embodies heterogeneous, and perhaps even contradictory, orderings of knowledge/power" (Lynch, 1991, p. 55). The disciplinary
practices documented here involve the achievement of an alignment, across such
a discontinuous ecology, of workspaces shared for the purposes of concerted action in the ongoing accomplishment of an accountable spatiotemporal order.

## Notes

1  All proper names are pseudonyms. The research reported here was conducted as a part of the
   Workplace Project at Xerox Palo Alto Research Center, through the sponsorship of Xerox and
   Steelcase Corporations. I am indebted to Francoise Brun-Cottan, Paul Drew, Charles Goodwin,
   Marjorie Goodwin, Brigitte Jordan, Emanuel Schegloff, and Randy Trigg for joint work on these
   materials.
2  For a full set of references to analyses of the operations room as a multiactivity work setting see
   Suchman, in press. See also Brun-Cottan et al., 1991; C. Goodwin and M. H. Goodwin, this volume.
3  For more on this project see Suchman, in press.
4  Different types of aircraft come in different sizes, thus the requirement that the stairs be ad-
   justable in order to reach the door of a given plane.
5  Any attempt at categorical description of the responsibilities associated with the various positions
   within the operations room is useful only as a gloss (whether for analysis or members). The account provided here is meant to serve as a resource for interpreting the analysis that follows, not
   as a description of the work.
6  Also in the room at the time are two researchers, here deleted from both the figures and the analysis.
7  In transcript segments colons ":" indicate prolongation of the immediately preceding sound and
   italics mark stress. A dot in parentheses "(.)" indicates an untimed pause, numbers in parentheses
   indicate elapsed time in seconds. An equals sign "=" indicates "latching," i.e., the beginning of
   one utterance following directly on the end of the prior one with no gap. Double slashes "//" indicate the onset of overlapped talk. Text in parentheses indicates uncertainty on the part of the transcriber.
8  Throughout, pronouns reflect the gender of the specific parties on this occasion.
9  While the work of operations is oriented to the gates, the room has no windows and therefore no
   visual access to the locations of most interest to Ops room workers. A technological solution to
   this problem is the placement of cameras at each of the gates, which feed a set of video images
   into a row of monitors aligned at the front of the room.
10 In fact, with the resolution of the trouble at gate 15, PP turns at the end of this sequence back
   to the monitors, saying to the room "How'd we do on fourteen, did we get that squared away?
   (.8) That's the one (the agent) didn't know what to do?" His question gets no response from his
   coworkers. After some time searching the gate area with the video camera, he apparently satis-
   fies himself that there is no outstanding trouble there and turns to other things. We infer, in retrospect, that the pilot who called in from gate 14 was not in fact reporting trouble at his own
   location, as we and the participants at first assumed, but rather reporting in as a witness to trouble at the gate next door. The pilot's construction of his trouble report, i.e. "would you send
   someone out here . . . the agent working the jetway here, . . . " seems to encourage the initial
   (mis)interpretation to the effect that his location and the location of the trouble are the same.
   Why he uses this construction remains a puzzle for us as analysis. For the participants, however, the puzzle seems resolved by the unfolding of events to the extent that continuing confusion
   is evident only in this question from PP, and he drops the question in the absence of any up-
   take by the others and the absence of any observable trouble at gate 14.

11 Note that it is the phone call that, for present purposes, constitutes "going to" Pacific. Shared workspace in this environment, given the extension of relevant activity systems across time and space, is continuously constituted in this way through the employment of mediating technologies, e.g., radios, telephones, video monitors, and computer systems.

12 There is a pervasive ambiguity regarding the exercise of power within a site like the operations room. Most profoundly, power lies in the anonymous discipline of the schedule, which defines the relations of time and space to which all participants by definition are dedicated (see Suchman, 1993; Suchman & Whalen, 1994). Within that discipline, the role of the supervisor includes certain corrective interventions in the activity of others, with implicit and explicit assessments unmistakably attached. At the same time, the supervisor can be viewed as a body in the service of those who work for him. That is to say, participants oriented to a specific line of action or even multiple lines of action rely upon the supervisor to take responsibility for the workings of the site as a whole and to reorient them when the need arises, thereby relieving them of some responsibility for monitoring the activity of others themselves. Insofar as one can be found to be unavailable or preoccupied for good reason, at the same time that mutual monitoring is an element of competent participation, the line between achieved disattention in the pursuit of one's duties and not paying attention is a subtle one.

13 Brun-Cottan (1991) points out the interactional requirements set up by radio technologies and the ways in which participants design their summonses with just such potential interruptions in mind.

14 The unremarkable status of the incident was indicated to us, for example, by the observation that a coworker coming in from the ramp shortly after the trouble's resolution, who inquired of one of the operations room workers present to the event, "What's happening," received the reply, "Oh, nothing much."

# References

Brun-Cottan, F. (1991). Talk in the workplace: Occupational relevance. In R. Hopper (Ed.) *Research on Language in Social Interaction.* Vol. 24, pp. 277–295.

Filippi, G. & Theureau, J. (1993). Analyzing cooperative work in an urban traffic control room for the design of a coordination support system. In G. Michelis, C. Simone & K. Schmidt (Eds.), *Proceedings of the Third European Conference on Computer-Supported Cooperative Work* (pp. 171–186). Dordrecht, The Netherlands: Kluwer.

Goffman, E. (1981). *Forms of Talk.* Philadelphia, PA: University of Pennsylvania Press.

Goffman, E. (1971). The Territories of the Self. In *Relations in Public: Microstudies of the Public Order.* New York: Harper and Row.

Goodwin, C. & Goodwin, M. H. (1995). *Formulating Planes: Seeing as a Situated Activity.* This volume.

Hanks, W. (1990). *Referential Practice.* Chicago: University of Chicago Press.

Harper, R. & Hughes, J. (1993). "What a F-ing System! Send 'em all to the same place and then expect us to stop 'em hitting": Making technology work in air traffic control. In G. Button (Ed.), *Technology in working order: Studies in work, interaction and technology* (pp. 127–144). London: Routledge.

Heath, C. C. & P. K. Luff (1992). Crisis and control: Collaborative work in London underground control rooms. *Journal of Computer Supported Cooperative Work, 1*(1), 24–48.

Hutchins, E. (1990). The technology of team navigation. In J. Gallagher, R. Kraut, & C. Egido (Eds.) *Intellectual Teamwork.* Hillsdale, NJ: Erlbaum.

Kendon, A. (1985). Behavioural foundations for the process of frame attunement in face-to-face interaction. In G. Ginsburt, M. Brenner & M. von Cranach (Eds.), *Discovery Strategies in the Psychology of Action* (pp. 229–253). London: Academic Press.

Lave, J. (1988). *Cognition in Practice.* Cambridge: Cambridge University Press.

Lynch, M. (1991). Laboratory space and the technological complex: An investigation of topical contextures. *Science in Context, 4*(1) 51–78.

Lynch, M., Livingston, E. & Garfinkel, H. (1983). Temporal order in laboratory work. In K. Knorr-Cetina & M. Mulkay (Eds.) *Science Observed* (pp. 205–238). London: Sage.

Schegloff, E. (1972). Notes on a conversational practice: Formulating place. In D. Sudnow (Ed.) *Studies in Social Interaction* (pp. 75–119). New York: Free Press.

Schegloff, E. (1990, November). *Body Torque.* Paper presented at the annual meeting of the American Anthropological Association, New Orleans, LA.

Suchman, L. (1993). Technologies of accountability: On lizards and airplanes. In G. Button (Ed.) *Technology in Working Order* (pp. 113–126). London: Routledge.

Suchman, L. Centers of Coordination: A case and some themes. To appear in L. Resnick, R. Saljo, & C. Pontecorvo (Eds.), *Discourse, Tools, and Reasoning* (in press). New York: Springer-Verlag.

Suchman, L. & Whalen, J. (1994). *Standardizing Local Events and Localizing Standard Forms.* Paper presented at the annual meetings of the Society for Social Studies of Science, New Orleans, LA.

Whalen, J. (1993, August). *Accounting for "Standard" Task Performance in the Execution of 9-1-1 Operations.* Paper presented at the annual meetings of the American Sociological Association, Miami.

# 4    Seeing as a situated activity: Formulating planes

*Charles Goodwin and Marjorie Harness Goodwin*

In order to focus as clearly as possible on some of the issues involved in the analysis of cognition in the workplace, this chapter will investigate a single, very simple, but very pervasive, activity performed by different kinds of workers in a medium-sized airport: looking at airplanes. Despite the brevity of individual glances, they are in no way haphazard. Workers look at planes in order to see something that will help them accomplish the work they are engaged in. Understanding that looking, therefore, requires analysis of the work activities within which it is embedded.

Powerful resources for the detailed analysis of mundane activities have been provided by the approach to the analysis of human interaction that encompasses Goffman (1963, 1971, 1974), Garfinkel (1967), Kendon (1990), and, most relevant to the work in the present paper, conversation analysis (Atkinson & Heritage, 1984; Drew & Heritage, 1992; C. Goodwin, 1981; M. H. Goodwin, in press; Goodwin & Heritage, 1990; Jefferson, 1973, 1984; Sacks, 1992; Sacks, Schegloff, & Jefferson, 1974; Schegloff, 1968). Moreover, in order to see the airplane in an appropriate, task-relevant way, workers use a range of different kinds of tools. A primary perspective for analysis of how human beings interact, not only with other human beings, but also with a material world shaped by the historical activities of others, can be found in activity theory (Cole, 1985, 1990; Engeström, 1987, 1990; Leont'ev, 1981; Vygotsky, 1962, 1978; Wertsch, 1985) and the work on distributed cognition that grows from it (Hutchins, 1990, 1995; Middleton & Edwards, 1990; Siefert & Hutchins, 1989). Analysis of the situated, technologically mediated, nature of seeing in complex work settings takes up themes raised in recent work in the sociology of science on representational practices (Latour, 1986, 1987; Latour & Woolgar, 1979; Lynch & Woolgar, 1988). One of the themes that will quickly become apparent in this paper is the way in which the ability to see something is always tied to a particular position encompassing a range of phenomena including placement within a larger organization, a local task, and access to relevant material and cognitive tools. Such focus on the embeddedness of knowledge within a plurality of diverse local perspectives explores issues raised in recent feminist scholarship on science (Haraway, 1988; Harding, 1986). By looking at how participants actually accomplish relevant seeing within specific tasks in local environments we will provide detailed analysis of what Star and Gerson (1987) call "performances" (see also Woolgar, 1988). Finally, the work provides a detailed investigation of the situated organization of action within the workplace (Suchman, 1987, this volume).

Investigating how airport personnel look at airplanes allows us to see how behavior as minute as a momentary glance is densely structured by larger organizational practices [i.e., how the body of a worker becomes an inscription point for what Foucault (1979) has called a discipline], as well as the tool-mediated organization of participants' access to the objects in their working environment, and the community that sustains such practices.

The work we report here is part of a long-term ethnographic study of work practices in a multiactivity setting – a midsized airport – initiated at Xerox PARC by Lucy Suchman. The project integrated ethnography with methodologies for studying human interaction developed within conversation analysis. In order to focus on what people actually did, rather than their reports about their work, we videotaped extensively, sometimes using as many as seven cameras to record distributed processes occurring in diverse locations. Whenever possible we tried to capture multiple perspectives in a single location, for example, using a wide-angle camera to record the interaction in the room and a close-up camera on the screens and documents with which the participants were working. One site that the project devoted particular attention to was the operations room used by each airline to coordinate ground operations (see Suchman, this volume).

### Seeing an airplane as a relevant organizational entity

Atlantic Hawk is a "commuter airline" that uses a fleet of small propeller planes to make flights to nearby airports. All of their planes look exactly alike and they are parked haphazardly (in the order in which they happened to arrive on this particular day) on a large section of runway some distance from the main gates.

Consider the tasks faced by someone responsible for loading baggage on an Atlantic Hawk flight to a specific destination, say Oakland. On the field in front of her are ten identical Atlantic Hawk planes (see Fig. 1). How is she to determine which plane to load, i.e., how can she see which of the ten planes is going to Oakland? Seeing the plane itself is not enough, since the plane she is looking for looks just like all of the other planes in her field of view.

For airport personnel, planes do not stand alone as isolated objects. Instead, they are defined by their positions in larger webs of activity. Thus, for the baggage loader a specific plane must be linked to another organizational entity, a *flight* going to a specific destination. To determine which of the planes in front of her is in fact going to Oakland, the baggage loader uses a tool called a "complex

Figure 1.

sheet," a grid that links flights and destinations to unique aircraft identification numbers:[1]

Complex Sheet

| Flight | Dest | Plane |
|--------|------|-------|
| 5231 | MRY | 462 |
| 5288 | OAK | 323 |
| 5246 | SBA | 287 |

The aircraft identification numbers are painted on the plane in several specified locations (for example, near the tail and nose). Thus, in order to find which plane to load, the baggage handler must: 1) look to her complex sheet to find the identification number of the plane going to Oakland and then 2) scan the collection of planes in front of her until she finds the one with that number (see Fig. 2).[2]

In order to see *a* plane in the manner that it is relevant to the tasks that she is engaged in, i.e., as *the* plane she is to load, the baggage handler must embed the object visible to her senses within a relevant organizational network, i.e., attach it to a flight going to a specific destination. Placing the plane in an appropriate network is not, however, automatic but requires both supporting tools (e.g., the complex sheet, the aircraft identification numbers, etc.) and specific situated

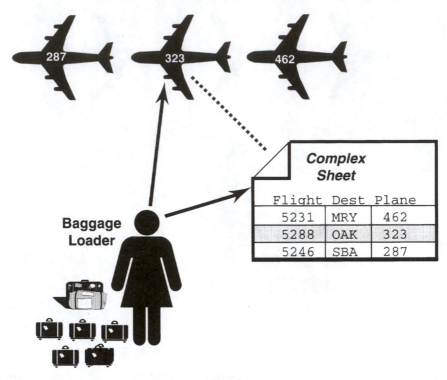

Figure 2.

work with those tools, an active course of seeing that juxtaposes the information on the complex sheet with the numbers painted on the plane.

The routine, but contingent and problematic, properties of this active process of juxtaposition cannot be overemphasized. In 1991, 34 people were killed when two planes crashed on the runway at Los Angeles International Airport after an air traffic controller "mistook another small plane that was halted short of the runway for the plane she had cleared to enter it" (Mydans, 1991, p. 9).

The complex sheet used by the baggage loader is the product of many different people's work. While the overall schedule is known well ahead of time, plane swaps are frequent (Jordan, 1990). The plane numbers must therefore be continuously updated as the day progresses. Shortly before each set of arrivals a ramp-crew chief goes into the Atlantic Hawk operations room, checks the computer, and makes a list of the latest aircraft numbers, which he posts on the ramp. Ramp personnel then update their own complex sheets. The glances being performed by each baggage loader thus build upon an elaborate social and technological infrastructure. An observer watching the baggage handler as she approaches the line of planes might see her as an isolated, solitary worker. However, by using the complex sheet, she builds upon the actions of coworkers who, though not physically present at the moment, provide organization for the looking she is doing.

Through the power of the complex sheet as a socially constituted tool, the actions performed by the baggage loader's body are linked in fine detail to the larger organizational structure of the airline.[3] The sheet mediates not only her access to the plane she is trying to find, but also, and simultaneously, it mediates her participation in the work of her coworkers and the larger organization within which her tasks are situated (see also Forbes, 1990).

One final point: from the perspective of the baggage loader, the plane as a relevant organizational object is defined by its position in the organizational network constituted by a flight. The flight is not, however, the only web that can be used to define a plane as a work-relevant object. Maintenance workers are most interested in the specific history of a particular aircraft, i.e., what work has been done on it in the past, what ailments it has had, when its servicing is next mandated, etc. This historical network is irrelevant to the baggage loader. For the tasks she faces, it is sufficient to know where the plane is going next, not what has happened to it in the past. Different work positions thus place the same physical object, a particular airplane, within different webs of accountability. The work structure of the organization defines a plurality of perspectives that entrain in differential fashion what alternative types of workers are expected to see when they look at an airplane. Quite frequently, perspectives overlap. For example Maintenance will allow a plane with a slight problem in its weather radar to fly as long as its route will not take it near thunderstorms. In such cases, the criterion central to the organization of the baggage loader's work, the plane's destination, becomes relevant to maintenance personnel as well. However, though both groups now attend to the same category, "destination," the detailed nature of the work that each group is doing differentially shapes how that category is to be perceived and what is to be seen in it. "Destination" for Maintenance is a complex object that encompasses multiple attributes (here, local weather conditions; on other occasions, altitude, distance, etc.), all of which are irrelevant to baggage. The situated perspectives of alternative work groups provide objects viewed in common with different horizons of meaning and relevance. Consistent with Wittgenstein's (1953, §66–67) analysis of "family resemblances," a category such as "destination" means different things in the different language games that make up the work life of the airport, though these separate senses have deep and overlapping connections with each other.[4]

## Gates and labels

The issues posed for the baggage loader faced with the task of finding a relevant flight are responsive to, and contingent upon, the detailed organization of the environment in which she is working. For example, the fact that the planes are scat-

Figure 3.

tered haphazardly on the runway requires that aircraft numbers be used to find the plane that constitutes a particular flight. At Atlantic Airlines, the large international airline that uses the Atlantic Hawk as a local subsidiary, planes are organized in space quite differently. Instead of being scattered on the runway, each plane is assigned to a specific *gate*. Thus, to see if a particular plane is in one does not have to scan the entire set of planes and read the aircraft number of each. Instead, one can look at the gate assigned to the plane and see whether or not it is occupied. Each plane/flight has been assigned a recognizable slot.

A video camera is mounted at each gate pointed at the position for the plane. The output of these cameras goes to the Atlantic Airlines operations room and into a line of monitors positioned on the front wall. Personnel in the Atlantic operations room can thus see the entire set of gates in a single glance (Fig. 3).

How is the task of seeing a plane accomplished in this environment? In the following, Ralph is teaching a new Operations apprentice, Val, how to do radio close-outs. In a radio close-out, an operations agent reads final flight information received over the computer to the pilot. A central piece of this information is the weights and balance report, which can only be computed after all doors to the plane have been closed and exact figures have been obtained for the weights of baggage, fuel, passengers, etc. In order to ensure speedy departures, operations personnel try to check their computers to see if the figures have been computed before the pilots actually call them as they approach takeoff position. Consider the sequence being examined here (see Fig. 4).

1. Ralph says "Let's see who's pushing" and shifts his gaze to the bank of monitors. While glancing at them he says "18." (i.e., a gate number).
2. He then moves his gaze to the computer system that is used to display flight information throughout the airport (i.e., flight, gate, destination, scheduled departure time, etc.). While reading it he says "18 is 1464" (i.e., he links a gate number to a specific flight).
3. He then turns to Val and says "He's off the gate. So let's go and see if 1464 has weight and balance."

Ralph's first task is to identify the gate of the departing plane. The label placed on each monitor (e.g., "18") ties the image on its screen to a particular gate. Linguistic anthropologists have devoted considerable attention to *texts* of various types (Hanks, 1989). However, the mundane, vernacular documents that constitute work spaces have largely been ignored (Goody, 1977). Some of these docu-

**Example (1)** *WE-9 13-Aug-90 2:01pm*

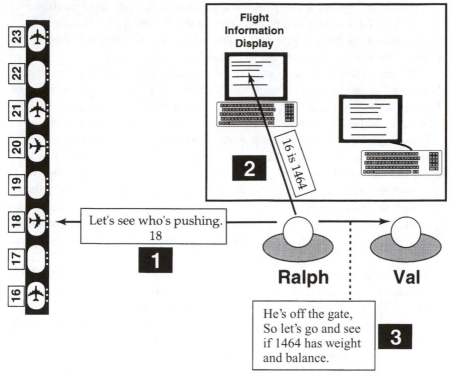

Figure 4.

ments have intricate forms of organization that are as complex as those attributed to traditional literary texts (note for example the complex, multilayered, socially distributed *authorship* of a form such as the complex sheet), whereas others, such as labels, might initially appear too simple and fragmented to merit serious analysis. However, the persuasiveness of such labels in work settings points to a set of complex practices through which workers annotate in locally relevant ways the worlds they inhabit (Engeström, 1990; Suchman, 1987). Ethnographers of science have devoted considerable attention to both the social organization of authorship (Mukerji, 1989; Shapin, 1989) and to a specific class of labels – captions on scientific diagrams (Bastide, 1988; Lynch, 1988). Bastide (1988, pp. 194–195) notes that without the caption to a scientific picture one would not know "what one is supposed to see in [the] Figure," e.g., whether the circular objects visible in the picture are stones in a river, pebbles on a wall, or phosphorus-rich calcium granules incorporated into the muscles of a sea worm. Note that the label under an operations room monitor provides a rather different type of information. Instead of identifying the content of the image on the screen, i.e., saying that this is an airplane, it specifies the location within a relevant organizational framework of that image, i.e., its location at a specific gate. The line of monitors is analogous to a row from a grid or spreadsheet and the label functions not to describe the contents of a cell, but to specify its relevant location.

Different airplanes move in and out of the same gate as the day progresses. Knowing the gate does not automatically identify the flight. Ralph thus moves his gaze to the flight information display, locates gate 18 on it, and by reading the other information on that line finds the flight he has been looking at. While actually looking at the monitors he saw a plane, not a flight. The flight information display functions much like the complex sheet of the baggage loader. Indeed, complex sheets are found in the operations room and could have been used to accomplish this seeing. However the flight information display was the relevant tool most at hand, the easiest one to use in Ralph's specific circumstances. Tasks can frequently be performed in a variety of different ways, such that problems (e.g., tying a plane to a flight) have multiple, locally situated solutions (Lave, 1988).

In speaking, Ralph does not in any way mention what was central to the baggage handler – the destination of the flight at issue. He is performing his search for the flight instantiated by the plane at Gate 18 in order to enter a weights and balance query into the computer. That command requires a flight number, not a destination (and indeed, in that the computer network covers the entire nation, there are multiple flights going to the same destination). Thus, a moment later Val types

Though both the baggage loader and the operations agent are faced with the task of tying a visible plane to a flight, the specific nature of the activity within which each of their searches is embedded provides alternative shapes for what will count as an appropriate solution to that query. Once again, the nature of the interconnections that will provide for an appropriate seeing of the plane is shaped in fine detail by the local structure of the activity in progress.

Aircraft operations provide one of the primary examples of rational technology in our society, and the computer networks that tie them together are among the most extensive in the world. However, neither these networks, nor the rational organization that sustains both the technology and the bureaucracy of the airline, provides a single all-encompassing view of what is happening in the airline. Instead of a master overview, one finds multiple, diverse local perspectives, each constituted through the combination of a specific array of tasks, an ensemble of tools for performing those tasks, and an entrainment of workers' bodies that encompasses not only their muscles but also phenomena as minute as acts of perception embodied in momentary glances.

### Seeing the status of an activity

Discussion has so far focused on the procedures used by airline personnel to tie a visible plane to a specific flight. Ralph's actions raise a second, related issue: finding the current status of the flight from the activities of the plane, i.e., the ability to see the flight as a process and to locate where in that unfolding process events currently stand. Investigation of such issues requires analysis of a local culture situated within the workplace. As a competent worker in the operations room Ralph knows the time frame within which a weights and balance report becomes both possible and relevant. It cannot be computed before all points of entry into the airplane (doors for passengers, baggage, fuel, etc.) have been sealed but must be computed before the plane reaches take-off position at the end of the runway. The gate monitors display both the plane and activity of people around it. By looking at that ensemble of activity a competent viewer can make inferences about how close the plane is to departure. For example, are the passenger stairs still connected to the plane? Are the baggage doors sealed? etc. In the present data, Ralph begins his search with a query about "Who's pushing."[5] Both the use of such seeable inferences as a constitutive feature of operations work and the way in which the ability to make them is developed within the culture of the operations room will be explored further later in this chapter. For the moment, we simply want to make three observations. First, being able to see relevant events on the screen is not in any way a transparent, "natural" ability (Lynch, 1988; Pasveer, 1990), but very much a socially organized element of culture that is instantiated within, and sustained by, a community of practice (Lave & Wenger, 1991). Second, insofar as glances reading the activity at a gate are used to further the work activities that operations personnel are engaged in (i.e., here Ralph looks to the monitors in order to determine which flight to call up on the computer), they are not isolated, individual acts of perception but instead function much like moves in the socially situated forms of life that Wittgenstein (1953) calls language games. Third, both the necessity of getting planes off on time and the regular sequences of action that mark different stages in that process have for those in the operations room a taken-for-granted character. However these phenomena have been actively constructed by larger social processes (e.g., airlines in the United States use "On Time" statistics to compete with each other for passengers). Rather than being natural constraints, these features are socially built and articulated, in part precisely through work such as that being examined here. By timing and tailoring their work to meet the constraints imposed by "On Time" departure, workers in the operations room collaborate in constituting that constraint as a pervasive feature of airline operations.

**The reflexive relationship between talk and tool-mediated seeing**

Central to the phenomena being investigated here is *context,* as exemplified in the endogenous activities participants are engaged in, the reflexive relationship between those activities, and the material artifacts that make them possible (Engeström, 1990, pp. 77–78). Context also encompasses the deployment of action within human interaction through which participants within a setting build frameworks of mutual accountability as they become environments for each other (McDermott, 1976). The major analysis of context as a phenomenon central to the organization of human interaction has been the study of the organization of talk in interaction provided by conversation analysis (CA). Work in CA differs radically from most approaches to the analysis of meaning developed in linguistics and related disciplines in that it starts from the assumption that sentences cannot be analyzed as isolated, self-contained wholes, but instead are forms of action that gain their intelligibility from the context in which they occur.[6] A major component of that context is the sequence of other talk from which a current utterance emerges and further develops. Thus, a first pair part, such as a question, makes relevant a particular type of next action – a reply – and creates a local environment for the production and interpretation of subsequent action (Schegloff, 1968; Schegloff & Sacks, 1973). The dynamic nature of context revealed by such a perspective cannot be underestimated. Thus Heritage (1984b, p. 242) notes that every utterance in conversation is "doubly contextual in being both *context-shaped* and *context-renewing.*" This dynamic interplay between context, interaction, and mutual intelligibility is found not only in how the talk of separate participants is organized relative to each other, but also *within* the production of single utterances. By including within the scope of analysis not only the talk of the participants, but also the visible displays of orientation, alignment, understanding, etc. provided by their bodies we (C. Goodwin, 1981; M. H. Goodwin, 1980; C. & M. Goodwin, 1987, 1992) have been able to demonstrate that even individual sentences occurring within single turns at talk can be dynamically reshaped as they are emerging through an ongoing process of interaction between speaker and recipient(s).

CA has not, however, included within the scope of its analysis of context the topic that has been so central to activity theory: interaction with a world of historically constituted artifacts. Much is to be gained by bringing these two strands of analysis together. The operations room is an appropriate place for attempting such an integration, since, on the one hand, the work done there is reflexively tied to the tool-saturated environment in which it occurs, while on the other hand, much of that work consists of talk. We now want to expand our previous analysis of how utterances are shaped by processes of interaction between speaker and hearers by looking at how a single strip of talk within the operations room embodies its speaker's dynamic articulation of the artifacts in her working environment as she attempts to determine the status of a specific plane. In the following, an arriving pilot radios the operations room to try to learn when the gate he is to go to will be free. Julie in the operations room replies. Data is transcribed according to the system developed by Gail Jefferson (Sacks, Schegloff, & Jefferson, 1974, pp. 731–733):[7]

**Example (2)** *WV-13 3-Nov-89 11:11pm*

|     |        |                                    |
|-----|--------|------------------------------------|
| 1.  | Pilot: | San Tomás Ramp?                    |
| 2.  |        | Atlantic two eighty six?           |
| 3.  | Julie: | Two eighty six.                    |
| 4.  |        | This is operations.                |
| 5.  | Pilot: | I understand gate 14 is occupied?  |
| 6.  |        | Do you have any instructions for (it)? |
| 7.  |        | (0.3)                              |
| 8.  | Julie: | Uh::m, (0.1)                       |
| 9.  |        | Should've left 10 <u>min</u>utes ago.= |
| 10. |        | Hopefully,                         |
| 11. |        | (1.0)                              |
| 12. |        | They <u>have</u> pulled the passenger stairs. |
| 13. |        | They should be leaving momentarily |
| 14. | Pilot: | Okay. Thanks.                      |

The operations room comes equipped with a rich array of material artifacts (e.g., computers, radios of various types, documents, telephones, video screens, etc.). However, different tasks require alternative local tool kits,[8] and, moreover, within each task, tools change as the activity progresses. A problem of *tool selection* is thus posed that cannot be solved by an external observer listing the contents of the room (cf. Engeström, 1990, pp. 171–178; Sacks, 1963). The operations room, with its equipment, is like a stage set for multiple courses of action. However, it is not yet action itself; to describe the reflexive relationship between available tools and the actions that constitute the work of the operations room requires analysis of endogenous local activities.

To explore such issues, we will focus on the exchange between the pilot and Julie that begins in line 5, after the call's opening mutual identification sequence. This exchange takes the form of one of the most pervasive types of sequential organization found in conversation – a request for information and its reply – a particular instance of the more general class of two-part sequences that Schegloff and Sacks (1973) have analyzed as adjacency pairs. The pilot's question sets a task for Julie – providing an answer to his request. We now want to look at the situated work Julie performs to provide that answer.

When the videotape is examined, one can see that throughout the course of the exchange Julie makes use of the tools and representations provided by her work environment. Gaze toward these resources can be mapped against developing talk. We'll begin with the pilot's talk in line 5:

5. Pilot:  I understand gate fourteen is occupied?

What Julie is gazing at is displayed just above the utterance. One word after the pilot says "gate," Julie shifts her gaze to the row of gate monitors. Even before she knows the precise problem she is dealing with, she begins to orient to tools (i.e., the gate monitors) that will be relevant to the solution of that problem. When she hears the pilot use the term "gate," Julie learns something about the work that the pilot is asking her to do. Even though the complete problem has not yet been specified, the term "gate" itself is enough to locate a particular subset of the tools in the operations room as relevant to the tasks of the moment. As the task becomes more completely specified, further tools may be located as relevant to its accomplishment; i.e., tools emerge as relevant within an expanding horizon of progressive action. The pilot's talk, by virtue of its context-building sequential relevance, sets an agenda for the next actions of its recipient. Dealing with this agenda involves selective operations on the materials in her environment, i.e., the selection of specific tools from a larger set in terms of their relevance to the task of the moment. Only through use of these tools can Julie see the gate that the pilot is talking about.

Previous work in CA has demonstrated that recipients do not wait until an utterance comes to completion before beginning to operate upon it; instead, they track its emergence on a moment-by-moment basis (cf. C. Goodwin, 1979; M. H. Goodwin, 1980; C. & M. H. Goodwin, 1987; Heath, 1986; Jefferson, 1973, 1984; Lerner, 1993). The present data shed further light on the complexities of this process. As Julie tracks the word-by-word unfolding of the pilot's talk, she is simultaneously attending to not only the talk itself, but also her work environment, finding the tools that will be relevant to the task she sees emerging. Talk-in-interaction and the tool-saturated work setting mutually inform and delineate each other.

In order to act as quickly as she does, to bring her gaze to just the right tool for the job, Julie is relying upon her *habitual knowledge* of the setting in which she is working. That habitual knowledge encompasses both awareness of how tools and personnel are distributed within her working environment (M. H. Goodwin, in press) and familiarity with the routine request sequences she can expect to participate in as an operations worker. Her glance is the act of a competent member of the setting that provides the home for the activities in progress. Routine ways of dealing with typical troubles, instantiated in the work practices that newcomers appropriate through apprenticeship, constitute a sedimentation of solutions to past problems that earlier inhabitants of the operations room pass on to their successors.

As the pilot continues to talk and she starts her reply, Julie shifts her gaze from the monitors first to some papers on her desk (presumably to her radio log which contains actual arrival and departure times), then to the Flight Information Display (FID) screen (which lists scheduled times of departure), and then back to her papers:

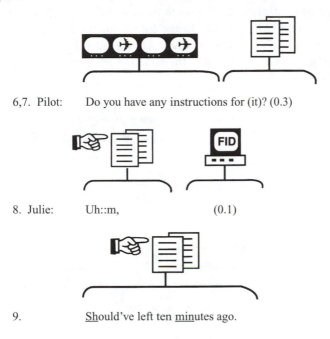

6,7. Pilot:  Do you have any instructions for (it)? (0.3)

8. Julie:  Uh::m,  (0.1)

9.  <u>Sh</u>ould've left ten <u>min</u>utes ago.

Though our camera is not able to read the papers on her desk[9] the talk she produces explicates the activities she has been performing. By saying "<u>Sh</u>ould've left ten <u>min</u>utes ago," she demonstrates that she has found the flight currently occupying gate 14, located its scheduled departure time, and compared that time with the current local time (clocks are visible in several places, near the flight information display screen and on the wall next to the gate monitors). The different types of technology clustered in her workspace provide structurally different kinds of information about the flight whose status she is attempting to decipher. The gate monitors show the plane itself still occupying gate 14, while the documents provide information about the flight instantiated in the plane, and the clock ties these events to the current situation, i.e., the plane shouldn't be at that gate now. The nature of the problem being dealt with is progressively reshaped as talk, tools, and documents mutually inform each other. Initially, all that Julie knows about the problem is that it concerns a particular gate. By looking at the monitors, she can find that there is indeed an aircraft at that gate. This then leads to a search for documents that might illuminate that status of that plane. As the representations provided by one tool are brought into play, the problem is reformulated, which leads to a search for further information through the interrogation of other tools.

To get a picture of the object that is the subject of her scrutiny – the status of the plane/flight at gate 14 – Julie must bring these multiple perspectives together. After discovering through her interrogation of the paper and electronic documents in front of her that the troublesome flight at gate 14 "<u>Sho</u>uld've left ten <u>min</u>utes ago," Julie returns her gaze to the gate monitors. She spans the move from the documents to the monitors with the word "Hopefull<u>y</u>:," – a term that indexes an optimistic expectation – that the situation projected in the documents will soon become actual:

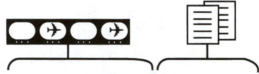

| 5. | Pilot: | I understand gate fourteen is occupied? |

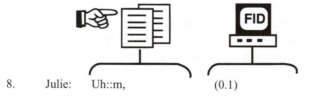

| 6,7. | Pilot: | Do you have any instructions for (it)? (0.3) |

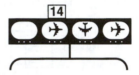

| 8. | Julie: | Uh::m,          (0.1) |

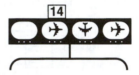

| 9. | | <u>Sho</u>uld've left ten <u>min</u>utes ago. |

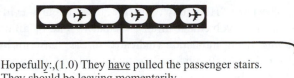

10–12.     Hopefully:,(1.0) They <u>have</u> pulled the passenger stairs.
13.        They should be leaving momen<u>ta</u>rily.

Languages provide speakers with a variety of resources that allow them to not only produce statements, but simultaneously take up stances toward what they are saying, for example, to comment on the status of what is being said. Such commentary can be provided in a number of different ways, for example by including in the talk *evidentials,* terms which explicitly mark the speaker's assessment of the reliability of what is being reported (Chafe, 1986), and through use of supersegmental phenomena such as intonation and aspects of voice quality that can provide displays about the speaker's engagement in both the talk she is producing and the tasks that the talk is embedded within.

Because perspective is so central to the work of airline personnel (e.g., workers who use separate tools to accomplish task-relevant perception at diverse locations see the same event from alternative perspectives), it is not surprising that evidential devices pervade their work-relevant talk.[10] Thus, in line 5 the pilot prefaces his report that gate 14 is occupied with "I understand," a preface that allows him to distance himself from full commitment to the accuracy of this statement while simultaneously cueing his recipient that he is not positioned to actually see the gate. For her part, Julie in line 9 uses the modal verb "should" to categorize the departure time 10 minutes ago as an expected or normative state of affairs, while allowing the speaker to distance herself from any claim that this event did in fact happen. By using the term "should" she displays her orientation toward a situation in which there is a marked discrepancy between what should be occurring and what is occurring.

Through the details of her speech production, Julie organizes her talk to explicitly display the way in which she is "catching information on the fly." The linguistic and paralinguistic devices she deploys reveal a progressive horizon of unfolding knowledge as she accesses different tools. When the pilot turns the floor over to her, she is still scanning the documents in front of her. By saying "uh::m" she accepts the floor while producing not the projected next action, an answer to his request, but a display of involvement in a search, a task that may be a prerequisite to providing the answer. Her involvement in the task of trying to figure out what is happening, and her own puzzlement as to why things are not as they should be, are made visible through the details of her continuing speech production. We do not have the technical resources to rigorously describe the sound quality of this speech but will impressionistically note that it seems to be spoken at a higher than normal pitch without the easy fluency that is found in her talk at the end of the sequence.

The term "Hopefully:," in line 10 is another evidential which displays its speaker's involvement in an anticipated state of affairs. It is pronounced with falling–rising intonation (indicated in the transcript by the comma), a contour that characteristically displays that the talk in progress has not yet come to completion. The term thus stands as the preface to an as yet incomplete course of talk. It is spoken as she moves her eyes from the documents to the gate monitors. It appears that what she will see on the monitors is relevant to the further elaboration of the description begun with "Hopefully:," Indeed, immediately after completing the word, she stares intently at the monitors for a second, and sees that the passenger stairs have actually been pushed away. What she says next is produced with a very different voice quality than the talk leading up it. "They have pulled the passenger stairs." is spoken at noticeably lower pitch and with much more authority. An utterance announcing the expected resolution of the problem "They should be leaving momentarily," is immediately latched to it. Its immediate, unproblematic production contrasts markedly with the hesitant, almost falsetto talk used to begin her turn in lines 8 and 9. By stating the expected time of departure as "momentarily" – a term used routinely by airline personnel to fudge exact time specification – Julie is able to display complete confidence in the imminent departure of the plane without specifying when precisely this will occur.

The unit begun with "Hopefully:," is abandoned without being brought to completion. One reason for this might be found in the contrast between the problematic, not yet actual character of the state of affairs that would be found in a description begun with a modal such as "Hopefully," (i.e., "Hopefully they'll be leaving soon") and the actual state of affairs she in fact reports: "They have pulled the passenger stairs." In essence, looking at the monitors enables her to see something that reformulates the epistemic status of the description she is providing the pilot, a state of affairs that requires the use of a different modality. The stress placed on "have" in line 12 not only highlights the fact that the stairs have been pulled, but through its contrast with the reduced verb in line 9, "ve" in "Should've," emphasizes that a change in the speaker's certainty about what she is saying has occurred. Julie's description of the pulling of the passenger stairs makes available the *warrant* she has for her eventual response to the pilot's questions – "They should be leaving momentarily." – in line 13.

Through use of particular lexical items (e.g., "momentarily"), evidentials (which are precisely articulated with gaze toward different representations of the plane's status), and the details of her speech production, Julie makes available to her recipient a progressively changing information horizon, one that has been shaped by her articulation of work-relevant tools. By constructing visibly different kinds of talk, Julie is able to display, within this single turn, a range of alternative stances toward the events made visible through her talk.

C. Goodwin (1981) demonstrated that processes of interaction between speakers and recipient(s) can lead to changes in the structure of an emerging sentence; for example, as the speaker shifts from one type of recipient to another she will change the emerging meaning of the sentence so that it maintains its appropriateness for its recipient of the moment. Here we find similar modifications of an utterance that has not yet come to completion. However, now, instead of adapting to her addressee, she changes the emerging structure of her talk in response to her interrogation of the tools and representations in her working environment. By including the work environment within which a query is framed, we gain a much richer understanding of the situated work that goes into the production of an appropriate answer.

Much research into the organization of linguistic and other cognitive processes has made inferences about the information-processing strategies being used by actors. Characteristically, these processes are conceptualized as occurring inside the mind, and thus are inaccessible to direct observation. By looking at how tools in a working environment are deployed to answer a query, we can investigate the articulation of relevant information, and the representations that encode that information, as accessible, visible phenomena.

Finally, these data demonstrate that the work-relevant perceptual event, the thing to be seen in order to accomplish the job at hand, doesn't exist apart from the heterogeneous work involved in assembling a set of relevant perspectives for viewing it, a process that encompasses the material technology that makes such seeing possible.

## Seeing absent events

We now investigate in more detail the cultural competence required to appropriately read a scene on a video monitor. The following provides a clear example of some of the issues involved. Stan, in the operations room, receives a query asking whether flight 722 is being fueled. To answer this query he 1) turns to another document to link the flight to a gate (line 1); 2) looks up to the appropriate gate monitor and finds that the place where a fuel truck would be is not visible; (line 3) and then 3) asks for help in using the controls in the operations room that pan and zoom the gate cameras, a move that is anticipated by one of his coworkers, Jay (lines 7–8). When the camera is panned (line 9) and gets to the place on the side of the plane where fueling is done, there is no truck in that place (line 10). Seeing this Stan reports back "No. It's not hooked up" (a ☎ marks talk spoken into the telephone receiver):

**Example (3)** *WE-73 26-Oct-90 6:32pm*

| ☎ | 1. Stan: | Let's see here. ((*Turns to complex board*)) |
|---|---|---|
| | 2. | Seven twenty two is gate seven. |
| | 3. | (0.8) ((*Looks at Gate Monitor*)) |

| ☎ | 4. |  | Uh I can't tell if there's a fuel truck hooked up to it. |
|---|---|---|---|

| | 5. | | Does seven twenty two have a fuel truck |
| | 6. | | hooked up to it. |
| | 7. | Jay: | [((*Jay gets up and starts to work monitor controls*)) |
| | 8. | Stan: | [Who's got these controls. |
| | 9. | | ((*Pan to side of plane where fuel is loaded*)) |
| | 10. | Jay: | Nope. |

| ☎ | 11. | Stan: | Uh no it's not hooked up. |
|---|---|---|---|

The fragment begins with another example of how an airline worker, faced with the task of finding the plane that instantiates a particular flight, accomplishes this task by turning to another document in order to link flight numbers to a specific gate (lines 1–3). What we want to focus on at present is how Stan is able to see something relevant when he eventually looks at the monitor. At least two classes of phenomena are relevant to the organization of such looking.

The first is the way in which the media being used for perception shape what can be seen through use of these media (cf. Lynch, 1988; Pasveer, 1990). Workers in the operations room are well aware that their cameras in no way give them a neutral, undistorted view of the events being looked at. As one of them says, when discussing with a coworker the problems involved in trying to direct the movements of plane visible on video: "Looking at the cameras you don't have any depth, or field, or perspective, or anything." For workers in the operations room such problems are practical, not theoretical. The communications equipment in the operations room, including the gate monitors, provides the workers with their primary perceptual access to the world of their work. They see and act upon that world through use of these tools. Thus, whatever the strengths and weaknesses of these tools, operations personnel are faced with the task of coming to terms with them, of learning how to see through them to do their work.

Second, operations personnel must see more in a scene than is actually visible on the gate monitor. This is particularly clear in the present data, wherein Stan and Jay are both able to see something that is quite literally not present, the *absent* fuel truck.[11]

How is such vision accomplished? Competent looking at the monitor is informed by applying knowledge of expected configurations of activity to the materials visible on the screen (the relevant activity being selected with reference to the task in progress at the moment). Thus, in these data both Stan and Jay demonstrate that they know where a fuel truck will be located when fueling is in progress. At the beginning of the sequence they are able to recognize that they cannot yet answer that question because the relevant place is not yet visible. They then move the camera to bring that place into view and use the fact that they see nothing there to see something relevant, i.e., that the plane is not being fueled.

The task of the moment makes particular features of the scene relevant and helps structure how they will be interpreted (cf. Heidegger, 1962, pp. 95–100).[12] To read the scene on the monitor in a work-relevant way, operations personnel bring to bear situated, local cultural knowledge.

The way in which Stan and Jay are each independently able to see the necessity of moving the gate camera demonstrates that applying activity configurations to the materials being studied is not an individual, psychological process, but a mode of practice, a shared competence implicated in the ongoing work of the room.

### Reading a scene as a social process

To further explore the social processes implicated in seeing images in a work-relevant way we will now turn to a more extended sequence. The events to be examined occurred two weeks after the airline had moved into a new terminal. The move to the new terminal involved a change in the way in which passengers boarded the aircraft. In the old terminal, they walked out onto the runway and climbed a set of stairs placed next to the plane. In the new terminal, they board planes directly by going through a tunnel at each gate called a Jet Bridge.

In the old terminal, activity around the passenger stairs provided operations personnel with resources for reading events on the ramp (cf. both Suchman in this volume and Julie's talk about the stairs being pulled away in Example 2); they are now going to have to learn how to read the jet bridge in a similar work-relevant way. The data we will now examine provide an extended example of how such seeing is developed by interaction between operations workers as they come to terms with the issue of appropriately interpreting a scene visible on one of their gate monitors. Present in the room are both a number of experienced operations hands and one newcomer, Stan, who is still being given instruction on the job. He is not an absolute beginner and was assigned a position to work on his own. However, whenever he encounters any difficulties, old-timers come to his aid. A particular "ethos" (Bateson, 1936) prevails in the room that greatly facilitates this process. Because of the respectful, and at times playful, way that the people in the room deal with each other, he freely admits the difficulties he is having with new tasks and is never put down as someone whose performance is defective. Figure 5 provides a diagram of how people and equipment are positioned in the room.

In addition to a computer terminal and telephone, each position also contains a new multichannel radio system. On the right side of the room is a complex board that lists plane numbers and gate assignments for all of the day's flights. In the old operations room this board was placed directly under the row of gate monitors.

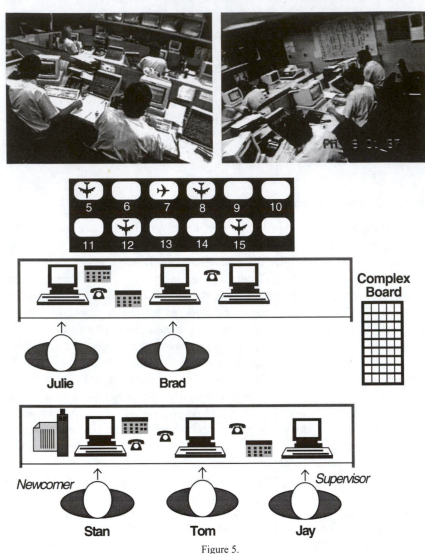

Figure 5.

*Seeable trouble*

In Fig. 6, Brad gets a radio call (which everyone in the room can hear)[13] about a problem with the jet bridge at gate A-12 (line 6). To separate the radio conversation from other talk in the operations room, boxes are drawn around talk within it and marked with walkie-talkie icons. The others in the room look to the A-12 monitor and then break into spontaneous laughter at what they see there (lines 15–17, and 22; "(h)" is used to transcribe within-word laugh particles).

**Example (4)** *WE-74 26-Oct-90 9:01pm*

| | | |
|---|---|---|
| Gate: | Operations, Come in. | 1 |
| | (2.4) | 2 |
| Brad: | Go ahead Mister Wilson. | 3 |
| | (3.5) | 4 |
| Gate: | Yeah Pete | 5 |
| | We _definitely_ have a problem here on this je:t bridge. | 6 |
| | (3.2) | 7 |
| Jay: | Which gate. | 8 |
| Brad: | What gate. | 9 |
| | (2.1) | 10 |
| Gate: | A: twelve. | 11 |
| | (2.0) | 12 |
| Brad: | Do you know what the: problem is. | 13 |
| Julie: | Uhoo: : : eh : : : | 14 |
| Julie: | It's covering ha lf of the ai(h)rpl(h)ane. | 15 |
| Jay: | Eh Heh Huh huh huh huh | 16 |
| Gate: | It's not taking ground power to the aircraft. | 17 |
| Jay: | Ah man. | 18 |
| Julie: | Ou: : : that's bad. | 19 |
| Gate: | A:n d, | 20 |
| Stan: | hh Ha Ha Ha °ha ha ha° | 21 |
| Gate: | the power presumably is not cutting | 22 |
| | off on it-on the je:t bri:dge. | 23 |

Figure 6.

The operations room is provided with two versions of the trouble at Gate A-12. In lines 17 and 22–23 the ramp worker at the gate provides a description of the trouble he is calling about: power isn't being supplied to the airplane. Meanwhile, the video camera at A-12 allows the operations room to look directly at the gate (see Fig. 7). For most of the people in the room, the problem visible on the gate monitor is absolutely transparent. They break into spontaneous laughter as soon as they see the position of the canopy (and indeed the ethnographers at the back of the room, who included one of the authors of this paper, silently joined into the laughter engendered by the scene).

Such transparent vision is subsequently shown to be deeply problematic. Six minutes later, after a talk with the ramp crew that reported the problem, Stan turns to the rest of the operations room and reports (line 5) that there is no problem whatsoever with the jet bridge. Instead the problem lies with a different piece of machinery, the ground power unit (see Fig. 8).

Julie's incredulous "*That's* not *nor*mal!" (line 9) goes to the heart of the anthropological concept of culture, i.e., the specification of what counts as normal within the lifeworld of a particular group. Indeed, in these data we are able to catch a glimpse of the social and historical processes through which a community accumulates experience of the habitual scenes that constitute their working environment, and articulates for each other how these scenes should be

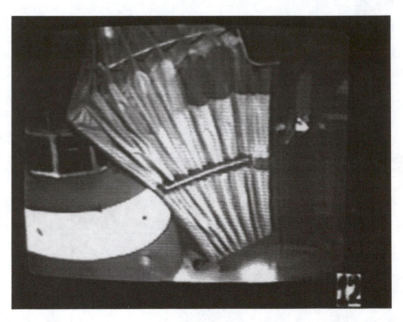

Figure 7.

**Example (5)** *WE-74 26-Oct-90 9:07pm*

```
 1  Stan:     Okay. Thanks a lot.
☎2              (1.0)
 3              Okay Bye Don.
```

4                    Yeah,

5         Don says there's no problem with the jet bridge at all.

6                    That was a <u>crew</u> chief calling in
7                    to say┌there was a problem with it.
                          │
8  Julie:        ─┘°Tell me that's   *((Looking at Gate Monitor))*
9         That's not┌normal!  ┐
                    │        │
10  Stan:          └With the ground power unit.

Figure 8.

properly interpreted. Through their work this night they come to see more clearly what constitutes the "normal appearance" of one of the objects that will figure repetitively in their work, the representation of a jet bridge on their gate monitors.

The fact that these very competent workers could so clearly see the image on the screen as abnormal, indeed laughable, poses the question of how such collaborative, multiparty, transparent seeing was accomplished. This process is analyzed in detail in a separate paper (C. Goodwin, in press). Briefly, the term "problem" in gate A-12's report (Fig. 6, line 6) provides instructions for interpreting the scene visible on the monitors. Consistent with what has been analyzed as the documentary method of interpretation (Garfinkel, 1967; Heritage, 1984b), these images in turn are used to elaborate and fill in the sense of "problem." Julie's response cry (Goffman, 1981) in line 14 and the laughter that follows from it not only provides further analysis of the image on the monitor, but also invokes a multiparty participation framework (M. H. Goodwin, 1990, chapter 10) that invites others to commit themselves to her vision of transparent trouble visible in the scene.

In the present paper we want to first investigate how the consensus about the clear visibility of seeable trouble on the screen was challenged, and second, how the status of what was visible there, for example its character as an emergency, was transformed as the representations provided by alternative tools situated the events on the screen within new perspectives.

*Multiple domains of expertise within the operations room*

At least one person in the room doesn't see the trouble on the screen. Stan repetitively asks "What's the problem with it" (lines 4, 5, 12, and 15) as Jay calls facilities maintenance to ask for a repair crew (see Fig. 9).

The party who doesn't see what the others see occupies a special position in the room; i.e., he is the newcomer, the novice who is being trained. This special position provides a plausible, default account, for his failure to see; i.e., he has not yet developed the work-relevant perceptual skills of a fully qualified operations worker. Meanwhile, his coworkers continue to treat the trouble as completely transparent. Julie (line 3) describes the situation on the screen as "good and ugly." When asked to describe the problem over the radio Jay (lines 16–17) says "The canopy has fallen away from the jet bridge on to the cockpit of the aircraft." Most tellingly, Stan's repeated queries about the nature of the problem are

**Example (6)** *WE-74 26-Oct-90 9:02pm*

```
  1  Jay:      Operations to Facilities Maintenance.

  2  Brad:     O-kay thanks.
  3  Julie:     └That's good en ugly.

  4  Stan:     What is the problem with it?
  5            What are they saying is the problem?

  6  Radio:    Yeah. They-
  7            They won't be here until ten o'clock.
  8                 (1.4)
  9  Jay:      We've got a problem with a jet bridge on alpha twelve
 10            right now.
 11            Anybody a:ble to handle that?

 12  Stan:     What is the problem with it.
 13  Jay:      Look at the: uh canopy.          ◄——

 14  Radio:    What's the problem with it?

 15  Stan:     ┌Yeah but-

 16  Jay:      └The canopy has uh: fallen away,
 17            from the jet bridge on ┌to the: (.) cockpit of the aircraft.

 18  Stan:                             └ They can still back it up.
```

Figure 9.

finally answered in line 13 with Jay's "Look at the canopy," a reply that treats the trouble as transparently visible on the monitor screen.

What Stan says next (lines 15 and 18) casts his failure to see the trouble in a new light. By prefacing his talk with "Yeah but" he offers a challenge to what he has just been told. He then proposes that, despite what can be seen on the screen, "They can still back it up." Subsequently, he and Brad have an extended debate regarding what can and cannot be done with jet bridges. Instead of being incompetent to see the trouble that the others in the room find so transparent, Stan is countering that viewing, actively resisting the interpretation that his colleagues have reached.

Each worker brings to the operations room a different work history and thus a range of different skills, producing a situation in which multiple domains of competence cross-cut the formal hierarchical organization of the work group. Jay is the supervisor for the evening and Stan is the low man on the totem pole, the newcomer who must repetitively ask others for help with routine computer work. However, jet bridges are brand new at this airport and even someone high in the local hierarchy may not have had much experience with them. By debating the details of jet bridge operation Stan displays competence in that domain of expertise. In the local arena of practice clustered around jet bridges, Stan claims expertise that Jay lacks, and challenges his analysis of the events visible on the gate monitor.

What consequences do Stan's claims have for the room's ongoing work with the jet bridge problem? Jay is unable to find anyone at facilities to fix the bridge. After listening to Stan debate the proper operation of jet bridges with Brad (lines 1–2), Jay suggests that if no one else can be found Stan himself should go down to the gate and "take care of it." Stan's expertise with jet bridges is thus not only acknowledged but called upon by his supervisor. What one finds here is an environment in which a plurality of contradictory viewpoints can be voiced. Though "only" a newcomer Stan is able to successfully challenge an interpretation of a situation that his more experienced colleagues treat as transparent. Instead of putting Stan in his place, ignoring the perspective of the most junior person in the room, Jay not only listens to what Stan has to say but draws upon the skills he displays. In view of the disparate problems sent to the operations room for resolution during the course of a workday (flight delays, inadequate meals, broken equipment, etc.) fostering an environment in which anyone, no matter how junior, with competence in a relevant area can make themselves heard can be quite valuable to the organization as a whole.

Looking at such phenomena from a slightly different perspective, it is important that the individual expertise that one party brings to the room be transformed into an element of social practice that can be used by others as well, i.e., that it become part of the working culture of the operations room. By articulating their interpretations of the scene being looked at through talk with their coworkers, workers in the operations room organize their work-relevant seeing within an arena of public discourse, one that is able to encompass multiple perspectives. Such openness to multivocality, and the ethos of the room that permits Stan to freely admit both his ignorance and his expertise without fear of censure, are quite consistent with other aspects of the way in which interaction is organized within the room. Thus operations personnel are expected to monitor what others in the room are doing (a call to one position may well have consequences for the work that others are expected to do) and frequently take action on the basis of such overhearing. The openness and accessibility of work in the operations room, and the inclusion of participants with heterogeneous domains of expertise, are quite relevant to the organization of situated learning by both newcomers and old-timers within it, i.e., it provides a productive arena for what Lave and Wenger (1991) call legitimate peripheral participation.

## Reframing the problem

As soon as operations learns about the trouble at the gate, personnel in the room mobilize to remedy it. Jay immediately calls facilities maintenance; when he learns that they won't be in for another hour, he has Stan call the gate itself. On getting no answer on the phone Stan tries to reach them on the radio. In essence, operations treats the trouble with the jet bridge as an emergency, and mobilizes multiple courses of action to fix it as soon as possible.[14] Multiple hypotheses about the precise nature of the trouble are kept alive and entertained by different participants in the room. Thus, at one point Brad points out to Stan that while Jay "noticed" the canopy, and reported that as the problem, the original call that Brad received located the trouble in the ground power unit. The status of the trouble as an emergency is not, however, debated but instead accepted as a default assumption as attention immediately focuses on finding a solution to the problem. Such quick response is valuable and useful for an organization that uses flight delays as one of its main measures of performance. However, as we saw earlier in this chapter, the mere ability to perceive an airplane with one's senses (here mediated through the video apparatus of the gate monitors) does not mean that one is apprehending it in the way that is relevant to the work life of the organization (for example as a flight going to some particular destination). In order to see the relevance of the plane, workers must juxtapose to it other kinds of information embodied in other tools: complex sheets, flight information display screens, etc. So far, that work has not been done for the plane at Gate A-12 (and indeed knowing where the plane is going does not in any way help fix the jet bridge).

After hearing that Stan has not been able to reach anyone at the gate (a location that would certainly be occupied for an outgoing flight), Jay turns to the complex board on the side of the room, queries the status of the flight, and finds that the plane at Gate A-12 is an "overnighter," i.e., a plane that will not depart until the next morning.

**Example (7)** *WE-74 26-Oct-92 9:04pm*
     ((*Jay looks to Complex Board*))
 1. Jay: ***What*** have we ***got*** at twelve anyway.
 2.    Is that an overnighter?
 3.     (1.5)
 4.    Oh! It's an over***nigh***ter.
 5.    There's no uh big deal about it. (0.4)
 6.    We could wait until Facilities (comes).

Looking at the complex board leads to a change in Jay's understanding of the problem at hand. Note that line 4 begins with a change of state token (Heritage, 1984a), the particle "Oh!" Through Jay's use of the complex board, the scene on the monitor is embedded within a new framework of meaning. Since the plane will be there all night, the emergency status of the work they are doing disappears. Instead, as Jay says in line 6, they can wait until the facilities crew comes on duty. The status of the plane as an overnighter solves other puzzles as well. Thus, a moment later Stan says, with reference to his failed attempts to reach someone at the gate, "So it's no wonder no one's there. They're not even departing." An even more radical reformulation of the trouble occurs three minutes later when, as we have seen, Stan reports that there is no problem whatsoever with the jet bridge (Example 5).

These data demonstrate once again that neither the plane, nor the image of it on the screen, are properly dealt with as isolated, self-contained objects. Instead, workers must use a heterogeneous collection of disparate technology to assemble a set of work-relevant perspectives for its proper interpretation, i.e., to see it in the way that is relevant to the work they are doing with it. What the object being worked with *is,* and their work responsibilities toward it, change as these perspectives change (cf. Lynch, 1982, pp. 516–518). Though situated within the organization of the operations room as systematic practices, the procedures required to place a plane within a relevant network of meaning are by no means automatic. Instead, assembling a set of relevant perspectives, i.e., properly seeing the plane, is an ongoing contingent accomplishment within a particular community of practice.

## Conclusion

This chapter has attempted to bring together within an integrated analytic framework phenomena that are typically studied in isolation from each other, including human interaction, tools, perception, and the details of language use. When actual courses of action are examined, it is found that all of these phenomena mutually shape each other. Thus, in Example 2 in order to answer the pilot's query about the occupied gate, Julie had to interrogate a range of alternative representations embodied in different tools, a contingent process within which her knowledge of what it was that she was working with was constantly changing. Her shifting evidential horizon was visible in the details of her speech production. Despite a few notable exceptions (for example Duranti, Goodwin, & Goodwin, 1991; Engeström, 1990; Hutchins, 1990; Latour, 1987; Middleton & Edwards, 1990; Ochs, Schieffelin, & Platt, 1979; Schegloff, 1992; Smith, 1990; Suchman, 1987) the contemporary social sciences typically conceptualize cognition within a Cartesian framework, as something located inside the individual mind, or in Searle's (1990) elegant phrase in "brains in vats."

All of the data examined in this chapter have displayed the interdependence of cognitive processes, tool use, and social organization. Thus, in the last example the conceptual object being worked with, the "problem" with the jet bridge, constantly changed as new representations were brought to bear upon it. These changes affected not only the definition of the problem (e.g., whether it resided in the jet bridge or the ground power unit) but also the work-relevant status of that trouble as an emergency. The cognitive operations involved in the resolution of this problem were not located in any single mind, but instead emerged through time as a contingent social process within which cognitive artifacts, such as the complex board, and historically constituted tools, such as the gate monitors, played a most important part.

For clarity we have focused our analysis on a single, very simple problem: looking at airplanes. However, as all the phenomena examined demonstrate, workers at the airport are never faced with the naked perceptual task of simply seeing an airplane. Instead that looking is always part of larger courses of activity, and it is these that are the focus of a worker's attention. Instead of seeing an isolated object with some attributes – a plane going to Oakland – the baggage loader is looking for the plane that she is required to load. This larger framework is not extrinsic to the act of perception but instead establishes the ground and relevance for such an act, while at the same time giving it shape (for example defining what will count as a solution to the perceptual tasks it poses). From this perspective, the activity of perception is a social rather than a psychological phenomenon.

The operations room constitutes a veritable electronic panopticon. On a scale undreamed of by Jeremy Bentham, it arrays the views of the scenes that are relevant to operations personnel into a single master grid (exemplified in very concrete fashion in the array of gate monitors); the vision provided by its cameras is richly augmented by a heterogeneous collection of computer and communication equipment. Each worker in the operations room has individual access to a nationwide computer network. Different kinds of radios and telephones connect them with planes, fuel trucks, mechanics, caterers, in essence any setting that might be relevant to airline operations. Documents of many different types provide them with representations of both the ideal, planned schedule and the actual status of each flight.

However, what one finds in this panopticon is not a single master view, but instead a heterogeneous collection of disparate views provided by the different tools for perception that happen to be available. To get a picture of the object that is the subject of her scrutiny, an operations worker must bring these multiple perspectives together. This does not happen in a single moment as the separate views dissolve into a single master perspective, but instead is a process that must be articulated through time as a worker shifts her gaze from the view provided by one tool to that offered by another (see for Examples 2 and 4–7). Her view of what is happening is the assembled product of a course of local action. Though this process is performed from a particular perspective, i.e., her position in the operations room, the seeing it produces is not homogeneous.

Both the objects being worked with, and the perspectival organization that provides relevant access to these objects, are tied to *participation in action*; configurations of participant, tool, perspective, and object are not haphazard but instead systematic components of the work setting that they help to constitute. Seeing in such an environment is not an unproblematic activity. Participants must learn how to see in organizationally appropriate ways the habitual scenes of the work setting.

Workers are continuously faced with the task of juxtaposing perspectives on whatever object is being worked with so as to situate it within a relevant web of meaning. While these perspectives are constituted through an ensemble of tools and positions, articulating a task-relevant view of the object requires active human *agency*. In that the object being worked with is defined in part by the perspectives brought to bear upon it, and in that juxtaposition of multiple relevant perspectives is a contingent, time-bound process, that object, and the responsibilities of workers toward it, change as the activity unfolds. This does not, however, provide evidence for extreme relativism. Instead, these various perspectives are articulated and constrained by the larger patterns of social organization, and the tasks of collaboratively achieving coordinated action, within which they are embedded.

Ethnographers of science (Lynch, 1988; Lynch & Woolgar, 1988) have provided insightful analysis of how graphic representations are used to shape the materials provided by the world into the phenomena of interest to a particular discipline. However, very little attention has been paid to the process through which alternative representations become relevant and are interrogated and tailored as actual tasks unfold contingently through time. A major task faced by workers at the airport is not just the production of such representations (e.g., the social construction of a complex sheet) but more crucially, the local *juxtaposition* of such representations to other phenomena in order to build relevant perspectives for the accomplishment of the work at hand. Analysis of such processes requires looking beyond the representation itself to the course of action within which it is embedded.

The most important representations used at the airport are documents of many different types. Few of these documents take the form of narrative accounts written in complete sentences and paragraphs. They thus differ dramatically from the kinds of texts typically investigated when literacy in the workplace is studied. However, as has been noted by Dorothy Smith (1990) it is such documents that tie local work into larger organizational structures. They thus constitute a most important locus for the analysis of not just literacy, but, more crucially, social organization and practice (Goodwin, 1994).

The mundane routine work of large organizations as strategic a site as rituals in traditional societies for the anthropological analysis of culture. Work tasks in such settings are one place where language, tools, documents, and human interaction interdigitate in such a fashion as to require analysis from an integrated perspective. Not only does this overcome old dichotomies such as that between cultural idealism (Goodenough, 1970) and cultural materialism (Harris, 1968), but, more importantly, it provides an opportunity to investigate dynamically and in detail how culture is constituted as a mode of practice (Bourdieu, 1977). The importance of apprenticeship (Rogoff, 1990) in these processes ties such analysis to current work investigating the relationship between language and socialization (Ochs, 1988; Ochs, Jacoby, & Gonzales, 1994; Ochs & Schieffelin, 1984; Schieffelin, 1990) and to work in linguistic anthropology that analyzes talk and the body as positioned within settings that culturally define a field of intelligibility for the production and interpretation of action (Duranti, 1992; Hanks, 1990). Central to all of these issues are processes of human interaction. In brief, the analysis of mundane action in the workplace constitutes a most important locus for the integrated study of language, culture, social organization, and the historically constituted material world within which these phenomena are embedded.

### Acknowledgments

Research for this chapter grew out of The Workplace Project, a collaborative research project devoted to the analysis of work as situated practice in multiactivity settings, which was initiated by Lucy Suchman at Xerox PARC and funded by the Steelcase Corporation. Conversations with other members of the project – Françoise Brun-Cottan, Kathy Forbes, Gitti Jordan, Lucy Suchman and, Randy Trigg – have deeply influenced our analysis. A very special debt is owed to Lucy Suchman for demonstrating to us the importance of including material settings in the analysis of human interaction and cognition as situated phenomena.

Françoise Brun-Cottan, Sandro Duranti, Kathy Forbes, Douglas Maynard, Susan Newman, Emanual Schegloff, Lucy Suchman, and Randy Trigg made helpful and valuable comments on an earlier draft. We presented this chapter at the

6th Annual Visual Research Conference sponsored by the Society for Visual Anthropology at the 89th Annual Meeting of the American Anthropological Association, New Orleans, 1990. Many thanks to Tom Blakely and Dick Chalfen for providing a forum for the presentation of this work.

## Notes

1  The complex sheet gets its name from the way in which it tracks the ground activity that occurs during a *complex,* the organizational entity that encompasses a bank of planes arriving from multiple destinations, staying on the ground while passengers and baggage are transferred, and then taking off again approximately an hour later for new destinations. The complex is a central component of an airline's hub and spoke system in which flights are funneled to a few central locations where connections are made. The *complex sheet* is the central document used to track ground operations during a complex. Because of its centrality, and the way in which different types of workers at the airport use it in quite different ways, it has received considerable study by The Workplace Project (see for example Forbes, 1990; Suchman & Trigg, 1993). For clarity of presentation, a very simplified version of the complex sheet is described in this chapter. There is also a large *complex board* in the Atlantic operations room that tracks gates and times for the entire day's complexes.

2  For analysis of the importance of juxtaposing documents in scientific practice see Latour (1987) and Woolgar (1988).

3  Latour (1990) raises the question of how events that are locally organized (for example, the glances of the baggage loader) are tied to larger structures that bridge local contexts. Forms, such as the complex sheet used by the baggage loader, are one of the systematic tools used to tie diverse local contexts into larger organizational patterns.

4  From another perspective, a category such as this provides an example of a *boundary object* (Star & Griesemer, 1989).

5  See the paper by Suchman in this volume for analysis of very elaborate collaborative disentangling of the scene visible on an operations monitor.

6  See the classic work within conversation analysis on recipient design (for example Goodwin, 1981; Jefferson, 1974; Sacks & Schegloff, 1979; Sacks, Schegloff, & Jefferson, 1974; Schegloff, 1972).

7  In the Jefferson transcription system, punctuation is used to mark intonation rather than grammatical structure. A period indicates a falling contour, a question mark indicates a rising contour, and a comma indicates a falling–rising contour. Colons indicate that the sound immediately preceding has been noticeably lengthened. Square brackets mark overlap onset. Bold italics indicate some form of emphasis. A degree sign marks lowered volume and a dash a sudden cut-off of the current sound.

8  We are using the term "tool" to refer to not only tools in the traditional sense, e.g., objects like hammers, but more generally any socially constituted structure used to accomplish a particular task, including documents and standardized work practices. "Tool kit" refers to the ensemble of materials deployed for the accomplishment of a particular task.

9  Events such as this also had a reflexive influence on our own developing work practices. In subsequent taping, we made special efforts to place multiple cameras so that we could capture both larger patterns of interaction in the room and the documents and computer screens that were the focus of the participants' attention.

10  For analysis of how evidentials are used to establish perspective in calls from the police see Whalen and Zimmerman (1990).

11  Work in conversation analysis has devoted considerable attention to the analysis of how relevant absences are attended to by participants as consequential events in the ongoing organization of their action (Schegloff, 1968; Pomerantz, 1984; Sacks, Schegloff & Jefferson, 1974).

12  See Edgeworth (1991) for very interesting analysis of the embodied looking being performed by a worker on an archaeological excavation.
13  For more detailed analysis of how listening to the talk and work of others is a central component of the work life of the operations room see M. H. Goodwin (in press), Brun-Cottan (1990, 1991), and Suchman (this volume).
14  For other analysis of how operations personnel quickly mobilize multiple trajectories when faced with an emergency see Suchman (this volume).

## References

Atkinson, J. M. & Heritage, J. (Eds.). (1984). *Structures of Social Action* Cambridge: Cambridge University Press.

Bastide, F. (1988). The iconography of scientific texts: Principles of analysis. In *Representation in Scientific Practice*. M. Lynch & S. Woolgar, (Eds.), pp. 187–230. Cambridge, MA: MIT Press.

Bateson, G. (1936). *Naven*. Stanford, CA: Stanford University Press.

Bourdieu, P. (1977). *Outline of a Theory of Practice*. Cambridge: Cambridge University Press (translated by Richard Nice).

Brun-Cottan, F. (1990, November). *Coordinating Cooperation*. Paper presented at the Invited Session on "Spacing, Orientation and the Environment in Co-Present Interaction" at the 89th Annual Meeting of the American Anthropological Association, New Orleans.

Brun-Cottan, F. (1991). Talk in the work place: Occupational relevance. *Research on Language and Social Interaction 24,* 277–295.

Chafe, W. (1986). Evidentiality in English Conversation and Academic Writing. In *Evidentiality: The Linguistic Coding of Epistemology*. W. Chafe & J. Nichols (Eds.), pp. 261–272. Norwood, NJ: Ablex.

Cole, M. (1985). The zone of proximal development: Where culture and cognition create each other. In *Culture, Communication, and Cognition: Vygotskian Perspectives*. J. Wertsch (Ed.), pp. 146–161. Cambridge: Cambridge University Press.

Cole, M. (1990, May). *Cultural Psychology: Some General Principles and a Concrete Example*. Paper presented at the 2nd International Congress for Research on Activity Theory. Lahti, Finland.

Drew, P. & Heritage, J. (Eds.). (1992). *Talk at Work*. Cambridge: Cambridge University Press.

Duranti, A. (1992). Language and bodies in social space: Samoan ceremonial greetings. *American Anthropologist 94*(3), 657–691.

Duranti, A., Goodwin, C., & Goodwin, M. H. (1991, November). *Communicative Acts as Socially Distributed Phenomena*. Preliminary Remarks Prepared for the Session on "Speech Acts as Socially Distributed Phenomena," American Anthropological Association, Chicago.

Edgeworth, M. (1991). *The Act of Discovery: An Ethnography of the Subject-Object Relation in Archaeological Practice*. A thesis submitted in partial fulfillment of the requirements for the degree of Doctor of Philosophy in the program in Anthropology and Archaeology at the University of Durham.

Engeström, Y. (1987). *Learning by Expanding An Activity – Theoretical Approach to Developmental Research*. Helsinki: Orienta-Konsultit Oy.

Engeström, Y. (1990). *Learning, Working and Imagining*. Helsinki: Orienta-Konsultit Oy.

Forbes, K. (1990, November). *The Complex Sheet*. Paper presented at the Steelcase Conference, Xerox PARC.

Foucault, M. (1979). *Discipline and Punish: The Birth of the Prison*. New York: Random House.

Garfinkel, H. (1967). *Studies in Ethnomethodology*. Englewood Cliffs, NJ: Prentice-Hall.

Goffman, E. (1963). *Behavior in Public Places: Notes on the Social Organization of Gathering*. New York: Free Press.

Goffman, E. (1971). *Relations in Public: Microstudies of the Public Order*. New York: Harper and Row.

Goffman, E. (1974). *Frame Analysis: An Essay on the Organization of Experience.* New York: Harper and Row.

Goffman, E. (1981). *Forms of Talk.* Philadelphia: University of Pennsylvania Press.

Goodenough, W. H. (1970). *Description and Comparison in Cultural Anthropology.* Chicago: Aldine.

Goodwin, C. (1979). The interactive construction of a sentence in natural conversation. In *Everyday Language: Studies in Ethnomethodology.* G. Psathas (Ed.), pp. 97–121. New York: Irvington.

Goodwin, C. (1981). *Conversational Organization: Interaction Between Speakers and Hearers.* New York: Academic Press.

Goodwin, C. (1994). Professional vision. *American Anthropologist 96*(3), 606–633.

Goodwin, C. (in press). Transparent vision. In *Interaction and Grammar.* E. Ochs, E. Schegloff & S. Thompson (Eds.). Cambridge: Cambridge University Press.

Goodwin, C. & Goodwin, M. H. (1987). Concurrent operations on talk: Notes on the interactive organization of assessments. *IPrA Papers in Pragmatics 1*(1), 1–52.

Goodwin, C. & Goodwin, M. H. (1992). Assessments and the construction of context. In *Rethinking Context: Language as an Interactive Phenomenon.* A. Duranti & C. Goodwin (Eds.), pp. 147–190. Cambridge: Cambridge University Press.

Goodwin, C. & Heritage, J. (1990). Conversation analysis. *Annual Reviews of Anthropology 19,* 283–307.

Goodwin, M. H. (1980). Processes of mutual monitoring implicated in the production of description sequences. *Sociological Inquiry 50,* 303–317.

Goodwin, M. H. (1990). *He-Said-She-Said: Talk as Social Organization among Black Children.* Bloomington, IN: Indiana University Press.

Goodwin, M. H. (in press). Announcements in their environment: Prosody within a multi-activity work setting. In *Prosody in Conversation: Ethnomethodological Studies.* E. Couper-Kuhlen & M. Selting (Eds.). Cambridge: Cambridge University Press.

Goody, J. (1977). *The Domestication of the Savage Mind.* Cambridge: Cambridge University Press.

Hanks, W. F. (1989). Text and textuality. *Annual Review of Anthropology 18,* 95–127.

Hanks, W. F. (1990). *Referential Practice: Language and Lived Space Among the Maya.* Chicago: University of Chicago Press.

Haraway, D. (1988). Situated knowledges: The science question in feminism and the privilege of partial perspective. *Feminist Studies 14*(3), 575–599.

Harding, S. (1986). *The Science Question in Feminism.* Ithaca, NY: Cornell University Press.

Harris, M. (1968). *The Rise of Anthropological Theory.* New York: Thomas Y. Crowell.

Heath, C. (1986). *Body Movement and Speech in Medical Interaction.* Cambridge: Cambridge University Press.

Heidegger, M. (1962). *Being and Time* (John Macquarrie & Edward Robinson). New York: Harper and Row.

Heritage, J. (1984a). A change-of-state token and aspects of its sequential placement. In *Structures of Social Action.* J. M. Atkinson & J. Heritage (Eds.), pp. 299–345. Cambridge: Cambridge University Press.

Heritage, J. (1984b). *Garfinkel and Ethnomethodology.* Cambridge, UK: Polity Press.

Hutchins, E. (1990). The technology of team navigation. In *Intellectual Teamwork: Social and Technological Foundations of Cooperative Work.* J. Galegher, R. E. Kraut & C. Egido (Eds.), pp. 22–51. Hillsdale, NJ: Erlbaum.

Hutchins, E. (1995). *Cognition in the Wild.* Cambridge, MA: MIT Press.

Jefferson, G. (1973). A case of precision timing in ordinary conversation: Overlapped tag-positioned address terms in closing sequences. *Semiotica 9,* 47–96.

Jefferson, G. (1974). Error correction as an interactional resource. *Language in Society 2,* 181–199.

Jefferson, G. (1984). On the organization of laughter in talk about troubles. In *Structures of Social Action.* J. M. Atkinson & J. Heritage (Eds.), pp. 346–369. Cambridge: Cambridge University Press.

Jordan, B. (1990). *The Organization of Activity and the Achievement of Competent Practice in a Complex Work Setting.* Paper presented at the Congress on Research in Activity Theory. Lahti, Finland.

Kendon, A. (1990). *Conducting Interaction: Patterns of Behavior in Focused Encounters.* Cambridge: Cambridge University Press.

Latour, B. (1986). Visualization and cognition: Thinking with eyes and hands. *Knowledge and Society: Studies in the Sociology of Culture Past and Present 6*, 1–40.

Latour, B. (1987). *Science in Action: How to Follow Scientists and Engineers through Society.* Cambridge, MA: Harvard University Press.

Latour, B. (1990, September). *Are We Talking about Skills or about the Redistribution of Skills.* Paper presented at Rediscovering Skill in Science, Technology and Medicine, University of Bath.

Latour, B. & Woolgar, S. (1979). *Laboratory Life: The Social Construction of Scientific Facts.* London: Sage.

Lave, J. (1988). *Cognition in Practice.* Cambridge: Cambridge University Press.

Lave, J. & Wenger, E. (1991). *Situated Learning: Legitimate Peripheral Participation.* Cambridge: Cambridge University Press.

Leont'ev, A. N. (1981). *Problems of the Development of the Mind.* Moscow: Progress Publishers.

Lerner, G. H. (1993). Collectivities in action: Establishing the relevance of conjoined participation in conversation. *Text 13*(2), 213–246.

Lynch, M. (1988). The externalized retina: Selection and mathematization in the visual documentation of objects in the life sciences. *Human Studies 11*, 201–234.

Lynch, M. & Woolgar S. (Eds.). (1988). *Representation in Scientific Practice.* First appeared as a special issue of *Human Studies.* Vol. 11, 2–3. Cambridge, MA: MIT Press.

Lynch, M. E. (1982). Technical work and critical inquiry: Investigations in a scientific laboratory. *Social Studies of Science 12*, 499–533.

McDermott, R. P. (1976). *Kids Make Sense: An Ethnographic Account of the Interactional Management of Success and Failure of One First-Grade Classroom.* Unpublished Ph.D. Dissertation. Stanford University.

Middleton, D. & Edwards, D. (1990). Conversational Remembering: A Social Psychological Approach. In *Collective Remembering.* D. Middleton & D. Edwards (Eds.), pp. 23–45. London: Sage.

Mukerji, C. (1989). *A Fragile Power: Scientists and the State.* Princeton, NJ: Princeton University Press.

Mydans, S. (1991). Air Controller Tells of Chaos in Fatal Los Angeles Collision. *The New York Times* February 9, p. 9.

Ochs, E. (1988). *Culture and Language Development: Language Acquisition and Language Socialization in a Samoan Village.* Cambridge: Cambridge University Press.

Ochs, E., Jacoby S., & Gonzales, P. (1994). Interpretive journeys: How physicists talk and travel through graphic space. *Configurations 2*, 151–171.

Ochs, E. & Schieffelin, B. B. (1984). Language acquisition and socialization: Three developmental stories and their implications. In *Culture Theory: Essays on Mind, Self and Emotion.* R. Shweder & R. LeVine (Eds.), pp. 276–320. New York: Cambridge University Press.

Ochs, E., Schieffelin, B. B., & Platt, M. L. (1979). Propositions across utterances and speakers. In *Developmental Pragmatics.* E. Ochs & B. B. Schieffelin (Eds.), pp. 251–268. New York: Academic Press.

Pasveer, B. (1990, September). *Pictures in Medicine: On Radiology, Tuberculosis, and Representing.* Paper presented at Rediscovering Skill in Science, Technology and Medicine, University of Bath.

Pomerantz, A. (1984). Pursuing a response. In *Structures of Social Action.* J. M. Atkinson & J. Heritage (Eds.), pp. 152–164. Cambridge: Cambridge University Press.

Rogoff, B. (1990). *Apprenticeship in Thinking.* New York: Oxford University Press.

Sacks, H. (1963). Sociological Description. *Berkeley Journal of Sociology 8*, 1–16.

Sacks, H. (1992). *Lectures*. G. Jefferson (Ed.). Oxford: Basil Blackwell.

Sacks, H. & Schegloff, E. A. (1979). Two Preferences in the organization of reference to persons and their interaction. In *Everyday Language: Studies in Ethnomethodology*. G. Psathas (Ed.), pp. 15–21. New York: Irvington.

Sacks, H., Schegloff, E. A., & Jefferson, G. (1974). A simplest systematics for the organization of turn-taking for conversation. *Language 50*, 696–735.

Schegloff, E. A. (1992). Repair after next turn: The last structurally provided defense of intersubjectivity in conversation. *American Journal of Sociology 97*(5), 1295–1345.

Schegloff, E. A. (1968). Sequencing in conversational openings. *American Anthropologist 70*, 1075–1095.

Schegloff, E. A. (1972). Notes on a conversational practice: Formulating place. In *Studies in Social Interaction*. D. Sudnow (Ed.), pp. 75–119. New York: Free Press.

Schegloff, E. A. & Sacks, H. (1973). Opening up closings. *Semiotica 8*, 289–327.

Schieffelin, B. B. (1990). *The Give and Take of Everyday Life: Language Socialization of Kaluli Children*. Cambridge: Cambridge University Press.

Searle, J. R. (1990). Collective Intentionality and action. In *Intention in Communication*. P. R. Cohen, J. Morgen, & M. E. Rollsik (Eds.), pp. 401–415. Cambridge: MIT Press.

Shapin, S. (1989). The invisible technician. *American Scientist 77*, 554–563.

Siefert, C. M. & Hutchins, E. L. (1989). Learning within a Distributed System. *Quarterly Newsletter of the Laboratory of Comparative Human Cognition 11*(4), 108–114.

Smith, D. E. (1990). *Texts, Facts and Femininity*. London: Routledge.

Star, S. L. & Gerson, E. M. (1987). The management and dynamics of anomalies in scientific work. *Sociological Quarterly 28*, 147–169.

Star, S. L. & Griesemer, J. R. (1989). Institutional ecology, "translations" and boundary objects: Amateurs and professionals in Berkeley's museum of vertebrate zoology, 1907–1939. *Social Studies of Science 19*, 387–420.

Suchman, L. & Trigg, R. (1993). Artificial intelligence as craftwork. In *Understanding Practice: Perspectives on Activity and Context*. S. Chaiklin & J. Lave (Eds.), pp. 144–178. Cambridge: Cambridge University Press.

Suchman, L. A. (1987). *Plans and Situated Actions: The Problem of Human Machine Communication*. Cambridge: Cambridge University Press.

Vygotsky, L. S. (1962). *Thought and Language*. (Translated by Eugenia Hanfmann and Gertrude Vaker). Cambridge, MA: MIT Press.

Vygotsky, L. S. (1978). *Mind in Society: The Development of Higher Psychological Processes*. Cambridge: Harvard University Press.

Wertsch, J. (1985). *Culture, Communication, and Cognition: Vygotskian Perspectives*. Cambridge: Cambridge University Press.

Whalen, M. R. & Zimmerman, D. H. (1990). Describing trouble: Practical epistemology in citizen calls to the police. *Language in Society 19*, 465–492.

Wittgenstein, L. (1953). *Philosophical Investigations*. (Translated by G.E.M. Anscombe). New York: Macmillian.

Woolgar, S. (1988). Time and documents in researcher interaction: Some ways of making out what is happening in experimental science. *Human Studies 11*, 171–200.

# 5     Convergent activities: Line control and passenger information on the London Underground

*Christian Heath and Paul Luff*

[T]he relevance of the works of the Chicago sociologists is that they do contain a lot of information about this and that. And this and that is what the world is made up of.

Sacks, H. (1964/1992, p. 27)

"Shared Agreement" refers to various social methods for accomplishing the member's recognition that something was said according to a rule and not the demonstrable matching of substantive matters. The appropriate image of a common understanding is therefore an operation rather than a common intersection of overlapping sets.

Garfinkel, H. (1967, p. 30)

## Introduction

Some of the finest work within the sociology of organizations began to emerge from Chicago following the second world war. Due in no small way to the lectures and essays of E. C. Hughes, social science witnessed the emergence of a substantial body of naturalistic studies of work and occupations that began to delineate the practices and reasoning that provide the foundation for tasks and interpersonal communication throughout a range of organizational settings. Hughes and his colleagues powerfully demonstrated through numerous empirical studies how organizational life is thoroughly dependent upon and inseparable from a tacit and emergent "culture" that is fashioned and continually refashioned in the light of the problems that personnel face in the routine accomplishment of their day-to-day work (see, for example, Hughes, 1958, 1971; Becker et al., 1961; Goffman, 1968; Roth, 1963; Strauss et al., 1964). This substantial body of research, and the conceptual framework developed by Hughes, has had a long-lasting and powerful influence not only on the sociology of work and organizations in the past three decades but also on numerous studies in related fields such as criminal justice or the sociology of health and illness.

Whereas the analytic and substantive concerns of the postwar Chicago School, filtered through the contributions of successive generations, continue to permeate social science, it is interesting to note that there is a corpus of research currently emerging within cognitive science that has many of the hallmarks of the postwar naturalistic studies of work and organizations. In the light of powerful critiques of goal-oriented, plan-based models of human conduct (for example, Suchman, 1987; Winograd & Flores, 1986), a growing interest in activity theory, and the emergence of distributed computing, we are witnessing the development of an exciting body of naturalistic research concerned with work practice and new technology in organizational settings, sometimes conceptualized in terms of "distributed cognition" (see, for example, Hutchins, 1985, 1989, 1990; Lave, 1988; Olson, 1990; Olson & Olson, 1991; Norman, 1988).

Although the Chicago School made a significant contribution to our understanding of work and occupational life, the ways in which they explain tasks and activities in institutional environments is not without its problems. For example, at a very general level, it is unclear how useful it is for sociological explanation to transpose metaphors used in one domain to characterize work and occupational life in another. More importantly, perhaps, while recognizing the importance of the mundane and routine in work, such studies, often by virtue of the conceptual framework then employ, ignore the ways in which tasks and work-based activities are accomplished in actual circumstances within organizational settings. In particular, despite Hughes's recognition of the importance of social interaction to the accomplishment of work and organizational life, the ways in which specialized tasks such as medical diagnosis or psychiatric treatment are produced in and through interaction remains unexplicated, glossed in terms of "organizational culture," "operational philosophies," "negotiation," or "taking the role of the other," etc. Perhaps as a consequence of subscribing to a model of human conduct that presupposes that social order rests upon shared meanings and understandings that remaining stable for brief periods of time, the sociointeractional and collaborative production of tasks and activities within organizational settings is largely lost from the analytic domain.

This chapter, like others in the volume, is concerned with continuing the rich ethnographic tradition in the sociology of work and organizations, but tries to realign the focus towards the sociointeractional foundations of task-based activities. Drawing on video recordings and field observation of work and interaction in the Line Control Rooms of the London Underground, it explores the ways in which personnel interweave and coordinate specialized work tasks within a relatively circumscribed division of labor. We wish to show how seemingly individual and specialized work tasks are produced with respect to the actions of colleagues and rely upon individual's ability to participate, simultaneously, in multiple activities. In this chapter, we are particularly interested in showing how line control and the provision of public information on the London Underground rest upon a body of practices and reasoning through which personnel produce, recognize, and coordinate their specialized actions and activities with the contributions of their colleagues.

Although such analysis falls within a longstanding sociological tradition, it is also of potential relevance to recent developments in computer science and human–computer interaction (HCI; see Baecker & Buxton, 1987; Carroll, 1991; Norman & Draper, 1986). Alongside the growing interest in developing systems to support collaborative work, we have witnessed the emergence of a research domain, CSCW (Computer Supported Cooperative Work; see Baecker, 1993; Galegher et al., 1990; Greif, 1988), in which it has been recognized that many innovative and advanced applications fail not so much as a result of technological inadequacy, but rather as a consequence of the systems' "insensitivity" to the ways in which individuals ordinarily interact and collaborate in the workplace (Grudin, 1988; Markus & Connolly, 1990; Galegher & Kraut, 1990; Moran & Anderson, 1990). Indeed, it is being increasingly argued that the requirements for complex systems need to be derived from a deeper understanding of real-world, technologically supported cooperative work, which in turn might lead to a distinctive, more social scientific, approach to user-centered design. Whether or not such developments can be drawn from work in the social sciences is unclear, but at this stage we can begin, on the basis of naturalistic studies of work and interaction, to chart some considerations for the ways in which we might reconsider a number of the central concepts in HCI and CSCW. In this chapter, as well as addressing how personnel in a particular setting "mediate" action and interaction through various tools and technologies, we wish to briefly suggest how we might begin to reconsider concepts such as "task," "user" and "collaboration," concepts that have driven design and research in HCI for a number of years.

### The technology in the control room

Drawing on materials from a number of Line Control Rooms on the London Underground, we focus in particular on the Bakerloo Line. The Bakerloo Line Control Room has recently undergone extensive modernization. Traditional manual signalling has been replaced by a complex computerized system, which is operated centrally by signal assistants who are based in the Line Control Room. It now houses the Line Controller, who coordinates the day-to-day running of the railway, the Divisional Information Assistant (DIA) whose responsibilities include providing information to passengers through a public address (PA) system and communicating with station managers, and two signal assistants who oversee the operation of the signalling system from Queens Park to the Elephant and Castle, the busiest section of the line. It is not unusual also to find a trainee DIA or Controller in the Control Room or a relief Controller when problems and crises emerge. Figure 1 shows the general layout of the Control Room.

The Controller and DIA sit together at a semicircular console that faces a tiled,

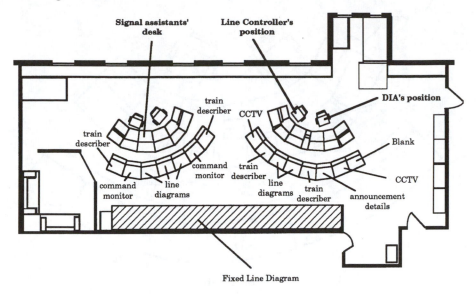

Figure 1.   The Bakerloo Line Control Room.

real-time, fixed-line diagram running almost the entire length of the room. The diagram indicates the location of trains on the northbound and southbound track between Elephant and Castle and Queens Park; lights illuminate on the board when the trains pass over different sections of the line. The console includes a radio phone system for speaking with drivers, the Public Address control keys, the headset and microphone, closed-circuit television (CCTV) monitors for viewing station platforms and their control keys, three monitors showing line diagrams and traffic, and a monitor listing the actual running times of trains. The console also contains two touch-screen telephones, which are operated by the user touching parts of a display of numbers and personnel names shown on the monitor (see Fig. 2). On occasion, a trainee DIA (tDIA) or a second Controller (Cii) will sit at this console. The signal assistants sit at a similar console alongside the Controller and DIA (see Fig. 1). They also have access to monitors showing real-time graphic displays of the line and its traffic, listings of running times, input monitors for making changes to the scheduled service, and touch-screen telephones.

   The Underground service is coordinated through a paper timetable that specifies the number, running time and route of trains, crew allocation and shift arrangements; information concerning staff travel facilities, stock transfers, vehicle storage and maintenance, etc. Each underground line has a particular timetable, though in some cases the timing of trains will be closely tied to the service on a related line. The timetable is not simply an abstract description of the operation of the service, but is used by various personnel including the Con-

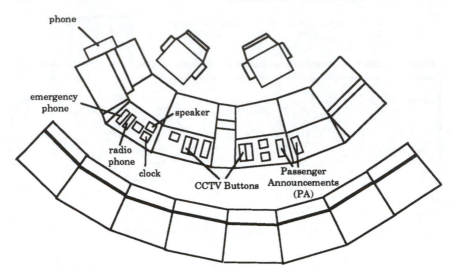

Figure 2.   Line Controllers' and DIAs' desks.

troller, DIA, Signalmen, and Duty Crew Managers, to coordinate traffic flow and passenger movement. In the Line Control Room, Controller, DIA, and other staff use the timetable in conjunction with their understanding of the current operation of the service to determine the adequacy of the service and, if necessary, initiate remedial action. Indeed, a significant part of the responsibility of the Controller is to serve as a "guardian of the timetable." Even if he is unable to shape the service according to the timetable's specific details, the Controller should, as far as possible, attempt to achieve its underlying principle: a regular service of trains with relatively brief intervening gaps.

The timetable is not only a resource for identifying difficulties within the operation of the service but also for their management. For example, the Controller will make small adjustments to the running times of various trains to cure gaps that are emerging between a number of trains during the operation of the service. More serious problems such as absentees, vehicle breakdowns or the discovery of "suspect parcels" on trains or platforms, which can lead to severe disruption of the service, are often managed by "reforming" the service, that is, by renumbering trains so that they are crewed by and follow the schedule of a different train. These adjustments and "reformations" are undertaken by the Controller. He marks the changes on the relevant pages of his timetable. The paper pages are covered with cellophane or laminated sheets to enable the Controller (and others) to mark changes in the timetable and then to remove them with a cloth when the trouble is over. The changes made by the Controller to the timetable have to be known by the DIA and Signal Assistants and communicated to Operators (Drivers), Duty Crew Managers, Duty Train Managers, and others outside the Line Control Room. It is critical that the DIA, relief Controller, signal assistants, and others receive information concerning changes to the timetable, otherwise they will misunderstand the current operation of the service and undertake inappropriate courses of action.

Despite important differences in the formal specification of the responsibilities of the Controller and DIA, the various tasks they undertake rely upon close collaboration. Indeed, Control Room personnel have developed a subtle and complex body of practices for monitoring each other's conduct and coordinating a varied collection of tasks and activities (see Heath & Luff, 1992). These practices appear to stand independently of particular personnel, and it is not unusual to witness individuals who have no previous experience working together, informally, implicitly, yet systematically coordinating their conduct with each other. One element of this extraordinary interweaving of sequential and simultaneous responsibilities and tasks is an emergent and flexible division of labor that allows the personnel to lend support to the accomplishment of each others' tasks and activities and thereby manage difficulties and crises.

## Assessing the service

The London Underground, like other rapid urban transport systems, does not provide the public with a timetable with which to schedule their journeys. Rather, passengers organize their travel arrangements on the assumption that trains will travel between particular locations at frequent and predictable intervals. On the Bakerloo Line for example, trains run approximately every two-and-a-half minutes during the "peak" period and between five and seven minutes at other times in the day. The DIA orients to the ways in which passengers organize their travel with London Underground and provides information when particular problems arise in the "normal" operation of the service. Such problems may vary from a slight delay as a result of absent staff, through to a major evacuation caused by the discovery of a "suspect parcel." The nature of such information varies with respect to the circumstances at hand; however, these public announcements do reveal recurrent characteristics.[1]

**Fragment 1 (10.7.91 9:45)**

> DIA: Good Morning this: is Bakerloo Line Information ↑ (0.3)
>
> DIA: The next train (just) left from Regents <u>Par:k</u> ↑ (0.6) (an) well be with you at Ba:ker Street (in) one mi<u>nute</u> (0.3) Marylebone (0.6) three minutes:, (.) Paddington in approximately six minutes:. (1.2)
>
> DIA: (Our) next train just left fro<u>m</u> (.) Re<u>gents</u> Par:k ↑ (1.2) <u>d</u>estination Harrow an Willsdo(w)n.

The actual advice is routinely foreshadowed by a series, or package, of actions that successively align the potential recipients to the upcoming information. These actions include a greeting and an official identification of the speaker. The

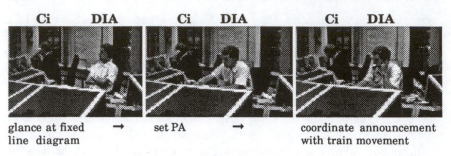

glance at fixed         →         set PA         →         coordinate announcement
line  diagram                                              with train movement

Figure 3.    Assessing the state of the service.

advice itself provides specific information to particular passengers, namely those
who are waiting at Baker Street, Marylebone, and Paddington, and who may be
waiting because of a delay in the service. The announcement appeals to the current or prospective experience of passengers and gains its significance by virtue
of the ways passengers organize their use of the Underground service. Thus,
even though the announcement is addressed to the "general public," it achieves
its performative impact—its relevance—through its design for specific categories of passengers; namely, those waiting at the particular locations on the
Bakerloo Line who are suffering a delay.

To produce timely and relevant information, the DIA monitors the service and
transforms his observations into carefully tailored announcements. In the case at
hand, the DIA glances at the fixed-line diagram and switches the CCTV monitor
to the northbound platform at Regents Park (see Fig. 3). He sets the PA system,
and as the train begins to leave the station, delivers the announcement. The specific advice the DIA gives is coordinated with the train's departure from a particular station and is based on the anticipated time it takes for a train to travel between the stations in question. The DIA's announcement is achieved by utilizing
various technologies in the control room. The fixed-line diagram allows the DIA
to assess the state of the service and, in particular, to notice any gaps or intervals
between the trains, and the CCTV monitor provides access to a particular train itself, at least as it appears on the screen, and allows the DIA to coordinate and design the announcement with the "actual" movement of the vehicle.

### "Monitoring" and discriminating action

Although the DIA does have independent access to various forms of information
concerning the operation of the service, such as the fixed-line diagram and the
CCTV screens, the assessments he makes and the various actions he undertakes
are often dependent upon the actions of his colleagues, and in particular the Line
Controller. It is relatively unusual however, for the Line Controller, the DIA or

the Signal Assistants, explicitly to provide information to each other concerning the problems they have noticed or the interventions they may have made. Indeed, given the demands on these personnel, especially when dealing with emergencies or difficulties, it would be impossible to abandon the tasks in which they were engaged in order to provide explicit information concerning what they were doing and why. However, it is essential that both Controller and DIA (and others) remain sensitive to each others' conduct, not only to allow them to coordinate specific tasks and activities, but also to enable them to gather appropriate information concerning the details of the current operation of the service.

To produce timely and relevant information for passengers, the DIA systematically monitors the service and the actions of his colleagues, and transforms these bits and pieces into carefully tailored announcements for passengers who are using the service at some moment in time. Consider the following instance, where the DIA delivers an announcement to warn the passengers at a particular station that their next train will be delayed.

**Fragment 2.1**

DIA: Hello: and good afternoon La(d)ies an Gentlemen ↑ (.) Bakerloo Line Information ↑ (0.3) (°hhh) We have a sli:ght gap in our Sou:th Bound Bakerloo Line Service ↑ (.) towards the Elephant an Castle, (1.6) Your next South Bound train: ↑ (0.6) should depart from this: station in about another three minutes::. (0.2) The next South Bound train ↑ (0.2) should depart from this station in about another three minutes::.

The announcement emerges in the light of the DIA overhearing the Controller's conversation with the driver, or operator (Op), and assessing its implications for the expectations and experience of travellers using the service.

**Fragment 2.2**

C: Control to the train: at Charing Cro<u>ss</u>: South Bound, <do you receive? (6.3) ((*C. Switches CCTV monitor to platform*))

C: Control to the train at Charing Cross South Bound, do you receive? (1.0)

Op: (( )) (°two four O:) Charing Cross S:outh Bound

C: Yeah two four O:: <we got a little bit of an interval behind you, (.) could you take a couple of minutes: in the platform for me please?

Op: (( )) Over

C: Thank you very much Two Four O:
(5.2)

DIA: Hello: and good afternoon La(d)ies an Gentlemen ↑ (.) Bakerloo Line Information ↑ (0.3) (°hhh) We have a sli:ght gap in our Sou:th Bound Bakerloo Line Service ↑ (.) towards the Elephant an Castle, (1.6) Your next South Bound train: ↑ (0.6) should depart from this: station in about another three minutes::. (0.2) The next South Bound train ↑ (0.2) should depart from this station in about another three minutes::.

The DIA transforms the Controller's request into a relevant announcement by determining who the decision will affect and what its consequences will be. In this case, this particularly concerns the passengers at Charing Cross whose train is being delayed as a consequence of a problem emerging on the Southbound service. A little later, the DIA produces a second announcement (not included in the transcript above) to inform passengers who have recently arrived on the platform of the delay.

The DIA does not wait until the completion of the Controller's call before preparing to take action. As the Controller begins his first attempt to contact the driver, the DIA glances at the fixed-line diagram, as if to seek an account for the Controller's intervention (Fig. 4, frame 2.1). As the Controller begins his second attempt to contact the driver, the DIA moves to a seat nearer the console and in reach of the PA system (Fig. 4, frame 2.2). On the phrase "couple of minu<u>te</u>s:," where the specific implications of the intervention become apparent, he begins to set the PA system to make an announcement to the passengers at Charing Cross (Fig. 4, frame 2.3). The DIA monitors the Controller's actions as they emerge in interaction with the driver, and using the various technological sources of information, particularly the fixed-line diagram, is able to account for the Controller's intervention and to assess its implications for passengers at a certain location.

The DIA overhears the Controller's emerging intervention and transforms his request for the Driver to "take a couple of minutes" in the platform, into a public announcement informing passengers that there will be a slight delay before the train continues its journey. The announcement "reproduces" certain features of the request to the driver, providing an explanation—"a <u>sli:</u>ght gap in our <u>sou:</u>th bound Bakerloo Line Service ↑"—which foreshadows the specific advice—"Your next South Bound train: ↑ (0.6) should depart from this: station in about another <u>three</u> minutes::." The Controller's intervention, therefore, appears to engender a specific activity by the DIA; an activity that systematically reformulates features of a conversation between two colleagues and presents the information to a particular category of passengers.

Despite the necessity to monitor closely the conduct of the Controller, the DIA maintains a certain "social distance," providing his colleague with what

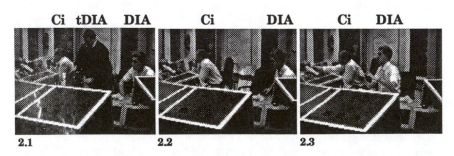

Figure 4.

Hughes (1958) might characterize as "the elbow room with which to fulfill his colleague's particular duties." As the DIA begins to "track" the call to the driver and prepare to make an announcement, he neither looks at the Controller nor watches the activity of his colleague. Moreover, as he changes positions and moves closer to the Controller, he avoids making his own activity visible or noticeable to his colleague; rather, the actions appear to be accomplished independently of the call to the driver, as if the DIA is engaged in some unrelated business. Through his bodily comportment and the ways in which he warily accomplishes his actions, the DIA preserves a careful balance of involvement, overhearing the Controller and monitoring his colleague's actions on the "periphery" of the visual field, while avoiding overt attention to the Controller's conduct.

Certain phrases or even single words addressed by the Controller to a driver or signalman on the telephone are often enough for the DIA to draw particular inferences and undertake relevant action. For example, in Fragment 2 the request to "take a couple of minutes" allows the DIA to infer that the Controller is attempting to reduce an interval on the southbound service, a problem that it is unlikely to have been noticed until the Controller called the driver. The DIA overhears the call, develops an account for intervention, and assesses its implications for his own conduct. In the following instance, the DIA, who is apparently engrossed in updating his own timetable, grabs the phone and calls the Station Manager at Piccadilly Circus on hearing the word "re:verse:."

**Fragment 3**

|  |  |
|---|---|
| C: | <u>Controller</u> ↑ to <u>Sou</u>th Bound <u>Two</u> <u>Three</u> <u>Three,</u> <do you receive? |
|  | (8.2) |
| Op: | Two Three Three receiving pass your message (. . .) (0.3) over ↑ |
| →C: | Yeah Two Three Three: (.) I'd like you to |
| → | re:verse: at Piccadilly:, (.) an: you'll also |
| → | be <u>re:for</u>med there: >I'll come back to <u>you::</u> when you get to Piccadilly:. |
|  | over. |
|  | (1.2) ((*Radio noise (0.3)* )) |
| Op: | O:kay >thankyou very much Contro<u>ller</u>: (0.2) |
|  | erm:: (.) can you ma(ke) (0.2) er:: (.) i(s)it |
|  | er: possible to make announcement (to the people) (when I get there) |
|  | over? |
|  | (0.7) |
| C: | Yeah: the D I: A:: will make announcements for: you, (.) Can you <u>con</u>‐ |
|  | <u>firm</u> you've just left <u>Re:gents</u>:? |
| Op: | Er:: Roger (.) no (I think) (I'm er::) (0.2) still at <u>Ba:</u>ker Street, Over on |
|  | the:: (.) on the (- - - -) South Bound, Over? |
| C: | hh <u>Yeah</u>:: we've received driver tha<u>nks</u>: very much, I'll tell the D I A:: |
|  | (who) will moni<u>tor</u> you down: te Piccadilly. |
|  | (0.3) |
|  | DIA:  Ye ah (.) Bakerloo Line Information Two <u>Th</u>rree Three is going |
|  |   to reverse with with you:, (0.2) South to North:, |
|  |   (2.0) |

DIA:　Two <u>Three</u> <u>Three</u>. He's at Baker: Street now::.

((*roughly 3 minutes later*))

DIA:　Good morning Ladies and Gentlemen ↑ (.) Bakerloo
　　　Line Informat<u>ion</u> ↑ (1.0) This train is for:: (0.4) Pic-
　　　cadilly Circus: ↑ only.(1.2) This tr<u>ain</u> (.) for: (.) Pic-
　　　cadilly Cir<u>cus</u> only.
　　　((*Successive announcements made at each station as
　　　the train in question arrives.*))

Before the Controller has finished speaking to the Driver, the DIA calls the Station Manager at Piccadilly and warns him that the 233 is to be "detrained." On completing the call, the DIA then produces a series of public announcements on each southbound platform between Baker Street and Piccadilly, warning passengers that the train is "for Piccadilly only." The photographs in Fig. 5 will provide a sense of the ways in which the DIA produces a series of actions on overhearing the Controller's request to the driver.

The DIA therefore overhears the Controller's intervention and assesses its implications for both staff and passengers. The Controller's request, and in particular the word "reverse," engenders sequentially relevant actions from the DIA; first to warn the station manager of the upcoming events, and second, to inform passengers who may join the train at a number of stations prior to Piccadilly that its presupposed destination has been changed. The driver himself is sensitive to the implications of "turning early" for the passengers, and asks the Controller to have the DIA make the relevant announcements. The Controller relies upon the DIA undertaking a specific set of sequentially appropriate actions with respect to particular types of action that he, the Controller, may undertake. Indeed, in the case at hand, if the DIA failed to warn the station manager or provide the appropriate passenger information, the absence of such actions would be noticeable and accountable.

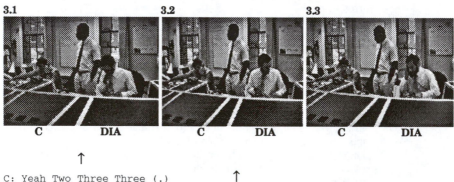

```
3.1                      3.2                      3.3




    C         DIA            C         DIA            C         DIA

          ↑
C: Yeah Two Three Three (.)                ↑
         I'd like you to re:verse: at Piccadily:,              ↑
                         (.) an: you'll be re:formed there:
```

Figure 5.

It is not simply that DIAs happen to remain attentive to the local environment of activity and are able to draw the relevant inferences from the actions of their colleagues. Rather, personnel within the Control Room organize their conduct so that while engaged in one activity, they simultaneously monitor or participate in the activities of others. This double-edged element of accomplishing these specialized tasks within the Line Control Room is an essential feature of their "collaborative work," demanding that participants design their activities so that while undertaking one task they remain sensitive to the "independent" actions of their colleague(s).

Producing an activity while simultaneously participating in the activities of another has implications for the ways in which personnel utilize the various tools and technologies within the Line Control Room. So, for example, the DIA may switch his CCTV monitor to a particular platform to enable him to read a number from the front of a train for the Controller, even though the DIA is engaged in delivering a public announcement and only happened to overhear that problems concerning the identity of particular trains are emerging. Or for example, it is not unusual to find the Controller or DIA switching the telephone handset to the other ear, to enable his colleague to overhear a conversation with a member of the Underground staff based outside the Line Control Room. Almost all tasks within the Line Control Room are produced by the DIA or Controller as they simultaneously participate in the concurrent activities of their colleagues. The various tools and technologies that are provided to support these tasks, are shaped, corrupted, and even abandoned, in order to enable Control Room personnel to participate simultaneously in multiple activities that more or less involve each other.

In both Fragments 2 and 3 we can see the ways in which phrases or even single words serve to engender particular actions and activities for colleagues within the Control Room itself. These words or phrases, while featuring in the accomplishment of specific actions in interaction on the radio phone, simultaneously embody particular activities for the DIA and allow him to produce sequentially appropriate conduct and provide a coordinated response to a problem or crisis. The DIA is not the "principal recipient" of the Controller's telephone talk, and yet is able to retrieve the necessary bits and pieces of information to enable him to produce "sequentially" relevant actions and activities. The production of conduct by the DIA (and others such as the Signal Assistants) relies upon a body of procedures and conventions that provide for, and engender, the relevance of particular actions given specific types of activity undertaken by the Controller. The very intelligibility of the scene for the DIA, and his colleagues, derives from their use of and orientation to a body of practice that informs the production, recognition, and coordination of routine conduct within the Line Control Room. So, for example, it is not simply that the DIA remains peripherally aware and sensitive to the whole gamut of "goings on" within the Control Room, but rather discriminates the local environment of conduct with respect to, for example, the routine implications of specific types of events for his own conduct. Interventions such as turning trains short, closing stations, delaying trains, taking trains out of service, and so on, in their different ways implicate specific trajectories of action for the DIA (and others). The procedures and conventions oriented to by the DIA and his colleagues in producing and coordinating actions, inform the ways in which they "monitor" and discriminate each other's conduct and remain sensitive to the local environment of "goings on."

## The production of convergent activities

Personnel within the Line Control Room are continually and unavoidably "monitoring" and "discriminating" the local environment of conduct, and by virtue of a body of indigenous practice and procedure, coordinate particular actions and activities with each other. Through these practices, personnel produce and preserve the mutual intelligibility of emergent events and activities and are able to recognize and make sense of each other's actions and the movement of traffic along the line. The natural history of specific events, such as the management of a "suspect parcel" or a "person under a train," even the natural history of the operation of the traffic "on this morning" and "on this day," provides for the intelligibility of actions and their relevance for particular conduct by particular personnel within the Line Control Room. In making sense of the actions of colleagues, the various information displays and the events at hand, the DIA and others orient to a body of practice that interweaves their particular actions and the ways in which those practices have configured and rendered intelligible the immediately prior events. Take, for example, a case in which a Controller might ask a DIA to perform a particular action. However "explicit" that request might be, it unavoidably relies upon the DIA's current understanding of the service, to assemble the sense of the action. Consider the following instance in which the Controller (Cii) requests the DIA to ask a driver of a train at Oxford Circus to continue his journey southbound.

**Fragment 4    Transcript 1**

                ((*Cii replaces one receiver and picks up another*))
                (2.5)
   Cii:    <u>T</u>ell him to go: (.) if you've got a clear
            sig$\lfloor$nal
   DIA:    $\llcorner$Yeah
                (6.4) ((*DIA resets the PA system*))
          DIA:   This is a <u>staff</u> announce:<u>men</u>:t ↑ (0.2) to the train operator (.)
                if you have a:: Green Signal: ↑ you may pro<u>ceed</u>. (1.4) If you
                have a Green Signal you may <u>pro:ceed</u>, Southbound.
                (1.2)
          DIA:   Staff announcement to the train driver. If you have a Green
                Signal you may proceed, (.) S<u>outh</u>bound.
                ((*The train leaves Oxford Circus*))

Until the delivery of the request, the Controller and the DIA have been engaged in distinct and apparently unrelated tasks. The Controller has been attempting to contact a driver who has unaccountably "sat down" at Oxford Circus for some minutes and caused a severe backlog of traffic on the southbound service. Meanwhile the DIA is preparing to make a public announcement concerning an unrelated difficulty emerging elsewhere in the service. On the failure of the Controller's third attempt to contact the driver at Oxford Circus, he abandons the radio phone and grabs the telephone in order to ask the station manager to go down to the platform and tell the driver to go. As the Controller looks for the Station Manager's number on the touch screen telephone, he "suddenly" turns to the CCTV monitor and asks the DIA to tell the recalcitrant driver to go.

Despite their involvement in distinct activities prior to the request, and the absence of any "communication" about the difficulty at Oxford Circus, the Controller assumes that the DIA knows who the "him" is and has some understanding both of the problem and why the DIA is being asked to help to solve it. The design of the utterance presupposes a common orientation to a particular domain and problem, and assumes that the DIA is in a position to immediately and efficiently contact the driver. The Controller's presuppositions prove well founded. The DIA demands neither explanation nor any additional information, but rather accepts the request, resets the PA system, and a few moments later delivers the announcement to Oxford Circus asking the driver to go "if he has a Green Signal." As the DIA accepts the request, the Controller turns to deal with another, unrelated problem. After making the announcement, the DIA witnesses the train leaving Oxford Circus and resets the Public Address system in preparation for a public announcement to tell passengers when their next train will arrive.

In part, the Controller's request achieves its intelligibility and performative impact by virtue of its position within the local configuration of the DIA's actions. Immediately prior to the delivery of the request, as the Controller searches the screen of the touch-screen telephone for the Station Manager's number, the DIA turns from the fixed-line diagram to the station CCTV monitor (with an intermediary glance at the PA monitor). As he turns from the fixed-line diagram to the station screen, a picture of the train at the southbound platform of Oxford Circus begins to emerge. Before the image has settled, the Controller looks up and produces the request.

**Fragment 4   Transcript 2**

```
                    looks at
                    station screen
                    ↓

Cii:    (1.3)      Tell him to go:-if you've (got) a clear signal
                                                        yeah
DIA:      ↑           ↑
        looks at    looks at
        fixed       station
        line        screen
        display
```

As the Controller delivers the request, both he and the DIA are looking at the train standing in the platform. The DIA makes sense of the utterance with respect to his own and the speaker's orientation towards the image on the monitor—the train standing in Oxford Circus southbound. Mutatis mutandi, the Controller reflexively invokes and constitutes a common referent by virtue of the design of the utterance and the coparticipants' orientation towards the CCTV monitor. The "common referent," namely "him," the driver of the train in the platform, is occasioned by the utterance, just as the accompanying visual orientation and the image on the screen serves to index the utterance. Each elaborates the other and feature in the production and the intelligibility of the utterance, in the way suggested by Garfinkel in his discussion of the "documentary method of interpretation" (1967, p. 77). In presupposing a common referent and designing the utterance accordingly, the Controller and the DIA reflexively establish a "scene in common."

Although the design of the utterance and the participant's visual orientation towards the screen provides a preliminary explanation for the success of the request, one or two questions remain unanswered. It is clear from the data that the image of the train at Oxford Circus station only begins to emerge a moment before the onset of the Controller's utterance (less than one-fifth of a second) and it seems unlikely that the request is designed (at least from its onset) in the light of the Controller seeing and recognizing the train. Moreover, though it is possible that the DIA could make sense of the request by virtue of the speaker's orientation towards the monitor, it seems unlikely that he would be able to undertake the relevant course of action unless he had a sense of the difficulties at Oxford Circus (that the Controller was attempting to solve). The question remains therefore, why (and how) can the Controller presuppose that the DIA is not only aware of the problem at Oxford Circus, but also may be in a position to contact the driver and effectively solve the immediate difficulties at Oxford Circus?

To answer this question it is worth briefly considering some of the activity in the Control Room that occurred prior to the event.

**4.10**            **4.11**            **4.12**            **4.13**

   ↑    ↑  ↑

  at fixed   at station Cii: Tell him to go:-if you've (got)..
  line display   screen

Figure 6.

In the few hours leading to the period from which Fragment 4 is drawn, the personnel within the Control Room have had to deal with a station closure, a fire on a train, a mechanical failure, and a missing driver. Because of these problems the personnel, including the signal assistants,[2] have lost the location of particular trains and are trying to maintain an adequate service irrespective of the timetable and scheduled running times of the traffic.

The following fragment begins approximately 15 seconds before the Controller's request to the DIA. We enter as the Controller (Cii) is having a heated discussion with his colleague (Ci), who is a relief Controller and has just entered the room, concerning the failure of a signalman (located outside the Line Control Room) to undertake various changes to the running times of the trains. During this discussion the telephone rings. The Controller (Cii) picks up the handset, but delays taking the call until an opportune moment arises in the discussion. On his colleague uttering "Oh for fucks sake" (Fig. 7, frame 4.4), the Controller (Cii) responds to the caller.

While the first call is being taken, a second phone rings (indicated by the arrow in Fig. 7, frame 4.2). The second call is answered by the relief Controller (Ci) after he finishes a brief discussion with the Signal Assistants concerning the identification of a train at Baker Street.

**Fragment 4    Transcript 3**

```
                (1.5)
          Cii:  Ye:s:
                (0.6)
 (Sii):   whats that at baker stree⌐t ↑ (Frank)
                                    |
   Ci:                              ⌊Ye:s:
                (0.6)
   Ci:    aint got a fucking clu:e
                (2.2)
   Ci:    aint got a clue
                (0.4)
          Cii:  Okay ri:ght ↑ (.) thank>you>very>much
                (0.1)
```

The first incoming call informs the Controller (Cii) of the difficulties at Oxford Circus. He grabs the radio phone and attempts to contact the driver. Cii makes three successive attempts to contact the driver on the radio and then turns to the conventional telephone in order to ask the station manager to ask the driver to go.

As the Controller begins his first attempt to contact the driver at Oxford Circus, the DIA and the Signal Assistant attempt to identify the train at Baker Street. He switches the CCTV monitor to Baker Street South and attempts to read the number from the front of train as it enters the platform. The DIA utters "all the two::s" and as the Signal Assistant returns to his own desk he calls out "two two two: " to his colleague (Fig. 8, frames 4.5 and 4.6). The DIA turns from the CCTV monitor (showing Baker Street) to the fixed-line diagram. The alignment

```
        .
        .
        .

Ci:   How could he have done it
      if he's taken the only
      (one round it)
      (0.4)

Cii:  said he (would not have)
      and then swapped them
      around behind the (Beeb)
      (0.5)

Ci:   Well (.) I just spoke to
      Mickey (.) Knight and I
      said (then) why didnt you
      do tha:t and he said he
      wouldnt
      (0.4)

Cii:  He (interferes a lot)
      (0.6)

Ci:   Oh f⌐or fucks sake
          ⌊
Cii:       Controller
          (1.5)

          Cii:   Ye:s:
                 (0.6)
```

Figure 7.

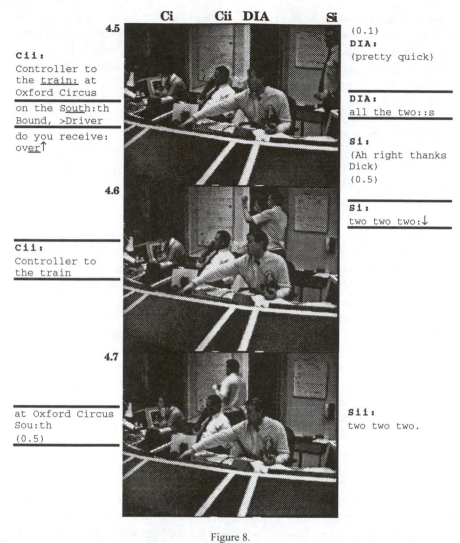

**Ci          Cii  DIA              Si**

4.5

cii:
Controller to
the <u>train</u>: at
Oxford Circus

on the <u>South</u>:th
Bound, >Driver

do you receive:
ove<u>r</u>↑

4.6

cii:
Controller to
the train

4.7

at Oxford Circus
Sou:th
(0.5)

(0.1)
DIA:
(pretty quick)

DIA:
all the two::s

si:
(Ah right thanks
Dick)
(0.5)

si:
two two two:↓

sii:
two two two.

Figure 8.

of gaze from one to the other "representation" of the traffic not only serves to
mark the completion of the previous activity but the onset of another, namely, an
assessment of a particular aspect of the operation of the service.

   This alignment of gaze cooccurs with the Controller's "Oxford Circus on the
South:th Bound" and with the DIA adopting a parallel orientation to the fixed-
line diagram to the Controller, an orientation that is directed towards Oxford Circus (Fig. 8, frame 4.5). As the DIA aligns his gaze towards the diagram, the Controller momentarily adjusts his orientation towards the area of mutual regard. The

position of the DIA's alignment of gaze, at the point at which the Controller voices the potential location of the "problem," coupled with its orientation towards the domain in question, suggests that as the one activity is brought to completion, the DIA is already sensitive to the attempts by the Controller to contact the driver and intervene in the operation of the service. Moreover, in the light of his colleague adopting a parallel line of regard, the Controller's reorientation may suggest that he is sensitive to the DIA's alignment towards his own attempts to contact the driver at Oxford Circus.

As the Controller begins his second attempt to contact the driver, he turns from the diagram to his desk. The DIA simultaneously turns from the diagram towards the console (Fig. 8, frame 4.7). As the Controller produces the word "Oxford" in "Oxford Circus South," the DIA moves his hand forward toward the key controls of the PA system in readiness for a public announcement.

The juxtaposition of the DIA's actions with components within the Controller's utterances that identify the locale of the problem, coupled with the ways in which his physical alignment and realignment parallels the actions of his co-participant, suggests and displays that the emergent activity of the DIA is convergent with the problem the relief Controller is attempting to address. Moreover, moving his hand to the PA controls serves to confirm, retrospectively, that the initial alignment by the DIA towards the fixed-line diagram is indeed a first action within an emergent trajectory of conduct. This trajectory being concerned with the delivery of an announcement to the passengers, who may be suffering because of the recalcitrant behavior of the driver at Oxford Circus. Through the use of particular tools at successive stages within the Controller's attempts to deal with the problem, the DIA's actions become visible and intelligible as part of a routine and recurrent activity that emerges in the light of interventions by the Controller in the operation of the service.

By the beginning of the Controller's third attempt to contact the driver, the DIA is setting the PA switches to enable him to deliver an announcement. As the Controller abandons the radio and grabs the telephone to call the station manager, the DIA is resetting the CCTV in preparation to witness the train finally leaving the station at Oxford Circus. This would enable him to provide precise information concerning the arrival of the train to the long-suffering passengers at Piccadilly Circus and beyond. While resetting the CCTV, the DIA glances at the fixed-line diagram, as if to assess, once more, the severity of the problem generated by the driver at Oxford Circus (Fig. 9, frame 4.10).

We can begin to see therefore, how the production and intelligibility of the request is not only achieved by virtue of the participants' mutual alignment towards the object in question, namely the train standing at Oxford Circus, but with respect to the interweaving of two interrelated activities. On the one hand, we find the DIA producing a trajectory of conduct that foreshadows a public announcement. On the other, we can see the ways in which the components of this

```
Cii:   at Oxford Circus Sou:th
       (0.5)
Ci:    on the sou:th↑
       (0.4)




Cii:   Yes ┌(I'm asking him)
Ci:        └Yeah.(0.2) (we're)
       just letting him go
       now:↓
       (0.3)
Cii:   Control(ler) to the
       tra┌in at Oxford Circus
Ci:       └(al)right
Cii:   South
       (.)
Cii:   Driver do you receive:,
       over?



       (1.1)
```

```
       ((Cii replaces one
       receiver and picks up
       another))

       (2.5)
```

Figure 9.

activity are coordinated with the Controller's attempts to intervene in the service, an activity that routinely engenders a sequentially appropriate activity from the DIA—a public announcement. The request itself is occasioned by the Controller's sensitivity to the DIA's alignment towards the problem at Oxford Circus and appears coordinated with the moment at which the DIA is able to deliver the announcement. In Fragment 4, therefore, we find the Controller to be sensitive to the DIA's monitoring and alignment towards the activity in which he, the Controller, is engaged, and that he exploits the alignment precisely at the juncture at which his colleague is able to deliver the announcement.

There is evidence to suggest that the Controller is not only sensitive to the DIA's alignment towards the problem with which he is attempting to deal, but also to the conduct of other colleagues within the Control Room and in particular the other Controller. As the Controller is attempting to contact the driver, the relief Controller (Ci) answers a second incoming call. It is another call from elsewhere in Oxford Circus station mentioning the problem on the southbound platform. The relief Controller utters into the mouthpiece of the telephone "on the sou:th ↑ " just as the Controller completes his second attempt to contact the driver (Fig. 9, frame 4.8). The Controller (Cii) overhearing "on the sou:th ↑ " turns away from the mouthpiece of the telephone and utters, "Yes (I'm asking him)." In overlap, the relief Controller informs the caller "Yeah (0.2) (we're) just letting him go now" (Fig. 9, frame 4.9).

While engaged in one activity, therefore, the Controller is able to produce a timely contribution to an activity in which his colleague is engaged. It may even be the case that the utterance "on the sou:th ↑ " is designed by the relief Controller not only to confirm the locale of the difficulty being reported by the caller, but also (through volume and intonation) to elicit, but not demand, confirmation from the Controller that he is indeed attempting to deal with the problem at Oxford Circus. Anyway, the Controller interjects an utterance in juxtaposition with the relief Controller's utterance, which provides the resources through which both the caller and the relief Controller are assured that the problem is indeed being dealt with.

For the Controllers and the DIA, therefore, who, until recently have been engaged in distinct and unrelated activities, the problem at Oxford Circus, momentarily becomes the primary focus of their conduct, as they establish distinct, but interrelated, orientations towards the "the problem at hand" and its management. Their various activities converge as they systematically monitor and participate in each other's actions and produce a coordinated response to the difficulties at Oxford Circus. A few seconds later, the Controllers address a range of other issues and only the DIA remains concerned with the problems generated by the delay at Oxford Circus (see Fig. 10).

The Controller's request to the DIA to tell the train to go, therefore, is embedded in a complex configuration of activities and mutual monitoring that provides

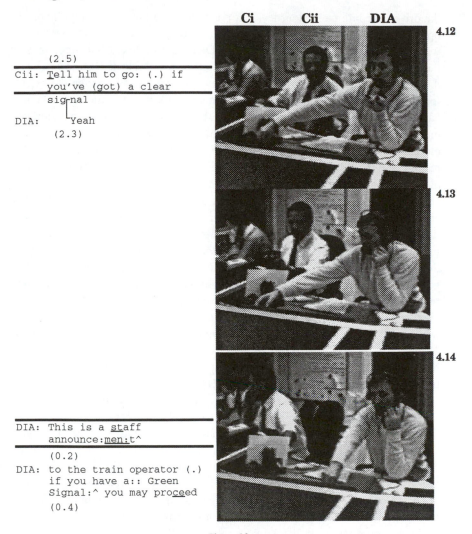

```
                                        Ci      Cii      DIA
                                                              4.12
        (2.5)
Cii:  Tell him to go: (.) if
      you've (got) a clear
      sig┌nal
DIA:      └Yeah
        (2.3)
```

```
                                                              4.13
```

```
                                                              4.14
DIA: This is a staff
     announce:men:t^
        (0.2)
DIA: to the train operator (.)
     if you have a:: Green
     Signal:^ you may proceed
        (0.4)
```

Figure 10.

for the intelligibility and impact of the utterance, and allows the participants to solve one of the more immediate problems at hand. In designing the request, the Controller presupposes that the image appearing on the monitor is the train that he is attempting to contact at Oxford Circus and the DIA disambiguates the utterance with respect to the Controller's orientation to the emergent scene on the CCTV monitor. The request, and the Controller's accompanying orientation, both invoke and accomplish a (presupposed) common referent, and provide the resources through which the DIA can address the problem at hand and encourage the driver to continue his journey. It is positioned at a juncture within the developing course of an activity undertaken by the DIA in order to provide passengers with timely and relevant information. The DIA scans the fixed-line diagram, sets the public address system to the relevant platforms, and selects Oxford Circus on the CCTV monitor to witness the train leave the station and provide precise information to passengers. Watching the train leave the station is the last move in a package or trajectory of action, which foreshadows the delivery of an announcement to passengers.[3] The Controller recognizes the trajectory of conduct and exploits the DIA's apparent orientation to the "problem" at Oxford Circus, and his readiness to make an announcement, in order to contact the driver and encourage him to continue his journey.

As Fragments 2 and 3 suggest, many of the activities undertaken by the DIA are engendered by actions of the Controller and in particular his interventions in the routine operation of the service. So, for example, in Fragment 2, the Controller holds a train at Charing Cross and the DIA provides information to warn the passengers of the delay. In Fragment 3, as the Controller intervenes to "reverse at Piccadilly," the DIA informs the station manager and then delivers a series of public announcements. The participants appear to orient to the sequential relationship between particular activities, the DIA undertaking specific actions with respect to the interventions of the Controller. In the case at hand (Fragment 4), the DIA undertakes a series of actions that foreshadow a public announcement. These actions begin as the DIA completes one activity and while the Controller is attempting to contact the train at Oxford Circus. The DIA's trajectory of conduct is not simply in immediate juxtaposition with the Controller's attempt to call the driver; suggesting a sequential relationship between the two activities. Rather, various actions within the developing course of the trajectory that typically foreshadow a public announcement, are coordinated with the Controller's conduct and his successive attempts to contact the driver. The routine organization of particular activities, the sequential relationships between the contributions of Control Room personnel, and the ability to mutually monitor each others' orientation towards particular sources of information, provide the foundation of the design of the Controller's request and the DIA's ability to render it intelligible and deal with the emerging crisis at Oxford Circus.

Finally, it is interesting to consider briefly the activity of the DIA following his success in encouraging the driver at Oxford Circus to continue his journey southbound. Indeed, the DIA returns to a sequentially appropriate activity that he was ready to begin when the Controller asked him to contact the driver. After he witnesses the train leaving Oxford Circus, he resets the PA system and delivers the following announcement to the passengers waiting at Piccadilly Circus and Charing Cross. It is worth noting that the anticipated times of arrival of the next train are precisely the journey times between the locations, excluding the time it has taken to prepare to make the actual announcement.

**Fragment   Transcript 5**

DIA:   (ev'ning) Ladies and Gentlemen ↑ (0.2) this is your Baker<u>loo</u> Line Information Serv<u>ice</u>.
(0.2)

DIA:   ( ) southbound train
(1.5)

DIA:   should arrive at Piccadilly Circus within <u>one</u> minute
(0.7)

DIA:   and at Charing Cross in two and a half minutes.
(0.5)

DIA:   Thank you.

## The coordination and mutual visibility conduct

It is widely recognized among both staff and management of the London Underground that it is very difficult to provide trainee personnel, in particular Line
Controllers, with formal instruction on how to work within the Control Rooms.
Indeed, even such essential tasks as reforming the timetable are not explicitly
taught, but rather left for trainees to learn in situ. Following a brief period of
learning rules, regulations, and technical procedures in the classroom, trainee
Controllers and Information Assistants are apprenticed to particular personnel
for three-week periods, during which time they attempt to learn the trade through
observation and instruction in the light of managing actual problems in the operation of the service. It is an extremely difficult process and more than 80% of applicants for the position of Controller fail to make the grade first time around.

The difficulty faced by trainee Controllers, Information Assistants, and Signalmen is not simply learning to undertake a body of relatively complex and specialized tasks, but rather learning to accomplish those activities with respect to
the real-time contributions and demands of personnel both within and outside the
Line Control Room. Following the classic essays of E. C. Hughes (1958, 1971),
we might think of the trainee's problem as one of becoming familiar with an unexplicated and tacit organizational culture, which might consist of skills, collective representations, defenses, mandates, ideologies, and the like. Although such
features may well inform occupational performance within the Line Control
Rooms, and perhaps in other work environments, the difficulties faced by the
trainees derive from the ways in which tasks are systematically coordinated in
real time with the actions and activities of colleagues. Indeed, it appears that individual tasks and activities are inseparable from, and thoroughly embedded in,
ongoing, concerted interaction with colleagues within the local milieu. Although
the sociointeractional foundations to task-based activities within the Line Control Room are paid tribute to by staff and management, the complex web of practices and reasoning upon which they rely are taken for granted and necessarily
remain an unexplicated resource, "seen but unnoticed" and are the foundations
of collaborative work and crisis management within the Control Rooms. The or-

ganizational culture is essentially a sociointeractional organization; tasks are ac-complished in and through interaction with others, and their competent and skilled performance is inseparable from the tacit practices and reasoning which inform their production, intelligibility, and coordination. The "situated" organi-zation of Line Control is the interactional and contingent accomplishment of a body of "routine" tasks.

One aspect of this sociointeractional organization is the ways in which person-nel coordinate, sequentially, particular tasks and activities. It was noted earlier that personnel appear to use, and orient to, conventional relations between partic-ular activities; the conduct of one participant engendering sequentially appropri-ate activities from others. So, for example, a Controller's intervention that delays the running time of a particular train leads to a series of public announcements undertaken by the DIA. Or, for instance, the Controller turning a train short de-mands that the DIA inform relevant personnel including station managers. The DIA's activities are seen as related to and engendered by the Controller's inter-ventions, just as the Controller's interventions project the relevance of a specific action or activity to be undertaken by the DIA. These procedures inform the ways in which personnel recognize the relevance or appropriateness of particular actions, as well as forming the foundation to their intelligibility or sense. They also feature in the ways in which individuals produce particular sequences or tra-jectories of action, and interrelate the "components" of an activity with the activ-ities and contributions of colleagues.

Collaborative activity within the Line Control Room however, does not sole-ly rest upon the sequential relationships that pertain between particular activi-ties. It is also dependent upon the ways in which personnel shape their partici-pation in the activities of their colleagues, even while they may be engaged in distinct and unrelated tasks. For example, we can see the ways in which the DIA systematically monitors the activity of a Controller to enable him to re-trieve the details of particular changes that are being made in the running of the service. In many cases, more active participation may be required. So, in Frag-ment 4, the Controller does not simply "monitor" the activity of his fellow re-lief Controller, but makes an essential and timely contribution to the communi-cation that his colleague is having on the telephone. The contribution is produced while the Controller remains "primarily engaged" in attempting to contact the driver at Baker Street. In other words, the production of a "task" is sensitive to the emergent activities of colleagues within the local milieu. The practices that personnel use and rely upon to participate simultaneously in more than one activity are not small additions to the formal procedures that "under-lie" their various occupational tasks. Rather, they are an essential feature of work in the Line Control Room without which personnel would be unable to accomplish their individual tasks or coordinate their activities with each other. These indigenous practices and reasoning are the resources through which personnel competently and reliably maintain the operation of the service, for all practical purposes.

Although Control Room personnel are undoubtedly sensitive to prescribed ways of undertaking specific tasks, such as delivering a public announcement or altering the destination of a train, undertaking competent and reasonable work demands that "individual" activities are produced with respect to concurrent actions of colleagues within the local milieu. This may be no more than delaying a public announcement so as to avoid disrupting a delicate negotiation between the Controller and a driver. Alternatively, it may involve coordinating the production of an activity with the concurrent actions of a colleague who is "engaged" elsewhere, so that, for example, a timely contribution can be interjected into a telephone conversation. Or it may necessitate producing actions in such a way that potentially private and specialized tasks, such as rewriting the timetable from "within" a crisis, are rendered visible to colleagues within the local milieu, enabling them to coordinate their own actions accordingly (cf. Heath & Luff, 1992). The production of activities within the Line Control Room, including relatively complex and specialized tasks, is coordinated with, and sensitive to, the concurrent actions of colleagues.

One way of conceptualizing the sociointeractional organization of task-based activities is to draw on Goffman's (1981) discussion of a participation framework. Goffman suggests that any activity is dependant upon a particular production format that establishes, or attempts to establish, the ways in which "those within the perceptual range of the event" will participate within the activity. In the materials at hand, we can begin to discern how the design of particular activities may be simultaneously sensitive to the potential demands of different "recipients," both within and beyond the local milieu. So, for example, while speaking to a signalman on the telephone to ask whether he has corrected the running order of a couple of "out of turn" trains, the Controller may not only articulate certain segments of his talk with respect to his conversation with the signalman, but shape particular words or phrases so that they are overhead by, and implicate certain actions for, the DIA. Indeed, even a single utterance may be designed to engender different actions by different colleagues who may be positioned at different locations within the organization. The production format of many activities within the Line Control Room is subject to multiple demands and implicates different forms of coparticipation from various personnel. The same activity can be systematically designed for different forms of coparticipation, and can even momentarily merge different ecologies within the organizational milieu.

## Technology in action

The usefulness of the fixed-line diagram, the computerized line displays, the CCTV monitors, and the various other tools designed to facilitate work within

the Line Control Room rely upon practices and reasoning through which personnel produce their own actions and make sense of the conduct of their colleagues.
In the light of these practices, Control Room personnel are continually and unavoidably, implicitly and explicitly, gathering and distributing information to
each other concerning the "current" operation of the service. Such information
informs the very intelligibility of various diagrams and representations they use
for seeing and assessing the service, and infuses the ways in which they recognize certain events and are able to develop a coordinated response. The use of the
technology to identify and manage the various problems that routinely emerge in
the operation of the service is dependent upon the routine ways in which personnel produce and coordinate their actions with each other.

For example, the fixed-line diagram displays the position of trains on the Bakerloo Line between Queens Park and the Elephant and Castle. Each train appears
as a strip of between two and six lights, depending on how many sections of track
the train is covering at a particular moment. At any time between 6:30 AM and
10:00 PM there are likely to be between 15 and 25 trains indicated on the board.
The diagram provides staff within the Control Room and, of course, visitors such
as management, with the ability to make, at a glance, an initial assessment of the
current operation of the service.

An even distribution of trains (lights) along the board with relatively few gaps

Figure 11.    The fixed-line diagram

between them, both on the South and North lines, tends to indicate that the service is running according to plan, i.e., the timetable. Yet, as any Controller knows, such an even distribution of trains along the line can conceal important problems that may later lead to difficulties. The fixed-line diagram does not tell whether the trains are in or out of turn, or which particular train is where. Neither does it provide information concerning an upcoming shortage of drivers, trains that are causing difficulties, stations that are closed "due to a London Fire Brigade investigation," nor does it reveal any of the complex body of timetable reformations that may have already been undertaken and which may lead to difficulties later. In short, the fixed-line diagram and the information it provides is a critical resource in control and crisis management, but only in the light of the natural history of the operation of the service on any particular day. Without knowledge of timetable reformations, out-of-turns, vehicle problems, station closures, that is, the incidents that have occurred and the ways in which they were managed, the technology is largely redundant. The sociointeractional organization of individual tasks and activities within the Line Control Room, and the ways in which personnel monitor and participate in each other's conduct, provides for the possibility of using the tools and technologies at hand.

In the light of practices that provide for mutual monitoring and coparticipation within the Line Control Room, the technology provides the Controller and DIA with the ability to assess the current operation of traffic and undertake, if necessary, remedial action or provide information to staff and passengers. The "public" availability of the technology within the Control Room, whether it is a fixed-line diagram, a CCTV screen, a screen-based line diagram or an information display, provides a critical resource in the collaboration between Controller, DIA, and Signal Assistant. For example, personnel are able to assume that they have equivalent access to the different technological sources of information and that, in principle, observations concerning the current operation of the service are mutually and commonly available. More importantly perhaps, personnel can use the common sources of information as a reliable means of accounting for a broad range of actions and tasks undertaken by others. So, for example, in Fragments 2 and 4 we noted how the DIA turned to the fixed-line diagram as a source of explanation for the Controller's intervention. Or, it was observed how the Controller could produce a request that is embedded within, and constitutes, a mutually available scene on a CCTV monitor. The mutual availability of the various information displays allows personnel to presuppose that information available to one is available to all; a presupposition that is dependent upon the systematic ways in which individuals monitor and participate in each other's actions and activities.

Although the mutual availability of particular sources of information is utilized in making sense of and coordinating actions with each other, it is the mutual visibility of the use of technology within individual activities that provides an important resource in the production of collaborative action. For example, a glance towards the fixed-line diagram, a gesture towards the radio phone, or a scroll through a display of the points at a particular junction, can all provide resources through which a colleague can recognize the action or activity of another. The use of a particular tool, even looking at a particular piece of text such as the timetable, can render the activity of a colleague visible, allowing others to coordinate their own actions with the apparent conduct of another.

Although the very use of tools such as the PA system, even before the onset of an announcement, can provide a relatively unambiguous sense of a colleague's conduct, the intelligibility of the use of a particular technology is embedded within the activity at hand. For example, switching a scene on the CCTV monitor may gain its particular sense by virtue of the immediately preceding actions, such as glancing at the fixed-line diagram and grabbing the PA microphone and headset.

The intelligibility of the action (involving the use of some particular tool or technology), may not only be embedded within the developing course of the individual's conduct, but also may be located with respect to a colleague's activity. So, for example, in Fragment 3, the intelligibility of the DIA's setting of the PA system is not only accomplished by virtue of the action's position within a developing trajectory of conduct being undertaken by the DIA, but also the action's location with respect to the concurrent conduct of the Controller. Or, for example, consider how in Fragment 4 the Controller presupposes that the DIA's orientation towards the CCTV concerns the driver at Oxford Circus. The location of the looking within the trajectory of the DIA's actions, coupled with the juxtaposition of the DIA's actions with the attempts to contact the driver, provide the resources through which the Controller can assemble the sense of the look and produce the request to contact the driver.

The visibility of a colleague's use of a particular tool or source of information, even if it consists of no more than a momentary glance at a line diagram, is made sense of by virtue of the action's location, not only within the colleague's emergent conduct, but also with respect to how that action, given its occurrence "here and now," may be sensitive to actions being undertaken by others within the local environment. So, whereas on the one hand the action may "naturally" emerge within a trajectory of a particular individual's conduct, it may also be simultaneously embedded in and coordinated with, the activities of other individuals within the Control Room. For the "relevant" sense of the action to be assembled, personnel have to be sensitive to colleagues' concurrent participation in multiple activities within the local milieu. The use of the various tools and technologies is embedded in the accomplishment of simultaneous and overlapping activities, which themselves are dependent upon an indigenous sociointeractional organization that provides for their production, intelligibility, and coordination.

The ways in which an individual's use of a particular tool or technology may be monitored by a colleague and feature in the production of multiple activities leads one to question the conventional wisdom in HCI that places the single user and his or her cognitive capabilities at the center of the analytic domain. Even more innovative conceptions of the "user" that aim to take into account the perceptions and attitudes of users who employ particular tools (e.g., Mumford, 1983), perhaps draw too sharp a distinction between a person handling a system and those others within the "local" environment whose actions may feature in the accomplishment of a particular task. For example, consider how the use of the CCTV monitor by the DIA occasioned a request by a colleague and provided the resources both for the design and impact of the utterance. Or how in Fragment 3 the DIA's use of the telephone to call the Station Manager during the request for the train to turn short allows the Controller to recognize his colleague tracking the activity, so that he can confidently inform the Driver that the "DIA will make announcements for you." So, whereas the "direct" use of a particular system may indeed be undertaken by a particular individual within the Line Control Room, the action may well be monitored by colleagues, and feature in their production of activities. Noticing another's noticing of one's own conduct, and sensing that another's actions are sensitive to one's own actions and activities, informs the accomplishment of tool-mediated tasks in which an individual is engaged. It is not simply that work within the Line Control Room is "collaborative"; it is rather that personnel, even within the accomplishment of apparently individual tasks, are sensitive to and participating in the activities of colleagues, and this participation is an intrinsic part of the organization of the task. The use of the various tools and technologies in the Line Control Room features in the accomplishment of these various activities and their coordination and provides resources through which potentially "private" actions are rendered visible within the local milieu. The various and complex ways in which the accomplishment of specialized tasks within the Line Control Room and other working environments (cf. Greatbatch et al., 1993; Suchman, 1993) is embedded in and inseparable from interaction with the concurrent actions of colleagues may lead us to question the usefulness of traditional approaches to the development of requirements for new technologies, approaches that place a single individual user with a relatively circumscribed set of tasks at the forefront of the analytic domain (Luff et al., 1994).

Although the sociointeractional organization of task-based activities within the Line Control Rooms might lead one to question the individualistic and psychologistic conception of conduct that underlies a substantial body of work in HCI and requirements analysis, it does not necessarily provide wholehearted support for recent initiatives in computer support for cooperative work, in particular the growing body of conceptual and technical work in CSCW. With its emphasis on cooperation and, in particular, technical support for "group" and cooperative activity, CSCW runs the risk of entrenching the distinction between the individual and the collaborative, allowing us to preserve a demarcation between particular tasks and their coordination. Observations of computer-supported cooperative work in real-world organizational environments suggest that it is both difficult and tenuous to delineate the individual from the collaborative. In the

Line Control Rooms, although different personnel have distinct responsibilities that are not undertaken by members of the other occupational categories, the competent accomplishment of their specialized tasks is dependent upon an indigenous organization that systematically shapes and coordinates their activities with respect to the contributions of others. The Controller and the DIA produce particular activities, even relatively complex tasks, with respect to the responsibilities and concurrent conduct of their colleague(s), tailoring their actions so that they preserve a mutually coordinated response to particular incidents and events. Moreover, while engaged in one activity, we find the Controller and DIA monitoring each other's conduct and able to discriminate the local environment with regard to contingencies which may be relevant to either their own conduct or the actions of their colleagues. Work within the Line Control Room does not simply necessitate that the participants distribute information and maintain a compatible orientation to the current scene. Rather, it requires that even the most apparently individual tasks are "ongoingly" accomplished, moment by moment, with regard to the conduct and responsibilities of the coparticipants. This may involve mutually focused interaction between Control Room personnel, but in a large part it requires Controller and DIA to engage in distinct tasks and activities while simultaneously participating in the conduct of their colleague(s). The activities of personnel within the Line Control Room continually flow between the private and the public, between the individual and the collaborative, so that any attempt to demarcate cooperative from individual work within the Line Control Room is unlikely to prove either reliable or conceptually fruitful.

## Summary

Within an organizational environment such as the Line Control Rooms on the London Underground, we can begin to discern how the performance of highly specialized and complex work tasks are embedded in, and inseparable, from a tacit body of sociointeractional practice and reasoning. Personnel unavoidably rely upon these competencies in producing, making sense of, and coordinating their actions and activities, and thereby in managing the problems and crises that inevitably emerge in the day-to-day operation of the service. These tacit competencies do not simply allow personnel to "apply" a body of specialized organizational knowledge and skill, but rather underlie the very ways in which particular tasks are produced and made sense of. The intelligibility of the scene and the possibilities of collaborative conduct emerge within the participants' abilities to "interactionally" accomplish their various specialized actions and activities. Although the organizational culture may well include "collective representations," "specialized vocabularies," and "codes and policies," routine work within the Line Control Rooms rests upon a complex foundation of sociointeractional practice and reasoning through which various specialized tasks are systematically and unproblematically accomplished.

Although the "situated" character of system use is widely acknowledged, there still remains a tendency to conceptualize human–computer interaction with respect to individual cognitive skills and competencies (see for example Young et al., 1990). The observations documented here, and related studies reported in this volume and elsewhere, suggest that even in circumstances in which the technology is primarily used to support the specialized tasks of particular individuals (such as medical practitioners; see Greatbatch et al., 1993), competent use of a system is embedded in conventional and routine ways of accomplishing particular activities, interactionally, within the organizational setting. The accomplishment of specialized tasks, and the conventional use of complex technologies to support those activities, are dependent upon a realm of tacit interactional competencies that inform the very production and intelligibility of organizational conduct. Tasks are accomplished in and through interaction, and it is only by detailing the socially sanctioned and "publicly" available competencies used by individuals within real-world situations that we will begin to uncover the systematics that undoubtedly underlie human–computer interaction and computer-supported cooperative work.

Although it is increasingly recognized that recent studies of work within complex technological environments have important implications for our understanding of concepts such as the "user," "task," and "collaboration," less attention has been directed towards their potential impact on more traditional research within the sociology of work and organizations. From its early beginnings in the lectures and writings of E. C. Hughes, naturalistic research concerned with work and organizations has recognized the significance of social interaction to work and organizational behavior; indeed Hughes suggests that the aim of his approach is

> to discover patterns of interaction and mechanisms of control, the things over which people in a line of work seek to gain control, the sanctions which they have or would like to have at their disposal, and the bargains which were made—consciously or unconsciously—among a group of workers and between them and other kinds of people in the drama of their work. (Hughes, 1971, p. 240)

Despite its commitment to placing interaction within the workplace at the forefront of the analytic agenda, the sociology of work and, in particular, naturalistic studies of organizational behavior, have, through successive generations, directed attention away from how personnel within institutional settings accomplish their specialized occupational activities in and through interaction with colleagues and clients. The sociointeractional foundations of work in real-world situations have remained unexplicated by virtue, one suspects, of the conceptual framework that has dominated naturalistic studies of organizations for successive generations. The observations discussed in this volume and elsewhere (Drew and Heritage, 1993), begin to chart the ways in which a concern with the interactional organization of work and occupations may lead to a respecification of the organizational conduct and some of its central ideas including "task," "performance," and "collaboration."

## Acknowledgements

The research discussed in this chapter was supported through project grants from the Joint ESRC/MRC/SERC Joint Initiative on Cognitive Science and Human Computer Interaction and the EC Commission RACE Programme (Project R2094), and by Rank Xerox Cambridge EuroPARC. The authors are grateful for discussions with David Middleton, David Greatbatch, John Gardner, Bernard Conein, John Gumperz, Isaac Joseph, Marina Jirotka, Rod Watson, and Liam Bannon concerning a number of the issues addressed in this chapter. We would also like to thank all those on the Bakerloo Line, London Underground, who so generously gave their wholehearted support for this research.

## Notes

1  The fragments are transcribed using the orthography developed by Gail Jefferson, which is widely used within ethnomethodology and conversation analysis. The talk is laid out turn by turn, speaker by speaker. The numbers in brackets consist of either pauses or silences measured in tenths of a second, the single stop in brackets referring to a minipause of, say, one tenth of a second. The colons capture the ways in which a sound is elongated. Brackets between speakers' utterances indicate that the talk is co-occurring, in overlap. Underlinings of part of a word, a word, or part of a sentence capture emphasis. For further details concerning the transcription system, see Atkinson and Heritage (1984), Boden and Zimmerman (1991), or Drew and Heritage (1995).
2  These are located on another console to the Controllers' and DIAs' right.
3  In particular, an announcement to those passengers waiting at Piccadilly Circus, the next station along the line.

## References

Baecker, R. M. & Buxton, W. A. S. (Eds.) (1987). *Readings in Human-Computer Interaction: A Multi-Disciplinary Approach.* San Mateo, CA: Morgan Kaufman.
Baecker, R. M. (Ed.) (1993). *Readings in Groupware and Computer-Supported Cooperative Work.* Hillsdale, NJ: Erlbaum.
Becker, H. S., Greer, B., Hughes, E. C., & Strauss, A. (1961). *Boys in White.* Chicago: University of Chicago Press.
Carroll, J. M. (Ed.) (1991). *Designing Interaction: Psychology at the Human-Computer Interface.* Cambridge: Cambridge University Press.
Drew, P. & Heritage, J. (Eds.) (1993). *Talk at Work: Interaction in Institutional Settings.* Cambridge: Cambridge University Press.
Galegher, J. & Kraut, R. E. (1990). Technology for intellectual teamwork: Perspectives on research and design. In *Intellectual Teamwork: The Social and Technological Foundations of Cooperative Work,* pp. 1–20. J. Galegher, R. E. Kraut, C. Egido (Eds.). Hillsdale, NJ: Erlbaum.
Galegher, J., Kraut, R. E., & Egido, C. (Eds.) (1990). *Intellectual Teamwork: Social and Technological Foundations of Cooperative Work.* Hillsdale, NJ: Erlbaum.
Garfinkel, H. (1967). *Studies in Ethnomethodology.* Englewood Cliffs, NJ: Prentice-Hall.
Goffman, E. (1968). *Asylums: Essays on the Social Situation of Mental Patients and Other Inmates.* Harmondsworth: Penguin.

Goffman, E. (1981). *Forms of Talk.* Oxford: Blackwell.

Greatbatch, D., Luff, P. K., Heath, C. C., & Campion, P. (1993). On the use of paper and screen in the general practice consultation. *Interacting with Computers, 5*(2), 193–216.

Greif, I. (Ed.) (1988). *Computer-Supported Cooperative Work: A Book of Readings.* San Mateo, CA: Morgan Kaufman.

Grudin, J. (1988). Why CSCW applications fail: Problems in the design and evaluation of organizational interfaces. In *Proceedings of CSCW 88,* 85–93, Portland, Oregon: ACM Press.

Heath, C. C. & Luff, P. (1992). Collaboration and control: Crisis management and multimedia technology in London Underground line control rooms. *CSCW Journal, 1*(1–2), 69–94.

Hughes, E. C. (1958). *Men and their Work.* Glencoe: Free Press.

Hughes, E. C. (1971). *The Sociological Eye: Selected Papers on Institution and Race (Part I) and Self and the Study of Society (Part II),* Chicago: Aldine Atherton.

Hutchins, E. (1985). The Social Organisation of Distributed Cognition. Unpublished Manuscript. San Diego: University of California.

Hutchins, E. (1989). A Cultural View of Distributed Cognition. Unpublished Manuscript. San Diego: University of California.

Hutchins, E. L. (1990). The Technology of Team Navigation. In *Intellectual Teamwork: The Social and Technological Foundations of Cooperative Work,* pp. 191–221. J. Galegher, R. E. Kraut, and C. Egido (Eds.). Hillsdale, NJ: Erlbaum.

Lave, J. (1988). *Cognition in Practice.* Cambridge: Cambridge University Press.

Luff, P., Heath, C. C., & Greatbatch, D. (1994). Work, interaction and technology: The naturalistic analysis of human conduct and requirements capture. In *Requirements Analysis Social and Technical Issues,* pp. 259–288. M. Jirotka and J. Goguen (Eds.). London: Academic Press.

Markus, M. L. & Connolly, T. (1990). Why CSCW applications fail: Problems in the adoption of independent work tools. In *Proceedings of CSCW 90,* pp. 371–380. Los Angeles, CA: ACM Press.

Moran, T. P. & Anderson, R. J. (1990). The workaday world as a paradigm for CSCW design. In *Proceedings of the Conference on Computer Supported Collaborative Work,* pp. 381–394. Los Angeles, CA: ACM Press.

Mumford, E. (1983). *Designing Human Systems for New Technology: The ETHICS Method.* Manchester: Manchester Business School.

Norman, D. & Draper, S. (Eds.) (1986). *User Centered System Design.* Hillsdale, NJ: Erlbaum.

Norman, D. A. (1988). *The Psychology of Everyday Things.* New York: Basic Books.

Olson, G. M. (1990). Collaborative Work as Distributed Cognition. Unpublished Manuscript: University of Michigan.

Olson, G. M. & Olson, J. S. (1991). User-Centered Design of Collaboration Technology. *Journal of Organizational Computing, 1*(1), 61–83.

Roth, J. A. (1963). *Timetables: Structuring and the Passage of Time in Hospital Treatment and Other Careers.* Indianapolis: Bobbs Merrill.

Sacks, H. (1992). Lecture 4: Fall 1964. In *Lectures in Conversation: Volumes I and II.* Oxford: Blackwell.

Strauss, A., Schatzman, L., Bucher, R., Ehrlich, D., & Sabshin, M. (1964). *Psychiatric Ideologies and Institutions.* London: Free Press.

Suchman, L. (1987). *Plans and Situated Actions: The Problem of Human Machine Interaction.* Cambridge: Cambridge University Press.

Suchman, L. (1993). *Technologies of Accountability: On Lizards and Aeroplanes.* In G. Button (Ed.), *Technology in Working Order,* pp. 113–126. London: Routledge.

Winograd, T. & Flores, F. (1986). *Understanding Computers and Cognition: A New Foundation For Design.* Norwood, NJ: Addison-Wesley.

Young, R., Howes, A., & Whittington, J. (1990). A Knowledge Analysis of Interactivity. In *Proceedings of Interact '90—Third IFIP Conference on Human-Computer Interaction,* pp. 115–120. 27th–30th August, Cambridge.

# 6 Users and designers in mutual activity: An analysis of cooperative activities in systems design

*Susanne Bødker and Kaj Grønbæk*

We are proposing and analyzing a cooperative prototyping approach wherein users are involved actively and creatively in design of computer applications. What we are suggesting is use of early prototypes in attempts to create and explore new work activities for the involved users. This chapter illustrates the approach by analyzing the design of computer support for casework in a technical department of a Danish municipality. Prototyping, as a design activity, is viewed as an ongoing learning process, and we analyze situations where openings for learning occur in the prototyping activity. Users and designers engage in this design activity, based on their different practices, and the development of the use activity is the primary focus of design. The situations that we are analyzing seem to fall into four categories:

1. Situations where the future work situation with a new computer application is simulated to investigate the future work activity.
2. Situations where the prototype is manipulated and used as a basis for idea exploration.
3. Situations focussing on the designers' learning about the users' work practice.
4. Situations where the prototyping tool or the design activity as such becomes the focus.

Lessons learned from the analysis of these situations are discussed. In particular, we discuss a tension between the need for careful preparation of prototyping activity and the need to establish conditions for user and designer creativity. Our approach to understanding these prototyping situations is inspired by activity theory, in particular the work of Engeström, wherein learning is seen as an expansion of work practice.

## Background and motivation

To understand our research background and tradition, it is necessary to look at the development of society in Scandinavia over the last couple of decades and the research projects concerning workplaces and computer technology carried out in interplay with this. Employee influence through unions and cooperation with management is a well-known part of the practice of social democracy in Scandinavia. In the early 1970s, this strategy was supplemented by projects set up by central and local unions independent of employer organizations and management. In these projects, workers, consultants, and researchers cooperated to develop a better platform for worker influence on the use of new technology at the workplace. New work practices, focusing on group work and the development of local resources for action, were of central concern. The first of these projects was the Norwegian NJMF project, followed by the Swedish DEMOS project and the Danish DUE project (Nygaard & Bergo, 1975; Ehn & Sandberg, 1983; DUE, 1981; Ehn & Kyng, 1987). These projects introduced worker participation in decisions about technology but the laws did little to shift the balance of power from a managerial perspective. And the rationalistic tradition of computer system development did little to help workers put forth their ideas with respect to the introduction of new technology.

By the early 1980s, a new generation of projects was initiated. An example of this was the Utopia project (Bødker et al., 1987), wherein the issues of quality of work, technological alternatives, and worker qualifications were emphasized. Computer system developers and researchers from a multiplicity of fields worked with typographers and printers to help them formulate ways in which computer technology could be used to enhance their skill and the typographic quality of newspapers.

For some of the researchers from Utopia, the focus, in the next phase of research, shifted to a theoretical one in which the experiences were digested and new ways of thinking about what we came to call cooperative design were outlined (Ehn, 1988; Bødker , 1991).

For the last three years we have been engaged in a research program on "Computer Support for Cooperative Design and Communication." Within this program we have undertaken several field studies of Cooperative Design, in particular, prototyping. We have discussed how, in current system design, descriptions and prototypes are developed by system designers utilizing users only as sources of information concerning the use domain (Grønbæk, 1989; Bødker & Grønbæk, 1991). However, we see prototyping with *active* user involvement as a way of overcoming problems that current approaches have in developing computer applications that fit the actual needs of the users. Such prototyping, using wood and paper mock-ups, was successfully applied in the Utopia project (Bødker et al., 1987; Ehn & Kyng, 1991). In several subsequent smaller projects this approach was applied using computer-based prototyping (Bødker & Grønbæk, 1989; Trigg, Bødker, & Grønbæk, 1990). Experiences from these projects led to proposals for a so-called *cooperative prototyping* technique (Bødker & Grønbæk, 1989, 1991; Grønbæk, 1990). Cooperative prototyping is meant to combine the use of computer-based tools for exploratory prototyping (Floyd, 1984) with approaches to design that allow users to participate in the modification of wood and paper mock-ups as described in Bødker et al. (1987).

The cooperative prototyping approach aims to establish a design process wherein both users and designers are participating actively and creatively based on their differing qualifications. Analysis and design activities are more closely coupled by rapid development of one or more prototypes early in the development process. The initial prototypes help make the participants' visions concrete. This requires that they relate to core work activities and that users' current skills must be confronted with new technical possibilities. These prototypes can then be modified, thrown away, or built anew in an iterative process that increases the participants' understanding of technological possibilities related to the users' work. The activities may serve one or both of the following goals: (1) idea generation and exploration and (2) work-like evaluation of the prototypes. When serving the first goal, the focus is on cooperative use of the prototyping tool and existing building blocks to create a prototype or extend an existing one. When serving the second goal, the designers must somehow let the users experience a fluent work-like situation with a future computer application. This can be done in a simulated future work situation or, even better, in a real use situation, if a fairly robust prototype has been prepared. The users first get introduced to its use and then an evaluation based on work-like use of the prototype is undertaken. *Break-downs* (Winograd & Flores, 1986; Bødker, 1991) in this use caused by faulty design lead to immediate modifications of the prototype. Breakdowns due to other causes are handled in other ways; for example, lack of training is handled by further training and by setting up training programs for future users. Ideally, cooperative prototyping should be performed by a small group of designers and users with access to flexible computer-based tools for rapid prototype development and modification. The (possibly simulated) functionality provided should make it possible to envision future work activities (Grønbæk, 1990; Bødker & Grønbæk, 1989). In the project described in this paper, the primary prototyping tool used was HyperCard for the Apple Macintosh.[1]

This chapter discusses experiences from a project that was set up to further investigate cooperative prototyping in realistic settings, in this case so-called casework in a Danish municipal office. Primarily, the project aimed to develop ways for users and designers to experience future use situations. The outcome of the project was not as anticipated, since it turned out that setting up ways for the users to experience future use was much more difficult than in our previous cases. However, the prototyping sessions did stimulate creative cooperation between users and designers, which will be discussed below.

Our process was well documented by means of notes and audio and video tape. In this chapter we will primarily focus on prototyping sessions wherein the users and designers worked with a fairly advanced prototype. These sessions were videotaped and analyzed (see also Trigg, Bødker, & Grønbæk, 1990) using interaction analysis techniques. Since our primary interest is in developing tools and techniques for cooperative prototyping, we have set up a framework to analyze the various situations and roles of users and designers of prototypes, and the sample data obtained in and between prototyping sessions. This yields a much more detailed analysis than we have achieved in our previous work.

## The project: Designing computer support for casework

This section briefly describes the cooperative approach to prototyping used in the design project, undertaken together with architects, engineers, and draftspeople in a technical department of a Danish municipality.

### Casework

A technical department has responsibility for tasks such as long-term urban planning, environmental inspection and advice, and so on. Beside these tasks a number of smaller requests from citizens are treated on a day-to-day basis. The architects, engineers, and draftspeople call their tasks "cases" and we use the term "casework" to describe their work. Thus, we call the architects, engineers, and draftspeople, "caseworkers." There is one caseworker in charge of a case. He or she handles external contacts and brings in a number of people with specific skills. The department currently possesses three different kinds of computer equipment. It has terminal connections to a common mainframe running shared databases for a number of municipalities. PCs are used for small-budget and environmental-inspection calculations and Xerox Viewpoint workstations are used for advanced text and picture processing. The different kinds of computer equipment are badly integrated and the caseworkers feel that better computer support could improve their work.

### The design process

Together with the caseworkers from the technical department we went through a process designed to take their work practice seriously and involve them in cooperative system design to influence technology development in their work environment. Elements of this process included studies of the workplace, brainstorming about problems and ideas, and cooperative prototyping activities. For a further discussion of the applied techniques refer to Greenbaum and Kyng (1991), which strongly inspired us when setting up the project.

Utilizing a previous contact in the technical department we presented a project proposal aimed at trying out our cooperative approach to system design. The benefit for the department was that it would receive an analysis of the possibili-

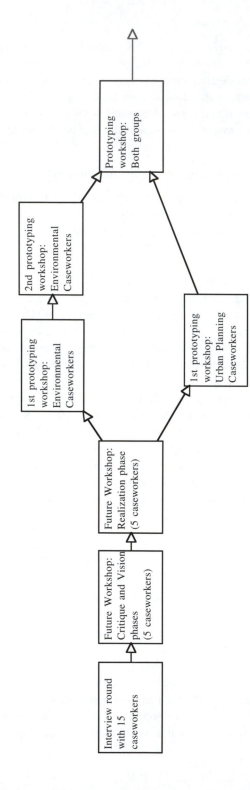

Figure 1. Overview of the design process.

ties for integrated computer support for casework. The caseworkers agreed to participate in order to gain insight into possibilities for improving their work, although the department did not at the time have money to start an actual development project.

We started by improving our understanding of the work activities. In this round we interviewed most employees from the urban planning and environmental offices and sent summaries of our impressions to all interviewed participants.

Based on the interviews, we arranged the workshops. The caseworkers chose from among themselves five representatives to participate. We call these caseworkers A, B, C, D, and E in the following analysis. Caseworkers A, C, and E are from the urban planning office, and B and D are from the environmental office.

We used the future workshop idea (Jungk & Müllert, 1987) as a frame for the two first workshops. The first day dealt with the critique and vision phases.[2] The participants were each asked to focus specifically on a central work task from their daily work in the presentations. Before the second workshop, we tried to focus the discussions by suggesting some specific problem areas. The caseworkers chose one of these, and in the second workshop we continued with the realization phase: the visions were made more specific with respect to the selected problem realizable in a prototype.

Following this, two initial prototypes[3] were set up, one for each of the groups: environmental caseworkers and urban planning caseworkers. The idea of making two prototypes was to focus on the specific needs of each group, as well as to get mutual inspiration from two rather different prototypes. The initial prototype for the environmental caseworkers was partly made by a group of students who had also attended the workshops.

The environmental prototype was first tried out by B and D in two consecutive half-day sessions. The urban planning prototypes were similarly tried out by A, C, and E in one half-day session. The prototypes were augmented cooperatively in the workshops and again revised by the designers between sessions. Following this, the prototypes were revised again and built together into one. This prototype was given to each caseworker to try out for one hour. They were to start out from the work tasks that they had chosen as representative earlier in the process. These tasks thus framed the evaluation, and we call them *frame tasks*. The researchers/designers were present at the sessions. In each session, one of the designers had the role as *primary designer,* i.e., he or she was sitting close to the caseworker(s) and the machine, taking responsibility for the interaction with both caseworker(s) and prototype. The *secondary designer* was sitting in the background, observing, taking notes, and intervening in the design activity when appropriate.

Inspired by Suchman and Trigg (1991) the five sessions from the final prototyping workshop were all videotaped to make it possible to analyze the problems and prospects of the prototyping approach. Results from the design process were

documented in a report that was given to the caseworkers in the technical department, and it was agreed that the caseworkers could get access to the prototypes if
they wanted to.

## Breakdowns and focus shifts

In the following analysis, we use the terms "breakdown" (Winograd & Flores,
1986) and "focus shift" frequently, thus they deserve an introduction in the context of prototyping. In Bødker and Grønbæk (1989) we described cooperative
prototyping as sessions in which users primarily experienced the future use activity and secondarily participated in modifying the prototypes when breakdowns required it. We distinguished between two levels of breakdowns present in
the situation: those related to the use process and those related to the in-session
modification of the prototype. Breakdowns related to the use process occur when
work is interrupted by something, e.g., when the tool behaves differently than
was anticipated. In these situations, the tool as such becomes the object of our
actions. Breakdowns in relation to the modification of the prototype occur when
the fluent conduction of the design activity is interrupted, e.g., because the user
loses interest in what is going on. By focus shifts we generally mean breakdowns
as well as changes of focus or object of the actions or activity that are more deliberate than those caused by breakdowns. For instance, a designer or a user may
have prepared to raise some issues in the session. Openings, e.g., pauses, in the
session may allow for a participant to deliberately shift focus.

The participating caseworkers each had their frame task to work on in the sessions. These tasks were representative of the work done by the caseworkers and
we aimed to create prototypes that would simulate support for these selected
work tasks. From the outset, we aimed to have the prototypes tried out in a work-
like situation lasting for an hour, following an introduction to and a demonstration of the prototype. We did not set up evaluation in the real work setting because we knew that our example material was far too limited for that. We found
that while the structure of the prototype was sufficient to support parts of the
work tasks, the sample data were too limited to keep the illusion of a work-like
situation going for a longer period.

In retrospect, viewing what went on in the prototyping sessions as a real work
activity is of little value. Only one or two of the caseworkers started out on
"their" frame task. Rather, the evaluation can be characterized as a step-wise,
hands-on evaluation of the prototype using the frame task as a guide for the evaluation. The sessions appeared as a mixture of caseworkers expressing expectations and trying out single features, and designers guiding the caseworkers
through the structure of the prototype. There was an on-going, vivid discussion
between the designers and the caseworkers participating in the session. The activities ranged from guided tours of prototypes, where the caseworker asked

questions and came up with proposals but touched the keyboard and mouse only when asked, to situations focused on the design of computer-based materials—forms, reports, plans, check-lists, etc.—used in the work.

The caseworkers in general never engaged in long-lasting, fluent simulated-use situations. Thus, our analysis shows few of the breakdowns in simulated use suggested by Bødker (1991). One breakdown occurred when we used an asterisk (*) as a hypertext link icon attached to a word, but to follow the link, the word marked with the * needed to be selected. Often, the caseworkers selected the * and got an error message, confusing them. Other breakdowns occurred, as mentioned above, when the users lost patience with the designers' attempts to fix something in the prototype. This issue will be discussed later.

Although the project activities differed slightly from our expectations, our material shows a richness of openings for learning that can be analyzed in terms of breakdowns and focus shifts. But restricting ourselves to the two kinds of breakdowns mentioned previously is far too simple to help us explain the rich variety of learning openings. Rather, we look for different kinds of potentials for focus shifts and breakdowns in prototyping activity than described in our earlier works. Focus shifts and breakdowns reveal the unpredictability of prototyping sessions that cannot be avoided. In most cases, they are not just "failure" indicators but rather they lead to new insights and trigger new ideas to be explored. We will give a number of such examples from our prototyping sessions.

## The theoretical framework

Our analysis of the prototyping situation is inspired by the application of activity theory to situations that range from empirical studies of physicians' work (Engeström, et al., 1988; Engeström & Engeström, 1989), to Bisgaard et al.'s (1989) application of the framework to system development. The key idea is that the design activity is a learning activity. The future work activity of the users, here the caseworkers, is its main object. Prototyping is a part of this, where, in our case, the detailed conduct of the work tasks-to-be are in focus.

Engeström and Engeström (1989) described patients' sessions with doctors as confrontations of two activities in quest of a mutual goal—to diagnose a certain illness based on the symptoms of the patient. The doctor in his or her diagnosis uses instruments such as X-rays, laboratory tests, the understanding of different diseases, and maybe even medical literature. The patient has access to the symptoms, the pain, and so on, but he or she may also interpret these in terms of folk medicine, etc.

We find many similarities between this situation and our prototyping sessions. The common goal of the prototyping session is to develop a computer application to function in work. The designers use instruments such as the prototyping tool, interview techniques, etc. They have an understanding of numerous technical issues relevant to the process and product, and some understanding of the work practice. The caseworkers, on the other hand have access to the instruments and materials that they employ in their current work situation. They also have an understanding of this, including also ideas for how they want things done differently. We see this framework as one application of the general understanding illustrated by Fig. 2.

We have found it fruitful to look at the actions that different involved actors take as part of their mutual activity [in some cases there is a very subtle difference between a cluster of such actions and a separation into several activities as described by Engeström and Engeström (1989); see Fig. 3]. In general, we find issues of sharing or not sharing instruments as well as understanding of the intentions of actions to be important for our analysis. For example, when a caseworker is deeply involved in some details of his or her work tasks, and the designer is looking impatiently at the clock, we interpret the caseworker to be focused on his or her work and the designer on the prototyping session. We will identify situations based on the intentions and foci by which they are characterized. We see roles as a cluster of actions that share an actor as well as focus/intention. Sometimes, such a cluster could rightfully be seen as a separate activity, similar to what is done in the doctors' case.

Engeström (1987), when looking at change processes in organizational settings, bases his analysis on *contradictions* within the activity and between this

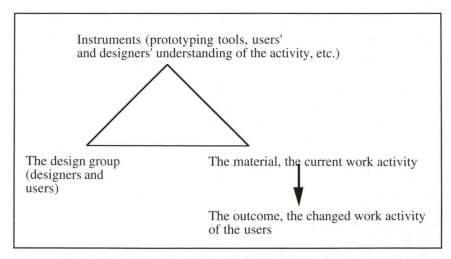

Figure 2.   The design activity. Designers and users act together with the mutual goal of changing the work practice of the users by introducing a computer application. The instruments of this change include prototypes and prototyping, programming and programming facilities, and so on, as well as the participants' mutual language and the preunderstanding that the participants have of the use activity as well as the design activity.

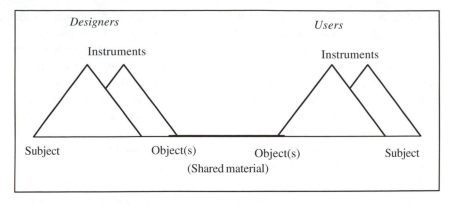

Figure 3.   Description of design situations. In our case, several caseworkers, as well as several designers, can appear on the scene. In some situations, the designers, for example, take action together; in some they do not. Actions have intentions and contribute to the goal of the activity. Operations always take place under certain material conditions and both, as well as the activity as such, are mediated by instruments.

activity and surrounding activities, since they constitute the basis for change. He looks at contradictions in how tools, objects, and subjects are seen and suggests studying contradictions between, for example, the tools currently used and the object created, or the norms that are part of praxis and the division of work. We use the idea of contradictions to understand changes in the design situation. The types of contradictions that are relevant for the triangles in Fig. 3 are—beside the ones mentioned already, where, e.g., the designer both feels part of a collective subject, and a need to act as individual—contradictions for one of the groups, between the instrument applied, and the object on which one is focusing. In the doctor's case, these could be situations where the symptoms of a patient do not fit the models of diseases that the doctor has in mind.

In our analysis, we will look both for such contradictions and for situations where a shift of focus occurs. In a breakdown situation, the object or focus of a certain actor changes (Winograd & Flores, 1986; Bødker, 1991). In our case, a breakdown often happens to one party, resulting in a change of this actor's focus. For example, the designer is changing the prototype. Something happens causing the designer to focus on the syntax of the programming language. This shift causes a later contradiction when the focus has become different for the two parties (e.g., the caseworker believes that they are still designing screen images, whereas the designer is fighting to get the syntax right).

Breakdowns are openings for learning and in our unhampered daily activity we can see some breakdowns causing a focus shift by which a daily activity becomes the object of our learning activity (Engeström, 1987; Bisgaard et al., 1989). Learning can take place in deliberate learning actions as well, where e.g., one of the actors teaches some other actor about his or her work practice. In the same way, the design activity can, as such, become the object of our activity.

We will use Vygotsky's notion of a zone of proximal development (see Engeström, 1987) to understand along which lines such a learning can take place. Vygotsky's idea is that besides from a person's present skills and understanding there is a zone within which the person is capable of or motivated to learn. In Engeström's reformulation, the zone of proximal development is "the distance between the present everyday actions of the individuals and the historically new form of the societal activity that can be collectively generated as a solution to the double bind potentially embedded in the everyday actions." We see prototyping as one way of uncovering the zone of proximal development, where the prototype is a means of exploring the historically new form of work activity of the involved users, as well as potential double binds of everyday actions (see Mogensen, 1990). Furthermore, prototypes can be used to explore and support the actual learning activity necessary for the participants and other future users of the artifact-to-be.

## Prototyping sessions: Situations and focus shifts

In this section we apply the framework to a variety of situation types and focus shifts experienced in the project. We illuminate examples of openings for learning that occur in cooperative prototyping sessions. We claim that these types of openings are worth paying attention to in cooperative design in general. The examples are grouped under headings that point to more general types of situations, but do not span all possible cooperative design situations.

### Focus on simulating future work actions

This section focuses on situations in which the primary focus is on the prototype as a medium for establishing work-like evaluation sessions by means of simulation. We discuss the conditions for, and problems in, setting up prototyping sessions wherein users pretend or play that they are in a future work situation.

*Fluent play of work-like actions.*   Our goal in cooperative prototyping is to evaluate prototypes in simulated work situations. Bødker and Grønbæk (1989) describe working with dental assistants to evaluate a prototype patient-record system this way. But the current project differs from this earlier case with respect to the success of establishing fluent work-like evaluation.

The caseworker sessions produced only short passages that resemble a fluent simulation of future work. In one such situation, the urban planning caseworkers (A, C, and E) were trying to navigate in the hypermedia structure combining maps and physical data on a certain area under consideration for buildings renovation. Caseworker A clicked with the mouse on compass arrows and buttons attached to scanned maps (see Figs. 4–6). The quality of the scanned maps was too poor for actual use, but he had no problem in pretending that he was navigating real digitalized maps linked to textual information. Later, when the caseworker had left the maps, he wanted to quickly pick up the most detailed map again. This was, however, not possible to do directly; he had to follow the links from the overview map and go several levels down. This breakdown led to a proposal for a facility to bypass the map hierarchy. This facility was built into the next version of the prototype. It proved to be useful in situations where caseworkers were resuming work on cases for which they could remember labels of detail maps. The hierarchical navigation was useful when they had to find a detail map for the first time.

The illusion of a fluent work-like situation only lasted for a short period of time; therefore, discourses caused by breakdowns in the simulated use in such situations were few.

One explanation of the difference between experiences in the two projects could be that the prototypes used in the dental assistants sessions were simpler than the ones developed in this project. But we see a more important difference in the characteristics of the work task and the need for sample data to get a work-like evaluation going. In the dental patient record system, little initial sample data was needed to get started on a work task. Also, in registering patients, patient data is a considerable part of dental assistants work. This implied that an important work task with the prototype was data entry, which meant that the dental assistants bootstrapped the prototype with sample data when evaluating it. In the dental assistant project, the material conditions to make a work-like evaluation take place were more easily brought about than in the case of the municipal

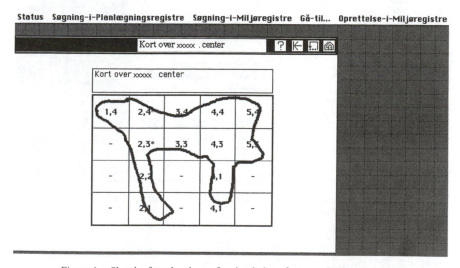

Figure 4.    Sketch of top-level map for simulation of map navigation.

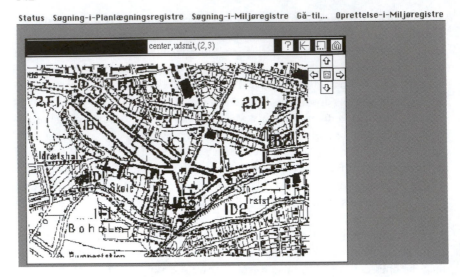

Figure 5.    Scanned map for simulation of map navigation.

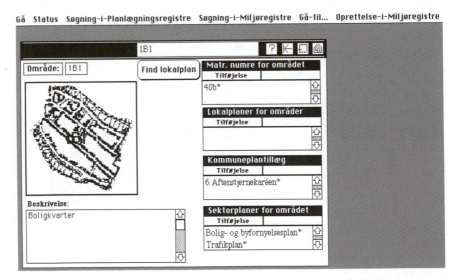

Figure 6.    Scanned detail map and data fields for simulation of map and database navigation.

caseworkers. Most casework in the technical department was concerned with the use of existing information that had to be gathered from paper files and computer databases. Entering new data into these files is a minor part of daily work. To let a caseworker get started on, for instance, modifying a local area plan required having access to nearly all of the long-term plans in the hypertext structure that we had built. These long-term plans consisted of several hundred pages of text.

*Point-wise play of work-like actions.*   When one of the caseworkers, A, went through his frame task with the prototype at the second prototyping workshop, it was clear that he was not in a fluent simulated work situation. Rather, we saw a performance of a sequence of actions that the caseworker associated with the frame task.

The caseworker used an important instrument in the prototyping situations: his understanding of how the information he worked on was organized in the real work situation. This understanding encompassed both structure and content of a large body of text. While looking for information in the prototype, a fluent work situation broke down because sample data was missing. But the caseworker performed an advanced play, in which he used terms from his work domain only when referring to the prototype. For instance, he said "I need to look at the 'preconditions section' of the municipality plan" when he pushed a link icon[4] and jumped to the place in the structure where he expected to find that section. He was also able to abstract from some kinds of breakdowns that happened in performance of such actions. This can be seen from A's reactions to a situation where the designers had entered sample data in wrong places of the structure. He said "let's just pretend that it was swapped . . . ."

Caseworker A maintained a focus on the frame task throughout the whole session. When he tried to perform an action that was not supported in the prototype, he continued, on his own initiative, a discussion of what he wanted to do with the prototype, using concepts belonging to the work domain (these issues are discussed further in a later section). For instance, he said at one point: "At this place I would like to be able to bring up a list of tasks that I have to do when treating a case (on a local area plan) . . . and I would like to be able to mark the task I have already done." Only in a few places breakdowns in actions were turning the focus to the prototype as an object detached from the frame task. These are cases where he needed instructions for how to continue. For instance he at some point wanted to follow a hypertext link backwards and asked "which button should I push?" And when he got the answer he pushed the button and replied: "Oh, it is this arrow I have to push."

*Discussion.*   The sessions with A show that a fluent work-like performance of the work task was difficult to set up at this early stage in the project, mainly due to lack of sample data. However, evaluation activities based on the frame task helped in maintaining a focus on the work task in a prototyping session. The close focus on work tasks brought up important issues such as the deficiencies of the hierarchical map navigation.

The fact that the overall activity was design and not use did not seem to disturb A. To some extent, he used his paper-based materials when the materials were not available on the computer. There is no doubt that he knew he was in a learning situation and not all the material conditions were as they should be, but the setting allowed him to try out certain future actions anyway.

Our general conclusion from the two examples is that it is important to simulate aspects of the future-use activity to some extent. The main purpose of this is to try out the future material conditions set up by the computer application. It is less important, though, to make this simulation work-like in all respects. Actually, we have seen demonstrated that a play-like situation may be useful.

*Focus on idea exploration*

Some situations from the prototyping sessions resemble brainstorming carried out by caseworkers and designers using the computer and prototype as instruments.[5] The prototype and computer are used to explore technological possibilities and for experimenting with design possibilities. In all such situations, the caseworkers were articulating their work tasks rather than doing them.

*Augmenting the current prototype.*    The session with one of the caseworkers, B, quickly turned from a work-like evaluation to idea generation and augmentation of the prototype. The frame task was an environmental case: checking hidden oil tanks and drinking water conditions on a site. To get started on the task, B found the data of a fictitious site with a key-word search on the database. She examined the sample data already there and said: "How do I find the site map?" We explained that we had not prepared, i.e., scanned, a site map for this task. Instead, she explained how she would examine the site map, and she entered some fictitious notes reflecting the examination of the site map and related data. In the middle of her formulation of a request for the name of the owner of the site, she said: "In general, we would like to be able to subtract a 'list of requests' on house owners; nowadays we have to remember the requests ourselves." B, on her own initiative, also took the mouse and attempted to use the existing key-word search function to search for house owners who have had a demand given to them by the environmental office. Now the focus shifted from the frame task to a discussion of how a reminder facility could be designed. A first attempt in designing the facility was made by the primary designer, who added two new fields—"deadline for fulfilling request" and "description of request"—to the current screen image. B tried to reformulate the request and used the fields. Then it was proposed that for a following session we prepare a report to generate the list of reminders on

requests with deadlines in the current month. We also noted that the reminder facility might be useful in general for the tasks that the other environmental caseworker, D, was performing. But B did not know at what level D made his request,
thus we decided to discuss this issue with D in another session. We turned the focus back to the initial frame task.

Later in the same session, B needed information from the Buildings File, a file
currently kept on paper. B pushed the button that brought her to the current
representation of the Buildings File in the prototype. B examined the data on
the screen and realized that there was no representation of the change applica-
tions/permissions that had been made for a building. B explained that each appli-
cations/permissions case consisted of a folder with letters and architectural
drawings sent in by the various house owners. According to B, it would be of no
use to enter this extensive material into the computer but it would be nice to have
a list of all the cases on a building and for each case a brief abstract describing
the case and telling where to find the material in the paper files. We started to design that facility. One of the application-oriented objects was a scrollable item-
list field that could be used as an index of abstracts for the applications/permis-
sions cases. An instance of this object was placed on the screen. B suggested a
prototypical headline for an applications/permissions case. We added an "abstract" screen carrying this headline and linked that to the item on the list. Now
the abstract could be brought up by a single click on the item in a list on the
overview screen. B tried that operation and seemed satisfied with the solution.

The examples described here shows that B, the caseworker, got a number of
ideas when confronting the frame task with a sketchy prototype that was supposed to support her work. The focus shifts in the session were not caused by
breakdowns in the simulated use activity, but rather by ideas that came to B when
she had to imagine the prototype being part of her future workplace. This way,
the prototype was used to create visions concerning the future computer application and changed work practice. Some of the proposals and ideas might have
come across in a paper-based design session, but it seems as if the confrontation
with the prototype triggered a more extensive idea generation. One explanation
could be that the prototype was viewed as an object to be developed in conjunction with investigation of the frame task and not viewed as something complete
that was brought into the office.

*Going beyond the current prototype.*    In the first urban planning workshop with
the caseworkers (A, C, and E) we were designing computer support for urban
and area planning. We considered A's frame task on local area planning for an
area where a small airport was proposed to be built. The initial prototype was
made to try out how to organize the information in database fields on a series of
screen images.

A general issue was raised by A: When working with a local area plan it was often necessary to look up certain issues in the long-term plans. These were kept as textual/graphical descriptions in paper folders. In general, the caseworkers found it hard to trace particular issues throughout these folders. Moreover, it was necessary to keep track of changes made between major revisions of the long-term plans. Such changes often had implications for a number of paragraphs, tables, and figures throughout the plans. It would be useful for the caseworkers to be reminded of such add-ons when retrieving information. This general issue led to a discussion on how to represent large text and graphics documents in combination with a conventional database design. For the designers, it seemed obvious that some kind of hypertext system was needed and one of the designers went to the blackboard and showed how sections and regions within sections of the long-term plan could be linked together as hypertext. At the same time, the other designer had opened a Guide hypertext document on the workstation.[6] A brief demonstration of Guide was given and one of the caseworkers tried to follow some links in the document. This example shows that it was possible for the caseworkers to relate already articulated problems concerning the material conditions and instruments of the work activity to the use of a prototype, and to be creative with respect to changing the situation. The conclusion of this session was that the designers, for the next session, should design a hypertext structure representing the long-term plan. In the second prototyping workshop, the caseworkers were provided with this hypertext structure representing the long-term plan and they worked rather painlessly with hypertext facilities without much further introduction.

*Discussion.*    The situations described in this section can be seen as examples of what Ehn (1988)[7] calls "creative transcendence of tradition," wherein the collectively created new takes shape. The caseworkers were able to go beyond their traditional skills when confronted with new technological possibilities such as prototypes and example applications. Moreover, the situations show how the caseworkers take the initiative to transcending their own skills in such prototyping sessions.

In the prototype modification situations the prototype had the role of an instrument to facilitate a concrete discussion of visions. Both caseworkers and designers were pointing at objects in the prototype and various facilities were discussed. Instead of using terms from the application domain, there was a higher frequency of computer-oriented terms such as "screen image," "fields," "buttons," and "arrows." This distance to the frame task was reduced a bit when reusing parts of the prototype already familiar to the caseworkers, but rarely were the parts to be reused referred to with a name familiar to the caseworkers. For instance, B could recognize how to use the scrollable item-list field when she saw it but she did not have a name for it because it did not correspond to something familiar to her.

When hypertext was introduced, the caseworkers easily adapted to the idea of browsing through text, using buttons, instead of key-word search facilities that were otherwise more common in the computer systems they were familiar with. The designers' introduction of hypertext represented a more advanced form of text representation than what the caseworkers themselves knew about, or would have imagined to be implementable, on the computer. At the same time, however, there was a clear need to impose a structure on the current texts to support efficient traversal and remind of crossing dependencies. The cooperative effort brought hypertext into the zone of proximal development for the caseworkers.

### Focus on current work practice

In several situations, the focus was on the caseworkers' current work practice. These were situations where caseworkers and designers used prototypes as instruments to trigger a further investigation of the current work practice. In these situations, the caseworkers were articulating their work tasks rather than doing them.

*Talk-through of the frame tasks.* C, B, and D did not simulate the future use of the prototype very much. Rather, the frame task was talked through while the prototype was examined. The role of the prototype became that of an object that was brought in to illustrate how certain parts of the frame task could be supported with a computer. The prototype never became an instrument for work actions.

An example of such situations was seen in sessions with D, who did environmental inspection of companies in the municipality. D's frame task for the session was "collecting information before an inspection visit at a company." The sessions started out with the designer giving a brief guided tour to the relevant part of the prototype. Then the initiative was given to D by the designer asking: "Show what you would start out with when you collect information for an inspection visit." D then took over and said: "First I'm checking whether the company has a 'Chapter 5 approval' and then I check whether I have made an earlier inspection visit at the company. I guess I'll enter this 'Chapter 5 approval' file." D clicked the mouse on the corresponding item in the table of contents menu of the prototype. When the screen image came up, D sat thinking for a while and said: "This is only an overview of approvals given—how do I find the detailed information? There ought to be information about heating technology, chimney size, and the like!" The designer thought for a short while and said: "But this information is kept in the file of 'inspection visit reports'—have a look!" The designer grabbed the mouse and jumped to the file of "inspection visit reports." D said: "Oh here they are . . . but this information is really needed in both places, because we have approvals on companies we haven't formally inspected yet." In this way, we recognized a need for making links between "Chapter 5 approval" documents and "inspection visit reports," and it was discussed how this could be done after the session.

From this breakdown, the session shifted into a talk-through of the frame task as D could recall it detached from his performance of the work. During this talk-through, we experienced other focus shifts that moved us into other kinds of situations. On the one hand, we moved into situations where we modified and augmented the prototype. On the other hand, we also experienced the need for getting more information on D's current frame task. This led to an interview-like situation with very little focus on future work, a kind of situation that is discussed in a following section.

In these talk-through situations the caseworker primarily demonstrated his own current role when going through a typical work task, the frame task, by "thinking aloud," i.e., expressing what he was doing as he was progressing through the task. This kind of thinking aloud is different from the way it is practiced in human interface studies, for example, those of Mack, Lewis, and Carroll (1987). In those studies the designers define a new task that the users are going to learn; the designers want to study how they learn the task, e.g., using a word processor. In our prototyping sessions, the caseworkers were going through a task they were already familiar with, even though they were detached from their normal performance of the task. The designers, on the other hand, were listening to understand the work task, to ask questions, and to introduce relevant parts of the prototype. Focus shifts or breakdowns typically occurred when contradictions in the caseworkers' and the designers' understanding of the frame task occurred. Some of these contradictions related to the prototype as described above, but they occurred as well when the caseworker progressed in the detailed talk-through of the frame task.

With the frame task it is possible to go through the work actions and articulate and investigate not only questions of what is done, or should be done, also questions of how and why, i.e., operations and the activity as such.

*Caseworkers teach designers about their work practice.*    In some situations, the focus shifted from design toward more analysis-like situations, because of contradictions between the participants' understandings of the frame task.

An example of such a situation occurred in the session with D when he was examining the "inspection visit reports." He realized that space was only allocated for making one query per visit. D explained that he typically made a number of queries on particular aspects such as chimney size or heating. The current forms used did not support this use and D made notes in the margin. This showed a misconception in the designers understanding of the queries. The focus of the session shifted to a situation where the caseworker was teaching the designers about his work. The designers were listening and occasionally questioning the caseworker about the different ways in which queries were used.

In Trigg, Bødker, and Grønbæk (1990) a more detailed video analysis of the session with caseworker E is discussed. Among other things, it was studied how confrontation with a prototype inspired E to tell short anecdotes from her work. These anecdotes illustrated her daily work more generally than the frame task. This was a similar but more indirect way of teaching the designers about her work practice.

*Discussion.*   In the above situations, the frame task and the prototype were used in different ways to help the caseworkers articulate problems with their current work practice. The situations were different with respect to the role of the prototype and the frame task. In the first one, the prototype was used to provoke articulation of work actions closely related to the frame task. In the second, the caseworkers taught the designers about their work. In these situations the designers took the pupil's role. The prototype assumed the role of an instrument to trigger the caseworkers' teaching and story telling about their current work practice, and the situations clearly demonstrate that we are dealing with a process of mutual learning, not one, as in, for example, Vygotsky's own definition of the zone of proximal development, where the designers are "adult guides" or "more capable peers."

These examples also illustrate situations wherein it could have been useful to supplement the prototyping techniques with other means to better document the caseworkers' articulation of their work. For instance, the anecdotes could easily be overheard by the designers, and making basic investigations of current work practice in front of the prototype can cause premature changes of the prototype.

### Focus on the prototyping tool or the session

We often experienced breakdowns in the session that moved all participants' foci towards the conduct of the session, the prototype, or the prototyping tool. These focus shifts are of little use as openings for learning with respect to the actual system to be designed. But with respect to improving the designers' understanding of how to prepare prototypes and improve prototyping tools they can be quite useful. We give examples of this kind of focus shift. In several situations we also see focus shifts when the designers are concerned about getting the session moving. These shifts are necessary to keep within time limits, but they can, as we shall see, easily disturb the prototyping activity.

*Lacking tool support.*   In situations wherein the prototype was augmented, breakdowns due to mismatch between the designers' ability to make modifications and the caseworkers' needs occurred. An example of such a situation happened with respect to use of prepared objects in the prototype. We had prepared a number of general objects, such as general search buttons, that could be parameterized and fields with special hypertext-supporting features. These objects were intended to be used with already existing screen images,[8] but a breakdown occurred when we wanted to start from scratch with the design of a new screen image. We needed a blank HyperCard screen that inherited properties similar to already existing screens. However, the way the tool was set up, it was not possible to get a blank screen, preserving, for instance, the browsing capabilities that all the screens in the application were supposed to have. Either one would get a blank screen with no functionality, or one would get a screen with contents similar to the current screen in use. This breakdown taught us to be better prepared for follow-

ing sessions by providing blank screen images that preserved operational properties for each screen type we could expect to reuse for design from scratch.

*Bugs in prototypes or sample data.*   Breakdowns due to regular programming
bugs and misplaced sample data occurred as well. Some of these were simple bugs
in details that caused little trouble. Either the fixing was simple or the bug could
be ignored when continuing the session while still focusing on the user's frame
task. In a session with one of the architects we, the designers, had swapped two
pieces of sample data in the hypertext structure, and after realizing that it was not
his fault, the architect said on his own initiative: "Let's just pretend they are
swapped." Other bugs, however, were more serious. For instance, a breakdowns
happened (see also Bødker & Grønbæk, 1989) when we were evaluating a report
design made before the session. The report generator would not select the data re-
quested in the query. After three attempts, the report generator created a system
bug that required reinstallation of the program in order to get started again. Meanwhile, the caseworker, who was in the beginning interested and active, became
more and more passive, as the designer moved into areas of the prototype that the
caseworker did not understand. In that situation we were forced to shift focus and
jump to another part of the prototype and continue evaluation there.

The focus shifts described here give the prototype the role of an instrument
that does not function well, either as support for casework or as a medium for the
design activity. The designer becomes a repair person, a programmer who uses
only computer-specific instruments to solve problems outside the scope of the
caseworkers' understanding. The caseworkers become passive observers who
watch a professional doing a complicated task. This kind of breakdown is not
very productive with respect to improved understanding of computer support for
casework. In this project, the prototype was not aimed at becoming part of a final
working system. Fixing the programming bugs also had little impact on the final
system. Thus this kind of breakdown should ideally be kept to a minimum in cooperative prototyping sessions. Careful preparation and good understanding of
what can be done in sessions to get around such breakdowns without spoiling the
purpose of the session is needed on the designer side of the table. This issue is
developed further in "Preparing for prototyping sessions" below.

*Conducting the session.*   In several situations, we saw focus shifts towards the
conduction of the session. Frequently, the designer who had the secondary role in
the session realized that the session activities did not serve their purpose and
started intervening in the situation.

In one example, the caseworker, A, was deeply involved in typing some piece
of information into a text node of the hypertext structure when the designers got
impatient and finally interrupted the caseworker. The caseworker was concerned
with correct spelling of words and language correctness. In contrast, the sec-

ondary designer was concerned about time frames and the evaluation as such and thought it was a pity if the caseworker spent all the time typing away on some details, instead of getting into some of the more "interesting" aspects of the prototype.

In other situations, the designers "pulled" the caseworker away from his or her focus because they wanted to get through the agenda for the session or simply because they were eager to explore some particular features of the prototype. In these situations, the designer often intervened and encouraged the caseworker to "have a look at this," "try this . . . ," or "try to write something here." This kind of designer intervention was not planned from the outset but happened often in situations where there was a break, a moment of silence, in which one of the designers lost his or her patience.

*Discussion.*    We have seen different types of situations wherein the design situation as such became the focus of the participants. When focus moved away from the frame task towards the sessions as an object this usually did not lead to learning about the caseworker's work or the computer system under design. However, we learned about how to plan and conduct sessions. In one of the situations, a breakdown occurred in the activity of the designers: the prototyping tool stopped working. This breakdown caused the designers to move away from the common activity, leaving the caseworker in a state of irresolution. In the other situation, one of the designers was reminded of his role as conductor of a session with limited time resources. This caused the designer to try to pull the caseworker out of the actions that were currently being carried out and thus to arrest the fluent acting.

One lesson learned from these focus shifts was that in taking the time limits seriously it would be useful to evaluate future work-like situations in a theatre-or movie-like fashion, where a scene indicates that some activity begins and quick scene shifts give the illusion that some long-lasting activity has taken place. Activities then continue in a following scene, leading to the assumption that time has passed and things are changed. We are actually facing a more general problem of how to reduce complexity of real work tasks without losing the important points that lead to good design. For the moment, we do not have concrete experience with that, but we believe it is important to consider this issue when setting up simulated work situations.

## Preparing prototyping sessions

We have discussed several types of situations that we observed in cooperative prototyping sessions. These situations have helped shed some light on the different learning activities going on in cooperative prototyping—learning with respect to the activity and the actions and the operations of the users, both with respect to the limitations of the current work practice and the possible changes that may occur when a computer application is introduced. But there is, of course, more to cooperative prototyping than what goes on in front of a prototype in sessions together with users. Before sessions, preparation and planning is needed; between sessions, clean-up and reconstruction of the prototype is needed; after a series of sessions, results need to be collected and documented in order to propagate them to continuing development activities. In this section, we briefly discuss lessons from the analysis with respect to setting up sessions and the activities that go on before and between sessions.

Each session needs to be prepared dependent on the current stage of the design process. Issues concerning preparation of prototyping sessions were discussed at a general level in Grønbæk (1989), where it was suggested to consider the following questions for preparation: What is the purpose of the session? How stable should the prototype be in advance? To what extent should in-session modifications be made? What setting should be chosen? How should the outcome be documented/evaluated? The analysis in this paper has improved our understanding of the richness of cooperative prototyping sessions. We have seen that prototyping sessions are somehow unpredictable due to inherent properties of creative activities. Although sessions were prepared to be rooted in a certain frame task, the focus shifted due to either breakdowns or more or less deliberate "pulling" of the focus by participants. We have analyzed a number of such situations and focus shifts. From these analyses, we conclude that users and designers should view focus shifts as openings of learning in the prototyping sessions rather than trying to avoid them. Of course, not all kinds of focus shifts are particularly fruitful openings for learning, as was pointed out.

We have pointed to a tension between careful preparation of prototyping sessions and their inherent unpredictable character. Being aware of such tension, a contribution from our analysis is an improved understanding of the variety of situations that may occur in prototyping sessions. This understanding can be utilized in the preparation of sessions, not to impose tighter steering on the session, but to prepare to better handle the most common and important types of situations and focus shifts. We briefly discuss a few examples of focus shifts to prepare for.

*Examples of lessons learned with respect to preparation.* The first example is from the situations discussed above in "Focus on simulating work actions." We saw that having extensive sample data was as important as the prototype in establishing fluent work-like evaluation. We find it important to pay attention to sample data early on in the prototyping process. Since the long-term municipal plans in this case didn't exist in computer-readable form, our only realistic possibility was to scan parts of the material into the prototype. This would help in situations where the caseworkers were navigating in existing information. But it would not help much in situations where the caseworkers needed to modify the material.

Another lesson could be to be less ambitious in cases where it is hard to provide sample data and only aim at a point-wise fluent performance of actions, as described above in "Focus on simulating work actions."

The second example is when ideas move the focus towards technological solutions beyond the current prototype, as described above in "Focus on idea exploration." We experienced a quite successful focus shift when we left the prototyping tool and experimented with the Guide hypertext system.[9] Guide happened to be installed on the computer that we were using in the prototyping session. We were not prepared for making such a focus shift, but in this situation it worked quite well. We got a shared hypertext example before we actually built tailored facilities aimed at the particular work of the caseworkers. Here this happened by coincidence. More generally, we would claim that is a good idea to prepare to be able to go beyond the current prototype. Such preparation requires some amount of good guessing by the designers; it is, of course, impossible for the designers to keep all sorts of example applications and be familiar with them. Thus, during preparation of sessions it is necessary to think of a repertoire of good example applications to have in stock for the next sessions. This corresponds to an attempt to anticipate potential directions of development for the group in the following sessions. Such anticipation is hard in general and cannot be directed by general guidelines. But based on the understanding of the work practice studied in the actual project, it may not be equally hard for the designers to make good guesses with respect to potential example applications to have in stock.

There are other ways of being prepared for such situations. We have seen that a less-fancy prototyping means such as mock-ups (see, e.g., Kyng, 1989; Bødker, 1991; Ehn & Kyng, 1991) can be a handy support—anything from simple screen images to more advanced slide- or video-based simulations to support design. Vertelney (1990) describes the use of a range of tools from simple drawings in flip-books to advanced video-based animations for storyboard prototyping. Earlier projects (Bødker et al., 1987) have shown that mock-up simulations are often easier set up for illustration than are computer-based prototypes. A disadvantage of mock-ups, however, is that it is harder for users to *experience* dynamic aspects of the future system than it is with a computer-based prototype simulation.

A third example of a type of situation/focus shift that we could have handled differently in the project is the situation where caseworkers teach about their work practice, as described above in "Focus on current work practice." There we realized that the designers needed to learn more about casework. The action changed from design to analysis. In one of the sessions, however, we kept sitting by the prototype, mixing the caseworker's teaching of his work practice with interview-like inquiries. This took place without proper tools and techniques to undertake and document such activities. In order to be better prepared, the designers could set up the sessions in a room equipped with pens and posterboard or a flip-over. From our experience with workshops, it seems to be a good idea to have simple means like these available because it can easily be carried away as documentation. To designers, a computer-based tool might be appropriate but in our experience users generally are more comfortable when using simpler, graphic means to illustrate aspects of their work. Moreover, the designers should be prepared to move temporarily away from the prototype, even though that is not always the best solution.

A fourth example of a situation type that the designers should be prepared for is, as described above in "Focus on the prototyping tool or the session," when the focus shifts towards conducting the session. In that kind of situation, it is typically one of the designers who starts acting to get the process going. It is important that the designers share beforehand an understanding of what they will do when, for instance, time limits seem to be violated in the session, or when either one of the users or one of the designers jumps to a level of detail that seems to be irrelevant for the session. Having discussed such issues previous to sessions may help smooth possible adjustments in the middle of sessions.

It is difficult to give general guidelines for what to do in these situations but for the preparation, there are important issues to consider. The number of participants and their roles are important. In the project described by Bødker and Grønbæk (1989), a single designer was working together with two to four dental assistants. In the current project, we always arranged sessions with two designers and a varying number of caseworkers. From these experiences, we conclude that it is clearly an advantage to have two (or more) designers participating in the sessions. Documenting the process and maintaining the session when states of irresolution occurred became much easier when the secondary designer took responsibility for some of these tasks. The primary designer could concentrate on the interaction with the caseworker(s) and the prototyping tool when modifications to the prototype were needed. The conclusion with respect to the number of users is less clear. When the focus is on establishing work-like situations, the nature of the frame task to some degree dictates the number of participants. However, it may be an advantage to have several users participating when the focus is on idea exploration and current work practice. The confrontation between the users' different understanding of the current work and the direction of development of the prototype can uncover issues that the designer wouldn't have realized from having contact with the users individually. A disadvantage of having more than one user participate in the session may be that some participants are too dominating and thus suppress important contributions from other participants. In the current project, we observed that the draftspeople were generally more active when they were *not* together with architects or engineers.

We also pointed to the possibility of making deliberate focus shifts, like scene shifts in a movie, to progress through the frame task in a condensed form due to time limits. The use of so-called storyboard prototyping as suggested by Vertelney (1989) and Andriole (1989) seems to provide a good flexible means for this.[10] Storyboards can be used to identify individual scenarios to be tried out with a prototype. Shifts to other scenarios can be discussed with direct reference to the storyboard. The storyboard techniques are inspired by scripting and storyboard techniques used in making movies and in choreography. The techniques seem intriguing with respect to getting a representation of the use scenarios to be considered in the evaluation. But a very strict planning of the scenarios may violate the idea of open-endedness (Trigg, Bødker, & Grønbæk, 1990), which is an important feature of cooperative prototyping.

A final example of situations for which it is hard to be extensively prepared for are situations (see "Focus on the prototyping tool or session") wherein the focus moves towards the prototyping tool. This happens in situations where we reach the limits of the prototyping tool or when regular bugs are found. Bugs cannot be totally avoided and no prototyping tools are without constraints. It can, however, be discussed beforehand what the designers should do when such focus shifts happen. For instance, questions such as: When is it worth fixing a bug in-session? When and how should unsuccessful programming attempts be stopped? could be considered. Focus shifts that have previously been experienced may lead to more general ideas for how to prepare subsequent sessions. For instance, we experienced several breakdowns because we could not pick a blank screen due to certain inherited program properties. We prepared the next session by making it possible to pick a blank screen for all the different categories in the prototype. Another issue is to be able to anticipate certain types of breakdowns. In Bødker and Grønbæk (1989), we discuss stopping an in-session modification, when the situation has become meaningless to the users and too complicated for the designers to get out of within a reasonable amount of time. In this case study, we have seen situations where the designers support each other in getting out of such situations and situations where they do not. The roles of the designers should clearly be discussed in advance. Often it is the secondary designer who can feel when the user is losing her or his patience. Clearly, the decision about when to stop must be weighed against the importance of the change, but, generally, the designers can avoid serious breakdowns in the sessions as such by understanding the extent to which in-session modifications make sense.

Limitations in the current prototyping tool may also trigger consideration of different tools. Grønbæk (1990) discusses a variety of tools to support cooperative prototyping.

The above examples are not claimed to span the space of possible situations and focus shifts but they illustrate how focus shifts in prototyping sessions can be viewed as openings to learning. Taking such openings seriously can improve our understanding of the cooperative design process in general. With respect to specific projects, this understanding can improve our ways of setting up subsequent cooperative prototyping sessions.

**Conclusion**

As pointed out in the first section, there is more to prototyping than rapid development of prototypes and demonstration of their features. To be beneficial, prototyping needs to be carried out cooperatively by users and designers (Grønbæk, 1989). This kind of cooperation is an interaction between two groups of subjects who from the outset possess different kinds of instruments and work toward different kinds of objectives aimed at different purposes. However, we claim that in designing computer support, new objects, tailored to the users' needs, have to be temporarily shared between the two groups or two skills. This implies that we as designers need to develop our instruments in a direction that enables us to deal with the objects of design as objects for a shared purpose. This is not easy, but techniques to perform cooperative system design experimentally are, from our point-of-view, the best solution. This is similar to the observation that the best way to improve the understanding of the usability of design proposals is to have prototypes tried out in actual use. The project that we have set up and analyzed can be seen as a contribution to make the development of designer instruments go in a cooperative direction. In particular, we have discussed the tension between the need for careful preparation of prototyping sessions and establishing good conditions for user and designer creativity. The message in this respect is that we need to be open to learn from focus shifts in sessions and not try to avoid them.

Compared to our previous work, the present study has illustrated a variety of situations wherein prototypes can be related closely to frame tasks. These are situations in which point-wise performance of work actions takes place, ideas are explored, and designers learn about the user's work practice, etc. This occurs even though work-like evaluation in early prototyping may be hard to do in some settings. To maintain the idea of work-like evaluation, the meaning of "work-like" needs to be modified somewhat: we find it inspiring to think of the prototyping activities as playlets, wherein the participants act out some situations, but skip others. The timing of which situations to act out and which to skip or condense in time seems to be of major importance for the development of this idea. In future research we will try out the emerging storyboard prototyping techniques.

**Acknowledgments**

The municipal caseworkers, students, and colleagues at Aarhus University are kindly acknowledged for their help with the project. Randy Trigg has played an important role in the later phases of our analysis and Jonathan Grudin has helped out with language and other comments. The historical introduction is a result of the authors' work with Morten Kyng on a separate paper surveying the strategies and techniques of our cooperative design approach (Bødker, Grønbæk, & Kyng,

1990). The work has been supported by The Danish Natural Science Research Council, FTU grant no. 5.17.5.1.30.

A version of this chapter was published in 1991 as Cooperative Prototyping: Users and Designers in Mutual Activity, *International Journal on Man-Machine Studies,* Special issue on CSCW edited by S. Greenberg.

## Notes

1 All trademarks are acknowledged.
2 Refer to Greenbaum and Kyng (1991) for a discussion on the use of the technique in a system-design setting.
3 The prototypes were built by means of HyperCard, Reports, a word processor and a spreadsheet application that could be linked together using HyperCard.
4 "Link icon" is the hypertext term (Conklin, 1987) for the button to push when the user wants to follow a link to a destination node in the network.
5 Some authors (e.g., Jordan et al., 1989) introduced the term "software storming" for a mixture of rapid prototyping and brainstorming techniques.
6 Guide is a hypertext system running on the Apple Macintosh. We acknowledge all trademarks. Compared to HyperCard it is better for illustrating hyper*text*, because it resembles a word processor extended by linking facilities. It mainly supports replacement links and pop-up notes as discussed in Conklin (1987) and Bannon and Grønbæk (1989).
7 Pages 451–453.
8 "Cards" in HyperCard.
9 All trademarks are acknowledged.
10 Both Andriole (1989) and Vertelney (1989) use the term "storyboard prototyping." But Andriole differs from Vertelney in only sketching the actual screen images of the human–computer interface in his storyboards and not the scenarios of use as Vertelney proposes.

## References

Andriole, S. J. (1989). *Storyboard Prototyping—A New Approach to User Requirements Analysis.* QED Information Sciences, Inc., Wellesley, MA.

Bannon, L. & Grønbæk K. (1989). Hypermedia: Support for a more natural information organization. In H. Clausen (Ed.), *Proceedings of the 7th Nordic Conference for Information and Documentation.* Lyngby, Denmark: Dansk Teknisk Litteraturselskab.

Bisgaard, O., Mogensen, P., Nørby, M., & Thomsen, M. (1989). *Systemudvikling som lærevirksomhed, konflikter som basis for organisationel udvikling* [Systems development as a learning activity, conflicts as the origin of organizational development] (DAIMI IR-88). Åarhus: Åarhus University.

Bødker, S. & Grønbæk, K. (1989). Cooperative Prototyping Experiments—Users and Designers Envision a Dental Case Record System. In J. Bowers & S. Benford (Eds.), *Proceedings of the first EC-CSCW '89,* London: Computer Sciences Company.

Bødker , S. & Grønbæk, K. (1991). Design in Action: From Prototyping by Demonstration to Cooperative Prototyping. In J. Greenbaum & M. Kyng (Eds.), *Design at Work: Cooperative Design of Computer Systems.* Hillsdale, NJ: Erlbaum.

Bødker , S. (1991). *Through the Interface—a Human Activity Approach to User Interface Design.* Hillsdale, NJ: Erlbaum.

Bødker , S., Ehn, P., Kammersgaard, J., Kyng, M., & Sundblad, Y. (1987). A Utopian experience. In G. Bjerknes, P. Ehn, & M. Kyng (Eds.), *Computers and democracy: A Scandinavian challenge,* pp. 251–278. Aldershot, UK: Avebury.

Bødker , S., Grønbæk, K., & Kyng, M. (1990). *Cooperative Design: Techniques and Experiences from the Scandinavian Scene*. Draft submitted for publication.

Conklin, J. (1987). Hypertext: An Introduction and Survey. *IEEE Computer, 20*(9), 17–41.

DUE. (1981). *Klubarbejde og EDB*. [Local Union Activities and EDP]. Denmark: Fremad.

Ehn, P. & Kyng, M. (1987). The Collective Resource Approach to Systems Design. In G. Bjerknes, et al. (Eds.), *Computers and Democracy—a Scandinavian Challenge*, pp. 17–58. Aldershot, UK: Avebury.

Ehn, P. & Kyng, M. (1991). Cardboard Computers: Mocking-It-Up or Hands-On the Future. In J. Greenbaum & M. Kyng (Eds.), *Design at Work: Cooperative Design of Computer Systems*. Hillsdale, NJ: Erlbaum.

Ehn, P. & Sandberg, Å. (1983). Local Union Influence on Technology and Work Organization. In U. Briefs, C. Ciborra, & L. Schneider (Eds.), *Systems Design For, With and By the Users*, pp. 427–437. Amsterdam: North-Holland.

Ehn, P. (1988). *Work-oriented design of computer artifacts*. Falköping, Sweden: Arbetslivscentrum/Almqvist & Wiksell International.

Engeström, Y. (1987). *Learning by Expanding*. Helsinki: Orienta-Konsultit.

Engeström, Y. & Engeström, R. (1989). Constructing the object in the work activity of primary care physicians. Unpublished manuscript.

Engeström, Y., Engeström, R., & Saarelma, O. (1988). Computerized Medical Records, Production Pressure and Compartmentalization in the Work Activity of Health Center Physicians. In *Proceedings of Conference on CSCW, Portland, Oregon, September 1988*, pp. 65–84. New York: ACM.

Greenbaum, J. & Kyng, M. (Eds.). (1991). *Design at Work: Cooperative Design of Computer Systems*. Hillsdale, NJ: Erlbaum.

Grønbæk, K. (1989). Rapid prototyping with fourth generation systems—an empirical study. *Office, Technology and People, 5*(2), 105–125.

Grønbæk, K. (1990). Supporting Active User Involvement in Prototyping. *Scandinavian Journal of Information Systems 2*, 3–24.

Jordan, P. W., Keller, K. S., Tucker, T. W., & Vogel, D. (1989). Software Storming: Combining Rapid Prototyping and Knowledge Engineering. *IEEE Computer 22*(5), 39–48.

Jungk, R. & Müllert, N. (1987). *Future Workshops: How to create desirable futures*. London: Institute for Social Inventions.

Kyng, M. (1989). Designing for a dollar a day. *Office, Technology and People, 4*(2), 157–170.

Mack, R. L., Lewis, C. H., & Carroll, J. M. (1987). Learning to use word processors: Problems and prospects. In R. M. Baecker & W. A. S. Buxton (Eds.), *Readings in Human-Computer Interaction: A Multidisciplinary Approach*. Los Altos, CA: Morgan Kaufmann.

Mogensen, P. (1990). Prototyping? In R. Hellman, M. Ruohonen, & P. Sørgaard (Eds.), *Proceedings of the 13th IRIS conference*, Reports on Computer Science & Mathematics no. 108, pp. 299–312. Åbo/Turkey, Finland: Åbo Akademi University.

Nygaard, K. & Bergo, O. T. (1975). Trade Unions New Users of Research. *Personnel Review, 4*(2).

Suchman, L. & Trigg, R. (1991). Understanding practice: Video as a Medium for Reflection and Design. In J. Greenbaum & M. Kyng (Eds.), *Design at Work: Cooperative Design of Computer Systems*. Hillsdale, NJ: Erlbaum.

Trigg, R. H., Bødker , S., & Grønbæk, K. (1990). A Video-based Analysis of the Cooperative Prototyping Process. In R. Hellman, M. Ruohonen, and P. Sørgaard (Eds.), *Proceedings of the 13th IRIS conference*, Reports on Computer Science & Mathematics no. 108, pp. 453–474. Åbo/Turkey, Finland: Åbo Akademi University.

Vertelney, L. (1989). Using video to prototype user interfaces. *SIGCHI Bulletin, 21*(2), 57–61.

Winograd, T. & Flores, F. (1986). *Understanding computers and cognition: A new foundation for design*. Norwood, NJ: Ablex.

# 7     System disturbances as springboard for development of operators' expertise

*Leena Norros*

## Introduction

Our research studies transitions that occur when new technologies are implemented in industrial work processes. We are particularly interested in analyzing the developmental dynamics of production processes, and are concerned with examining the production process as a "sociotechnical system."

The effect of technology can be seen to be mediated by social activity in two senses. First, any technology is itself socially constructed and therefore only one alternative of several possible ones. Second, the technology takes its concrete shape through use and is therefore influenced by the choices of the users. In this chapter we especially concentrate on the latter aspect of the social mediation of technology; i.e., we examine the role of operators in constructing the sociotechnical system through the use of technology as a tool of activity.

### The dynamics of change in sociotechnical systems

Due to the principal difficulty, even impossibility, of anticipating precisely the functional and economic constraints of a system in its future operation, which is also reflected in internal difficulties in organizing the design process, a system in design deviates from one in operation. The more complex the system is, and the more flexibly it is expected to function in future use, the more difficult it is to predict and specify during design.

As a consequence, there exists a need to develop the design activity (Rouse & Cody 1988; Martin et al., 1990). As the design process has become an object of research, the inadequacy of different formal design models to comprehend the actual design activity has become apparent (Rouse & Cody, 1988; Hyötyläinen et al. 1990). On the basis of discovered problems and unofficial design practices, we can identify a general demand for better interactiveness in design activity in two senses. First, interaction is needed between areas and disclipines of design within the design process itself. Second, enhanced interaction between design and operation is also needed. Aspects of operating the system should be considered more directly during design. Another aspect of this is that design praxis should include institutional structures for better feedback from operative experience and, among other things, direct participation of the users in design. We have used the term "operation-oriented design" (Norros et al., 1989; Hyötyläinen et al., 1990) to signify this type of design activity. During such a design process, a trade-off between functionality and economic criteria takes place and the constraints of the future work processes are defined. Seen from a dynamic point of view, these processes in design activity form the "top-down" effect of the technological change.

However good the design is, unpredictability of the future operational demands of a complex system and direct faults in design create uncertainty in the process. This becomes apparent in different kinds of everyday problems, deviations and disturbances of the planned normal operation. It is the operators who directly face these problems, and as a result of their handling problems they identify features that complete the design. The more complex the system, the more difficult it is to anticipate such problems. At the same time, for safety and economic reasons, it becomes more important to identify them. Thus, operators' handling of difficulties is not restricted to identifying problems that are predictable but also includes that operators define the world of the possible.

In the sociology of work it is widely acknowledged that no production system can work without human intervention. The concept of tacit knowledge has been used to view this activity as some silent maintaining of the status quo (of the production, division of labor, and the users' way of working) (e.g., Kusterer, 1979; Manwaring & Wood, 1985). In contrast, we have interpreted users' intervention as an opportunity for them to complete the design and continue to construct the system. Through handling of problems, a potential for learning is opened up for the user. We have used the term "design-oriented operation" to indicate the developmental potential of the disturbances. Clearly, this activity of the users is the "bottom-up" process in the development of sociotechnical systems.

The intersection of the top-down and bottom-up mechanisms are the *distur-bances* caused by the unanticipated behavior of the system. Disturbances have a double nature. On the one hand, they are *threats* to the proper functioning of the system, and, on the other hand, they include the *possibility to develop* the system. As this possibility must and can be exploited by the users, it is also the opportunity for the users to *construct their expertise*. How this opportunity is realized is the problem of our study. We have tried to tackle it in two empirical studies, one in manufacturing industry and the other in nuclear power production. The first study is used in this chapter to demonstrate our approach.

## Disturbances, disturbance handling, and users' expertise in flexible manufacturing[1]

A case study was carried out on implementation of flexible manufacturing system (FMS) in tooth-gear production in a firm producing diesel engines. The management of the plant had decided to replace the traditional technology and organization of tooth-gear manufacturing by a middle-sized FMS comprised of four robotized NC-cells,[2] a tempering plant, automated storage lift, and central computer for controlling the functioning of the system. The new production was to be organized in the new "skill-based" manner. That is, the six (later seven) users and their foreman were supposed to form a highly and homogenously skilled team with no fixed division of labor. The change in work was expected to be quite dramatic to the users who did not have previous experience of NC-machining. Our problem was to define and analyze the transition space. Our methodological assumptions about the role of disturbances in the dynamics of this transition were developed during the empirical study. In the next section we demonstrate the sequential phases of applying our dynamic model of the transition to new modes of working.

It is a typical system-theoretical idea to study systems' functions from the point of view of their deviations. This approach is well known in the field of industrial safety, where it is applied to controlling occupational accidents (Kjellen, 1987). In their book *Individual Behaviour in the Control of Danger*, Hale and Glendon (1987) refer to a number of accident-sequence models (e.g., MacDonald, 1972 and Kjellen, 1983) based on this concept. These models define different sequential states that a system may take leading to a disturbance. Not only the functions of the technical system but also system operators' activities have been analyzed from this point of view. There are a wide range of models of human-error mechanisms from which taxonomies of errors are derived (Rasmussen, 1982; Reason, 1987).

These models refer to the first aspect of disturbance, i.e., disturbance as a threat to the functionality and safety of the system. The deviation is typically interpreted as a state that is filling out of the set norm, which can be, e.g., the planned functioning of the system. When analyzing disturbances, interest is concentrated on the deviation process itself, e.g., failure causes and mechanisms are studied and disturbance classifications constructed. In this context, user activity is only considered as a possible cause of system failure. On the basis of identification of failure causes, it becomes possible to prevent the threat caused by the deviation. This embodies the idea that this feedback control is realized by design engineers, not users of the system. The disturbance process can be summarized in a simple flow model as depicted in Figure 1.

As a consequence of the assumptions of the model, a general reduction of dis-

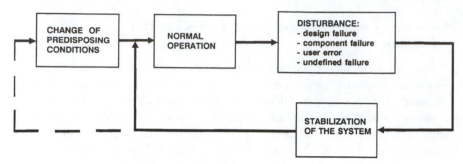

Figure 1. Orthodox model of system disturbances.

turbance rate as a function of time can be predicted. More precisely, a high disturbance rate during implementation, a steady low rate in normal operation due to the feedback control of disturbances, and an acceleration of disturbance due to normal wear during later years of system's operation can be predicted. These assumptions are based mainly on experience of single machines and can be summarized in a broad U-shaped curve called the "bathtub" curve.

## Disturbances of the system

We first examined the disturbances of the new manufacturing system. The implementation of the new system was very long; 26 months from the installation of the first manufacturing cell to three-shift, full-scale production. During this period, different research interventions and a follow-up after one-and-a-half years of normal operation were carried out by the researchers.

Disturbance data was collected during both implementation and operation of the system. Disturbances were registered by the operators themselves for the last 15 months of implementation with the help of log books kept for each cell. This method was not designed to register every single disturbance but, instead, the operators were instructed to notice each novel disturbance as it first occurred. Thus, this data does not give us direct information on the failure rates but it can be used in the analysis of typical disturbance causes.

The functioning of the FMS in normal operation was studied after 18 months of full operation of the whole system. This time a 24-hour intensive follow-up was carried out and the disturbances were registered by the researchers. Both the rate and cause of disturbances can be analyzed from these data.

The rate of disturbances is one indicator of the control of the system. As was mentioned above, the rate is supposed to follow the "bathtub" curve, i.e., after a high disturbance frequency during implementation a stable low-frequency level is expected during normal operation. According to our data, the rate of distur-

Table 1. *Disturbances according to cause in implementation and normal opera-*
*tion. The table includes all the different disturbances that occured during the ob-*
*servation period*

| Cause of disturbance | Observation period | |
|---|---|---|
| | Implementation (15 months) (%) $n = 110$ | Normal operation (24 hours) (%) $n = 36$ |
| Design-based failure | 34 | 42 |
| Component failure | 31 | 25 |
| User error | 20 | 19 |
| External cause | 7 | — |
| Undefined cause | 8 | 14 |
| Total | 100 | 100 |

bances in normal operation was three disturbances per hour. When the duration
of the disturbances is taken into account, it is found that disturbance time accounts for 25% of the total time. Even though data on the failure rates during implementation were not available and, consequently, it is not possible to examine
the development of the disturbance rate as a function of time, this high rate in
normal operation can be considered as counterevidence to the "bathtub" curve
expectations.

Both the disturbances in implementation and in normal operation were classi-
fied according to their cause. A classification commonly used in mechanical and
safety engineering was used. The results are indicated in Table 1. As usual in this
kind of analysis, repeated disturbances are not included in the data.

When comparing the distributions of the disturbance causes in implementation and normal operation, a general consistency in the cause profile can be
found. This result is contrary to the expectations of the orthodox system-disturbance handling model in Figure 1 and the "bathtub" curve in several respects.
First, the persistence and high proportion of design-based disturbances after one-
and-a-half years of normal operation is not in accordance with the common expectations of getting rid of the "childrens' diseases" during implementation of
the system. Second, on the basis of the system-disturbance model and "bathtub"
curve it would be assumed that disturbances of undefined cause were eliminated
by the time of the latter measurement. Third, the proportion of the component
disturbances has slightly decreased, as could be expected, but the general level of
occurrence of these failures violates the expectations.[3]

The above data become more comprehensible if we take into account the unpredictability of complex systems. When analyzing in detail the design-based
failures it was found that only part of the cases could be considered design failures in the strict sense, i.e., that it could have been possible to make a better de-

sign decision. Instead, some of these disturbances were caused not by *deficient* but rather by *limited* design. In other words, unpredictability of some functional requirements and unanticipated interactions of the complex system had made complete design unattainable. The high rate of design-based disturbances would thus indicate that new questions and knowledge of the system had been created during the operation period.

It can also be assumed that unknown interactions in the system and unantici- pated operational constraints cause unexpected component failures. This would explain the observed high rate of these failures, which was said to violate normal expectations (which are based on experience of less-complex, single-machine systems). As these unknown interactions are only gradually revealed through us- ing the system, the occurrence of undefined failures can be expected.

Given that the data support the assumption of the unpredictability of a com- plex system and the existence of disturbances as the more or less "normal" state of the system, it would further imply that there exist pressure on and opportuni- ties for the users to develop the system during operation, i.e., disturbances should also be taken into account as bases for innovation and change. Of course, this hypothesis is in contradiction with the above disturbance model or typical assumptions of work psychology that after implementation (learning phase) the develomental demands of a new system decrease and operators' activity becomes routinized (Tuominen et al., 1989).

### Disturbance handling as operators' activity

It is an obvious conclusion from the above that the actual handling of distur- bances by operators should become the focus of investigation. We shall next de- scribe a study that aimed to do this. It might also be concluded that our data af- ford a simple extension of the orthodox model of system disturbances. However we suggest that such an extension is inadequate the more it is concerned with ac- counting for the elimination of disturbances as a deviation from adequate func- tioning. We will argue that it is necessary to reconceptualize system disturbances as an essential feature rather than merely an eliminable feature of system func- tioning.

The rate of disturbances in normal operation of the FMS was high. In our analysis we found that during the 24 hour observation period each operator in the shift used on average 1.5 hours, i.e., 21% of his working time, for disturbance handling. Considerable differences among individual operators were, however, found. The proportion varied from 0% to 47% of the total working time depend- ing on each shift's interpretation of the official division of labor.

These facts demonstrate, of course, that disturbances threaten the functionality of the system. They also suggest individual differences in reacting toward them. It is now claimed that depending on the users' choices in reacting toward the disturbances, the developmental challenges of the present system can be exploited to greater or lesser extent. In a disturbance situation the system is, in a sense, restored back to its design phase. The problem situation tells the users that design is not yet completed and that something can and must still be done. To catch the decision space and the learning potentials of users' problem-solving activities, we have defined five optional problem orientations (Figure 2) (Norros, 1989) that can act as a heuristic for exploiting the developmental potential of system disturbances.

Two aspects are important in evaluating the optional orientations that operators might adopt when handling a problem or disturbance. First, it should be asked how the problem is defined and its extent within the system, i.e., what is conceived as the object of disturbance-handling activity. The decisive distinction is whether the disturbance is conceived and handled locally as a temporary deviation from the normal situation or globally, including diagnosis of the problem and feedback to the system in the normal situation. Second, it can be asked who actually handles the disturbance and how widely distributed the activity of disturbance handling is, i.e., who is the subject of the disturbance-handling activity. Our model is based on these two criteria.

The optional orientations toward the system disturbances are socially constructed. Adopting an orientation option is a contradictory situation of problem solving and decision making. The contradictions to be coped with are already top-down structured by technoorganizational design, but they are also social contradictions within the management, between it and the shop floor, and within the shop-floor organization itself, as well as psychological contradictions of its individual members. Methods that could be used for analyzing these dynamics are currently being constructed in our further studies. The following example of our data indicates how an operator develops his orientation to a particular problem and how the solution to the problem is gradually found (Toikka et al., 1990, p. 63).

*Phase 1. Routinized problem solving*

At 22:33 one of the two operators notices a disturbance in the machining cell. The robot is placing the work piece inadequately into the mandrel of the machine and the machine stops. The operator removes the slanted work piece, resets the machine manually and updates the status information in the robot control The time used for troubleshooting is 2 minutes. The user remains by the robot for the next operating sequence in order to check if the disturbance should repeat. It does not and the operator can pass on to other tasks.

The disturbance was handled as a simple, fast routine without a diagnosis of its cause. At first, this seems to be sufficient. At 22:51 the disturbance reappears. The above routine is used to tackle it. This is repeated again at 22:52, 23:07 and 23:18.

*Phase 2. First diagnosis: Deficient sensor element*

At 23:36 the disturbance occurs for the sixth time. The operators are loading work pieces on pallets and they both go immediately to the place of disturbance. Meanwhile, as they routinely eliminate the disturbance, they also discuss its cause and optional methods of tackling it. Thus, a first diagnosis is formulated.

Having finished loading the pallet at 23:59 the first operator starts to work on the disturbance according to the first diagnosis. He adjusts a particular sensor element that is supposed to be dislocated and to have caused the trouble. This seems to help but then the disturbance occurs again at 00:30.

*Phase 3. Second diagnosis: Fault in robot control*

As a reaction to the last disturbance, a new diagnosis is formulated and a new procedure to tackle the problem started. This time the operator makes small adjustments to the robot program to change the robot trajectory. This is carried out in several phases interlaced with other tasks.

At 01:10 the above changes in the trajectory lead to a new disturbance, i.e., the work piece slips out from the robot grip. Further adjusments in the program are made and the disturbance is eliminated.

*Phase 4. Third diagnosis: Fault in the mandrel*

The operator starts to investigate more thoroughly how the work piece is placed into the mandrel. He makes manual transportations of the work piece and notices that it has a tendency to become stuck in the mandrel from its lower part. He then assumes that there is a burr in the mandrel that prevents the work piece from being placed adequately. He grinds it with sandpaper. This seems to help until the disturbances reappears again at 3:30 and 3:38.

*Phase 5. Stabilization of the second diagnosis and final elimination of the disturbance*

The disturbance has appeared 13 times. After carrying out other tasks the operator returns to the robot to make some adjustments into the program. He is now convinced of the adequacy of this diagnosis and spends much more time than earlier to tackle the problem. After 30 minutes of work he believes he has succeeded in the eliminating of the problem. This appears to be the case, since the problem does not reappear during the following 10 hours of observation.

At 04:24 the user had struggled with the problem for almost six hours and used one hour and 23 minutes of his working time.

With the help of the above example we can now define some features of the five optional orientations in our model.

## 1. Withdrawal from disturbance handling

This option refers to the possibility that an operator does not handle the disturbance when it occurs. The basis of this orientation is thought to lie in acquisition of a deterministic representation of the system through direct tacit learning of normal operation routines. Restricting activity to mere normal execution of routines is a rather extreme orientation. It might express workers' attempts to achieve short-term efficiency in work, or it might also be an indication of workers' active resistance. Besides being a possible individual choice, this orientation can also be due to Tayloristic organizational principles. The extreme cases of this orientation are to be found in rationalized industrial mass production, but it also occurs in process industries where unqualified operators may be used to carry

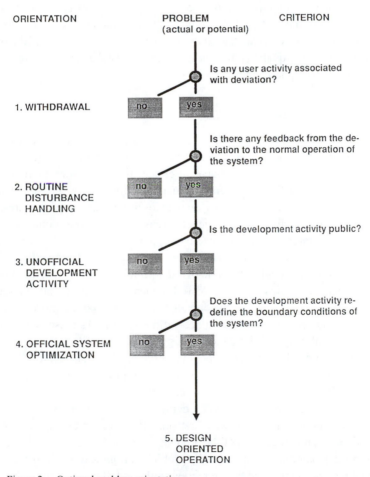

Figure 2. Optional problem orientations.

out routine operations and monitoring, specialized trouble shooters taking care of any exceptional situations.

The top-down limits of the withdrawal orientation are met when the restricted capability and motivation of the operators get economic weight that is big enough. The bottom-up need to overcome the withdrawal from disturbance handling is a result of the meaninglessness of this orientation from the users' standpoint. This is a case wherein the personal costs of this type of activity (i.e., monotony and frustration of underutilization, stress caused by the contradiction of responsibility for expensive technology, feeling of inability to adequately respond to unexpected situations) exceed the benefits.

In our case study, this type of problem orientation was principally ruled out by management through its choice of a flexible organizational strategy that emphasizes homogeneous and high expertise. However, we did observe withdrawal during the implementation period. As production pressures increased during the implementation of the system, the training rotation, which was designed to produce the homogeneous expertise, had to be stopped. As a result some of the operators did not acquire the qualifications to intervene in disturbance situations. Training rotation was continued later.

## 2. Routinized disturbance handling

Normal work of the user is interpreted as carrying out prescribed tasks. Part of this is handling disturbances in a routinized way without making an attempt to analyze the causes of the disturbance or change the system or situation.

The user is identifying problems and carrying out trouble-shooting, reacting to some familiar disturbances one by one, according to known procedures, and locally, without searching for any general reason or systemic connection behind them. The operators possess a sense-based, partial, and algorithmic model of the system. As these models are formed through repetition of procedures in repeating situations, they tend to become overdeterministic and are prone to be biased by judgment heuristics (Tversky & Kahneman, 1982). Restrictions and inadequacies of the model prevent the operators from anticipating more complex and latent interactions and possible failures of the system. As these were said to become essential in system-based technology, thus also in FMS, the type-2 orientation is expected to be the inadequate minimum level orientation in FMS. In more complex automated processes, as in chemical or power plants, the limitations of type-2 orientation are even more severe.

Some of these dynamics could be demonstrated in the above example of our data. The routine orientation was first prevailing in our example. However, as was demonstrated, repetition of the problem increased pressure to change the orientation. The attempt to diagnose the problem, an indicator of a more advanced orientation, was facilitated by interaction with the fellow operator.

## 3. *Unofficial development activity*

The transition to more developed management of disturbances takes place when this reactive disturbance orientation loses its meaning for the user and anticipation of disturbances and activities to change the system replace them. This is the case when the routine becomes too arduous (takes too much time, gets too dull) or challenges his safety, and the user invents a better way to solve the problem by making improvements in the system. The users are privately taking the authority to define their tasks or make a change in the system aiming at making their jobs smoother. Such an activity prerequires relational models of the system for systematic collection of experiences in order to consider the competing functional goals of the system. Activity is still in most cases triggered by repeated problems or in some cases acute demands of the situation.

In transition from the routinized disturbance handling to this level of orientation, the operator is making a diagnosis of the disturbance. It involves reflecting on and redefining the constraints and possibly the goals of activity in the problem situation. In a way, the user unofficially adopts the authority of the supervisor and even that of the designer. Paradoxically, this secret developmental work is maintaining the traditional division of labor between operation and design by preventing the revealing of the design deficiencies. This also means that the operator takes personal responsibility for the improvements, which in many cases include the risk of making errors. This is why in complex risk processes, the users are advised to rely on the design and operative experience rather than to invent their own improvements. This conflict creates pressure for public and cooperative development activity.

## 4. *Official system optimization*

If the unofficial development efforts do not lead to sufficient improvements in the system, and as, simultaneously, it becomes clear that the user's knowledge is not efficiently exploited, a tendency to officially establish the user participation might appear. At this stage, the design efforts are directed to optimizing the system functions within the given boundary conditions.

From the operators point of view, this orientation requires maintenance of the disturbance as a problem and object of development activity, and explicit knowledge of the system as the condition of its optimization. Learning can remain mainly experiential and on-the-job but some conceptual elements (e.g., adoption of common planning and working routines, independent use of process-oriented quality control systems, use of documentation systems for collecting operation experiences) might be needed. Explicit rules are made for group working and for the relationship between work groups and the rest of the organization. Critical to this is the transition from the traditional resistance of the mass production or craft work culture into participation in official development activities of the organization and cooperation with management.

This kind of orientation has been typically the case in the humanization of work and in the original sociotechnical experiments. The top-down condition of this transition is the orientation of management to allow more autonomy to workers for motivational reasons or for making use of their unofficial skills.

Evaluation of the FMS operators' disturbance orientation was carried out in normal operation with the help of a checklist including the characteristic features of disturbance orientation from the cognitive and cooperative points of view in different sequential phases of disturbance handling. We evaluated those activities that were carried out as a reaction to the above mentioned 36 different disturbances during 24 hours of intensive observation (Table 1). Further information of operators' disturbance orientation was obtained in interviews held two weeks after the intensive observation.

The major criterion used to make a distinction between routinized disturbance handling and higher orientation levels was the existence of a diagnosis and the operator's attempt to have an effect on the functioning of the system or change his own activity. When using this as an indication of the feedback to normal system, we obtained the result that 24 (67%) of the disturbances were handled in a routinized way, whereas in the remaining 12 disturbances (33%) a more advanced orientation was typical. We also found that if a disturbance was a repeating one it was more likely to be handled in a nonroutinized way, as shown in the previous example.

When asked about the decision criteria for starting to construct diagnoses or new disturbance-handling measures, the operators referred to personal aptitudes like studiousness. The significance of the novelty and complexity of a disturbance could not be studied in this context.

As developmental activity had, according to the organizational concept, been accepted as an official task of operators, all those disturbances that exceeded the second type of orientation (12 cases) could principally be considered to be official optimizing measures. On the other hand, a bottom-up criterion for distributed optimizing activity would maintain the disturbance as a problem after the acute disturbance situation is over and discuss it collectively. Initiating further analysis and development measures and creating means and cooperation for solving the problems would signify the fourth option of disturbance orientation. This information was not obtainable from the 36 disturbances due to the cross-sectional nature of the data.

On the basis of the operators' and the system leaders' interviews we were, however, able to collect information on 16 developmental measures that had been initiated by the operators during the one-and-a-half years of normal operation (Table 2). According to the operators' description, it was estimated that 69% of the developmental measures were optimizing activities without direct connec-

Table 2. *Operators' developmental measures according to their cause in implementation and normal operation*

| Cause of the measure | Normal operation (%) $n = 16$ |
|---|---|
| Design-based failure | 31 |
| Component failure | — |
| User error | — |
| Optimization | 69 |
| Total | 100 |

tion to disturbances. The rest of the cases were immediate reactions to the pre-ceeding disturbance.

According to common expectations, it was shown that users participate in system development during implementation. But the data indicates, further, that the acquired developmental orientation was also maintained during normal operation. Moreover, not only disturbances but increasingly also anticipated problems trigger these activities. This tendency is related to the bottom-up pressure to reach the type 5 disturbance orientation, design-oriented operation.

## 5. Design-oriented operation (system development)

In problem-orientation development activity is not limited to optimization of the system functions within the given constraints but instead is directed to redefine the boundary conditions of the system. Operative experiences are systematically collected and fed back into the development of the structure, functional principles, and organization of system. Thus, the users are, for the first time, adopting systematic conceptual-design methods; the design tasks include the socioeconomic and technical basis of the production and new work methods are created to organize the cooperation between designers and users.

As the continuous development of the system through its lifetime becomes an economic and functional necessity (product quality, safety, ecological effects, etc.) the sporadic cooperation between design engineers and users becomes insufficient. The integration of the expertise of these two actor groups has to become institutionalized through top-down decisions to form new organizations and a common system of conceptual tools and working methods must be created. This development includes coping with conflicts of power and social relations as, e.g., Shoshana Zuboff has demonstrated in her case studies (Zuboff, 1988).

Among the developmental measures we were able to register there were two indicating that the operators had unofficially approached the fifth orientation option as they clearly challenged the framework of the given system. These included measures to overcome bottlenecks in the production and development of the control system which were not achievable within the present framework, but still close enough to be within reach if new design decisions were considered. However, our interview data also elaborates power issues related to the users' increased abilities to develop the system. The impression of the users was that their proposals and ideas for the future development of tooth-gear manufacturing were not especially welcomed by management. This attitude of management became even more apparent through direct omission of engineering resources that were needed to carry out the development suggestions. A further phase of the study had been planned to create tools for systematic analysis of operational experience. It was later cancelled by management.

### Developing the disturbance model

The results of the implementation of flexible manufacturing systems seem to support our assumptions about the bottom-up dynamics of sociotechnical systems. One of our starting points was the system-theoretical idea of the role of disturbances in the development of the system. As was indicated earlier, in the orthodox system-disturbance model deviation is, however, interpreted as a threat to the proper functioning of the system and feedback as a possibility of eliminating deviations. Moreover, improvements of the system based on feedback are understood as design activities that represent top-down control of system construction. We insist, however, that the deviations also include another aspect: the developmental possibility, which prerequires inclusion of the users, or an operative view, in the construction process. Only when both top-down and bottom-up processes are included can we conceive of the development of a sociotechnical system. Thus, a redefinition of the initial disturbance model could be proposed by including the activity of the users in the model. This implies that mechanisms mediating between the technical system characteristics or disturbance mechanisms (analyzed by the present disturbance models) and the operators' disturbance-handling activity should be made explicit. We did this in the model depicted in Figure 3.

In the new model, operators' orientation to the disturbances is included as an element in the disturbance sequence. As can be seen from Figure 3, the previous disturbance model covers the case in which an operator adopts routinized disturbance handling and thus leaves the system intact. This is the implicit normal case assumed in disturbance models like the one presented in Figure 1. Figure 3 demonstrates however, that there are both less-developed and more-developed options actually open for the operators.

In particular, we are interested in those options in which an orientation exceeding the routine disturbance handling is included. These orientations are supposed to lead to system development, as indicated in the model, and activity for preventing already identified failures can be carried out.

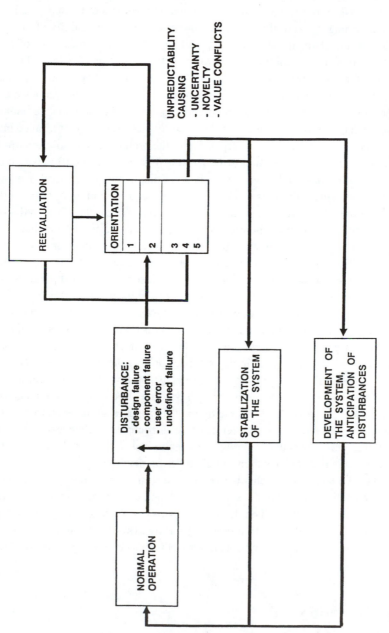

Figure 3.   System disturbances as developmental possibilities. (The numbers in the figure indicates the different orientation options.)

The upper feedback loop in the model is supposed to indicate reorganization of operators' own activity when the demand to deviate from routine disturbance handling is identified. As a result, a reorientation toward the present situation may occur. On the basis of our FMS study the basic man–machine inconsistency causing pressure to disengage from the previous routines is the unpredictablity of the system. This system characteristic can lead to situations that invoke feelings of novelty, uncertainty, or conflicting values among the operators (Schön, 1988). It seems to us that there are two principal ways to release the imbalance of the situation. First, the operators might try to apply procedures that have proved adequate in other problem situations. It may, however, appear that the methods are unoptimal and inadequate for solving the problem completely and the disturbance may reappear repeatedly. Forced by the repetition of the problem a new solution might be developed gradually. The other principal way of solving the conflict is to construct a new solution straight away on the basis of diagnosing the general structure of the problem. This solution is more effective but requires comprehension of the general features of the problem in the particular problem case. This is activity that is often called "judgment" in uncertain situations. It can be assumed that these idealized options to act in a problem situation are more or less intertwined in a real disturbance-handling activity. In our FMS study, indications of this were registered during the intensive observation period. A close study of the operators' activities in a disturbance situation is required to reveal the actual forms of realization of these mechanisms. A study of nuclear power plant disturbance handling was carried out with the aim to solve these problems (Hukki & Norros, 1993).

Moreover, we assume that reevaluation may also effect the "cause" of the failure. Thus, our disturbance data indicated that not only the design-based failures but also the other failure types may require consideration of the constraints and wider interactions of the system in order to become effectively handled, i.e., design activities are demanded to tackle them. Thus, as a result of operators' high-level disturbance orientation, smaller or more restricted disturbances, even early signs of problems may actually "grow" into design-based failures (Figure 3). This is the mechanism through which anticipation of disturbances on the basis of knowledge of disturbance mechanisms and system interactions may be developed. Prevention of disturbances that never occurred, i.e., control of risks and a proper safety culture may be founded on this mechanism (Norros & Reiman, 1994). This requires adequate top-down activities, e.g., training in system dynamics and organizational measures that promote cooperation between design engineers and operators.

### Concluding remarks

We have tried to develop and test our approach to understand the dynamics of production transformations. The basic structural idea of this approach is that there are two intertwined control processes – the top-down activities of the designers and managers and the bottom-up activities of the users of the technology. Further, the concrete mechanism that realizes the interaction between the two developmental processes is the disturbance caused by the unanticipated behavior of the system. In the FMS study, we could demonstrate the persistence of disturbances in a system's normal operation. A plausible explanation for this observation was that unpredictability, as a general system characteristic of FMS, is a source of disturbances through the lifetime of the system. As with disturbances, attempts to fight against them are also continuous. The users of the system play a decisive role in controlling this threat, as was shown in the study. The significance of the users' disturbance-handling activity, not only for maintaining the designed functionality norms, but also for the development of the system, is usually not acknowledged. This means that the bottom-up development mechanism of a man–machine system is either considered self-evident or neglected. Whatever the truth, both attitudes are inadequate. Thus, we have argued that in disturbance handling the operators both open the opportunity to design the system and, in connection with this, to develop their own professional expertise. Five optional orientations towards a disturbance were described. These are supposed to define the extent and strength to which the users are exploiting this demand and possibility. In present industrial work, the transition from a routinized disturbance orientation to a higher one has gained importance and interest. Implications of the orientation-based approach to disturbance handling on the conception of expertise are elaborated in a further paper (Norros, in press).

## Notes

1  This study on implementation of flexible manufacturing was carried out in collaboration with Kari Toikka and Raimo Hyötyläinen of the Technical Research Center of Finland.
2  NC-cells is the industry term for production cells utilizing numerically controlled machines, i.e., machines that are controlled by computer programs.
3  The evident difference in level regarding the number of novel disturbances in the two measurements presented in Table 1 probably reflects the difference in the methods of acquiring the data. We assume that during the long registration period (15 months); the operators heightened the disturbance threshold in implementation. Thus, even though log-book registrations were reviewed and discussed with the researchers every three weeks, many disturbances must have remained unreported. This might be considered an indication of disturbances becoming "normal" and being handled tacitly by the operators. Instead, in the operation phase, during the intensive study of the operators' activity, disturbances were made explicit and registered by an outside observer.

## References

Hale, A. R. & Glendon, A. I. (1987). Individual Behaviour in the control of danger. Amsterdam: Elsevier Science Publishers.
Hukki, K. & Norros, L. (1993, May). Diagnostic judgement in the control of disturbance situations in nuclear power plant operation. *Ergonomics, 36,* (11), 1317–1328.
Hyötyläinen, R., Norros, L. & Toikka K. (1990). Constructing skill-based FMS – A new approach to

design and implementation. 11th IFAC World Congress "Automatic control in service of mankind." Talinn, Estonia August 13–17.

Kjellen, U. (1983). The deviation concept in occupational accident control theory and method. Occupational accident group, Royal Technological University, Stockholm.

Kjellen, U. (1987). Deviations and the feedback control of accidents. In: Rasmussen, J., Duncan, K. & Leplat, J. (Eds.), New technology and human error, pp. 143–156. Chichester: Wiley.

Kusterer, K. C. (1979). Know-how on the job: The important working knowledge of "unskilled" workers. Boulder: Westview Press.

MacDonald, G. L. (1972, March). The involvement of tractor design in accidents. Research reports. Department of Mechanical Engineering, University of Queensland, St Lucia.

Manwaring, T. & Wood, S. (1985). The ghost in the labour process. In: Knights, D., Willmott, H. & Collinson,, D. (Eds.), Job redesign pp. 171–196. Brookfield: Gower.

Martin, T., Kivinen, J., Rijnsdorp, J. E., Rodd, M. G. & Rouse, W. B. (1990). Appropriate automation–integrated technical, human, organizational, economic, and cultural factors. Plenary paper held at the 11th IFAC World Congress "Automatic Control in Service of Mankind." Talinn, Estonia August 13–17, 47–65.

Norros, L. (1989). Responsibility for system development as an element of process operators' professional expertise. Second european meeting of cognitive science approaches to process control. October 24–27, Siena, Italy, 11–28.

Norros, L. (in press). An orientation-based approach to expertise. In: Hoc, J-M, Cacciabue, P. C. & Hollnagel, E. (Eds.), Expertise and technology: Cognition and human-computer cooperation. Hillsdale, NJ: Erlbaum.

Norros, L., Toikka, K. and Hyötyläinen, R. (1989). Constructing skill based FMS – Lessons for design and implementation. IFAC/IFIP/IMACS symposium on skill based automated production. November 15–17, Vienna, Austria.

Norros, L. & Reiman, L. (1994). Organizational assessment of maintenance department at a nuclear power plant. In: Apostiolakis, G. E. & Wu, J. S. (Eds.), Proceedings of the PSAM II, March 20–24, 107:7–12. San Diego CA.

Rasmussen, J. (1982). Human errors. A taxonomy for describing human malfunctions in industrial installations. *Journal of Occupational Accidents, 4,* 311–333.

Reason, J. (1987). A framework for classifying errors. In: Rasmussen, J., Duncan, K. & Leplat, J. (Eds.), New technology and human error, pp. 5–14. Chichester: Wiley.

Rouse, W. B. & Cody, W. (1988). On the design of man machine-systems: Principles, practices and prospects. *Automatica, 24,* (2), 227–238.

Schön, D. A. (1988). Educating the reflective practitioner. San Fransisco: Jossey-Bass.

Toikka, K. Norros, L., Hyötyläinen, R. & Kuivanen, R. (1990). Control of disturbances in flexible manufacturing. Tampere, Technical Research Centre of Finland and The Finnish Work Environment Fund (in Finnish).

Tuominen, E., Seppälä, H. & Koskinen, P. (1989). The impact of technological change on qualification and control. IFAC/IFIP/IMACS Symposium on Skill Based Automated Production. November 15–17. Vienna, Austria.

Tversky, A. & Kahneman, D. (1982). Judgement under uncertainty: Heuristics and biases. In: Kahneman, D. Slovic, P. & Tversky, A. (Eds.), Judgement under uncertainty: Heuristics and biases. New York: Cambridge Press.

Zuboff, S. 1988. In the age of the smart machine. The future of work and power. Oxford: Heineman.

# 8 Expert and novice differences in cognition and activity: A practical work activity

*Edith A. Laufer and Joseph Glick*

## Introduction

> All work activities involve complex forms of practical and creative thinking. Whether that work is work of filling milk cases or writing computer programs. In my view, all work has some intellectual aspect to it. (Scribner, 1990)

Prevailing theories of expertise and the classic model of the difference between expert and novice are predicated on a logical/rationalist model of thinking. Although at present there is no single definition of expertise based on this classic model, "expert" and "novice" are assumed to be fixed psychological categories defined by some "cognitive ideal." The theory of expertise has been developed primarily in the context of intellectual tasks, wherein specific standards have to be met, e.g., chess (Chase & Simon, 1973), physics problems (Larkin et al., 1980), and medical diagnosis (Patel & Groen, 1986), and recently summarized by Ericsson and Charness (1994). The focus of this research has generally been on problem solving in "well structured" problem domains that lend themselves readily to problem descriptions and identification of linkages between problem representations and linear solution strategies. But does this logical/rationalist model of thinking apply to the more mundane tasks that people face in their everyday life and work? What constitutes problem solving in real-world activities?

The research described in this chapter seeks to address these questions and explore the application of activity theory to the investigation of expert/novice differences in an everyday work task. By employing an activity approach, the choice of what is acceptable as data, data collection methods, and data interpretation differs here from other studies in the field. An activity approach allows for an examination of work practices, as performed by people within natural settings. Categorical distinctions between expert and novice appear naturally from the analysis of the work activity. This shift in perspective, as this analysis will demonstrate, allows aspects of the work activity to be revealed that may not be visible when interpreted as problem-solving from a logical/rationalist model of thinking. With an activity model, there is no one "ideal" way of problem solving. It is the "individual" located in concrete activity and embedded within a social and cultural milieu who functions as the ideal.

*Logical/rationalist model of thinking*

Expert and novice performances differ in some meaningful ways (Glaser, 1986). For instance, in comparing solution strategies of experts and novices, researchers have found that experts differ from novices in the quality of their problem representation (Chi, Glaser, & Reese, 1982; Chi, Feltovich, & Glaser, 1981; Larkin et al., 1980; Simon & Simon, 1978). Experts use information in the problem statement to develop a more complete and cohesive representation of the problem than do novices (Simon & Simon, 1978; Chi et al., 1982). Experts perceive the "deep structure," whereas novices perceive the "surface structure" of a problem. The representations, which are cognitive structures, guide actions.

Perhaps the most significant difference between novice and expert problem solvers is the sequence of steps that are employed to obtain a solution. Experts use information in a problem statement to work forward through a problem in a systematic unidirectional way. Novices, in contrast, adopt a working backward approach. Their solution pattern begins with the goal and works backwards toward the beginning with repeated checking and retracing of steps (Simon & Simon, 1978; Larkin et al., 1980).

Although problem solving theories have contributed significantly to the understanding of expert/novice differences, the main focus has been on a cognitive model of excellence in the world. These theories do not address the issue of how and where knowledge is acquired. More importantly, they fail to address the significance of social and motivational aspects of problem structuring. Because of this, extensions of the logical/rationalist model of thinking to the study of everyday activity in natural or work settings have been particularly problematic (Lave, 1988).

*Activity approach to work*

In contrast to a classic model of analysis, which looks at levels of functioning with respect to well-defined domains, activity theory looks first to the structure of activity within an activity domain. This may include the rationalities that apply in the classic model, but may also include elements of personal sense in relation to organizational meaning that may produce performance domains with different properties.

There are a growing number of studies that employed an activity approach to examine work activity. There have been investigations of work tasks or goal-directed actions such as bartending (Beach, 1985), house-cleaning (Engestrom & Engestrom, 1985), dairy-product assembly (Scribner, 1984a,b), and more recently, navigation (Hutchins, 1994) and blacksmithing (Keller & Keller, 1994). Scribner's (1984b) investigation of a product assembly problem-solving task performed by novice and expert dairy-plant workers is an important departure from the longstanding logical/rationalist tradition of research on work skills and problem solving. Scribner designed a model of practical thinking based on problem solving and found that the performance of experts was characterized by flexibility. According to Scribner, "modes of solutions changed with experience" and knowledge. Dairy loaders began their jobs by using literal solutions for dairy orders. With experience, these solution procedures were transformed into nonliteral solutions. Thus, experts "freed themselves from rules, and invented flexible solution strategies" (Scribner, 1983, p. 22). Most important, the novice/expert shift went from the mastery of the general to the concrete.

As far-reaching as this approach has been, it nonetheless does not take into account a fundamental aspect of work activity—that activities are done for some purpose, and that the purpose is not always clear from the formal specification of the activity in "job description" terms.

Consider, for example, a seminal study by Lewin and Rupp (1928). These researchers viewed the machine, the worker, and their specific interaction as a dynamic unit in the course of a concrete work activity within a natural setting. Lewin and Rupp investigated the real-time interplay of textile workers using spinning machines and concluded that novices made poor use of the machines because they lacked the proper organization of actions. Expert workers, on the other hand, organized their actions so that they had "more free time for relaxed preparation and because of their good performance and the good work situation they did not have to exert themselves as much" (p. 13). Interestingly, Lewin and Rupp also examined how the worker's "personal goals" had an effect on their work actions:

> She (the expert) does not approach the machine as a neutral observer (like the novice), but with certain goals which she wants to achieve, namely to achieve as much work as possible and earn a lot of money. Thus, the significance of the individual objects and events on the machine is essentially determined by the events which affect the increase or limitations of earning, i.e., the continuation or standstill of the work activity. (p. 15)

Summarizing what seem to be the most interesting findings of the Lewin and Rupp study, it is apparent that there are two sets of differences between experts and novices. On the one hand, the expert is indeed more expert in knowledge-organization terms. But equally important, on the other hand, is the fact that experts and novices differ in the "what for" the knowledge is about. It is perhaps this latter issue that may be the more important issue to come to grips with.

The present research also represents a departure from the classical–rationalist model of research in employing the activity–action–operation scheme (see Wertsch, 1981). As a way of looking "up," to the relation of the molecular to the molar, it shifts the unit of analysis to include motivation and social interaction as objects of analysis. This research considers the work activities of employees not only in real work settings – their jobs – but also includes aspects of those settings that can be neglected in "expertise-oriented" studies, e.g., how they interact with others and with artifacts in achieving their expertise.

We conclude that traditional methods and explanations, stressing some standard or cognitive ideal, lose much of their predictive power when applied to the knowledge domain of telephone sales work once one includes within the analytic view some representation of motives, quasimotives, and other aspects of an individual that are traditionally neglected.

### Research aims

In employing the activity approach as a theory and as a methodology, our aims were to consider the implications of this framework for (a) examining work activities in their natural settings and, (b) in examining the nature of the novice/expert shift in a work activity including both the structure of knowledge and motivation.

### Activity and its setting

The sites chosen for this study consisted of five small-to-medium-sized industrial precision-parts distributor companies. Such a setting is an environment well-suited for carrying out an investigation of practical work activity (Scribner, 1986). The office component of these work sites and the task of telephone sales was the focal point of this investigation. The prototypic office environment shown in Fig. 1 illustrates the layout of a telephone sales office. Represented in this diagram are areas coded for "function" and "possible function" in supporting this activity. However, a setting and a diagram do not in themselves talk to the structure of activities that may occur within the settings. That requires a detailed functional analysis of how jobs are done.

### Method

A four-phase multimethod approach was employed (see Scribner, 1984b, 1986). The first phase involved obtaining ethnographic information through interviews and observations of all office workers and upper and middle management. The second phase consisted of a quasinaturalistic task designed to model the work activity. Customer orders, based on ethnographic analysis, were carefully selected to reveal important aspects of functioning and were placed by the experi-

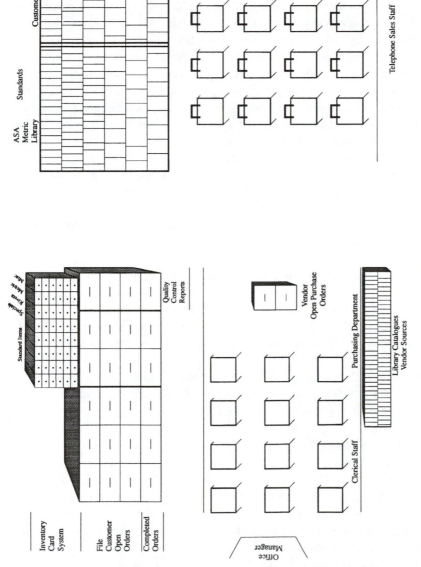

Figure 1. Prototypic office layout.

menter. The third phase consisted of an experimental task to more formally examine how workers organize their knowledge of precision parts (see Laufer, 1990a, 1990b). A final phase consisted of one-hour posttest interviews.

## Ethnographic information

The first phase of this research consisted of informal naturalistic observations of ongoing activity, taped interviews, and weekly "bull sessions" with employees. These provided the information for the descriptive data. According to Leontiev's activity theory (1981b), this is the first level of analysis involved with the "activity" of work embedded in a sociocultural environment. Observations revealed that few workers, whether file clerks or top management, sat at their desks for any length of time. The office was a center of constant interaction – workers with other workers, or with inventory files, order files, prints, and catalogs. This suggests that there is a relationship between internal and external uses of knowledge and that social interaction may be an important factor for this work activity. More importantly, social, cultural, and material interaction seem to occur within a background of a changing collective industry-specific knowledge. New and improved products, materials, and production methods are always developing in this industry. Individual corporate organizations, such as the sites examined here, are continually discovering new suppliers, different overseas markets, and cheaper sources. This knowledge is often specific and private to each company.

*Telephone selling.* The position of telephone sales has no formal requirements and learning takes place primarily in the context of the worker's daily activity. Management hesitated to disclose what specific qualifications they looked for when hiring telephone sales clerks: "I look for a person with telemarketing experience and telephone personality. The rest is knowledge, stuff you learn here."

Telephone selling involves: (a) obtaining orders from buyers, (b) checking inventory to fill these orders, (c) buying products from other manufacturing sources if not found in stock, and (d) pricing items.

*Filling product orders.* Taking and filling orders for precision parts ideally requires a sales clerk to question customers carefully and obtain a record of all the information needed. Each promise to a customer is based on a combination of factors such as product availability from suppliers, time required to manufacture the item, plating, secondary processes, etc. Bills of materials are broken down into types of items and either drawn from inventory or ordered from suppliers. This is a formal item-oriented description. The actual working environment of these companies is much more complicated, as will be shown.

*Participants*

Participants in this study included management and telephone sales clerks. Telephone sales clerks were selected and ranked according to their proficiency in two areas: sales volume and dollar earnings. These were then correlated to the number of years of experience. On that basis, and to prevent overlap, 24 sales clerks were selected who fell into two groups, 12 novices having less than three years of experience and 12 experts having more than seven years of experience.

*Order processing: A quasinaturalistic task*

The measures employed in this task were designed with the direct help of management and telephone sales clerks in the companies studied. Although no other literature is available for the task devised here, measures were constructed so as to closely reflect company norms within the industry. There are no official training programs in this industry and learning takes place informally. The example task consisted of two parts.

First the investigator acted as customer and asked the major participants what information they needed to fill a hypothetical order based on an actual work order. All participants were asked to "think aloud" and explain each step of the process. They were permitted to ask the advice of other employees or managers, use the inventory, reference material, catalogs, calculators, and pencil and paper. In contrast to traditional methods, participants here were free to perform the same task in a host of different ways. All verbalizations were recorded using an audio cassette recorder and later transcribed for analysis. The investigator noted every action, i.e., going to the inventory, looking up a file, etc. These observations were inserted into the protocol data.

The order consisted of five special precision parts, carefully chosen with the help of two expert sales clerks and representing four major categories and different levels of difficulty in respect to specification. An adequate description of these special items demands very specific information. This enabled participants to ask a wide range of questions and display their knowledge and know-how.

To meet the prevailing corporate standards consistent with the requirements of the nationally recognized American Society of Mechanical Engineers (ASME), a participant ideally had to ask 65 customer questions to fully specify all five items. Standard parts can be mass-produced and prices are listed in catalogs. Nonstandard unlisted or special parts are made of bar stock, require special tooling, and are more costly and "cost-blind" items. From a logical/rationalist model perspective, experts should ask nearly all questions, and novices may only be able to ask a few questions. Fig. 2 lists the official or ideal prescribed information needed to fully specify the first item.

A coding system was devised in order to examine every step of the problem-solving process relating to filling the hypothetical order. A "step" was defined as

---

**8/32 × 2 Pan head captive m/s, steel[a]**

*Attributes*

1. head diameter: .3125 ± .005 = .3175–.3075
2. head height: 0.95 ± .005
3. slotted or Phillips drive: slotted
4. slot width: .062 ± .003
5. slot depth: .062 ± .003
6. diameter of captive section: .130 ± .002
7. length of captive section: ½" ± .005 length
8. length of threaded section: 1½" ± .005
9. thread series and fit: class 3 fit (class 2A std.)
10. type of point: cone point
11. angle 60 degrees: ± 1 degree
12. material: special type 1018 steel
13. plating—zinc .002

*Tolerances[b]*

K 14. length of captive section: ± .005
K 15. diam. of captive section: ± .002

*Note.* Off spec. – Receive off spec. permission but not in keeping with 0 defect concept.

[a]Cannot manufacture or modify from standard – unless customer accepts diameter approved by quality control engineer.
  1. Class 3 is special fit (class 2A is standard fit)
  2. Head diameter is special
[b]Tolerance is defined as the total permissible variation of a size; the tolerance is the difference between the limits of size.

---

**Figure 2**. Official attribute knowledge required for salesworker to fill an order on the first product item

a means, either a self-generated (s.g.) question or one involving external means, directly related to some physical aspect of the item in question, leading to price initiation by either the participant or the investigator. Actual price computations were not counted as steps. Each item had a specific number of dimensions. Some of these were standard dimensions and others were special. In order to understand which dimensions were standard and which dimensions were special, a participant had to ideally ask "all" the questions to fully specify the item.

The questions regarding each of the five items in the verbal protocols were coded by assigning sequentially each "means" of obtaining the required information about the item with a number, starting with number one. For example if a participant's first question was: "What is the diameter of the part?" this question was assigned number 1 and was the first means of asking the customer information without external aids. If, thereafter, the participant decided to look up a dimension in a catalog, this action was then assigned number 2 and counted as a step using external means to obtain information, etc. Thus, each step was assigned a number for: (a) a verbalization via a question stemming from the knowledge the participant had; (b) an external behavioral act involving external resources, e.g., going to the inventory file or checking catalogs; and (c) a communicative act such as asking the help of another person. The participant received a score reflecting how many of these steps s(he) used. The purpose of numbering the steps was to determine how knowledge is organized in the ongoing process of filling this simulated order.

In the second part, participants were asked to "guesstimate" price for the first item, thinking aloud and explaining how they arrive at their answers. Guesstimating price on the other four items depended on whether the customer (investigator), or the sales clerk participant initiated pricing.

## Results

*Question-asking and analysis of steps*

Sixty-three percent of the first three steps taken by the novice group, for all items, were external steps and of those 25% involved other workers. This suggests that from the very beginning of the problem-solving process novices needed external resources and the help of other people. In marked contrast, experts took 10% external steps using the material objects of the office.

As expected, generally, experts also performed significantly better than novices by asking more customer questions than novices. Novices also required significantly more external aids, such as asking another person and checking inventory or catalogs to generate their questions. Intriguing, however, was the fact that experts, generally, asked less than half the number of required customer questions.

*Trigger questions*

In keeping with the multimethod approach, further observation and interviews at the work sites shed light on the less than optimal performance of the experts. In these interviews, it was suggested that experts often asked questions that are particularly pertinent to issues of pricing – "trigger" questions. Trigger or price-sensitive questions focus on dimensions that are responsible for the cost of production. Experts bypassed many required questions because they concentrated on those dimensions that were highly price sensitive. Novices, in contrast, thought that they had to know all the dimensions in order to price the items. These findings suggest that novices performed closer to a linear logical/rationalist model of thinking when asking customer questions.

*Questions and goals*

Viewed from the perspective of the activity model, when experts asked trigger questions, they were placing upon the question-asking task another system that had more to do with price than with the concrete dimensions of the items. By asking themselves: "What dimensions do I need to know to determine how much this item will cost me?" the expert changed the goal of the action, no longer observed the single realm of the officially prescribed company norms, but focused on the multidimensional unwritten rules of the company.

In this case, the goal for expert was different from that of the novice, which suggests that experts and novices may have been performing different tasks. It suggests, furthermore, that the design of the task may have truncated the need for further information before arriving at a price. Interview data showed that in their daily work activity these sales clerks often ask customer questions after pricing and obtaining the order.

These results indicate that experts may have had many avenues available to them in acquiring and filling an order, allowing them to risk guesstimating prices without obtaining all the standard information. More important, it suggests that experts may often be employing a way of "working backwards" by seeking to price first and then obtain answers to questions pertaining to the item's dimension.

*Pricing, guesstimating price, and working backwards*

Additional support for the conclusion that experts could employ ways of working backwards, whereas novices were only able to work forwards, came from the pricing part of the task and interviews. Novices were significantly less likely to initiate guesstimating prices than experts. This suggests that novices either perceived the question-asking and pricing-task phases as two tasks or that they were reluctant to guesstimate due to their limited knowledge. Experts on the other hand, by initiating pricing, perceived the question-asking and pricing phases as one task. Pricing, for them, as previously noted, was not as dependent on the physical dimension of the items as on other factors. One expert stated: "I work backwards and don't need to ask questions."

Eight experts actually confided that they worked backwards in pricing most items, particularly special items not listed in catalogs. Working backwards took various forms. One form of working backwards was asking a few trigger questions and then guesstimating price. Another form of working backwards meant first quoting a price to the customer then, if the customer objects, negotiating the price downward, or if the profit margin is not sufficient for the company, renegotiating the price downward with the supplier. An expert described the process as follows: "I guesstimate and get the order. If it isn't right then I will make it right by working backwards and negotiating with the supplier or customer for a better price." Another expert joked:

> If I guesstimate wrong, I bullshit. I don't just want go back to the customer and say: "I made a big mistake – I didn't know the damn things were so expensive." That makes me look incapable of doing the work I am supposed to do. So you go back and say: "There's a shortage of this type of material, right now – they are not going to have the material for another eight weeks. If you want it in four weeks you have to pay a premium price to get the stuff sooner," or "This is not a common, standard, off-the-shelf-type item. I presumed that it was. There are certain tolerances and certain dimensions that are not standard, which changes the price."

When asked why none of the novices discussed price in this way the expert responded:

> I negotiated with the supplier really to cover my mistake in judging the right price. The novice would not think this way. The novice does not know that he can negotiate with suppliers. He hasn't been exposed sufficiently to buying and selling and wheeling and dealing. He knows only that if something costs $1.00 he must get $1.50–$1.60. I can approximate price based on my past experience with similar items and knowing the type of customer and who my vendors are. Novices are afraid to take a chance.

Guesstimating price by knowing your customers and vendors represents another form of working backwards. When asked if novices are taught "wheeling and dealing" or the standard methods of pricing, the expert replied: "First you must know the standard procedures and have the technical knowledge. Once you have that in place, you can deviate from that system. First you have to know the standard way to deviate from it."

This suggests that with the acquisition of technical knowledge, novice sales workers become free to develop and exercise "business acumen," i.e., feel more comfortable negotiating with customers and suppliers.

### Knowledge and outside information in pricing

On closer analysis of the protocols, there was a significant difference on how much outside information experts and novices needed to avail themselves of to guesstimate a price. Table 1 allows us to compare the two groups with respect to the following three categories. First, participants who used exclusively "outside information" – defined as any information obtained from files, books, and catalogs in the office or from vendors and people working within the company. Second, participants who employed "part outside information/part personal knowledge." These participants, for example, were able in part to guesstimate price but required some outside information such as the cost of plating to calculate the final price. Finally, participants who completely guesstimated the price of the item and came under the category of "internal knowledge."

Table 1. Internal knowledge and outside information in the total number of price guesstimations*

| Information | Novice | Expert |
|---|---|---|
| Outside information only | 36 (85%) | 3 (5%) |
| Part outside information, part internal knowledge | 2 (5%) | 20 (36%) |
| Internal knowledge | 4 (10%) | 33 (59%) |

*Instances of arriving at one or more prices: novice, $n = 42$; expert, $n = 56$.

According to Zinchenko and Gordon (1981):

> . . . the initial and fundamental form of human activity is external practical activity. The internal plane of activity, inner mental operations and actions, is formed in the process of internalization. Internalization is the "transition" in which external processes with external, material objects are transformed into processes that take place at the mental level, the level of consciousness. During this transition these processes undergo specific changes – they become generalized, verbalized, abbreviated; and most importantly, they become the means for further development that transcends what is possible with external activity. (p. 74)

Table 1 shows that experts use a predominance of internal knowledge and novices use predominantly external information. This suggests that experts and novices employ different but functional equivalent means to reach a goal. These findings are especially interesting if viewed from an activity perspective because the course of transition from external to internal is made so visible.

There was also a significant difference between the two groups on how many participants priced, the price quoted, and the number of prices they gave for each of the five experimental items. Experts more often gave a price than did novices. More importantly, experts were flexible and gave several prices based on factors such as availability, type of customer, quantity, etc., whereas novices thought that the task required one right answer. The frequency scores are shown in Table 2.

Novices underpriced most items, either because they thought the items were standard or they were afraid to risk losing the customer. One expert gave the following account of pricing by working backwards:

> I always have a 75% markup. I like to work on a minimum of 50–55%. So I like to use the 20–25% as a "margin of negotiation." Then, if a customer asks me to come down 15–20% in price, I can tactfully come down on my price. I will, however, always say that I will have to call him back. Even though I could give the customer the lower price right away, I don't want to because he may think that I took advantage of him. I call him back after a while and say, for example: "Look, I spoke to the plater, and he can put this in with other items and will give me a lower price, so I think that I can meet your price."

The conclusion that experts have the ability to reason backwards and novices don't represents a major departure from that of current problem-solving research

Table 2. Price calculation of the five items*

|  | Novice | Expert |
|---|---|---|
| No price | 18 | 4 |
| One price | 32 | 24 |
| More than one price | 10 | 32 |

*$n = 60$ instances; 12 participants × 5 items.

in other domains (Simon & Simon, 1978; Larkin et al., 1980). Furthermore, tasks employed in all of the investigations of physics problem solving (e.g., Chi et al., 1981; Larkin et al., 1980), have been problems with one known solution and are usually referred to as well-defined problems. In this study, results suggest that the representation established by the novices was guided by the company norms requiring one price, whereas experts guesstimated prices relating to the one price that they thought would result in an order.

This suggests that order-processing may present well-structured problems for novices but frequently ill-defined problems for experts. According to Reitman (1965) and Simon (1973), writing from an information point of view, ill-structured problems are those that draw highly variable responses and experts can find solutions by reducing them to well-structured problems. In the present study, if considered from an information-processing point of view, the reverse is true. Experts took well-structured problems in terms of formulation and standard prices and transformed them to ill-structured problems. However, from an activity perspective, the issue is more complicated. The experts, in fact, transformed the problem to be solved. Giving the "one right price" did not always constitute a solution for experts.

### An activity approach

The unit of analysis on the level of the whole person engaged in a concrete type of activity or task, i.e., fulfilling a sales order, is the object of this study. This unit on the level of activity was chosen because it allows for an examination of expert/novice differences in the development of structure and content of the activity. The unit of analysis must be relative to the domain and how it is investigated. Selecting the unit of analysis on the level of activity enabled the study of components that possess characteristics of the whole.

*The first level of object activity: Reorganization of goal motives from novice to expert*

Findings culled from observations, interview data, and explanations given by participants suggested that goal motives, which are defined as conscious motives, played a central role in differentiating experts from novices. Although motives cannot be directly observed they can be "derived by analyzing other activity components" (Hakkarainen, 1986, p. 74). According to Leontiev (1979, 1981a), motivation does not spring from inside the person but comes about through and in the course of participating in socially constructed activity. Contrary to traditional theories, this shifts the boundaries from inside the head to the "objects" in the world and defines motives in a more concrete way. For example, interview data showed that the personal goal motive and the company agenda of novices converged on one object, i.e., doing what is best for the company. The object of activity for the novice was primarily to process orders according to company standards. For the novice, personal sense and organizational meaning were one.

Experts were different. The pattern of responses suggests that in the course of working, the work activity of experts changed and became more directed towards often-conflicting objects. This shift of the work activity upward to order-bound skills, i.e., decisions and responsibilities often associated with managerial tasks, reinforced in the expert an unrealistic perception or illusion of achieving an entrepreneurial state which, however, was not borne out by their current pecuniary returns (their paycheck). Comments by expert sales workers reflected this shift. When asked how their goals compare with those of the company, novices typically responded:

> Novice 2
> Company agenda: "I am happy if I get a good account for the company." Personal goal: "Company does well and is happy with me."

> Novice 4
> Company agenda: "Improve service along with improved quality. Satisfy the client." Personal goal: "My goal is the same as that of the company. Satisfying the client gives me personal satisfaction."

> Novice 5
> Company agenda: "Increase sales for the company." Personal goal: "To become more experienced, gain knowledge. Be more comfortable on the phone talking to customers. I get a little nervous and want to overcome that nervousness."

For the expert, the structure of the relationship between company agenda and personal goal is different and often in tension or contradiction.

> Expert 15:
> Company agenda: "I want to be sure I give competitive prices and meet delivery dates." Personal goal: "Make money from commissions. Get out of here. Sometimes I don't know why I'm here. I should be doing this for myself."

> Expert 17:
> Company agenda: "My goals are those of the company but they should also keep my goals in mind." Personal goals: "There is not much further that I can go in the company unless there are drastic changes. If that happens, yes, I can go a

lot further. I don't see a great future here for myself. Sometimes I feel 'boxed in.' My goal other than that is to make money and higher commissions."

Expert 20:
Company agenda: "The goal of my job is to serve my customers in the best possible way that is beneficial to the company." Personal goals: "It is kind of contradictory working for someone else. I try to make the most commission possible."

Expert 23:
Company agenda: "My goal is to ship the item on time, on or before the in-house date and not to antagonize the customer." Personal goals: "It's not just making money. My goal is to become somebody . . . a big business man. Right now I have to survive. I have a family to support and I want a stable company. On the side I own a small part of a real estate company. I want to advance here and make more money. Money always comes first."

As these protocol excerpts illustrate, societal meaning and personal sense became separated for many experts. In other words, experts were often caught in the conflicting demands between personal and company needs, indicating that they had several objects and "simultaneous relations to reality" (Leontiev, 1979, p. 73). This suggests that for experts the activity involved is structured differently from that of the novices by the organization of their motives both on an individual level and as they relate to the societal or company level.

Figure 3 illustrates schematically the relative place of cultural meanings and personal sense of telephone sales activity for the company and for the workers. As shown, there are several ways of viewing the ideology[1] of the workplace. Novices replicated the surface ideology tied to the materials, and adhered strictly to official standards, whereas experts employed a deeper ideology – that of maximizing profits for the company and for themselves (Laufer, 1990a, 1990b). These apparent multiple ideological forms coexisted and sustained the business practice.

First, for the company, telephone sales were based on multiple official and unofficial variables such as availability of the item, the quality and quantity of items required, and negotiation with customers and suppliers. Second, for the novice, telephone sales' goal motive conformed to the official norms of the company, i.e., use a company-established markup in pricing and fully specify the item. Finally, telephone sales for the expert had multiple aspects. Their objectives were grounded in the norms set by the organization (official and unofficial). Overriding and sometimes against this broad-based system of official and unofficial meanings was apposed and opposed another system, a system of individual or personal sense. This personal sense kept developing for the expert and was never quite complete in its formulation. It lived in the "future of possibilities," i.e., to get promoted, start a business, or be more challenged. For these workers, the immediate goals and overall motives became separated. This raises

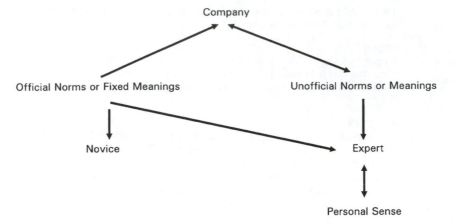

Figure 3. Model of company and novice/expert sociocultural difference in business practice. Official norms or meanings include the stable quality of the organization, i.e., technical knowledge; standard prices with standard markup; and social exchanges shared by
every member of the organization.
  Unofficial meanings include "feeling the customer out," "low-balling," "wheeling and
dealing," etc.
  Personal sense includes what the job means to the worker and the personal goal motives that have developed from their activity, i.e., going into one's own business, getting
promoted, being challenged, etc.

the possibility that the transition from novice to expert leads to the differentiation
of societal meaning from personal sense.

*Transformation from surface to complex multilayered social relations*

All experts agreed that friendship plays an important part in being an expert.
Eight experts felt that even more important was to feel the customer out, listen to
the tone of the voice, and from that gain information on competition and previous costs, etc. This pattern may best be referred to as the "feeling out interaction," defined as sales clerks, customers, and suppliers each feeling the other out
for some privileged information. This suggests another form of working backwards. Here are some examples:

> Expert S: "Anticipating what your customer wants and feeling your way in
>   terms of this back-and-forth of price . . . you know how to price because of
>   your customer's reaction and voice."
> Expert L: "You know right away from the tone of the voice and from the few
>   questions you ask. If someone says: 'Can I please have sales?' It's a quick
>   tone. 'I have to place an order. I need it right now.' That means the customer
>   is very desperate. You can charge a high price."

Here are some examples in response to the question: "What do you consider necessary to be an expert telephone salesperson?"[2]

Novice L: "Be charming and nice to the client. Persuade them to give you an order. Agree with the specifications and delivery time. Talk about other than technical things, e.g., plans for the weekend."

Expert S: "It's being able to size up a situation. It's the art of getting underneath the initial conversation. The art of extracting information and then doing something about it to modify the situation to your advantage as opposed to just going ahead and attacking the task without extracting important information."

Expert R: "90% of this business can be learned the first year. The other 10% takes you the next 20 years."

Some of the themes that emerge from these responses indicate that the major expert/novice difference in the social character of the workers centered around the patterns of their relationships. From their descriptions, novices endeavored primarily to have a monologue-like, superficial, friendly relationship with their customers. Experts' responses, on the other hand, suggest that they had many different levels of simultaneous relations in their work world. For example, they developed more significant social interactions with their customers, and their apparent friendships often functioned also as instruments to get orders and achieve some kind of advantage over their competition. This suggests that experts generally developed deeper, more dialogic and dynamic relationships with their customers and suppliers than did novices. In other words, their relations were finely tuned to particular people and situations. These private relationships often had a sentient component and were not solely bound up with sharing technical information. These interactions are reminiscent of Volosinov's (1973) and Bakhtin's (1986) concern with the social role of verbal utterances and dialogical exchange.

Table 3 shows the three-tiered novice/expert shift suggested by the data. On the general level of work activity, novices were participating in what may be called "clerical sales," which was reflective of the monologue-like quality of their work activity and because the major component of their daily actions was routine and clerical in nature. Experts, on the other hand, participated in work activity that may be called "telephone sales" because their day-to-day actions consisted of dialogue-like telephone communications, i.e., negotiating with customers and suppliers.

## Expert/novice differences on the level of actions and operations

As shown in Table 3, with the movement to more order-bound skills by the expert, there was a simultaneous qualitative shift to the next lower level in the activity structure compared to the novice. For example, findings indicated that when the inner and outer means, i.e., forms of mediation, and their transitions are examined, they demonstrate a novice/expert shift. Novices employed external means, like asking other coworkers to help them define the items, whereas experts transformed the novice's external actions into internal operations, i.e., self-

Table 3. The novice/expert shift from an activity perspective

| Work activity | Novice (clerical sales) | Expert (telephone sales) |
|---|---|---|
| Level 1 | | |
| Practical activity 1 | Order processing | Order getting and pricing |
| Practical activity 2 | Pricing | |
| Object or goal motive(s) | Learn to fill orders | Make money; get promoted; be |
| | Price according to company | challenged; take profitable |
| | standards | orders for the company |
| Level 2 | | |
| Actions—Task 1 | Questions asking actions | Communicative actions; negoti- |
| | | ate with suppliers and customers; |
| | | guesstimate price |
| Actions—Task 2 | Calculate standard markup | |
| | with pencil and paper | |
| Goal 1 | Learn to fully specify items | Price according to each situation; |
| | | get order at highest price without |
| | | losing order or customer |
| Goal 2 | Complete the order by | |
| | quoting one price | |
| Level 3 | | |
| Operations | Write up orders; calculate | Ask s.g. question to specify |
| | price with component costs | item; calculate price without |
| | given by coworkers; clerical | external means |
| | skills | |

generated questions (s.g.). For the novice, the goal was to define the characteristics of the item and this then structured how the item was priced. The goal of the expert, on the other hand, was to guesstimate price; price structured their question-asking. For the expert the question asking was the means (operation) to a goal, not a goal in itself. They superimposed upon the question-asking component of the task an aspect of their business practice as, for example: "How can I out-price a competitor?"

In sum, price was structured by the total business practice. Question asking, social relations, motivation, and goals all contributed. Even meaning and sense condensed into the price, in the case of experts. In general, experts became part of the industrial, corporate culture and reflected that culture. They could afford to take a risk because they had many alternative ways of doing things available to them. Generally, for most novice, the goal was to ask *all* the questions. They could not take risks. Their actions were constrained and limited by their goal.

It was, interestingly, the patterns of the novices' social interactions that were similarly constrained by their singular object and goal, as reflected in their friend-ly but monologue-like surface relationships with customers and suppliers. On the other hand, on the level of actions, the moment-to-moment dialogic interaction with customers and suppliers resonated the experts' multiple objects and goals.

*What is problem solving in telephone sales?*

That experts did not present one right price or solution reflects the multiple so-cial and material connections of their activity in telephone selling. What was the goal motive of their pricing action? The real issue here is what constitutes a prob-lem and a problem-solving situation in contrast to a situation that presents a mul-tiplicity of goals? In the present study, having the goal of giving the one and only right price constitutes a solution for the novice but not always for the expert. The single price is characteristic of the normative standards (that most novices ad-hered to) of the industry and closer to the solutions provided in the more tradi-tional experimental problem-solving tasks defined by the linear logical/rational-ist model of thinking.

For many experts, operating in multiple realities, such as having the customer repeat the order, getting the right price from the supplier, and at the same time making money, etc., represent multiple goals. The fact that experts personally or-dered and edited prices depending upon the type of customer and situation, re-flected aspects of their motivation and values. It is this difference that shaped their business practice and was most indicative of the fact that experts and novices performed different tasks. In other words, the proportion of social and material constituents changed from novice to expert. For the novice, the socio-cultural structure of the office and the people in it provided the major resource for the order-filling activity. For most experts, order getting was a multilevel, multipurpose phenomenon that generated a qualitatively and quantitatively dif-ferent interplay of actions and operations from that of the novice and encom-passed a whole social network of resources beyond the confines of the office set-ting. It had a rationale all its own that could not be understood by solely invoking a linear, logical/rationalist model of thinking. According to Leontiev's principle (1981) and the activity model, it is the need objects (motives) that guide and di-rect activity. As these change, so does the activity and the components in it. As the forms of mediation change, in the course of becoming an expert, there is also a shift in the locus of knowledge and the structure of the activity components.

## Conclusion: Redefining expert and novice as expertness and noviceness

Knowledge of industrial precision parts, although necessary, cannot be employed as the sole measure of expertise. The larger data base liberates the salesperson and facilitates the development of expertise through the acquisition of social and cultural experience effecting an integration and structural reorganization of technical knowledge with social skills.

For example, novices usually start out as clerical workers, bringing with them the knowledge they acquire in school. The more experienced coworkers usually delegate the humdrum rote or routine aspects of telephone sales to these newcomers to get rid of the tedious details of this business. With time and experience, the technical aspects and standard procedures are mastered by the novice workers. Within traditional rationalist theories, these workers are now considered experts. From an activity approach, however, after the technical aspects are in place, the sales worker is then free to integrate all other aspects of the task, such as the more situation-specific realizations of business practice, i.e., bargaining with suppliers, guesstimating prices for customers, working backwards, etc.

Thus, the notion of expert/novice differences is not exhausted by looking solely at qualitative and quantitative differences or the organization of knowledge, customarily associated with a logical/rationalist model of thinking, but focused on the variations in what might be called the use of business acumen, which is a way of reproducing and instantiating the culture and meaning of business.

Therefore, expertness and noviceness cannot be isolated from the individual who is the expert or novice. To be an expert one must participate in a particular work activity and transform it and in the process be transformed oneself. In the present study, the job of telephone sales is different for the expert and novice because the activity is different and the subject (the worker) and object (need object) are different. This represents a major shift from one activity system to another activity system. Theoretically, truly expert workers reproduce the culture or societal meaning in their work activities and then bring to it their own personal sense.

In conclusion, despite the emerging new technologies, such as the integration of computer-aided design and manufacturing resource planning, history allowed a brief moment in time to gather data on this work activity, a last look before many of the old patterns of psychological and social experiences of these workers will be transformed into or inexorably altered by "paperless," "personless" transactions. The kind of knowledge and activity examined here is on the eve of its transformation. With the creation of new job demands, the knowledge organization, personal relations, and negotiations discussed here, will change.

Where will these experts go? Future studies must address what will happen to these experts with their broad and deep complex kind of practical knowledge. What is important in this research is the examination of a rapidly changing particular individual activity within a system of social relations embedded in a particular culture at a particular time in its historical development.

## Acknowledgments

Portions of this chapter were presented at the Second International Congress for Research on Activity Theory, Lahti, Finland, May 21–26, 1990.

I would like to express my deep gratitude to my late mentor and committee chair, Dr. Sylvia Scribner, for her invaluable direction throughout the course of this research and for inspiring me to operationalize the concept of activity.

## Notes

1 The term "ideology" refers to a "level of social meaning with distinct functions, orientation and content for a social class or group" (Hodge & Kress, 1988, p. 3).
2 While descriptions do not include first-hand documentation of customer–sales clerk interactions, participants' accounts present additional evidence for the transformational effect of work experience on these relationships.

## References

Bakhtin, M. M. (1986). *Speech Genres and Other Late Essays.* Austin: University of Texas Press.

Beach, K. (1985). *Learning to become a bartender: The role of external memory cues at work.* Paper presented at Eastern Psychological Association, Boston, MA.

Chase, W. G. & Simon, H. A. (1973). Perception in chess. *Cognitive Psychology, 4,* 55–81.

Chi, H., Feltovich, P. J., & Glaser, R. (1981). Categorization and representation of physics problems by experts and novices. *Cognitive Science, 5,* 121–152.

Chi, M., Glaser, R., & Rees, E. (1982). Expertise in problem solving. In R. Sternberg (Ed.), *Advances in the Psychology of Human Intelligence.* Hillsdale, NJ: Erlbaum.

Engestrom, Y. & Engestrom, R. (1986). Developmental work research: The approach and an application in cleaning work. *Nordisk Pedagogik, 1,* 2–15.

Ericsson, K. & Charness, N. (1994). Expert performance: Its structure and acquisition. *American Psychologist, 49*(8), 725–747.

Glaser, R. (1986). On the nature of expertise. In F. Klix and H. Hagendorf (Eds.), *Human Memory and Cognitive Capabilities.* Amsterdam, Holland: Elsevier.

Hakkarainen, P. (1986). Learning motivation and the theory of activity. In M. Hildebrand-Nilshon & G. Ruckriem (Eds.), *Proceedings of the First International Congress on Activity Theory,* pp. 71–82. Berlin, West: Druck und Verlag System Druck.

Hodge, H. & Kress, G. (1988). *Social Semiotics.* Ithaca, New York: Cornell University Press.

Hutchins, E. (1994). Learning to navigate. In S. Chaiklin & J. Lave (Eds.), *Understanding Practice: Perspectives on Activity and Context.* Cambridge: Cambridge University Press.

Keller, C. & Keller, J. (1994). Thinking and acting in iron. In S. Chaiklin & J. Lave (Eds.), *Understanding Practice: Perspectives on Activity and Context.* Cambridge: Cambridge University Press.

Larkin, J. H., McDermott, J., Simon, D. P., & Simon, H. A. (1980). Models of competence in solving physics problems. *Cognitive Science, 4,* 317–345.

Laufer, E. A. (1990a). *Practical work activity in the industrial fastener industry: A study of expert/novice differences in cognition and activity.* Unpublished dissertation. Cuny, Graduate Center.

Laufer, E. A. (1990b, May). An activity approach to office work in an industrial setting: Expert/novice differences. Paper presented at the First International Congress on Activity Theory, Lahti.

Lave, J. (1988). *Cognition in Practice.* Cambridge: Cambridge University Press.

Leontiev, A. N. (1979). *Activity, consciousness and personality.* Hillsdale, NJ: Erlbaum.

Leontiev, A. N. (1981a). *Problems of the Development of the Mind.* Moscow: Progress Publishers.

Leontiev, A. N. (1981b). The problem of activity in psychology. In J. H. Wertsch (Ed.), *The Concept of Activity in Soviet Psychology.* New York: M. E. Sharpe.

Lewin, K. & Rupp, H. (1928). Untersuchung der Textile Industrie. (Examination of the textile industry.) Psychotechnisches Zeitschrift Heft 2 & 3. (Unpublished translation by E. Laufer.)

Patel, V. L. & Groen, G. J. (1986). Knowledge based solution strategies in medical reasoning. *Cognitive Science, 10,* 91–116.

Reitman, W. (1965). *Cognition and Thought.* New York: Wiley.

Scribner, S. (1983). *Mind in Action: A Functional Approach to Thinking.* Invited lecture, Biennial Meeting, Society for Research in Child Development.

Scribner, S. (1984a). Studying working intelligence. In B. Rogoff & J. Lave (Eds.), *Everyday Cognition: Its Development in Social Context.* Cambridge: Harvard University Press.

Scribner, S. (1984b). Cognitive aspects of work. *Quarterly Newsletter of Laboratory of Comparative Human Cognition.* San Diego: University of California.

Scribner, S. (1986). Thinking in action: Some characteristics of practical thought. In R. J. Sternberg & R. K. Wagner (Eds.), *Practical Intelligence: Nature and Origins of Competence in the Everyday World.* Cambridge: Cambridge University Press.

Scribner, S. (1990, May). *Manufacturing Resource Planning.* Paper presented at the Second International Congress on Activity Theory, Lahti.

Simon, H. A. (1973). The structure of ill-structured problems. *Artificial Intelligence, 4,* 181–201.

Simon, D. P. & Simon, H. A. (1978). Individual differences in solving physics problems. In R. Siegler (Ed.), *Children's Thinking: What Develops?* Hillsdale, NJ: Erlbaum.

Wertsch, J. V. (Ed.) (1981). *The Concept of Activity.* White Plains, NY: M. E. Sharpe.

Volosinov, V. N. (1973). *Marxism and the Philosophy of Language.* Cambridge, MA: Harvard University Press.

Zinchenko, P. I. & Gordon, V. M. (1981). Involuntary memory and goal directed nature of activity. In J. V. Wertsch (Ed.), *The Concept of Activity in Soviet Psychology.* White Plains, NY: M. E. Sharpe.

# 9     The tensions of judging: Handling cases of driving under the influence of alcohol in Finland and California

*Yrjö Engeström*

## Introduction

Expert work has become an object of increasing attention among cognitive scientists (e.g., Chi, Glaser, & Farr, 1988; Ericsson & Smith, 1991). This research tends to view expertise in a social and cultural vacuum. More specifically, the following three dominant underlying ideas may be identified in mainstream cognitive research on expertise (see Engeström, 1989, 1992). First, expertise in a given field is seen as universal and invariant; differences are noticed in the degree of expertise, but differences in content and quality are largely overlooked. Second, expertise is viewed as consisting of individual mastery of discrete tasks and skills; the broader collaborative practice in which individuals are embedded is overlooked. And third, the development of expertise is seen as consisting of gradual accumulation of individual experience under the guidance of established masters; the reconceptualization of existing practice and collective generation of new models is overlooked.

On the other hand, social scientists have identified broad structural forms of the social organization of expertise; professionalism, bureaucracy, and corporatization. These pervasive forms are commonly depicted as structures that leave little room for construction from below. In a way, the lack of social context in cognitive analyses of expertise is complemented by a lack of agency in many social analyses of the organization of expertise.

Attempts to overcome and bridge this dichotomy of individualism and structuralism focus on local socially distributed activities (e.g., Chaiklin & Lave, 1993; Lave, 1988; Middleton & Edwards, 1990). In this chapter, I will present another attempt to transcend the dichotomy. I will focus on the three aspects of expertise usually overlooked in mainstream cognitive research, namely on its multivoiced, collectively embedded, and creative nature. In this endeavor, I will employ conceptual tools from the cultural–historical theory of activity (see Vygotsky, 1978; Leont'ev, 1978; Wertsch, 1981; Engeström, 1987; Hildebrand-Nil-shon & Rückriem, 1989).

I will analyze legal work conducted in municipal courts, taking the work and expertise of the judge as my point of departure. I will use data from two different cultural settings; a municipal court in a mid-sized city in Finland and a municipal court in a large city in southern California. I will restrict my analysis to the handling of cases of driving under the influence of alcohol (DUI). In both cultures, these are considered common, simple, and routine cases.

There is, however, a marked difference in the general attitudes toward drunken driving in these two cultures. In California, drunken driving is defined as a misdemeanor, and in legal practice it is not regarded as a serious offense. As Gusfield (1981, p. 140) observes, "in day-to-day enforcement and adjudication DUIA, is treated *as if,* like other traffic offenses, it is the normal behavior of motorists." In Finland, drunken driving is a crime, quite clearly distinguished from other traffic violations in legal practice. In both cultures, there is political pressure toward introducing tougher laws. (For extended analyses of DUI as a social and criminological phenomenon in the American society see Gusfield, 1981; Jacobs, 1989.)

Courts are intimately connected to our notions of power, Judges are almost emblems of ultimate secular authority. Several authors have studied how professional experts, such as judges, may effectively suppress the concerns and dialects of their lay clients. Such analyses of the asymmetrical power relations between professionals and their clients (e.g., O'Barr, 1982; Harris, 1989) illuminate an important aspect of interaction in courts. However, such analyses do not focus on the work of the experts themselves. Far from being a straightforward exercise of power, the work of judges is internally multifaceted and contradictory. In this chapter, I will focus on the multiple dialects, disturbances, and tensions in the work of judges, interpreting those features as dynamic possibilities of learning, change, and development.

The data for this chapter were collected in 1990. The data from Finland are from a case example taken from a large database consisting of complete sets of official case documents, videotaped court hearings, and audiotaped interviews of the judge and other relevant participants in a number of different criminal and civil cases from two municipal courts located in mid-sized cities. The data from southern California consists of audiotaped court hearings and complementary field notes as well as audiotaped interviews with the judge and a team of public defenders. The case analyzed in this chapter is one chosen from 53 DUI cases, the hearings of which we recorded during one week in the court. In both settings, the research teams spent a considerable amount of time in the field, getting acquainted with the local officials and customs. While the analyses reported in this chapter are limited exploratory case studies, they are also part of ongoing interaction with the courts in question.

**Judges – referees, inquisitors, or more?**

Susan Philips (1990) has recently pointed out that in much of the social-scientific literature on courts, the American trial judge is either invisible or cast in the role of a rather passive referee who assures that procedural law is followed. This corresponds to the notion that there are two basic types of legal procedures: the Anglo-American "adversarial" system and continental European "inquisitorial" system. According to that notion, continental European judges question witnesses from each side of the case and are generally much more active and dominant in the hearing than their American counterparts.

Philips herself challenges such a dichotomy and provides evidence of American trial court judges taking more active and versatile roles than the standard referee notion would predict (Philips, 1990; see also Yngvesson & Mather, 1983). While I endorse this argument, I would like to inquire further into the contents, characteristics, and contextual prerequisites of such versatility in the judge's work.

Hogarth (1971) and others (e.g., Gibson, 1978; McKnight, 1981) have shown that there are important substantive differences in judges' "penal philosophies" and "role orientations" within one and the same culture. On the other hand, Philips (1990, p. 208) observes that "a single third-party intervenor may employ the strategies of more than one [ . . . ] kind of remedy agent, depending on the situation." In other words, one approach (Hogarth and others) has identified a variety of relatively discrete philosophies or viewpoints among judges, while the other approach (Philips) contributes the idea of multiple parallel roles used by one expert. When these ideas are brought together, we get a picture of the judge employing several complementary but possibly also contradictory substantive strategies or orientations in managing the complex trajectory of a court case.

The notion of *voices* (e.g., Silverman & Torode, 1980; Mishler, 1984; Wertsch, 1990) is particularly suited for the analysis of varieties of talk in organizations, reflecting various underlying normative orders and social positions. Conley and O'Barr (1990) have recently used the notion of voices in their analysis of discourse in informal courts. According to them, most voices are eventually silenced in the legal process and "the purported voice of legal authority is in fact the voice of social power" (Conley & O'Barr, 1990, p. 170). Conley and O'Barr found, however, that within the voice of legal authority, judges differ in their orientations. They identified five orientations: (1) the strict adherent to the law, (2) the law maker, (3) the mediator, (4) the authoritative decision maker, and (5) the proceduralist. The orientations manifest themselves in talk. In this chapter, such qualitatively different ways of talking within the voice of legal authority will be called *dialects*.

Conley and O'Barr point out that there is considerable discord in informal courts. They mention several sources of discord, all associated with the litigants' expectations that the court cannot meet. These discordances are described as dissonances between the ideologies of the litigant and the judge. While such dissonances may certainly be seen in the data of Conley and O'Barr, this may be an unnecessarily restricted account of the nature of discord in courts. In most courts there are multiple parties and participants whose complex interactions may give rise to various kinds of communicative glitches, errors, breakdowns, and conflicts. In this chapter, all such deviations from the formally expected smooth script of the court procedure will be called *disturbances.*

Complexity is here the key issue. Heydebrand and Seron (1990; see also Seron, 1990) present a compelling account of the rationalization of American courts in the 20th century as a response to the tension between growing caseloads and shrinking resources. According to Seron, the dominant developmental trend in courts has been "from traditional–professional case processing with the focus on adjudication to technocratic case processing with the focus on administration" (Seron, 1990, p. 462). This has important implications for the judge's work. First, the traditional division between judicial and nonjudicial, professional and clerical labor is giving way to a new, emergent organizational model that relies on teamwork between judge, magistrate, and law clerk. Secondly, judges are increasingly urged and trained to "think of the court as an organizational and coordinated 'system' in which they are encouraged to take a proactive posture toward pretrial and to encourage and raise settlement when appropriate" (Seron, 1990, p. 462).

What kinds of effects will the development described by Heydebrand and Seron have on the nature of the judge's expertise? It may be hypothesized that the more intricate the division of labor in the processing of a court case, the more likely it is that the judge will have to employ and combine various parallel dialects and the greater the likelihood of numerous systemic disturbances requiring repair and proactive measures from the judge. The present study is an inquiry into these two issues.

### The courts as administrative and physical systems

The two municipal courts from which I take my examples were quite different administratively and physically. The following description is necessarily sketchy and greatly simplified.

The court, located in Finland (hereafter referred to as the Finnish court), employed 16 judges. The court was divided into eight departments, of which all but two handled both civil and criminal cases. Different types of cases had different combinations of judicial personnel handling them, all the way up to the "full composition" of three judges. Driving under the influence of alcohol was a routine criminal case, handled in this court by one judge and a clerk, occasionally also by a judge intern (a law school graduate acquiring his or her judge's qualification by serving an internship in a court). Only a year earlier, DUI cases were still handled by the full composition of three judges. After we collected our data, the rationalization proceeded further and all routine criminal cases not requiring the full composition were assigned to one department only.

In simple cases such as DUI, the judge commonly dictated and compiled the court minutes while conducting the hearing; the clerk sometimes kept notes but those were usually only supporting material. The judge used the original police report in which the defendant's story (along with the arresting officer's account) was recorded in a narrative form as a key component of the minutes. The prosecutor's complaint, also in a free narrative form, although more condensed and formal, was another key component of the minutes.

The Finnish court has no jury institution in the American sense. In certain types of cases (not in DUI cases), lay members participate in the hearing, but in practice they have little input in the actual decision-making. Also it is quite common that in simple cases such as DUI, the defendant uses no defense attorney but represents him- or herself. There is a system of municipal public defenders, and the court may grant a free trial to a person with limited financial means. There is no plea bargaining in Finnish courts. The Finnish penal code differentiated between DUI cases involving driving under the influence and those involving severe or gross driving under the influence. The lower limits of punishable blood alcohol level were 0.05 and 0.15%, respectively. The judges used a simple unofficial table to standardize the sentences. According to the table, when the blood alcohol level was between 0.05 and 0.10%, the sentence would be 20 to 30 daily fines and four to seven months suspension of the driver's license. When the blood alcohol level was between 0.10 and 0.149%, the sentence would be 30 to 50 daily fines and five to eight months suspension of the driver's license. The amount of the daily fine was determined progressively, on the basis of the defendant's taxable monthly income. In 1989, the court we studied gave verdicts in 290 cases of driving under the influence and 333 cases of severe driving under the influence. The caseload of the court was not excessive. There was an atmosphere of relative tranquility, tradition, and stability.

The layout of the Finnish courtroom used in the DUI hearing analyzed in this chapter is depicted in Fig. 1. The first noticeable feature in Fig. 1 is that there were only five people in the courtroom. As is usual in these cases, the defendant used no defense attorney. There was no audience. In the back of the room, there were empty seats that could be used by spectators, but in a regular DUI case there are very seldom any. The authority of the court is not very strongly emphasized by the physical setup. Each participant, including the defendant, sits at a desk. The defendant also answers questions sitting down. The judge's bench is somewhat higher and bigger than the other desks and there is a large open Bible on a stand attached to the front of the bench (it is used when witnesses give their oaths; nobody touched it in this hearing). On each desk, there is a fixed micro-

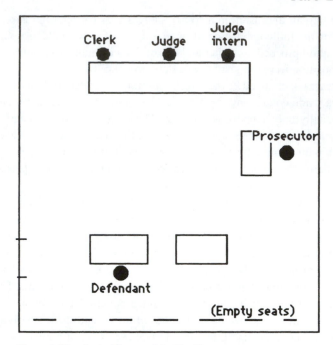

Figure 1. The physical layout of the Finnish courtroom.

phone, for the purpose of taperecording the hearings. The judge wears no special outfit. In this case, the judge was a male, wearing a regular gray suit. The judge intern, also male, wore a sweater and a tie.

The court located in southern California (hereafter referred to as the California court) was a separate part of the municipal court, called Traffic Arraignment Court. It was located in a different part of the city than the main municipal court building. It handled exclusively traffic misdemeanors; felonies were automatically relegated to the next level, called Felony Arraignment Court.

Each of the 26 judges employed by the municipal court had to complete a "tour" fairly early in his or her career as judge. The "tour" consisted of two months in Traffic Arraignments, then two months in Misdemeanor Arraignments, and finally another two months in Felony Arraignments. The same single judge handled all the cases in the given arraignment court during the "tour." This way, the large bulk of routine cases were delegated exclusively to only a few judges at a time, relieving the rest of the judges to work on more demanding criminal and civil cases.

In the Traffic Arraignment Court, four or five main types of cases were handled: reckless driving, speeding, failures to appear, driving on a suspended or revoked license, and driving under the influence. DUI cases were the most serious ones handled in that court. Every weekday, the morning session of the court was dedicated to the less serious cases and the afternoon session mainly to DUI cases. It was common that 20 to 40 DUI cases were heard and decided, or else sent forward to trial setting, during one afternoon session lasting roughly two-and-a-half hours. The task of the arraignment court was to ensure speedy sentencing, given that the majority of the defendants entered a guilty plea. In other words, this court functioned as a filter and buffer, preventing an overflow of cases into full-scale jury trials. Roughly 10% of the DUI defendants pleaded not guilty and were automatically sent to trial setting, but around 90% were actually sentenced in the Traffic Arraignment Court.

The Traffic Arraignment Court did not have a jury; the defendants pleading guilty waived their right to a jury trial. In principle, the judge alone made the decisions. However, the system was dependent on the effective functioning of a plea bargaining machinery. The prosecutors (assistant district attorneys) filled out an offer form for each defendant. The large majority of the defendants were counseled by public defenders in cubicles in the hall outside the courtroom. The defendant and the counseling public defender went through the offer and filled out a plea form in which the defendant pleaded either guilty, not guilty, or no contest (the latter meaning guilty but implying that the plea cannot be used in any future civil trial concerning the same incident). They also went through and signed a form acknowledging the defendant's having been advised of his or her constitutional rights. Some, actually very few, defendants hired a private lawyer to represent them. Some, even fewer, chose to represent themselves. The plea bargaining process involved more counseling between the defendant and the public defender than interaction between the public defender and the prosecutor. The latter occurred, too, but only occasionally, when misunderstandings or disagreements surfaced.

The court was obviously under pressure due to the large caseload. A complex division of labor between the judge, the prosecutors, the public defenders, the clerks, the bailiffs, and the interpreters had been erected to cope with this pressure. In the hearing, the judge relied on a case file containing the prosecutor's complaint and the forms filled out by the defendant and the public defender. In order to prevent the case from being reopened due to technicalities (which would mean additional pressure), the judge had to make sure that all the forms were correctly and completely filled out. The judge did not keep and formulate the court minutes; that was the task of the clerk. And the minutes were not a narrative that would need much writing or dictating. Instead, the clerk filled out a rather detailed form, titled Misdemeanor Docket–Judgment/Traffic, in which there was a blank for every possible element of the sentence. Contrary to the Finnish practice, the police report describing the actual incident in a narrative form never entered the hearing. It remained a background document on which the prosecutor based the complaint and the offer. The DUI complaint was a fixed

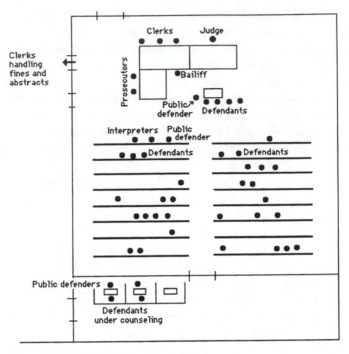

Figure 2. The physical layout of the California courtroom.

form in which the prosecutor filled in the blanks for the date of the incident and
the blood alcohol level of the defendant.

The sentences given to DUI offenders were standardized, much like they were
in the Finnish court. The legal maximum blood alcohol level was 0.08% in California. For a first offense, the legal sentence was 180 days in jail, but the judge
regularly granted probation for five years. The mandatory conditions of probation included a fine of $390 to $1000, completion of an alcohol or drug treatment program, and either (a) a minimum of 48 hours in jail or (b) a 90-day driver's license restriction, allowing driving only to and from work and to and from
the court-ordered treatment program. The court could enhance the sentence if the
blood alcohol level exceeded 0.20%. In practice, the fine for the first offense was
regularly about $1000 and virtually no one chose the 48 hours in jail because the
Department of Motor Vehicles automatically suspended the offender's driver's license for four months anyway, regardless of the contents of the court sentence.

The layout of the California courtroom is depicted in Fig. 2. The first striking
feature of Fig. 2 is the large number of people in the courtroom. It was common
that 40 to 50 people were present. And there was an audience, often quite large.
The audience, people sitting on the benches in the courtroom, consisted of de-

fendants waiting for their turn and of people accompanying the defendants. The cases were not usually handled one at a time. The bailiff or the clerk called three or four defendants to step to the podium at the same time, and the judge went through these three or four cases as one batch, thus speeding up the procedure.

The locus of intensive action was not limited to the courtroom as it was in the Finnish court. In front of the courtroom entrance, public defenders counseled defendants in small cubicles, and this went on even while the court was in session. The defendants left the courtroom usually through the door on the left, entering an adjacent room where clerks received fines and gave out abstracts of court record, little slips containing condensed information on the sentence and a notice of payment of fine (the defendant needed such an abstract in order to get the Department of Motor Vehicles to return his or her driver's license.)

Interestingly enough, the California court highlighted its authority more visibly than the Finnish court. As the judge entered the room, the bailiff, wearing a uniform, called everybody in the room to come to order and stand up. The judge wore a black robe. The judge's bench was very high; others in the room literally had to look up to her (in the case analyzed below, the judge was a woman). The defendants always stood up at the small podium in front of the bench when the judge discussed their cases.

## Two DUI hearings

In the following, I will present the verbatim transcripts of the spoken interactions of two DUI hearings, one from each setting. I will use a minimum of technical notation. Ellipses ( . . . ) in the middle or at the end of a sentence indicates that there is a small pause or hesitation in the speech. Necessary explanatory remarks are inserted in the text within brackets [ ]. The letters ADA refer to assistant district attorney in the Finnish court. The letters PD refer to public defender in the California court. One US dollar is currently (1995) worth about 4.25 Finnish marks.

I have translated the contents of the Finnish hearing into English myself, knowing full well that it is impossible to provide a translation that would accurately convey all the meanings and nuances across cultures.

*Transcript of the Finnish DUI trial*

| 001 | Judge: | Next, case number five, the people versus HK. All right, you |
|-----|--------|---|
| 002 | | are HTK. Please take a seat there. R90 dash 125, prosecutor |
| 003 | | district attorney EK, defendant machinist HTK, complaint |
| 004 | | driving under the influence of alcohol. New paragraph. You |
| 005 | | can give me the birth certificate. [Pause] The prosecutor gave |
| 006 | | the birth certificate and the appendices to the police report |
| 007 | | one to two. New paragraph. After this the prosecutor read |

| 008 | | and gave the complaint, appendix three. Go ahead, please. |
| 009 | ADA: | HTK, on the 5th of March 1990 in the City of L, on M Street, |
| 010 | | drove a passenger car, register plate number ACX-297, after |
| 011 | | having consumed alcohol so that at the moment of testing his |
| 012 | | blood alcohol level was at least 0.058%. Therefore I |
| 013 | | demand that K will be punished for driving under the |
| 014 | | influence of alcohol, according to the Penal Code paragraph |
| 015 | | 23:1. Additionally I demand that K shall pay restitution to the |
| 016 | | state for the cost of the blood alcohol test, 262 marks. |
| 017 | Judge: | You are K, born twenty-five dash ten fifty-two? |
| 018 | Mr. HK: | Yes. |
| 019 | Judge: | The social security number is 059 and the address is still this |
| 020 | | 30 T Street? |
| 021 | Mr. HK: | Yes. |
| 022 | Judge: | Dependents one child. Is the income 7400 Marks per month |
| 023 | | still true? |
| 024 | Mr. HK: | Yes. |
| 025 | Judge: | Then you have told the following in the police interrogation: |
| 026 | | On the fifth of March, 1990, around five o'clock PM I had |
| 027 | | drunk one bottle of beer in a party. Between eight o'clock and |
| 028 | | eight forty I was in Bar T where I drank three bottles of beer, |
| 029 | | the last one just before driving away. I had not drunk other |
| 030 | | alcoholic beverages during the day. I did not have so-called |
| 031 | | head start, and I have not used any medication. The |
| 032 | | passenger car ACX-297, which is in my permanent possession, |
| 033 | | was parked in front of Bar T, from where I then drove away |
| 034 | | in my car at eight forty. From there I then drove to a nearby |
| 035 | | kiosk, about one hundred meters away, in order to go and |
| 036 | | buy something to eat. Immediately after arriving in the kiosk |
| 037 | | yard I was tested with a breathalyzer by a police officer who |
| 038 | | had driven behind me, and at that point I was found to be |
| 039 | | under the influence of alcohol. From there I was taken to a |
| 040 | | blood test, after which I was released. In my own opinion, I |
| 041 | | was not drunk when I started driving, and my intention was |
| 042 | | to drive home. This is your story. Is it correct? |
| 043 | Mr. HK: | Yes. |
| 044 | Judge: | Then you were taken to this blood alcohol test and the blood |
| 045 | | alcohol level at the time of the test has been 0.058%. |
| 046 | | And then your driver's license was suspended on March |
| 047 | | 19, 1990. This is correct? |
| 048 | Mr. HK: | Yes |
| 049 | Judge: | So you confirm the information recorded in this police report? |
| 050 | Mr. HK: | Yes. |
| 051 | Judge: | The defendant K admitted that the information in his vital |
| 052 | | statistics is valid and repeated his story, which is recorded in |
| 053 | | the police report. What do you say about the complaint? Do |
| 054 | | you admit it's correct or do you dispute it? |
| 055 | Mr. HK: | The complaint is correct, yes. |
| 056 | Judge: | And he admitted that the complaint is correct. Do you have |
| 057 | | anything else to state? |
| 058 | Mr. HK: | Well, only that I'd ask that I'd get the driver's license back as |
| 059 | | soon as possible because I need to drive in my work. |

060  Judge:     What kind of work do you do?
061  Mr. HK:    Well, my main occupation is machinist, but this is such a
062             small firm that we must go and do installation and service
063             work, too.
064  Judge:     Trips . . . ? [inaudible]
065  Mr. HK:    Yes, in this city, one necessarily needs a car.
066  Judge:     And he asked that the suspension of the driver's license
067             would be ordered to be as short as possible in duration
068             because in his work he must visit different locations in the
069             city and needs a car for this purpose. Do you have anything
070             else to say?
071  Mr. HK:    No.
072  Judge:     Has the prosecutor anything to say?
073  ADA:       Nothing to add.
074  Judge:     Well, if you would step into the hall for a moment and wait,
075             the verdict will be made.

[Pause; everyone except the judge, the judge intern and the clerk leaves the courtroom.]

076  Judge:     You may now take seats. HK is sentenced for driving under
077             the influence of alcohol to pay 20 daily fines of 74
078             marks each, in other words, to pay a fine of 1480 marks,
079             and in accordance to the penal code paragraph 23.1, to have
080             his driver's license suspended until June 26, 1990. K must
081             pay restitution to the state for the costs of the alcohol test, 262
082             marks. The court considers it proven that on March 5, 1990, K
083             has driven a passenger car ACX-297 in the city of L on M
084             Street after having consumed alcohol so that his blood alcohol
085             level at the time of the test was at least 0.058%. The
086             proof is the alcohol test and the confession of the defendant.
087             Therefore, the court has sentenced as stated above. A party
088             dissatisfied with this verdict may appeal to the superior court
089             of P within 30 days in writing, and this court must be
090             informed of the dissatisfaction by next Wednesday at the
091             latest. Here you get these forms for paying the fine and
092             instructions for appealing if you express your dissatisfaction.

While in the Finnish court, the single case of Mr. HK is clearly a unit with a well-marked beginning and an end, this is not so in the California court. The cases are handled in batches. In the following example, the batch contains four cases. In order to save space, I will include here only the first part of the handling of this batch, the part that contains the entire process for the first of the four defendants, Mr. IJ.

*Transcript of the California DUI hearing*

001  Bailiff:   Following people please approach the microphone. These are
002             more DUI matters. IJ, RF, GS, CJ.
003  PD:        DH on behalf of Mr. J, Mr. F, Mr. S and Mr. J. They've all been
004             advised of their constitutional rights and signed

| 005 | | acknowledgement forms to that effect. They've all been |
| 006 | | advised of the charges against them and they waived further |
| 007 | | reading, they will each be entering pleas of guilty to Vehicle |
| 008 | | Code 23152A. Balance and charges to be dismissed. Their |
| 009 | | counsel has advised with them of the nature of the charges |
| 010 | | against them, possible defenses to those charges and the |
| 011 | | consequences of the plea of guilty. Each has initialed, signed |
| 012 | | and executed a plea form waiving their constitutional rights |
| 013 | | thereon with the exception of their right to counsel, and their |
| 014 | | counseling to join in their plea and waivers to have been |
| 015 | | entered knowingly, voluntarily, and intelligently. |
| 016 | Judge: | Did you have an opportunity to discuss your case with your |
| 017 | | counseling attorney, Mr. J? |
| 018 | Mr. IJ: | Yes. |
| 019 | Judge: | Mr. F? Am I saying your name right? How do you say your |
| 020 | | last name? |
| 021 | Mr. RF: | [Utters the correct pronunciation]. |
| 022 | Judge: | [Repeats the pronunciation]. Okay, and your answer was, |
| 023 | | yes? |
| 024 | Mr. RF: | Yes. |
| 025 | Judge: | Mr. S? |
| 026 | Mr. GS: | Yes. |
| 027 | Judge: | Mr. CJ? |
| 028 | Mr. CJ: | Yes, and I got, ah, I was readvised to, ah, change my plea to no |
| 029 | | contest. |
| 030 | Judge: | Okay. I'll hand the form to counsel and you can make that |
| 031 | | change right now. |
| 032 | PD: | Is this for Mr. S, your honor? |
| 033 | Judge: | Mr. CJ ... is changing his to no contest. Do you have any |
| 034 | | questions concerning the contents of the plea form or the |
| 035 | | entry of your plea, Mr. IJ? |
| 036 | Mr. IJ: | Pardon? |
| 037 | Judge: | Do you have any questions concerning the contents of the |
| 038 | | plea form or the entry of your plea? |
| 039 | Mr. IJ: | Ahm ... just how much I'm supposed to pay. |
| 040 | Judge: | Okay, that's when we get to the sentence, I'll tell you about |
| 041 | | that. Do you have any other questions? |
| 042 | Mr. IJ: | No. |
| 043 | Judge: | Okay. Mr. F? |
| 044 | Mr. RF: | No. |
| 045 | Judge: | Mr. S? |
| 046 | Mr. GS: | No. |
| 047 | Judge: | Mr. CJ? |
| 048 | Mr. CJ: | No. |
| 049 | Judge: | Do you understand the mandatory maximum and minimum |
| 050 | | penalties for a conviction for this offense and any later |
| 051 | | conviction for a same or similar offense, Mr. IJ? |
| 052 | Mr. IJ: | Yes. |
| 053 | Judge: | Mr. F? |
| 054 | Mr. RF: | Yes. |
| 055 | Judge: | Mr. S? |
| 056 | Mr. GS: | Yes. |

057  Judge:      Mr. CJ?
058  Mr. CJ:     Yes.
059  Judge:      To the charge that you violated Vehicle Code Section 23152A,
060              how do you plead, guilty or not guilty, Mr. IJ?
061  Mr. IJ:     Guilty.
062  Judge:      Mr. F?
063  Mr. RF:     Guilty.
064  Judge:      Mr. S?
065  Mr. GS:     Guilty.
066  Judge:      Mr. CJ?
067  Mr. CJ:     No contest.
068  Judge:      Mr. IJ, the complaint alleges that on or about September 24,
069              1990, you violated Vehicle Code Section 23152A, by driving a
070              motor vehicle while under the influence of alcohol with a
071              blood alcohol level of 0.30; is that what you did?
072  Mr. IJ:     Yes.
073  Judge:      Mr. F, the complaint alleges that on or about July 31, 1990,
074              you violated Vehicle Code Section 23152A, by driving a motor
075              vehicle while under the influence of alcohol with a blood
076              alcohol level of 0.17; is that what you did?
077  Mr. RF:     Yes.
078  Judge:      Mr. S, the complaint alleges that on or about September 23,
079              1990, you violated Vehicle Code Section 23152A, by
     driving a
080              motor vehicle while under the influence of alcohol with a
081              blood alcohol level of 0.19, is that what you did?
082  Mr. GS:     Yes.
083  Judge:      Mr. CJ, the complaint alleges that on or about September 8,
084              1990, you violated Vehicle Code Section 23152A, by driving a
085              motor vehicle while under the influence of alcohol with a
086              blood alcohol level of 0.19, are those the facts you're not
087              contesting?
088  Mr. CJ:     Yes, your honor.
089  Judge:      The court accepts your pleas, makes the findings in order as
090              set out on the plea form directly above the court signature.
091              The people's motion to dismiss the balance of each complaint is
092              granted. Mr. IJ, I sentence you to 180
093              days in the custody of the sheriff. Execution of sentence
094              suspended for five years in the following terms and
095              conditions of probation: that you violate no laws, that you
096              obey the standard alcohol conditions, that you attend the first
097              conviction program, that you pay a fine of 939
098              dollars plus 51 dollars to the crime-victims
099              fund, that your driver's license be restricted for 90 days,
100              that you do 20 days of volunteer work. Do you accept
101              probation on those terms and conditions?
102  Mr. IJ:     Yes.
103  Judge:      All right, that will be the order. For what organization do you
104              want to do the volunteer work?
105  Mr. IJ:     Ahm . . . Little League Park.
106  Judge:      Little League?
107  Mr. IJ:     Yeah, . . . Park.

| 108 | Judge: | Little League Park. |
| 109 | PD: | [Inaudible; requests a sidebar conference with the judge.] |
| 110 | Judge: | All right. If you really think it's necessary. [Goes to the |
|     |        | side to confer with the PD and the prosecutor.] |
| 111 | PD 2: | Your honor. |
| 112 | Judge: | Yes? |
| 113 | PD 2: | May I . . . [inaudible]. [Calls five defendants to |
| 114 |        | counseling.] GM, AF, EH, EJ, LH. |
| 115 | Judge: | [Returns to bench.] Okay, Mr. IJ, that sounds like a fine |
| 116 |        | plan for volunteer work. Ahm, do you need time to pay the |
| 117 |        | fine? |
| 118 | Mr. IJ: | Yes. |
| 119 | Judge: | How much time do you need? |
| 120 | Mr. IJ: | Ahm . . . what's the maximum? |
| 121 | Judge: | Ahm . . . well are you employed? |
| 122 | Mr. IJ: | No . . . [inaudible]. |
| 123 | Judge: | Okay, how about one year? |
| 124 | Mr. IJ: | Yes. |
| 125 | Judge: | Okay? Try to make . . . |
| 126 | Mr. IJ: | I can do it before. |
| 127 | Judge: | Do the best you can but in . . . in no event longer than one year, |
| 128 |        | okay? |
| 129 | Mr. IJ: | Okay. |
| 130 | Judge: | But you might want to try to make periodic payments, |
| 131 |        | although I'm not going to make that a requirement, okay? |
| 132 | Mr. IJ: | Okay. |
| 133 | Judge: | All right, and I asked, did I ask? Do you accept probation on |
| 134 |        | all these terms and conditions that we just talked about? |
| 135 | Mr. IJ: | Yes. Okay, on probation? |
| 136 | Judge: | You're going to be on probation for five years. |
| 137 | Mr. IJ: | With a pro . . . probation officer? |
| 138 | Judge: | No, not with a probation officer. |
| 139 | Mr. IJ: | Okay. |
| 140 | Judge: | What that means is, if you get another violation for driving |
| 141 |        | under the influence in the five years, your probation can be |
| 142 |        | revoked and you can be ordered to serve the custody. 143 |
| Mr. IJ: |     | . . . hmm. |
| 144 | Judge: | So for that whole five-year period you want to do all of the |
| 145 |        | things that you are supposed to do, okay? |
| 146 | Mr. IJ: | Yeah. |
| 147 | Judge: | All right, that will be the order. Good luck. |
| 148 | Mr. IJ: | Hmm. |
| 149 | Judge: | Mr. F, I sentence you to 180 days in the |
| 150 |        | custody of the sheriff. Execution of sentence suspended for |
| 151 |        | five years in the following terms and conditions of probation: |
| 152 |        | that you violate no laws, that you obey the standard alcohol |
| 153 |        | conditions, that you attend the first conviction program, that |
| 154 |        | you pay a fine of 939 dollars plus 51 |
| 155 |        | dollars to the crime-victims fund. That your license be |
| 156 |        | restricted for 90 days, that you perform five days of |
| 157 |        | public work service. Do you accept probation on those terms |
| 158 |        | and conditions? |

```
159  Mr. RF:   Yes.
160  Judge:    All right, that will be the order. Ah . . . do you need time to pay
161            the fine?
162  Mr. RF:   Yes, I need six months.
163  Judge:    All right, that will be the order.
164  Clerk:    Ah . . . six months, your honor?
165  Judge:    Yes, six months to pay the fine. On the last case, . . . ah . . . Mr.
166            IJ, I didn't say how long he should have to do his volunteer
167            work. Let's make it six months.
168  Clerk:    Okay.
```

As I pointed out above, this excerpt is not an intact unit in the judge's work. Even the batch of cases is not such a unit with clear boundaries – there is no pause between the batches and fragments of upcoming batches appear in the middle of ongoing batches (see lines 111 to 114 above). It seems that the unit for the judge is an entire session. This was confirmed by the judge in her interview.

> Judge: In fact, I think I probably take it by the session, morning and afternoon.
> Interviewer: So that's the unit of your work?
> Judge: Yes, every session is a new beginning and an end.

## The multiple dialects of the judges

Perhaps the most striking feature about the Finnish hearing is the extent to which the compilation and dictation of the minutes dominates the interaction. In his interview, the judge himself pointed this out at the outset:

> Everything is focused on the minutes. The most important thing is that the minutes are right, more important than anything else, because nobody pays attention to anything else except to the correctness of the minutes. . . . So the technical aspect takes most of the time.

There are large segments in the transcript in which the judge is addressing his speech primarily to the emerging minutes (via the taperecorder), not to any of the people present in the courtroom. I call this "*the dialect of document making.*" The judge quite abruptly switches from this dialect to the more familiar "*dialect of adjudication,*" and back again. The very beginning of the transcript provides good examples of such switches.

```
001  Judge:   Next case number five, the people versus HK. All right, you
002           are HTK. Please take a seat there. R90 dash 125, prosecutor
003           district attorney EK, defendant machinist HTK, complaint
004           driving under the influence of alcohol. New paragraph. You
005           can give me the birth certificate. [Pause] The prosecutor gave
006           the birth certificate and the appendices to the police report
007           one to two. New paragraph. After this the prosecutor read
008           and gave the complaint, appendix three. Go ahead, please.
```

Here the judge first talks to the defendant in the regular dialect of adjudication. He then switches over to the dialect of document making – here printed in italics. He then says to the prosecutor, "You can give me the birth certificate" in the regular dialect of adjudication, to return again to the dialect of document making, and to finish again in the dialect of adjudication ("Go ahead, please").

There is one passage in the transcript where the judge talks in a way that doesn't fit either one of the two dialects identified above. From line 058 to line 065, the judge and the defendant discuss the latter's request to get his driver's license back as soon as possible because he needs it in his work. The judge asks, "What kind of work do you do?" (line 060) and subsequently another question about the trips involved in the work (line 064). These questions go beyond the restricted legal script of a standard DUI hearing in that they are not questions to which the police report would already contain answers, only to be confirmed by the defendant. In fact, the first question is nicely paradoxical: the police report tells that the defendant's occupation is machinist; machinists do not by definition need to drive in their work, yet the defendant says he needs to drive in his work – hence, *what kind of work does he really do?* I call this "the dialect of socioeconomic adjustment." It is the dialect of finding out about the defendant's lifeworld and adjusting the sentence accordingly.

The dialect of adjudication is essentially that of proceeding toward the sentence according to the standard legal script. The dialect of document making is that of preparing a document that will fulfill the standard requirements of clear and complete court minutes. These two dialects are different in that the dialect of adjudication follows, above all, the logic of substantively correct legal procedure, whereas the dialect of document making follows the logic of appropriate documentation regardless of the contents to be documented. Thus, even when the dialect of adjudication if temporarily abandoned, as in the passage concerning the defendant's work, that exceptional piece of conversation is faithfully reproduced in the dialect of document making, as happens in lines 066 to 069.

It is interesting to note that the Finnish court procedure routinely offers to the judge a fair amount of information pertaining to the defendant's socioeconomic situation: occupation, income, and number of dependents. All these are data that the California judge does not encounter in the hearing. Similarly, the Finnish fine is based on the income of the defendant while the California fine is fixed and the same regardless of the economic means of the defendant.

The California Judge speaks in the dialect of adjudication, in this case obviously not selecting between the arguments of adversaries but simply proceeding according to the script toward the standard sentence. On lines 103 to 132 of the transcript, she also speaks richly in the dialect of socioeconomic adjustment. Her use of this dialect is not limited to questions about the defendant's living conditions; she actually engages in a negotiation of a workable plan for carrying out the volunteer work and paying the fine. However, she also uses dialects that are missing in the Finnish hearing. These include *the dialect of prevention, the dialect of monitoring,* and *the dialect of instruction.*

The dialect of prevention is very closely related to the dialect of socioeconomic adjustment – these two are practically flip sides of the same coin. When the judge gives the defendant a year to pay the fine (lines 123 to 132), she not only wants to take the defendant's life situation into consideration. She is also attending to the "business" of the court system in processing the caseload:

> What we can't afford to do is keep seeing these people over and over and over again. So, the reason I say how much time do you need to pay is that I am very, very liberal in the amount of time I'll give them to pay. I am real hard on the people who come back and have had a long time and still haven't paid.

And further:

> It is too hard on the system to have them keep coming back. . . . My philosophy is how can I help the system to become law-abiding, how can I make being law-abiding accessible. Because if it's not accessible, then they are going to be non-law-abiding, they are going to break the law. I want everybody, as soon as possible, to have driver's license and to have insurance, to have registration.

In other words, the judge wants to prevent the sentence from becoming a cause for new offenses and new visits to the court, which would further increase the pressure on the court. Failures to pay the fine within the given period of time lead to new hearings and thus to an increased caseload. Thus, the judge wants to make sure that the defendant expresses a clear and unambiguous commitment to fulfilling the terms of probation. In the hearings, this dialect becomes dominant, typically when the judge emphasizes an exact date by which the fine must have been paid. In the case analyzed here, this dialect surfaces briefly on lines 127 to 128: "in no event longer than one year, okay?"

Admittedly, this is not a strong example of the dialect of prevention. In other hearings conducted by the same judge, there are clearer examples. The judge acts as if alerted and changes her dialect noticeably whenever there is ambiguity concerning the date by which the fine must be paid. The following example is a case in point.

> Judge: You are going to have to give a higher priority to this matter. I appreciate that you have a limited amount of income and that you want to pay your bills, but this is probably your only creditor who can put you in jail and revoke your probation. I am willing to work with you and give you more time, but you haven't done anything and you're still not offering me anything except a vague statement that maybe in December you'll have some money. I, I need concrete facts, "on this date I will pay X number of dollars and I need this much more time to pay the balance," then I'll work with you but not with vagaries.
> Defendant: I . . . I can pay it on the first of December.

This excerpt is interesting in that the judge's dialect of prevention actually acquires a flavor of the dialect of instruction when she didactically tells the defendant how to be concrete. It may also be pointed out that the judge talks about "working with" the defendant, a phrase highly unlikely to be used by the Finnish judge.

The dialect of monitoring is a "metacognitive" dialect of supervising, coordinating, and planning, as well as checking and pointing out errors or omissions in the forms produced and actions performed by the public defenders, prosecutors, clerks, and interpreters, as well as by the judge herself. In the case selected for the present analysis, there are two minor examples where the judge uses the dialect of monitoring her own actions. On line 133, she asks: "All right, and I asked, did I ask?" And later, on lines 165 to 166, she says, " . . . ah . . . Mr. IJ, I didn't say how long he should have. . . . "

The use of the dialect of monitoring others is, however, much more common throughout the hearings. These situations often involve collaborative checking and troubleshooting. On lines 28 to 33 of the transcript, we see one such example, involving an exchange between the judge, the defendant, and the public defender. Here is a further example from another hearing on the same afternoon:

> Judge: All right, that will be the order. I don't have an advisal slip of constitutional rights from Mr. H, so I'll need that before he goes into the clerk's office.
> PD: Ah . . . don't we also need a victims', for the victims' names . . . ?
> Judge: All right, and we need a victims list. Okay. Same counsel will take care of the matter of the victims' names. You may go into the clerk's office.

Here the judge's initial monitoring about the missing advisal slip leads the public defender to notice the missing victims list. In the interview, the judge comments on such events.

> Judge: The public defenders are overworked, trying to counsel every single person who comes in every morning. So they, being human beings and being overworked, tend to make a lot of mistakes on the plea forms that they fill out. The prosecutor seems to make fewer errors. But it is the same thing; they are overworked, too, and so, as I am the one with the responsibility, I guess I'm the one who has to make sure that it all falls together.

And later she explains why the monitoring tends to happen in a collaborative manner.

> Judge: Normally a judge wouldn't do that. Normally the judge would just reject the paperwork, say go away and fix it and come back. But we can't do that here, because we don't have time. And also it's not the defendant's fault, it's the fault of the attorney. So my philosophy is I just try to fix it.

The dialect of instruction is evident in the transcript on lines 140 to 146. The defendant asks a question that indicates to the judge that he has not quite understood what the sentence implies. She then rather didactically explains the legal contents of the sentence. This may be a dialect that is partially replaced in the Finnish court by the meticulous practice of document making. Listening to the judge dictating the minutes may have an unintended didactic function. And the

Table 1.   Dialects employed by the Finnish judge and the California judge

| The Finnish judge | The California judge |
| --- | --- |
| The dialect of adjudication | The dialect of adjudication |
| The dialect of document making | The dialect of instruction |
| The dialect of socioeconomic adjustment | The dialect of socioeconomic adjustment |
| | The dialect of prevention |
| | The dialect of monitoring |

availability of detailed minutes may in many cases help the client understand what actually was the content of the sentence and on what grounds was it decided.

Table 1 sums up the multiple dialects the judges were found to use in these two court hearings. These findings open up interesting questions about the impact of rationalization on expertise. Traditionally, rationalization has been seen as process of deskilling, reducing expertise to standardized routines. In the California court, such effects are visible.

> Judge: Oh, and the other thing that I am ashamed to say on a tape recording, is that my brain is in suspended animation, practically. It doesn't even do things it used to do. So that I see so many people that they can go into the bail office, they come back five minutes later and I do not remember them. Or, if I remember them, I don't remember what they are there for.

But these effects don't seem to be the most important and interesting ones. The really interesting feature is the emergence of new dialects, of new "mental registers" that the judge must employ in order to cope with the complexity. These new dialects don't seem to have much to do with the traditional prestigious core of judicial expertise and legal thinking. They are mundane dimensions of daily routine. And yet they seem to be key cognitive components of what Seron (1990, pp. 461–462) calls "a more activist judicial posture toward management of cases," associated with the ongoing "systemic push" in courts.

**The standard actions of the judges**

Both judges handled the DUI case in the courtroom by proceeding through certain standard actions. By standard actions I mean procedural steps that follow the legal script of a minimal, disturbance-free case. The script and sequence of these actions were, however, significantly different in the two cultural settings.

In the Finnish court, the standard actions proceeded as follows:

1. Presenting the case (lines 001 to 016)
2. Matching the defendant with the file (lines 017 to 057 and 069 to 073)
3. Deliberating the verdict (lines 074 to 075)
4. Sentencing (lines 076 to 092)

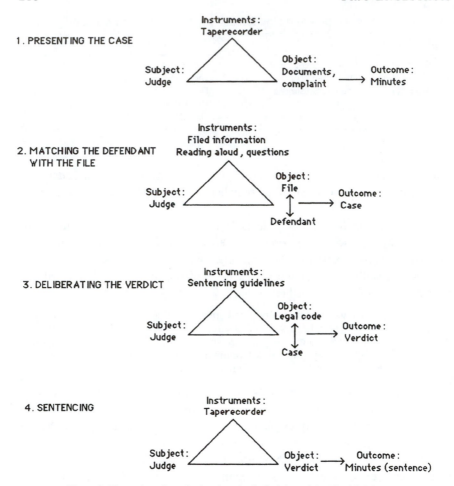

Figure 3. The script of standard actions in the judging of the Finnish DUI case.

In graphic form, the logic of these actions is depicted in Fig. 3. The first action – presenting the case – is actually aimed at producing the first section of the minutes, consisting of the birth certificate of the defendant, the police report, and the complaint. The second action – matching the defendant with the file – is aimed at producing a sentenceable case, i.e., one in which the documents and the defendant in flesh-and-blood merge together through the latter's confirmation of the validity of the documents. The third action – deliberating the verdict – is a rather empty anachronism in this type of case, where the verdict is reached through a simple, highly schematized matching between the penal code and the case. The unofficial sentencing guidelines adopted by the court function here as a pretty clearcut instrument (in more complex cases, legal precedents are typical instru-

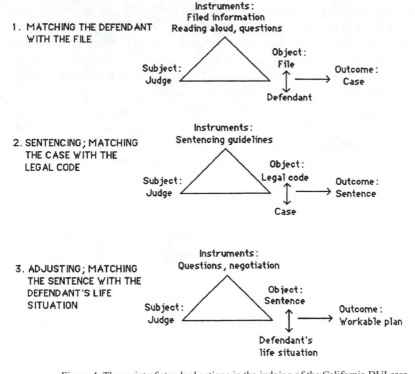

Figure 4. The script of standard actions in the judging of the California DUI case.

ments). Finally, the fourth action – sentencing – is again aimed at producing the minutes, this time the sentence part.

In the California court, the sequence of standard actions looks like this:

1. Matching the defendant with the file (lines 003 to 018, 049 to 052, 059 to 061, and 068 to 072)
2. Sentencing, or matching the case with the legal code (lines 092 to 102)
3. Adjusting, or matching the sentence with the defendant's life situation (lines 103 to 104 and 116 to 117)

This sequence can again be depicted with the help of a graphic model (Fig. 4). Here, too, the sentencing is highly constrained by its instruments. On the other hand, deliberation is eliminated as a separate action. The big difference in comparison to the Finnish case is the third standard action, adjusting. The script used in the California court required that each defendant was asked about the time needed for the payment of the fine, and many defendants were also asked about the organization where they wanted to serve their volunteer work service. Volunteer work was used in the cases when the defendant was not considered able to do more strictly supervised and physically demanding public service work. Even in the cases involving public service work, the defendant and judge often discussed issues such as where and within what time period the work service had to be completed. In Finnish courts, public service work and voluntary work have thus far not been legal options, and the defendant's ability to pay has been assumed on the basis of the reported income. Thus, no action of adjusting has been included in the standard script for handling DUI cases.

Now that we know something about the multiplicity of the dialects used by the judges and about the sequence of their standard actions, we may ask: What in the actions' sequences prompts the judges to change their dialects? What makes them expand and step into registers that are outside their traditional roles?

### Disturbances, repair actions, and learning in the handling of DUI cases

In the Finnish DUI hearing, only one phase stands out as a deviation from the script. It happens at the end of the second standard action, matching the defendant with the file.

| 056 | Judge:  | And he admitted that the complaint is correct. Do you have |
| 057 |         | anything else to state? |
| 058 | Mr. HK: | Well, only that I'd ask that I'd get the driver's license back as |
| 059 |         | soon as possible because I need to drive in my work. |
| 060 | Judge:  | What kind of work do you do? |
| 061 | Mr. HK: | Well, my main occupation is machinist, but this is such a |
| 062 |         | small firm that we must go and do installation and service |
| 063 |         | work, too. |
| 064 | Judge:  | Trips . . . ? [inaudible] |
| 065 | Mr. HK: | Yes, in this city, one necessarily needs a car. |
| 066 | Judge:  | And he asked that the suspension of the driver's license |
| 067 |         | would be ordered to be as short as possible in duration |
| 068 |         | because in his work he must visit different locations in the |
| 069 |         | city and needs a car for this purpose. Do you have anything |
| 070 |         | else to say? |
| 071 | Mr. HK: | No. |

Although in practice it has become quite common that DUI defendants express wishes regarding the length of the suspension of their driver's licenses, the standard script would assume that to the judge's routine question on lines 057 and 058, the answer would be "No." Thus, the defendant's question is a mild disturbance. The judge's repair action is that of assuming temporarily the dialect of socioeconomic adjustment (lines 060 to 064), only to return to the script through the gateway of the detached dialect of document making (lines 066 to 069). The question, "Do you have anything else to say?" (on lines 069 to 070) is, in effect, a repetition of the question that started the disturbance (on lines 056 to 057) and it signals the closing of that episode and a return to normalcy.

This disturbance did not lead to a substantive reconceptualization of the object of the judge's work. In other words, it was resolved in regressive manner. When viewing the videotaped hearing, the judge commented on the defendant's request as follows.

> Judge: Well, one doesn't always have to take it . . . what the defendant says, whether it's true or not. I mean, he can just as well say that yes, he needs the license. . . . Sometimes they even have some papers and certificates showing that they need it. So that is relatively . . . . But it's always considered, because the law requires it, if it's because of the occupation. And here the suspension of the license would have been longer if it had not been taken into consideration a little bit, so it would have been. Our minimum has been four [months], and here if I recall he got probably only three, about three months. Since a part of that time had already passed, he'll get it back already at the end of May, so it won't be long anymore.

Actually, the judge remembers the date wrong. The defendant will get his license back only at the end of June, not at the end of May. The judge thought that he took the defendant's request into consideration and it had some effect on the length of the suspension. The defendant, however, thought otherwise.

> Mr. HK I need it, I need my driver's license. I must . . . . I've driven a car for 19 years, so it . . . it goes like that. You don't even remember that you don't have it. Since it doesn't affect your driving performance in any way, whether you have the license or not. I don't understand why the judge cannot give it back. I don't know what the minimum penalty is – is it three? Or not necessarily anything.
>
> Interviewer: What do you think, was your request taken into consideration?
>
> Mr. HK: Not at all, in my opinion. . . .
>
> Interviewer: Do you have an opinion about what would be a just sentence here, or a decision you'd be satisfied with?
>
> Mr. HK: Well, I've been without my license for two months, and now I've got about 1500 to 1600 marks fines to pay. I think it's a pretty hard sentence for such a small excess [in the blood alcohol level].
>
> Interviewer: You mean that would be a sufficient sentence?
>
> Mr. HK: Yes, I think that two months without the license and 1500 marks fine, it's pretty appropriate.

Interestingly enough, the defendant quite clearly hints at the possibility that being without the license leads him to break the law again by driving without a license. Later the interviewer asked whether the defendant thinks that the judge understood what defendant's request was.

> Mr HX: Yes, I think it should have become quite clear to him. I mean, I could not tell the judge that I'm forced to drive without the license. If I had said that, he would have given me more.

This aspect is not considered by the judge in his interview answers. The judge was asked about his view of the meaning of the sentence to the defendant.

> Judge: You mean the meaning of the sentence for me or for him? For me it does not . . . .
>
> Interviewer: No, I mean for the defendant.
>
> Judge: No, they usually know it. Usually they anticipate what they'll get.

There is no trace here of the dialect of prevention. In fact, there is a wide gap between the defendant's notion of an appropriate sentence and the judge's basic conception of DUI cases.

> Judge: I think driving under the influence is a bad crime. I mean even a case like this. . . . So driving under the influence, when you ask for my personal opinion, it is a terrible crime.

The judge actually states that the defendant "seemed to be quite satisfied, no problem." But he quickly adds:

> It [the sentence] is given, and then it won't be changed anymore. . . . I say in court that this case is so and that's it. [Jokingly:] That's the way it is at home, too. No negotiation, it's like this.

What is regressive about the resolution of the disturbance is not that the judge and the defendant disagree. The regressiveness stems from the fact that there is no shared elaboration of the sentence in relation to the defendant's life situation. If the judge elaborates on the defendant's request, he does it alone during the deliberation, not interactively. This allows for no mutual reinterpretation of the situation and, correspondingly, calls for no explicit commitment from the defendant. The judge regards a DUI case like this as a strictly scripted, unalterable unit.

> Interviewer: How did the decision making happen in this case?
> Judge: There is not much to it. It is almost like a rubber stamp case.
> Interviewer: So the only thing was that request of his?
> Judge: Well, even that wasn't anything as such. These DUI decisions one could almost give like with a rubber stamp. There was no real deliberation.
> Interviewer: Are these necessary hearings, then?
> Judge: Well, one must sentence them. There is no other instance to do it.

This attitude may also have something to do with routinization through extensive experience. The Finnish judge had worked for 16 years as municipal court judge.

In the California hearing, there are altogether six disturbances and associated repair actions. The first two take place in connection to the first standard action, matching the defendant with the file. Interestingly enough, they are launched by almost the very same question that launched the only disturbance in the Finnish case.

> 033  Judge:  Mr. CJ . . . is changing his to no contest. Do you have any
> 034            questions concerning the contents of the plea form or the
> 035            entry of your plea, Mr. IJ?
> 036  Mr. IJ:  Pardon?
> 037  Judge:  Do you have any questions concerning the contents of the
> 038            plea form or the entry of your plea?
> 039  Mr. IJ:  Ahm . . . just how much I'm supposed to pay.
> 040  Judge:  Okay, that's when we get to the sentence, I'll tell you about
> 041            that. Do you have any other questions?
> 042  Mr. IJ:  No.

Here the first disturbance is utterly simple: on line 036, instead of answering "No" like a script-abiding defendant should, Mr. IJ answers "Pardon?" indicating that he has either not understood or not heard the question. The judge's repair action is equally simple: she repeats the question (lines 037 to 038). However, that immediately launches another disturbance: instead of answering "No," the defendant asks how much he's supposed to pay. The judge's repair action uses the dialect of instruction: "Okay, that's when we get to the sentence, I'll tell you about that" (lines 040 to 041). Here, the relatively novel dialect of instruction is evoked by the disturbance. It should be noted that at this point, the judge doesn't realize that there is anything exceptional about the defendant, Mr. IJ (see below).

The next disturbance occurs in connection with the third standard action – adjusting, or matching the sentence with the defendant's life situation.

```
103  Judge:   All right, that will be the order. For what organization do you
104           want to do the volunteer work?
105  Mr. IJ:  Ahm . . . Little League Park.
106  Judge:   Little League?
107  Mr. IJ:  Yeah, . . . Park.
108  Judge:   Little League Park.
109  PD:      [Inaudible; requests a sidebar conference with the judge.]
110  Judge:   All right. If you really think it's necessary. [Goes to the
              side to confer with the PD and the prosecutor.]
111  PD2:     Your honor.
112  Judge:   Yes?
113  PD2:     May I . . . [inaudible]. [Calls five defendants to
114           counseling.] GM, AF, EH, EJ, LH.
115  Judge:   [Returns to the bench.] Okay, Mr. IJ, that sounds like a fine
116           plan for volunteer work. Ahm, do you need time to pay the
117           fine?
```

Here, instead of giving a name of an acceptable organization, the defendant names the Little League Park as his volunteer work site (line 105). The judge is baffled. Then the public defender steps in and asks for a sidebar conference with the judge. In other words, the first repair action is collaborative. The judge grants (line 110) and holds the sidebar conference, which is joined by the prosecutor, too. In the interview, I asked the judge about this episode.

Judge: His mother was with him and he was very limited in what he could do.
Interviewer: I suppose he was mildly retarded, or . . . ?
Judge: Right, so I decided to let him do whatever he wanted to do.
Interviewer: I just wondered why the public defender did not inform you clearly about the nature of the case and that he actually had to have a side bar.
Judge: I know. I don't know.
Interviewer: As soon as the man started walking, you could see that he was somehow handicapped. But when he was standing there, there was no way you could see?
Judge: No, I didn't. I didn't know. That's why I thought "Little League," for crying out loud!

As the judge returns to the bench, she further repairs the disturbance by using the dialect of socioeconomic adjustment in a very determined manner: "that sounds like a fine plan for volunteer work" (lines 115 to 116). Another related disturbance follows immediately, as the defendant, instead of requesting a certain amount of time for payment asks "what's the maximum?" Now the judge systematically works in the dialect of socioeconomic adjustment, negotiating a very flexible plan for the defendant (lines 121 to 132).

The next disturbance is curiously connected to the second standard action, sentencing or matching the case with the legal code.

| 133 | Judge: | All right, and I asked, did I ask? Do you accept probation on |
| 134 | | all these terms and conditions that we just talked about? |
| 135 | Mr. IJ: | Yes. Okay, on probation? |
| 136 | Judge: | You're going to be on probation for five years. |
| 137 | Mr. IJ: | With a pro . . . probation officer? |
| 138 | Judge: | No, not with a probation officer. |
| 139 | Mr. IJ: | Okay. |
| 140 | Judge: | What that means is, if you get another violation for driving |
| 141 | | under the influence in the five years your probation can be |
| 142 | | revoked and you can be ordered to serve the custody. |
| 143 | Mr. IJ: | . . . Hmm. |
| 144 | Judge: | So for that whole five year period you want to do all of the |
| 145 | | things that you are supposed to do, okay? |
| 146 | Mr. IJ: | Yeah. |
| 147 | Judge: | All right, that will be the order. Good luck. |
| 148 | Mr. IJ: | Hmm. |

This time, it is not the defendant but the judge herself who initiates the disturbance. She has already once asked the defendant whether he accepts the probation on the given conditions (lines 100 to 101) and she has received the scripted "Yes" answer (line 102). But the complexity of the situation makes her forget that, and she asks the question again. Now the defendant expresses uncertainty about understanding the sentence (lines 135 and 137) and the judge repairs the disturbance by using the dialect of instruction. Although her closing comment on line 147 ("All right, that will be the order. Good luck.") is exactly according to the script, the presence of disturbance is not totally ruled out, as may be seen in the defendant's reaction: "Hmm" (line 148).

The last disturbance is also self-initiated by the judge. It is related to the third standard action, adjusting, or matching the sentence with the defendant's life situation.

| 165 | Judge: | Yes, six months to pay the fine. On the last case, . . . ah . . . Mr. |
| 166 | | IJ, I didn't say how long he should have to do his volunteer |
| 167 | | work. Let's make it six months. |
| 168 | Clerk: | Okay. |

Here Mr. IJ has already left the courtroom. But in the middle of the next case, the judge suddenly remembers that she failed to agree with Mr. IJ on the amount of

Table 2. The distribution of disturbances in DUI hearings
during one session in the California court

| Standard action | Number of disturbances |
| --- | --- |
| 1. Matching | 13 |
| 2. Sentencing | 13 |
| 3. Adjusting | 6 |

time given to complete the volunteer work. She quickly repairs that using what I interpret to be the dialect of socioeconomic adjustment. Since that dialect is inherently dialogic and the dialogue partner is no longer present, the judge uses the clerk as a substitute partner: "Let's make it six months." And the clerk responds: "Okay."

In order to obtain a more representative picture of the disturbances and repair actions, I analyzed the transcripts of all the DUI cases with guilty or no-contest pleas handled during the afternoon session that included also the case of Mr. IJ. There were 21 DUI cases during that afternoon. In 14 cases, a plea of guilty or no contest was submitted. In those 14 cases, I identified 32 disturbances. This means an average of 2.3 disturbances per case. The disturbances were connected to the three standard actions, as shown in Table 2.

In the corresponding repair actions, 35 distinct uses of dialects were identified (in three repair actions, the judge used two dialects). The distribution of those dialects is shown in Table 3.

Table 3 shows that the standard actions of matching and sentencing elicited mainly disturbances that led to repair by monitoring, and to a lesser degree to repair by instruction. The standard actions of adjusting elicited disturbances that led to repair by socioeconomic adjustment, prevention, and monitoring. In other words, the action of adjusting the sentence to the life situation of the defendant had qualitatively different implications from the other two standard actions. This poses an interesting question about the Finnish court, which had no such action of adjusting in its standard script.

Furthermore, Table 3 shows that the dialect of monitoring was quite dominant in the repair actions of the California judge. This reflects the fact that there were a large number of minor problems with the paperwork and also with translations both in matching the defendant with the file and in formulating the sentence. These disturbances commonly required active involvement and collaboration of two or more persons in the courtroom.

From the examples analyzed above, it seems clear that disturbances tend to push the judges into taking up novel, nonscripted dialects such as the dialects of socioeconomic adjustment, instruction, and monitoring. Such moves to adopt novel dialects are crucial forms of learning. Such learning is not simply learning

Table 3. The distribution of dialects used by the California judge in repairing
disturbances

| | Dialect used in repair action | | | | |
|---|---|---|---|---|---|
| Standard action | Adjudication | Instruction | Adjustment | Prevention | Monitoring |
| 1. Matching | 1 | 3 | — | — | 9 |
| 2. Sentencing | — | 2 | — | — | 12 |
| 3. Adjusting | — | — | 4 | 2 | 2 |

by "tuning" and perfecting the standard performance (see Norman, 1982). The
adoption of novel dialects seems to require stepping out of the ordinary routine,
into the realm of experimentation and construction (see Engeström, 1995).

These expansive moves are certainly partly spontaneous situational responses
to unexpected contingencies. However, there are indications that such moves
may also become conscious innovative strategies. In the California court, the dialect of socioeconomic adjustment seemed to be part of the routine script. But in
her interview, the judge clarified the issue as follows.

> Not all judges do that. For example somebody else was here yesterday [as a sub-
> stitute] and the clerks told me that that judge said that I don't want to talk to
> anybody about converting any fines into public work service, I don't want to
> talk to anybody about time to pay, and he also ordered the clerks not to have any
> pauses between the cases. . . . But the reason I do that. . . . I have a lot of reasons
> why I do that. One of them is that a lot of the cases on my calendar are people
> who were sentenced before by another judge. Since I've only been here 30 days
> and, well, not even 30 days, and I'm only going to be here 30 days more, I see, I
> don't know, 10 or 20 people a day who are sentenced by other judges, probably
> more than that, and haven't done what they said they were going to do. I sin-
> cerely believe that if the last judge had worked with them a little bit more when
> they were being sentenced, they might have been more realistic at the outset and
> they wouldn't be back seeing me again. . . . would rather they took a really long
> time to pay than that they came back to the court over and over and over again.
> So I'll give anybody six months to pay a driving under the influence fine, which
> is about $1000. The guidelines before I got here from the last judge were four
> months. I don't think four months is enough time. I would have a hard time pay-
> ing a fine of $1000 in four months and I think that I'm probably better situated
> than a lot of these people.

The judge's answer indicates that the standard action of adjusting could quite
well be performed by using the dialect of regular adjudication – that is, by simply
stating how much time the defendant is granted for paying the fine ("I don't want
to talk to anybody about time to pay") and where he or she must perform the voluntary work. Here the judge was consciously stepping out of such previously established and commonly used script, to construct a novel script for her own work.
This expansive move cannot be attributed to a lot of direct experience. To the
contrary, the judge had worked in this setting for less than a month and as munic-

ipal court judge only a year. One is tempted to hypothesize that the very lack of routine was here a precondition for innovative learning (see Sternberg & Frensch, 1992).

## Contradictions behind disturbances

What causes the disturbances to appear in the first place? First of all, our observations indicate that the disturbances described above were not just accidental and arbitrary. They seem to be systemic. Perrow (1984) has written about "normal accidents," failures and breakdowns that are caused by the complexity of the system itself. His material is drawn from large-scale technological systems in which disturbances often reach a spectacular scale. Courts are not very large organizations and they rely on low-level technology, yet their social organization is complex. Consequently, their disturbances are typically local rather than global and commonplace rather than spectacular. But they are no less systemic and "normal."

To understand how systemic disturbances arise, one needs conceptual tools to analyze the activity system of the court. I will here employ an extended version of the triangular model I have already used above in Figs. 3 and 4 (for theoretical background of the model, see Engeström, 1987; for prior examples of application, see Engeström, 1990, 1993). I will take one more close look at two key disturbances in the examples used above: the defendant's request for short suspension of his driver's license in the Finnish hearing (lines 056 to 071), and the defendant's suggestion of Little League Park as the organization of his volunteer work in the California hearing (lines 103 to 117). In interpreting the causative background of these disturbances, I will hypothetically identify certain contradictions in the activity systems of the respective courts.

In both cases, the disturbance was launched by the defendant's request. In other words, its point of initiation was the *object* of the judge's work. The defendant's request went beyond the information recorded in the file and thus created a mismatch. In the Finnish court, that mismatch was only heard and recorded in the minutes. The judge repaired it regressively, by using the dialect of document making. But the mismatch was not elaborated interactively because the rules of the scripted procedure excluded such interactive elaboration. There was a systemic contradiction between a fundamentally *unpredictable object* and *inflexible procedural rules*. This contradiction is schematically depicted in Fig. 5 (which is an extension of the second action in Fig. 3). Tensions between the components of the activity system are indicated with the help of two-headed lightning arrows.

In the California court, the defendant's initial request was elaborated interactively. But the elaboration was first blocked by missing information. The judge did not know why the defendant presented such an unusual request ("Little League Park").

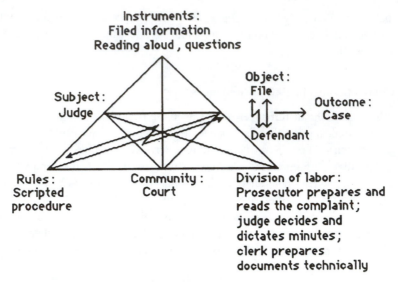

Figure 5. The contradiction behind the disturbance in the Finnish court.

The documents in front of the judge did not give her the needed information. The documents were highly standardized forms in which almost all information was in the form of filled blanks. Additional freely formulated information was practically excluded. In other words, there was a systemic contradiction between a fundamentally *unpredictable object* and *inflexible instruments*.

In her interview, the judge touched upon this contradiction when asked what would be the first thing she would like to have changed in the court's operation:

> We need to automate. If we were automated, I think it would make all the difference in the world. .... I know that some things are automated but this is something that just cries out for it because of the volume. If we were automated, I would assume that the judge would have a computer on the bench and that when a defendant appeared, would be able to plug it in and everything would be there and wouldn't need all of this paper. If that happened, then the clerk wouldn't have to spend two to three hours pulling all the files every morning and I wouldn't have to spend all the time I do thumbing through this trying to figure out why the people are there, and neither would the prosecutor and neither would the public defender.

Computerization may not solve the problems quite the way the judge hopes. Our previous research in the use of computerized medical records (Engeström, Engeström, & Saarelma, 1988) indicates that while computerization of manual forms may make the workflow more speedy and efficient, it often at the same time aggravates and makes more visible the problems produced by a compartmentalized division of labor in the activity system.

In the case of Mr. IJ, the forms had been filled out by the prosecutor, the pub-

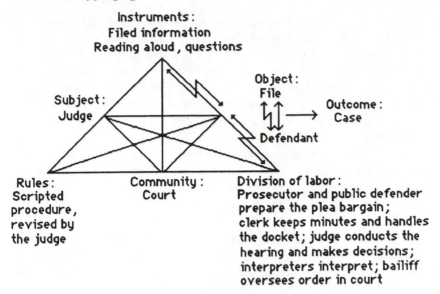

Figure 6. The contradictions behind the disturbance in the California court.

lic defender (together with the defendant), and the clerk. The disturbance launched by the "Little League Park" request was a product of a division of labor in which these members of the activity system were somehow working as if in their separate compartments, not realizing that the judge might need additional information concerning the defendant's disability. Thus, in addition to the contradiction between the object and the instruments, there was a systemic contradiction between a fundamentally *unpredictable object* and *inflexible division of labor.* These two contradictions are schematically depicted in Fig. 6 (which is an extension of the first action in Fig. 4).

The disturbance was repaired with the help of a *collaborative action* – the sidebar conference between the judge, the prosecutor and the public defender – and subsequently with the help of the judge's determined use of the dialect of socioeconomic adjustment.

At this point, the contradictions identified above are only hypothetical constructs. Their validity must be tested and their nature further elaborated in analyses of more extensive and versatile data.

Keeping this reservation in mind, it is still instructive to consider the implications of the contradictions. In the Finnish court, the crucial component causing tension seemed to be the rather inflexible procedural script. The script made it difficult for the judge to adjust the sentence to the life situation of the defendant. In this script, there was one strategic component that potentially invited disturbances, namely the question "Do you have anything else to say?" at the end of the second standard action. The expected standard answer was "No." But there was a qualitative difference between this "No" and other "Yes/No" answers the defendant was expected to give. The other answers had already been recorded in the documents and the judge was only checking that the defendant confirmed what he or she had previously stated. However, the answer to the question "Do you have anything else to say?" was by definition not previously recorded. In that sense, this question always carried a possibility of an unexpected deviation from the script.

Prevention of repeated or accumulated offenses by adjusting the sentence to the life situation of the defendant was not a built-in feature in the procedural script of the Finnish court. However, Mr. HK's interview indicates that driving without a license – which invites an accumulation of offenses – was a very real possibility.

In the California court, the procedural script, revised by the judge, was more flexible, corresponding to the much bigger and more complicated caseload and the crucial issue of repeat offenders. But this flexibility was not reflected in the instruments and in the division of labor. To the contrary, the instruments, above all the standard forms contained in the case file, were so streamlined that they seemed to make it nearly impossible to store and transmit more freely formulated, content-rich information about the case. And the division of labor effectively compartmentalized the judge, the public defenders, and the prosecutors into their own relatively closed niches, making it difficult for them to see the activity and its emergent situations from each other's viewpoints.

This latter point may be compared with Seron's (1990) observation according to which the new organizational model of American courts relies increasingly on teamwork. In the California court analyzed here, teamwork between the different professional groups surfaced only as an emergency measure to repair disturbances by calling a sidebar conference. Seron may well be right when she notes that teamwork will eventually transcend bureaucratization and deprofessionalization in courts (Seron, 1990, p. 461). But, at least in the setting analyzed in this chapter, this transcendence has yet to take shape.


## Acknowledgments

Although this chapter speaks in the voice of the first author, it is a product of collective work. The following members of my research groups collaborated with me in the preparation of this chapter: In Finland, Juha Pihlaja and Vaula Haavisto, both of University of Helsinki. In the United States, Katherine Brown, Ritva Engeström, Judith Gregory, Robert Taylor, and Chi-Cheng Wu, all of the University of California, San Diego. The research reported in this chapter has been financed by grants from the Finnish Ministry of Justice and from the Committee on Research of the University of California, San Diego. Views expressed in the chapter are solely those of the author. I am grateful to the judges, other personnel, and clients of the two courts from which the data in this chapter was collected. Michael Cole, Charles and Marjorie Harness Goodwin, David Middleton, Bud Mehan, Don Norman, Roger Säljö, and Lucy Suchman have given valuable comments on the different versions of this chapter.

## References

Chaiklin, S. & Lave, J. (Eds.) (1993). *Understanding Practice: Perspectives on Activity and Context.* Cambridge: Cambridge University Press.

Chi, M. T. H., Glaser, R. & Farr, M. J. (Eds.) (1988). *The Nature of Expertise.* Hillsdale, NJ: Erlbaum.

Conley, J. M. & O'Barr, W. M. (1990). *Rules Versus Relationships: The Ethnography of Legal Discourse.* Chicago: The University of Chicago Press.

Engeström, Y. (1987). *Learning by Expanding: An Activity-Theoretical Approach to Developmental Research.* Helsinki: Orienta-Konsultit.

Engeström, Y. (1989). Developing thinking at the changing workplace: Toward a redefinition of expertise. University of California, San Diego. Center for Human Information Processing. Technical Report #130.

Engeström, Y. (1990). *Learning, Working and Imagining: Twelve Studies in Activity Theory.* Helsinki: Orienta-Konsultit.

Engeström, Y. (1992). Interactive expertise: Studies in distributed working intelligence. Helsinki: Department of Education, University of Helsinki. Research Bulletin #83.

Engeström, Y. (1993). Developmental studies of work as a testbench of activity theory. In S. Chaiklin & J. Lave (Eds.), *Understanding Practice: Perspectives on Activity and Context.* Cambridge: Cambridge University Press.

Engeström, Y. (1995). Innovative organizational learning in medical and legal settings. In L. Martin, K. Nelson & E. Tobach (Eds.), *Sociocultural Psychology: Theory and Practice of Knowing and Doing.* Cambridge: Cambridge University Press.

Engeström, Y., Engeström, R., & Saarelma, O. (1988, Sept. 26–29). Computerized medical records, production pressure and compartmentalization in the work activity of health center physicians. In CSCW 88: Proceedings of the Conference on Computer-Supported Cooperative Work. Portland, Oregon. New York: The Association for Computing Machinery.

Ericsson, K. A. & Smith, J. (Eds.) (1991). *Toward a General Theory of Expertise: Prospects and Limits.* Cambridge: Cambridge University Press.

Gibson, J. L. (1978). Judge's role orientation, attitudes, and decisions: An interactive model. *The American Political Science Review 72,* 911–924.

Gusfield, J. R. (1981). *The Culture of Public Problems: Drinking-Driving and the Symbolic Order.* Chicago: The University of Chicago Press.

Harris, S. (1989). Defendant resistance to power and control in court. In H. Coleman (Ed.), *Working with Language: A Multidisciplinary Consideration of Language Use in Work Contexts.* Berlin: Mouton de Gruyter.

Heydebrand, W. & Seron, C. (1990). *Rationalizing Justice: The Political Economy of Federal District Courts.* Albany: State University of New York Press.

Hildebrand-Nilshon, M. & Rückriem, G. (Eds.) (1989). *Proceedings of the First International Congress on Activity Theory.* Vols. 1–5. Berlin: Hochschule der Künste.

Hogarth, J. (1971). *Sentencing as a Human Process.* Toronto: University of Toronto Press.

Jacobs, J. B. (1989). *Drunk Driving: An American Dilemma.* Chicago: The University of Chicago Press.

Lave, J. (1988). *Cognition in Practice: Mind, Mathematics and Culture in Everyday Life.* Cambridge, MA: Cambridge University Press.

Leont'ev, A. N. (1978). *Activity, Consciousness, and Personality.* Englewood Cliffs: Prentice-Hall.

McKnight, C. (1981). Subjectivity in sentencing. *Law and Human Behavior 5,* 141–147.

Middleton, D. & Edwards, D. (Eds.) (1990). *Collective Remembering.* London: Sage.

Mishler, E. G. (1984). *The Discourse of Medicine: Dialectics of Medical Interviews.* Norwood, NJ: Ablex.

Norman, D. A. (1982). *Learning and Memory.* San Francisco: Freeman.

O'Barr, W. M. (1982). *Linguistic Evidence: Language, Power, and Strategy in the Courtroom.* New York: Academic Press.

Philips, S. U. (1990). The judge as third party in American trial court conflict talk. In A. D. Grimshaw (Ed.), *Conflict talk: Sociolinguistic Investigations of Arguments in Conversations.* Cambridge: Cambridge University Press.

Perrow, C. (1984). *Normal Accidents: Living with High-Risk Technologies.* New York: Basic Books.

Seron, C. (1990). The impact of court organization on litigation. *Law and Society Review 24,* 451–465.

Silverman, D. & Torode, B. (1980). *The Material Word: Some Theories of Language and Its Limits.* London: Routledge & Kegan Paul.

Sternberg, R. J. & Frensch, P. A. (1992). On being an expert: A cost-benefit analysis. In R. R. Hoffman (Ed.), *The Psychology of Expertise: Cognitive Research and Empirical AI.* New York: Springer.

Vygotsky, L. S. (1978). *Mind in Society: The Development of Higher Psychological Processes.* Cambridge, MA: Harvard University Press.

Wertsch, J. V. (Ed.) (1981). *The concept of activity in Soviet psychology.* White Plains, NY: Sharpe.

Wertsch, J. V. (1990). The dialect of rationality in a sociocultural approach to mind. In L. C. Moll (Ed.), *Vygotsky and Education: Instructional Implications and Applications of Sociohistorical Psychology.* Cambridge: Cambridge University Press.

Yngvesson, B. & Mather, L. (1983). Courts, moots, and the disputing process. In K. Boyum & L. Mather (Eds.), *Empirical Theories about Courts.* New York: Longman.

# 10 Talking work: Argument, common knowledge, and improvisation in teamwork

*David Middleton*

## Introduction

This chapter examines collectivity in teamwork. The analytic concern is with how collective action is accomplished in team members' conversations. The example sequences were recorded in a multidisciplinary Child Development Centre (CDC) located within a large National Health Service (NHS) hospital in the United Kingdom. Multiprofessional teamwork is central to the provision of diagnostic and coordinated therapeutic services for children with developmental difficulties. At the time of the study, the physical surroundings of the Centre and its associated daily routines afforded many opportunities for informal discussion between team members concerning their work and case loads.[1]

## Multidisciplinary professional services for children

Multidisciplinary professional practice has been widely advocated in the British Isles for organizing the provision of services for children with complex developmental problems (Court Report, 1976; Warnock Report, 1978). It provides a "single gateway" to assessment and therapeutic services. Although widely taken up as a model of professional practice, there has been little evaluation of how such teams actually develop the ways of realizing their daily work activity in a multiprofessional manner. What research there is has either focused on the consultation process between professionals and their clients (e.g., Silverman, 1987; Sharrock & Anderson, 1987) or has examined the flaws in professional practice that surface as a result of professional jealousies and rivalries (Tomlinson, 1981). Such inter professional tensions are interpreted as detracting from good professional practice (Tomlinson, 1981). Research can also be found articulating an ideal that aspires to eliminate professional barriers and to equalize status relationships between professional expert and layperson (Gleidmann & Roth, 1980; Cochran, 1986; Wolfendale, 1986). The question of how multiprofessional teams develop modes of practice that are more than some arbitrary togetherness and actually come to realize their practice in a collective manner has, however, not been investigated directly.

## Teams

"Teams" are an organizational concept. In the literature on "organizations" it is possible to find different kinds of accounts about their "nature" and organizational impact. Morgan (1986) and Jirotka, Gilbert & Luff (1992) have identified a whole range images deployed as versions of organization, for example: organizations as hierarchical structures, networks, environments, information processors, coalitions, and cultures. Applied to teams, such images, or metaphors, frequently fail to account for a range of commonly acknowledged features central to the coordination activities in team practice, especially within multiprofessional settings. Such features include the trade-off between the informal and formally declared procedures, people's use of tacit and informal practices, the conventionalization of the formal from the informal, the handling of uncertainty and unpredictability, the improvisation of change, and the incorporation of innovation into existing practice.

Both Morgan (ibid.) and Jirotka, Gilbert & Luff (ibid.) note their images are all in their own terms plausible accounts of organizations that participants may use as part of their "doing organizational life." Morgan (op cit.) recommends that "effective managers and professionals in all walks of life, whether they be business executives, public administrators, organizational consultants, politicians, or trade unionists, have to become skilled in the art of "reading" the situations that they are attempting to organize" or manage (p. 11). For Morgan, such an "art" involves treating organizations as "text." Morgan (op cit.) argues for a "dialectical analysis" of organizational contradictions. Such an analysis is claimed as showing a way forward in handling "the management of contradiction" (p. 266).

Morgan's recommendations involve improved reading skills. The suggestion here is that the analysis should do more than that. It should allow both the participants and analysts the opportunity to examine how the dilemmatic features of organizational life become both a topic and a resource for doing organizational life. The analysis presented also aims to move beyond the sorts of organizational analysis of teams that is concerned with patterns of information flow, role demarcation, interprofessional jealousies, leadership, working cultures, etc. (see, for example, Levine & Moreland, 1989). The critical issue remains how to conceptualize team expertise and practice as accomplished in the social actions of team members in dialogue with each other rather than as some bureaucratic summation of individual expertise and how to study teamwork as the accomplishment of "dialogical" rather than "monological" expertise. To understand such dialogical expertise involves examining the way the team structure, patterns of coalition, information, etc. are formulated as matters of ongoing concern by agents within organizations. How they become performed rather than merely read in the communicative action of everyday practice. Jirotka, Gilbert & Luff (op cit.) argue that it is necessary to examine how that interpretative work is done in order to produce a situated understanding of "doing organizational life."

**Previous work**

Although interest in communicative activity in medical and pediatric contexts has been the focus of previous research projects (see for example Beale, 1976; Davis & Strong, 1976; Rittenberg, 1986; Silverman, 1987) the range and nature of unscheduled communications ("corridor talk") had not figured in attempts to evaluate the nature of multidisciplinary teamwork (see for example Stacey, 1980; Crocker, 1982; Thomas et al., 1984; Bax & Whitmore, 1985). The precursor to the work reported here was a "diary" study to establish the extent and significance of what we termed "titbits and work-related gossip" for the creation and maintenance of common knowledge concerning details of current and past cases, and in the creation of interim solutions to unforeseen problems that occur in multidisciplinary teams (Middleton & MacKinlay, 1987). Team members logged their communicative activities over two one-week periods. Analysis of these schedules revealed extensive use of incidental talk in achieving working solutions to unanticipated problems. The majority of those problems concerned children who were additional to the children "officially" scheduled to attend for developmental assessment and therapy at the Centre. Initial examples of this type of conversation were recorded and the significance of incidental talk for the team's capacity to glean information and react in a flexible manner to unexpected issues was discussed.

Since that initial study, further examples of the team's conversations have been recorded. This chapter extends the analysis of these spontaneous and informal commentaries on team practice. As Rittenberg (1985) points out, citing the work of Garfinkel (1967) and McHugh (1968), team members in health care settings habitually collaborate in a process of defining their current situation without any evident self-conscious reflection. However, when problems arise, the work of defining what is currently happening becomes an object of debate and awareness (Kleinman, 1980). Rittenberg (op cit.) was concerned with identifying and illustrating the way locally realized situation definitions could extend to become part of, and indeed structure, the shared concerns and practices in a pediatric ward. However, in that study the consolidation of shared understandings concerning the culture of ward practice is drawn as one negotiating a consensus of agreement between members where argument is suppressed and quieted. The contrary position is adopted here. Argument is presented not as something to be resolved before negotiated understandings of what the current object of work practices is or should be, but crucially involved in the accomplishment and maintenance of what team members take to be common understandings. This is not to argue that the generative potential of argumentation is necessarily and inevitably an instrument of positive consequence for team practice. Arguments can be deployed in both the "opening up" and in the "closing down" of options in team practice.

## Argument and argumentation

A distinction can be drawn between individual argument and social argument. Billig (1987) points out that there is an ambiguity in the meaning of what we understand by the word argument. It can refer to a piece of reasoned discourse that any individual may elaborate in establishing a particular case or point of view. As Billig puts it, "(A)s one articulates a point of view, one can be said to be developing an argument" (p. 44). Equally, the argument can also refer "to a dispute between people" (p. 44), wherein "opinions, or individual chains of reasoning, clash in the context of a social argument" (p. 44). Billig exploits this variability in usage of the term to demonstrate that "any individual argument is actually, or potentially, a part of a social argument," in that any individual argument is potentially controversial in the social arena. Equally, in team talk, although people can put up individual lines of justification for plausible ways of proceeding, these can lead to socially constituted disputes; the move to consensus is one created through argumentation. This chapter examines how such social argumentation provides the basis for team practice that has collectivity and joint accountability as a primary focus of concern.

## Team talk

Talk by team members about their work is of interest because as "situated action" (Suchman, 1987) it is used both to construct versions of what the team is currently doing and constitutes ways to act that respond to those versions. Accounts of past practice in the present become a resource in defining future practice. There has been no shortage of discussion in a range of literatures on this point; see, for example, discussions of "situated action" (Suchman, 1987); "cognition in practice" (Lave, 1988); "distributed cognition" (Hutchins, 1985, 1990); and computer-supported cooperative work (CSCW, 1986, 1988). All these discussions have argued for detailed ethnographically informed data as a basis for understanding the nature of communities of practice. Some (e.g., Suchman, op cit.) go further and have incorporated insights drawn from ethnomethodology (e.g., Garfinkel, 1967) and conversation analysis (e.g., Sacks, Schegloff, & Jefferson, 1974; Atkinson & Heritage, 1984; Drew & Heritage, 1992). Insights from ethnomethodology are also to be found in the discourse-analytic orientation of this chapter (Gilbert & Mulkay, 1984; Potter & Wetherell, 1987; Billig, 1987; Edwards & Potter, 1992). They highlight a significant inversion in the study of human action. What it is to know is just as much a concern for the subjects of any analysis as it is for any analyst. The way participants construct and account for what they do is a resource and a topic for both participants and analysts. The analytic perspective adopted here examines "team practice" as a *topic* of concern within teams. This involves taking account of the way members formulate what is "to do" the teamwork they find themselves involved in.

## Dilemmas in teamwork

In dealing with uncertainties in the representation of practice, team members' talk gives voice to contradictory and dilemmatic aspects of team practice. Attempting to evade or resolve such contrary themes can be seen to involve argumentation in the way speakers accounted for their practice and were able to distance themselves from the contradictory consequences of their accounts. The overall suggestion here is that teams should be understood performatively as constructed in and through the multiple occasions on which members define them and debate their definitions. Such kinds of definitional work can be found as a routine part of work. This is illustrated in the following transcription of a sequence of teamwork talk recorded within the multidisciplinary Child Development Centre referred to earlier.[2]

*Sequence 1*

*Context:* Sister's (nurse's) office used as a general meeting room. Sister (S) and one of the unit physiotherapists (PTU) discussing a problematic case.[3] PTC refers to community physiotherapist, a physiotherapist who works within the community who has a base within the CDC. PTD refers to the district physiotherapist, the person in overall charge of physiotherapy within both the community and the CDC.

> S: (. . .) teacher at um at (school) (&)
> PTU: u:m
> S: (&) and {1} she had a child that was (condition) (&)
> PTU: u:m
> S: (&) and {2} she was wanting more physio {3} she took the child off to get a private physio involved and Jane (PTC) {4} said {5} well if another physio's involved then I can't be{6} because (&)
> PTU: yes yes
> S: (&) {7} we both probably will be doing different things saying different things {8} she has not the team approach and I don't think that it should be done and and I think that {9} you should involve Anne (District PT) certainly Jane (PTC) did and and I think Jane (PTC) was saying exactly what you're saying about this case *exactly* what you're saying and I feel um you ought to go through it with Jane (PTC) (&)
> PTU: she did actually talk to Anne (District PT) about it

> S: she is {10} a very dynamic lady and um it it's extremely difficult I think Jane
> (PTC) had quite a few sleepless nights over it
> PTU: u:m
> S: but uh she was sticking in exactly the same way as you were and I I think if
> you have a chat with her and a chat with Anne (District PT) I am quite sure
> that uh
> PTU: yeah
> S: OK

This sequence displays a number of rhetorical resources for "doing" team work. For example, the notion of what it is to be a "team" is used {8} to argue for a particular course of action in relation to this problematic case. "(T)he team approach" is identified as a distinctive feature of this organizations practice. The Sister focuses on the team's practice and objectifies it as a feature that illustrates a potential distinction between the individualization of private practice and the collective nature of their state-funded team practice.

Being part of a team is more than a bureaucratic resource; it is a discursive resource in the argument over the direction of future practice in that problematic particular case. The Sister, in representing a previous case, engages in acts of (re)presentation in working up and arguing her view of a potential line of action that might help to resolve current difficulties. Such acts of (re)presentation form an important feature of creating a "working intelligence" concerning practice that is crucial to teamwork as collective action. This point will be discussed in more detail shortly. For the moment, the issue is the way this example represents a series of arguments concerning what might be an appropriate course of action in a particular case; at the same time, a version of what constitutes organizational life and team practice is constructed. The communicative work in the example involves the Sister improvising the grounds for recommending possible lines of action in a particular case: seek the advice of another physiotherapist (PTC); consult with the district physiotherapist in overall charge of the physiotherapy service in the area. The Sister employs a number of rhetorical devices to support her recommendation, one of which is to formulate organizational life and the obligations that make it up, as constituted by "the team approach." In using such devices, the Sister's (re)presentation of the situation attends to a number of overlapping dilemmas of practice: parental versus professional rights; individual versus team provision of service; state versus private practice; egalitarian versus authoritarian decision making. However the participants do more than a passive reading of "preexistent" ideological and practical dilemmas (Billig et al., 1987). Their conversation provides the basis to elaborate the significance of the dilemmas of practice they currently face. If we extend beyond the notion of "reading" their organizational circumstances, they can be characterized as "authoring" a way forward (Shotter, 1990).

The Sister, in identifying some actors who do and some who do not have the team approach, and enjoining PTU to liaise with someone who does, is doing more than merely discursively representing the organization. She is recommending courses of action and associations between actors that would literally create a new organizational form. This analytic perspective views organizations not as some object of an ostensive definition that we might know of in spite of the ignorance of participating agents, and more the outcome of a series of trials and contests in which various parties (analysts included) lobby each other for the version of team organization that they wish to have stick. "Teams," then, becomes performatively defined [cf. Latour's (1986) discussion of the powers of associations and "actor network theory"; Grint, 1991].

Team members' talk continually handles uncertainties concerning their work; for example: what should they be doing next in relation to problematic cases?; are there any misunderstandings of purpose between the various professionals involved and between team members and the families?; what further information might be required to cope with an emergent problem?; whose responsibility might it be to instigate and monitor a recommended line of action? Solutions to such issues are always only provisional. The children's needs and family circumstances change. Uncertainty can always return and this gives team members talk about their work its contradictory and dilemmatic quality. Dealing with contrary themes of practice can be seen to involve argumentation. Dilemmas are a topic of concern that unfold in ways that reveal speakers attending to those dilemmas without falling prey to them while accounting for practice. Team members' talk about work therefore gives voice to contradictory and dilemmatic aspects of team practice.

## Common knowledge and "working intelligence"

As stated earlier, the analytic intention of this work is to examine and illustrate the way collectivity in team practice is accomplished and organized for in the argumentative structuring and content of conversations between team members. Two specific issues will now be discussed. The first concern is the way the rhetorical structuring of informal conversations between team members affords the generation and maintenance of common knowledge for current cases and procedures. The analysis then moves on to illustrate the rhetorical resources available to team members for improvising interim solutions to unexpected problems.

What might be understood by "working intelligence" or "understandings held in common"? "Classically," cognition refers to representations and the transformations that representations undergo. This is very clear in contemporary cognitive science, where terms such as "know," "think," "believe," and other "mental language" are unpacked by reference to operations on representations of the world that occur, in some sense, "inside" agents or "inside" the organizations that agents make up. Not only does this raise the issue of how organizations or agents can be individuated so that we might speak of their "insides" in contrast to their "outsides" (cf. Cooper, 1986), we cannot invoke representation nonproblematically (Woolgar, 1988).

Consider again Sequence 1. It has already been pointed out that the topicalization of "teamwork" is a rhetorical resource for handling dilemmas of practice. Closer examination of the sequence reveals ways in which uncertainty of representation are managed rhetorically. The line of the Sister's argument leads to her establishing grounds that are borne of the experience of other team members in equivalent cases. The (re)presented experiences of other team members becomes a resource for establishing equivalence between current and past circumstances. Such equivalence is crucial in justifying the lines of action being recommended by the Sister.

She has to find grounds on which to establish her claim that there exists an equivalence. In so doing we see an invocation of the team's "working intelligence," the working of a distributive reasoning of problematic circumstances through renarration embedded in the voice of another team member of the particulars that establish that equivalence (4: *Jane (PTC) said well if another physio's involved then I can't be because . . . .*). Rather than accept a number of voices of equivalent status of acceptance, the Sister's talk addresses the possibility that other competing representations might be possible. This is achieved by accomplishing a relation between voices that brings off a construction of equivalent cases. The Sister, in recruiting another team member as a potential ally, so frames her recommendation that it can be heard as not just hers. To defeat this recommendation, PTU would now have to undo not merely the words of the Sister but also of the Sister's rhetorically invoked ally, Jane. In this way, her talk handles the potential defeasibility or undoing of her claims for equivalence.

We represent the world in contexts where we might be opposed as others mobilize alternative versions of events, objects, and agents and try to assemble support for them. In addition to constructing the argument through the voice of another person, a variety of other devices are deployed in handling uncertainties of representation. Initially, the Sister's argument is couched in terms of formulating another's circumstances, intentions, and actions as equivalent.

The initial focus of the Sister's recorded intervention involves the use of others to establish some form of equivalence between the present case and a previous case. A comparison is made to the mother with equivalent circumstances from a previous case the team had handled. Three aspects of the cases are argued to be equivalent: that "she" (the mother) is presented as having an equivalent *"child that was (condition)"*{1}; that her motives are equivalent because *"she was wanting more physio"* {2}; that she followed an identical course of action *"and took the child off to get a private physio"* {3}. In this way, representing the cases in terms of circumstances, intentions, and actions, and establishing the pertinence of just these features of the cases will head off, for all practical purposes, the possibility of further disagreement.

But this will be the case for only so long as the Sister's formulation of circumstances and issues invoked are taken as reliable and not contestable. Here again, the recommendations' rhetorical base is made larger and more secure. To disagree would now involve undoing three more things (sets of representations) over and above a claimed equivalence: the Sister's account of the circumstances, actions, and intentions of the mother in question.

It was at that point that the Sister used the voice of the person whom she was recommending should be consulted to further bolster the claim that the cases are comparable and merit comparative consideration as a means of moving beyond a "sticking" point.

The voice of the physio accomplishes further argument in relation to the identity of the cases and also to suggest what the nature of the sticking point in the present case might be. The evidence evinced in the voice of the physio is also couched in directly argumentative terms *"well if"* {5} qualified by a reason *"because"* {6}. The Sister introduces through the voice of the physio a completely new line of comparison that relates to the practicalities of servicing any particular case: the difficulty of having more than one therapist of the same kind involved on the same case (*"well if another physio's involved then I can't be because"* {5}). This difficulty is justified because two therapists might *"be doing"* and *"saying different things"* and thereby violate the consensus and unitary nature of recommendation and action that are the hallmarks of team practice.

It is only after the concluding comment in the voice of the physio that two persons should not be included on this particular case that the Sister puts forward a suggestion of her own. It is only now that speaking "matter of factly" about a course of action becomes feasible. The Sister's suggestion is immediately qualified using a further argument based on equivalence with the previous case: *"I think that you should involve Anne (District PT) certainly Jane (PTC) did,"* the District Physiotherapist being the person in overall control of the physiotherapy service in the whole of the health district in which the hospital is situated. This then is a plea to involve a higher authority in seeking a resolution to any impasse in this particular case. But even that recommendation is only stated in terms of a conditional modality (*"I think"*) and the way forward is located in the action of another (*"you should . . . "*). In this way, a voice is adopted that, while handling current uncertainties through speaking factually, is not so committed that future outcomes could not be articulated in terms of a revised **in**equivalence between the two cases.

This controversial work is the arena in which improvisatory interim solutions to recurring problems are argued for in terms of the uncertainties of representation that are only provisionally managed at any particular point in time. This provisionality arises through the uncertainties being ineradicable. However, it also allows for flexibility in how future outcomes might be dealt with and represented in their own turn. From these examples, we see how accounts of teamwork should allow for the emergent rhetorical means by which the uncertainties of representation get managed. In addition, and this seems to be particularly significant in framing an approach to collectivity in practice, just "how far" the management of uncertainty proceeds needs to be understood in terms of how much future practical and representational flexibility is required. We must not construct an authoritative voice now if the refutation of its certainties at some time in the future would then leave the team "voiceless." Not only are representations future directed (e.g., through leading to the specification of courses of action) but so are the strategies themselves by which uncertainty is managed. This suggests that the management of uncertainty is always provisional, and as uncertainty can always potentially return, everyday life often has a dilemmatic quality (cf. Billig et al., 1988). This entails understanding representation performatively.

### Rhetorical emergence of common knowledge

Further examples will now be discussed to illustrate how a multidisciplinary team talk about work accomplishes an up-to-date "intelligence" concerning the current activities of the team. This common knowledge or "working intelligence" can be seen to be collectively accomplished in the team's conversations. The second conversational sequence illustrates the rhetorical organization of uncertainties concerning the status of current information relevant to team activities. Teams such as the ones working in CDC's are continually having to incorporate into their program of work new clients for assessment and therapy, address issues relating to established cases on their "books," and adapt to staffing changes both within and around the unit that are an endemic feature of hospital organization. In Sequence 2 the Nursing Sister in Charge of the daily running of the CDC had just finished a phone call. As she terminated the telephone conversation she indicated to whom she had just been talking. The colleagues she addressed were not assembled in the room for the purpose of being told that information.

### Sequence 2

*Context:* Sister (S) at the finish of a telephone conversation addresses physiotherapist (PT) and nursery nurse (N).

```
1 S:   (name) from the (name) School
2 PT:  who?
3 S:   (name) from the (name) School
4 N:   I thought she was retiring
5 PT:  no she's not its the school nurse isn't it?
6 S:   the school nurse has gone
7 PT:  has she gone?
8 S:   yes
```

Here we see the passing on of current information concerning links with the outside world. The rhetorical structure and content of this sequence derives from the way people argue for their version of what they argue to be the status of the world beyond the Unit. The Sister commentates her recent activity in naming whom she had just been talking to (line 1). This is queried by the physiotherapist and that elicits a repetition of the commentary (lines 2–3). The subsequent exchanges establish that the particular person is still potentially in place and that another member of the school staff had infact retired. It is the conditionality of the nursery nurse's interjection, "I thought" (line 4) and the conditionality of the Physiotherapist's interrogative response, "Isn't it" (line 5), that gives both the exchange as a whole and individual contributions their argumentative structure and content. The physiotherapist's contribution is interesting because in the same utterance she argues both for a particular version and then opens up the possibility of an alternative construction on the circumstances. Neither the nursery nurse nor the physiotherapist are trading bald statements of "fact." They give and take around possible uncertainty. There is also a rhetorical ambiguity in the physiotherapist's question, "Has she gone?" in response to the Sister's statement, "The school nurse has gone." The Physiotherapist's response has the potential of being read both as questioning the "facts of the matter" concerning who has retired and at the same time affording a confirmatory reply – "yes" – by the Sister.

This exchange is an example of the collective realization of a working intelligence. The outcome is a product of the joint construction of a version of what is happening in an external institution. An apparently simple mismatch of information that crops up in an incidental conversation serves to keep the status of the unit's common knowledge of the world of professional personnel beyond the Centre up to date. There is nothing extraordinary about this information nor about the fact that the team includes it in their talk to each other. It is in consideration of how team members commentate that very ordinariness that we can explore further the way in which argumentation is implicated in the construction of shared common knowledge concerning what is going on within and beyond the team.

## Common knowledge in commonplace dilemmas

Later in this chapter, the improvisatory consequences of team talk will be discussed. However, the constructive and generative consequences of talk need not be improvisatory. Indeed, with respect to the function of these sorts of conversations in establishing a working intelligence in the unit, it is more usual to find that the conversational activity focuses on prosaic aspects of the unit's work, such as comments on a phone call, noting the birth of a child to one of the parents who already attends the unit, and arranging the timetable of appointments. Billig (1987) cites how, in discussions of rhetorical argumentation to be found in the classical literature, "common places" (loci communes) and points of "invention" (loci inventio) are two important aspects of argumentation. The collective (re)presentation of commonplaces in team activity is one way the common knowledge of what is currently happening and has happened is made available and maintained. For there to be argument, there does not have to be the invention, improvisation of new procedures, or innovative interpretation of past cases. The collective (re)presentation of the team's activity can be argumentatively structured around the dilemmas of representations concerning mundane and commonplace features of team practice.

The following Sequence 3 has these properties. On this occasion, the issue that emerges focuses around the relative rights of team members to determine the nature of the case load of other members of team. At first reading it would appear to be a simple matter of coordinating an appointment for a child to see the consultant, but it turns out to be more complicated than that.

*Sequence 3*

*Context:* Sister's office, which is used as a general meeting area. Participants include a community physiotherapist (PTC) who works out of the unit, a unit physiotherapist (PTU), a nursery nurse (N), and the Sister of the unit (S).

```
 1 PTC:   um please could we have an appointment for (Forename Surname) to
          see Mr. (Consultant)
 2 PTU:   ah ah (&)
 3 ?:                ah yes
 4 PTU:   (&) I was just coming say she has got one for next week I did not re-
          alise
 5 PTC:   oh has she ( . . . ) she's got (condition)
 6 N:     she has got an appointment (&)
                              |
 7 ?:                         yes
 8 N:     (&) and she should have one 6 months ago and we are waiting for a
          referral letter for Mr. (Consultant) and as soon as that's done she has
          got an appointment and it is provisionally in for next week
                |
 9 ?:           yes
10 ?:     24th?
11 N:     and all we need oh sorry a week on Tuesday
12 PTC:   I am going to ring mum ( . . .) to forewarn her
13 N:     do you think you ought to yet (&)
14 S:     (PTU) have you had words with (PTC)
15 N:     (&) I think you might worry her
16 PTC:   ( . . . ) needs to be monitored ( . . . )
17 N:     um because I think if you ring her before she sees Mr. (Consultant)
          she going to whittle for fortnight
18 PTC:   ( . . . ) next Tuesday
19 S:     (PTC) I think (PTU) needs to talk to you
```

```
20  PTU:  yeah
21  S:    to have words with you
22  N:    (PTC) a week on Tuesday 24th
23  PTU:  oh a week on Tuesday sorry
24  PTC:  oh that's that's alright then I shan't bother ( . . .)
25  N:    so who's doing the referral letter (1) are you
26  PTC:  I I I'll do it (1) I don't mind
27  N:    thank you I didn't realize that you were seeing her and I asked (PTU)
          cos she used to so I'm sorry
28  ?:    ( . . .)
29  PTC:  24th
30  N:    u m
31  PTC:  ( . . .) and I'll do the letter
```

This sequence starts with the community physiotherapist (PTC) requesting an appointment for a child to see a consultant at the hospital because a particular condition is suspected (lines 1 and 5). The condition had not been confirmed with the parents via any medical consultation with a consultant who dealt with the type of condition. This evokes a response from one of the unit physiotherapists (PTU) that the child in question has indeed got an appointment but that she "did not realize" that this had been made (line 4). This query is taken up by the nursery nurse who recapitulates details concerning appointments for the child (line 8). The full significance of the nursery nurse's contribution to the working intelligence of the team only becomes apparent toward the end of the sequence (line 27). Only at that point is it explicitly revealed why there might have been confusion over the making of the appointment. The nursery nurse declares that she had not realized that the community physiotherapist was already seeing the child and that she had gone ahead and made a provisional appointment with the consultant in the name of the unit physiotherapist rather than in the name of the community physiotherapist.

Again we see a conversation constructed in accordance with the dilemmas of uncertainty in teamwork activity. A commonplace in the team's culture of team-work concerning who has appointments when and for what purpose is not just a simple exchange of information, it is information evoked interactionally in con-versation that handles delicate problems of taking responsibility without usurp-ing the authority or democratic rights of other members of the team. Three inter-related aspects of team practice are handled in this exchange: potential confusions of demarcation over therapeutic responsibility and the initiation of a consequent letter requesting that the consultant make an appointment for the child; a practical confusion over the actual date of the appointment (it was in two weeks rather than one week); and, finally, the manner in which the mother of the child should be forewarned of the potential significance of the child's handicap-ping condition. The nurse's position on the confusion over appointments and the advance information to the mother involves some delicate footwork with respect to her initiatives both in terms of initiating appointments (the general spacing of

appointments in time, when they are specifically, who is the responsible therapist), and in terms of advising a therapist as to the probity of a particular course
of action.

The nursery nurse's initial contribution concerning the letter of referral man-
ages a potential conflict of interest between the two physiotherapists that was a
consequence of an initiative that she had taken on behalf of a child attending the
Centre. Her actions have only been of a provisional nature though, "it is provisionally in for next week" (line 8). It can be argued that is that very proviso that
keeps her initiative in check. Provisionality provides acceptable grounds for taking initiative that is the hallmark of an egalitarian team ethos while at the same
time leaving open for a later date the process of ratification that acknowledges
the rights and privileges of other team members.

However, before the uncertainty of role demarcation and situated authority can
be resolved, an inaccuracy in the way that nursery nurse reported the date of the
provisional appointment creates the conditions for the subtopic introduced by the
community physiotherapist. She gives warning that she will attempt "to fore-
warn" (line 12) the mother of the child as to the possible outcome of the consultation. The nursery nurse employs delicate footing (Goffman, 1981)[4] of personal
pronoun, person shift, and conditionality in warning the community physio
against telephoning the mother of the child ("do you think you ought to yet I
think you might worry her um because I think if you ring her before she sees . . .
she is going to whittle . . . ) (line 13). The nurse is constructing a plausible argument for and against a course of action that skirts around baldly telling someone
what they should or should not do. She distances herself from that recommendation by representing it as a possible thought of the person she is addressing ("do
you think"). That attributed thought is only conditional though ("you ought"). Finally, the conclusion of the argument is conditionally accepted as her own ("I
think") but it is stated in terms of the consequences for a third person's mental
state – the mother ("she is going to whittle").

Finally, when the immediate timing of the appointment has been worked out
and the appropriate course of action in respect to the mother determined, (line
24) then the original "commonplace" of getting a referral letter written comes
back into focus. The nursery nurse couches the initiative in such a way that does
not place her in the position of making the decision. She essentially asks for a
volunteer ("So who's doing the referral letter") (line 25). This is qualified with
the question "are you?" It is couched in diplomatic terms of "are you doing this
already" rather than "will you do this in the future." When the referral letter has
been resolved, we see articulated the very issue around which this working intelligence was constructed. The nurse apologizes to the community physiotherapist
for having involved the unit physiotherapist without prior consultation. She
would not have done this had she known that the community physiotherapist was
already seeing the child as a client. Her action had been premised on the fact that

on previous occasions the unit physiotherapist had also seen the child. Her apology is structured in the form of an argument addressing uncertainties of demarcation (line 27) ("I didn't realize . . . I asked cos . . ."). The emergent common knowledge made available in their conversation is accomplished through the management of contingent uncertainties concerning who may or may not have organized the commonplace action of making the appointment.

The analysis now moves on to examine the way common knowledge necessary for collectively accountable team action both emerges and is maintained in repair through team members' arguments to resolve variations between different accounts of details and procedures. Such common knowledge is more than the sum of any recollections individual team members might bring to the work situation. It is a property of the team's conversational rememberings concerning details of those cases and previous activities and outcomes of the team (for a more detailed discussion of remembering as a jointly realized activity see Edwards and Middleton, 1986; Orr, 1986; Middleton, 1987, 1991; forthcoming; Middleton & Edwards, 1990; Edwards, Middleton, & Potter, 1992). Again, the main point to note in this context is that both aspects of the collective nature of the team's working intelligence are emergent aspect of handling uncertainties in accounting for the apparent "facts of the matter."

## Situated improvisation and innovation in teamwork

Teamwork has to be improvisatory if it is to succeed in flexibly coping with a changing case load of frequently idiosyncratic cases within general procedures and expertise. Such improvisatory flexibility is discussed in the work of Sharrock and Anderson (1987). Their concern was to account for opportunistic handling by pediatric consultants of the specific and idiosyncratic issues of particular cases they dealt with. They examined how the flow of work in a pediatric clinic is realized through the routine orderliness of everyday forms of talk and conversation that constrains and gives form to the work of the clinic. Their studies were concerned with the way work "flows" out of the orderliness of conversational exchanges in pediatric settings. Improvisation is dealt with in terms of the specific orderliness of work tasks. Such tasks have no predetermined order. Sharrock and Anderson aim to demonstrate how they come to have specific order in the particular circumstances of a particular situation, what they term "situational contingencies." Their suggestion is that "it is in the opportunistic handling of such contingencies that the routine character of work resides" (p. 250). Sharrock and Anderson put forward an account of how the work of the consultation process can be improvised within the orderly flow of expected aspects of the consultation situation. "The same orderliness which characterizes their (participants in a consultative exchange) organization in talk, is on view in the way in which they are used to organize work tasks" (p. 259).

It is a matter for further speculation whether such flexible opportunisms, borne of situational orderliness, can provide a full account of the total range of novelty and difference that is handled in the routine work of such clinics. The social constitution of work activity in these contexts must surely extend beyond what is to be expected. The examples presented here are an attempt to demonstrate that there are other features in the improvisatory process of work activity. Talk about work is of interest as situated discursive action that is used both to construct versions of what the team is currently doing and constitutes ways to act that respond to those versions. Accounts of past practice in the present become a resource in defining future practice.

## Innovation as part of mundane practice

It is important to note that no special status is being accorded to "innovatory" practices as distinct from mundane features of team member's social relationships and "normal" working practice. "Innovation" in organizational practice is examined not as some extraordinary and potentially "endangered" marginal feature of the changing social organization of work but as formulable as part of the "commonplaces" of improvisation within ordinary everyday practice.

## Improvising potential innovations in practice

In addition to the generation and maintenance of common knowledge constituting working intelligence, it is possible to examine how arguments focused through dilemmas of uncertainty provide a basis for the improvisation of new procedures and, as will be outlined next, the articulation of interim solutions to problems confronting team practice. The aim is to illustrate how the team's incidental conversations open up "spaces for the improvisation" of possible interim solutions in the light of plausible arguments concerning the future. Of particular interest are the specific rhetorical resources available in ordinary conversation for achieving improvisations in team practice.

Sequence 4 is an example of rhetorically structured improvisation. It also demonstrates that such talk can lay the basis for innovations in practice. The conversation was recorded on a different occasion from Sequence 2 but in the same general meeting place at the Child Development Centre, the Sister's office. "P," a pharmacy assistant, entered the room and immediately addressed "N" one of the nursery nurses on the team.

*Sequence 4*

1 P:  Sally I have split it into two bottles and given two syringes
2 N:  yes
3 P:  one for school and one for home
4 N:  that's great thank you

5 P: and I didn't split the tablets because with it being a twice daily dose I presumed they would be taking both doses at home

6 N: yes yes yes I would think so thank you

7 P: OK then (about to leave)

8 N: I'll put them in that cupboard (indicating one in the room)| Dad might come straight round to you for it because I think he usually does normally| we give the prescriptions and leave it and he is picking it up tomorrow so I'll I'll lock it in that cupboard so if he turns up

9 P: do you want me to take it back to the pharmacy

10 N: he is more likely to come straight to you for it

11 P: alright then as long as long I don't want him somebody want somebody just to pick it up (&)

| 

12 N: you didn't want somebody not to explain

13 P: (&) without explaining but if we keep it it will be

14 N: if you keep it you will make sure you explain it

15 P: yes and if ever they want to write that you know to split it in two its OK

| 

16 N: will you be open
tomorrow it is Good Friday (possible holiday) is the Pharmacy open

17 P: no no

18 N: I'd better ring him and ask him to come up for it this afternoon then alright

19 P: yes do you want (offering the drugs back)

20 N: I will give him a ring now I'm just um when I have finished talking I will ring Dad and ask him to come up this afternoon but I won't be here

21 P: right so collect it from us then (&)

| 

22 N:        so it is best at Pharmacy

23 P: (&) and we explain that

24 S: alright then thanks

25 P: OK thanks a lot (leaves room with drugs)

Neither of the two participants had planned this exchange. The pharmacy assistant had brought over some prescribed drugs to the Centre. The nursery nurse happened to be the person who was available to discuss the logistics of getting the drugs to the family and the reason for why the drugs and the syringes had been packed in the way they had.

This brief sequence of dialogue illustrates the importance of such conversations in the socially coordinated activity of the hospital. However, it is more than a simple exchange or transfer of information concerning a particular case and set of circumstance between individuals representing the CDC and the pharmacy. The interactional accomplishment of the conversation is the improvisation of a solution that was a best fit to what were plausible interpretations and representations of the father's expectations of where the drug would be made available, and the wider constraints of an impending public holiday. It is this interactional work expressed through argumentation as to what might be a plausible resolution of the practical dilemma of coordination that is of particular interest: how to get the drugs to the family with the appropriate instructions. That rhetorical work handles a range of uncertainties within the situation and lays the basis for future innovations in working practice with respect to coordination between the team within the CDC and the pharmacy department.

The whole sequence was obviously part of a rolling "co-text" (Brown & Yule, 1983) of shared understanding concerning that particular family's immediate requirements. The pharmacist made no effort to contextualize what she said and the nurse demanded no such background. Their interaction commences with the pharmacist informing the nursery nurse of what they have done (lines 1–6). But through that declaration a discursive context is established that affords the possibility of joint argumentation concerning the reasons why they have done what they did for one set of drugs but not for the other. Even the statement elaborating the reasons for the idiosyncratic method of dispensing the prescription is couched in the form of an argument (*"I didn't . . . because,"* line 5). This argumentative structure is extended to the "presumption" that a *"twice daily dose"* would not entail the necessity to *"split"* the tablets.

For the moment, the concern is with how the argumentative structure and content of the exchange allows for an elaboration of what it was necessary to do in order to achieve effective coordination in the handing over of the drugs. The plausibility of the argument expressed in the pharmacy assistant's assertion is accepted by the Nurse – ". . . *yes I would think so"* – as a likely condition or assertion. Interestingly, further considerations are raised by the nursery nurse just after the pharmacy assistant is on the point of departure – a standard conversational location for raising ancillary or contingent concerns (Schegloff, 1972; McHoul, 1986).

The conditionality of what *"might happen"* is taken up by the nursery nurse: *"Dad might . . . does normally . . . if he . . ."* (line 8). This expression of conditionality is a commentary couched in the form of an argument about the specific intended operation of placing the drugs in a convenient cupboard. The argument in the commentary works on the plausible implications of a course of action that involves allocating the responsibility to the Centre for realizing the handing of the drugs to the father: the father would normally be handed a prescription for the drugs by the Centre, which he would pick up at the pharmacy department. This in turn opens up the possibility of another course of action that embodies an alternative allocation of responsibility: return the drugs to the pharmacy for collection by the parent. That was expressed in the pharmacist's specific suggestion (line 9) of *"take it back to the pharmacy."*

In accepting that as a possibility, a second problem was identified: who should take responsibility for explaining the idiosyncratic way the drugs have been prescribed. The pharmacy department has the local "intelligence" for "dispensing" both the reason and the drug. It was jointly ratified in the conversation that it was essential to have those idiosyncratic circumstances explained by someone who was in the know: *"you did not want somebody not to explain"* (line 12); *"if we keep it it will be"* (line 13); *"if you keep it you will make sure you explain"* (line 14). The locating of the drug with the appropriate department creates the conditions of realizing a solution of successfully communicating the information to the family.

It is at that point in the local improvisation of solutions that manage uncertainties in the situation that a potential general principle or interactionally situated "script" is formulated concerning coordination on future occasions is raised. Out of the specific details of this case, a general innovative principle is suggested: *"Yes and if you mention to the doctor that if ever they want to write that you know split it in two that's OK"* (line 15). This principle is not "written" into any "code of practice" outlining the procedures to be adhered to in the prescription of drugs in a nonstandard manner; it inheres in the rhetorical organization of the situated interaction of the current circumstances.

However, at that point another set of specific conditions becomes apparent, the impending public holiday, and the "innovation" of routine is not taken up as a topic of further concern. A practical contradiction becomes apparent. Allocating the responsibility to the pharmacy for giving both the drugs and the information about their use could mean the parent coming on a day when the pharmacy was closed: *"will you be open tomorrow . . . ?"* (line 16). Again the specific operational logistics are thrown into the melting pot of the discussion: *". . . do you want"* (offering the drugs back) (line 19). A resolution is suggested in line 20 with the nurse agreeing to telephone the father immediately and to get him to collect the drugs *"this afternoon but I won't be here"* (line 20). That sealed the logistics of how to achieve both the giving of the drugs to the father, that afternoon, and informing him of the reasons concerning the manner of their prescription: *"so it is best at the Pharmacy and we can explain"* (line 22). The reasoning is not contingent upon individual perceptions or cognitive schema concerning what people might have done in the past, or may do in the future, but is jointly constructed as part of the social reasoning of their talk about their work.

The important point to be made about the foregoing analysis is that a possibility for future practice was formulated precisely when an anomalous circumstance was identified. In this respect, a potential innovation in practice was proposed as an upshot of improvisation. In turn, an improvised solution was required exactly because uncertainty returned over how a course of action should be formulated and over what Dad might do. Thus, uncertainty is far from being the enemy of innovation. On the contrary, its return within everyday practice is both innovation's resource and provocation.

## Conclusion

The aim of this discussion has been to demonstrate the implications of the rhetorical nature of talk about teamwork for mediating the way multiprofessional teams accomplish common understandings of their work activity and in the way they improvise interim solutions, and sometimes new procedures, for dealing with the unique aspects of their case loads. It is unnecessary to accord any special status to "innovatory" practices as distinct from mundane features of member's social relationships and "normal" working practice. As indicated earlier, "innovation" in organizational practice can be understood not as some extraordinary marginal feature of the changing social organization of work but within the "commonplaces" of improvisation that occur in ordinary everyday practice. Such a performative perspective points us to the analysis of social practices and the way in which they produce and reproduce individuals and social forms.

The organization of this team talk, frequently unplanned "corridor talk," centers on how to represent and account to others the relationships between different professionals and between professionals and their clients. The arguments people have in their attempts to resolve or evade the dilemmas that emerge in representing and accounting for their working life appear crucial to the coordination of team practice, as are the maintenance of past experience as the working intelligence for that practice, and the definition of appropriate ways forward in particular cases and in terms of team procedures in general.

The suggestion that team conversations constitute a key element in multidisciplinary practice is not to suggest that such conversations provide a route to the "real" structure of the organization or definitive versions of team member's beliefs and identities. The critical point is that conversational argument both constructs a jointly ratified version of events and achieves some coordinate action in response to that version. Variation in the lines of argument managing the dilemmas of practice opens up options for future team practice – a product of collective deliberation. In addition, variability in the way versions get instantiated opens up the possibility of improvising a variety of means of going from given circumstances to new. The accounts constructed in the conversations of team members are the resource that is locally grounded and is drawn upon in their subsequent action.

The argumentatively constructed accounts of team practice afford not only the possibility of a productive and flexible creation of the *object* of team activity but also the constitution of team activity as a collective enterprise (see also Lerner, 1993). Collectivity is afforded because arguments, whether embodied in the statements of individual team members or in disputation between team members or between the team and its clients, express opinions or positions that are controversial in some social arena. Consideration of the interactional organization of team talk and the rhetorical work team members engage in order to evade or attempt to resolve the dilemmas of team practice elaborates the notion of any socially constituted joint cognition in team practice.

The consequences of all this is that approaching team practice from such a discourse-analytic perspective changes the focus of the research enterprise. Instead of studying teamwork as an unambiguously definable activity or process that has determinate functions or effects, teamwork is studied as something shaped by peoples' attempts to grapple with the uncertainties of presentation and representation associated with their work as practitioners and experiences as participants. The way they interactionally (re)present their work in talk, and engender a variety of discursive positions and devices to accomplish membership in teams, is a major resource in accomplishing collectivity in teamwork.

## Acknowledgments

The help and cooperation of Dot MacKinlay and Hilda Topliss is gratefully acknowledged. My thanks also to members of the Loughborough Discourse and Rhetoric Group (including Malcolm Ashmore, Michael Billig, Derek Edwards, and Jonathan Potter); to members of the Communication Department, UC San Diego Graduate Seminar on Work Research (including Katherine Brown, Yrjö Engeström, and Judith Gregory); and Aaron Cicourel, for their critical comments. I am also most grateful to John Bowers for his suggested amendments.

## Notes

1 The team occupied one L-shaped wing of a single-story building adjacent to the Paediatric Outpatients Department of the hospital. A significant feature of the building was a 3 m wide corridor. This corridor gave line of sight access to a large waiting and play area near the main entrance. The corridor space was used by children, parents, and unit members as a place to congregate and converse. This resulted in an extensive amount of unscheduled contact between people visiting and working in the unit.

2 At the time this study was conducted, the team consisted of 11 core members whose principal work at the hospital was based within the Child Development Centre. These include a Sister appointed to be in daily charge of the management of running of the unit, staff nurse, nursery nurse, occupational therapist, speech therapist, two physiotherapists, two clerical assistants, a pediatrician with overall clinical responsibility for medical decisions, and a clinical child psychologist (half-time). In addition, the unit housed associated medical services offering optometry, audiology, dentistry, neurology, and further pediatric services. It also provided a base for a variety of community workers who attended the unit on a part-time basis to coordinate services including physiotherapy, health visiting, and social work.

3 Transcription conventions. Numbers in { } are reference markers for use in subsequent discussion. (.) Indicates pause less than 1 second; ( ) pause in seconds; coincident speech; (&) continued speech; (details) substituted; (. . .) indecipherable talk; italics indicate emphasis; ? signals question intonation irrespective of grammar; (:) extension of vocalization, i.e., u:m.

4 Goffman (1981) has discussed this general phenomenon in his discussion on "footing." He pointed out that commonly "words are heard as representing in some direct way the *current* desire, belief, perception, or intention of whoever animates the utterance" (p. 147). Many utterances are not of that form. Although speakers may represent themselves through "the offices of a personal

pronoun, typically 'I'," that "I" can be diactically displaced within the utterance in time and place. We can both quote ourselves as situated in other times and places and we can quote others to animate our words. Such displacements are more than a matter of convenience and variety in the organization of talk; they reveal its rhetorical and argumentative organization.

# References

Atkinson, J. M. & Heritage, J. (Eds.) (1984). *Structure of Social Action: Studies in Conversation Analysis.* Cambridge: Cambridge University Press.

Bax, M. & Whitmore, K. (1985). District Handicap Teams: Structure, Function and Relationships. Report to the D.H.S.S., London.

Beale, G. (1976). *Practical Sociological Reasoning and the Making of Social Relationships among Health Centre Participants,* pp. 61–75. In M. Stacey (Ed.). The Sociology of the N.H.S. Monograph 22, University of Keele.

Billig, M. (1987). *Arguing and Thinking: A Rhetorical Approach to Social Psychology.* Cambridge: Cambridge University Press.

Billig, M., Condor, S., Edwards, D., Gane, M., Middleton, D., & Radley, A. (1988). *Ideological Dilemmas: A Social Psychology of Everyday Life.* London: Sage.

Brown, G. & Yule, G. (1983). *Discourse Analysis.* Cambridge: Cambridge University Press.

Cochran, M. (1986). The parental empowerment process: Building on family strengths. In J. Harris (Ed.), *Child Psychology in Action.* London: Croom Helm.

Cooper, R. (1986). Organisation/Disorganisation. *Social Science Information, 25*(2), 299–355.

Court Report (1976). Fit for the Future. Report of the Committee on Child Health Services DHSS (Department of Health and Social Security). London: HMSO.

Crocker, P. (1982). An Examination and Evaluation of the York Child Development Centre. Unpublished synopsis of research, Department of Social Administration, University of York, England.

CSCW (1986 & 1988). Proceedings of Conference on Computer Supported Co-operative Work. ACM, New York.

Davis, A. G. & Strong, P. M. (1976). Aren't children wonderful? A study of the allocation of identity in developmental assessment. In M. Stacey (Ed.), *The Sociology of the N.H.S.,* pp. 156–175. Monograph 22, University of Keele.

Drew, P. & Heritage, J. (Eds.) (1992). *Talk at Work: Interaction in Institutional Settings.* Cambridge: Cambridge University Press.

Edwards, D. & Middleton, D. (1986). Joint remembering: Constructing an account of shared experience through conversational discourse. *Discourse Processes, 9*(4), 423–459.

Edwards, D. & Potter, J. (1992). *Discursive Psychology.* London: Sage.

Edwards, D., Middleton, D., & Potter, J. (1992). Towards a discursive theory of remembering. *Psychologist 5,* 439–455.

Garfinkel, H. (1967). *Studies in Ethnomethodology.* Englewood Cliffs, NJ: Prentice Hall.

Gilbert, G. N. & Mulkay, M. (1984). *Opening Pandora's Box: A Sociological Analysis of Scientists' Discourse.* Cambridge: Cambridge University Press.

Gliedman, J. & Roth, W. (1980). *The Unexpected Minority: Handicapped Children in America.* New York: Harcourt Brace Jovanovich.

Goffman, E. (1981). *Forms of Talk.* Oxford: Basil Blackwell.

Grint, K. (1991). *The Sociology of Work: An Introduction.* Cambridge: Polity Press.

Hutchins, E. (1985). The Social Organisation of Cognition. Unpublished manuscript, San Diego, Institute for Cognitive Studies. San Diego: University of California.

Hutchins, E. (1990). The technology of team navigation. In J. Galagher, R. Kraut & C. Egido (Eds.), *Intellectual Teamwork.* Hillsdale: Erlbaum.

Jirotka, M., Gilbert, G. N., & Luff, P. (1990). On the Social Organisation of Organisations. *CSCW: An International Journal, 1*(1–2), 95–118.

Kleinman, A. (1980). *Patients and Healers in the Context of Culture.* Berkeley: University of California Press.

Latour, B. (1986). The powers of association. In J. Law (Ed.), *Power, Action and Belief.* London: Routledge and Kegan Paul.

Lave, J. (1988). *Cognition in Practice: Mind, Mathematics and Culture in Everyday Life.* Cambridge: Cambridge University Press.

Lerner, G. H. (1993). Collectivities in action: Establishing the relevance of conjoined participation in conversation. *Text, 13*(2), 213–245.

Levine, J. M. & Moreland, R. L. (1989). Cognitive integration in work groups. Paper presented at the conference on Socially Situated Cognition, Learning Research and Development Centre, University of Pittsburgh.

McHoul, A. (1986). The getting of sexuality: Foucault, Garfinkel and the analysis of sexual discourse. *Theory, Culture and Society, 3,* 65–79.

McHugh, P. (1968). *Defining the Situation: The Organization of Meaning in Social Interaction.* New York: The Bobbs-Merrill.

Middleton, D. (1987). Collective memory and remembering: some issues and approaches. *LCHC Quarterly Newsletter, 9*(1), 2–5.

Middleton, D. (Ed.) (1991). Activity and Collective Memory: Introduction. *Activity Theory, 9/10,* 3–5.

Middleton, D. (forthcoming). *Social Remembering.* London: Sage.

Middleton, D. & Edwards, D. (Eds.) (1990). *Collective Remembering.* London: Sage.

Middleton, D. J. & Mackinlay, D. (1987). Gossip and Titbits in Team-Work: Conversation as an Instrument of Multi-disciplinary Practice in Child Development Centres. Paper presented at the Nordic Society for Educational Research Conference on *Activity, Work and Learning.* Karja, Finland.

Morgan, G. (1986). *Images of Organisation.* London: Sage.

Orr, J. (1986). Narratives at work, story telling as a co-operative diagnostic activity. Proceedings of *Conference on Computer-Supported Co-operative Work,* pp. 65–72. MCC Software Technology Program, Texas.

Potter, J. & Wetherell, M. (1987). *Discourse and Social Psychology: Beyond Attitudes and Behaviour.* London: Sage.

Rittenberg, W. (1985). Mary: Patient as Emergent Symbol on a Pediatric Ward: The Objectification of Meaning in Social Process, pp. 141–153. In R. A. Hahn and A. D. Gaines (Eds.). Dordrecht: Reidel.

Sacks, H., Schegloff, E. A., & Jefferson, G. (1974). A simplest systematics for the organisation of turn-taking in conversation. *Language, 50,* 596–735.

Schegloff, E. A. (1972). Notes on a conversational practice: Formulating place. In D. Sudnow (Ed.), *Studies in Social Interaction.* New York: Free Press.

Sharrock, W. & Anderson, B. (1987). Work flow in a paediatric clinic. In G. Button and J. R. E. Lee (Eds.), *Talk and Social Organisation.* Clevedon Philadelphia: Multilingual Matters.

Shotter, J. (1990). The manager as author: A rhetorical-responsive, social constructionist approach to social-organisational problems. Epilogue. In J. Shotter (Ed.), *Knowing of the Third Kind.* Utrecht: ISOR/University of Utrecht.

Silverman, D. (1987). *Communication and Medical Practice: Social Relations in the Clinic.* London: Sage.

Stacey, M. (1980). Charisma, power and altruism: A discussion of research in a child development centre. *Sociology of Health and Illness, 2*(1), 64–90.

Suchman, L. (1987). *Plans and Situated Action: The Problem of Human Machine Interaction.* Cambridge: Cambridge University Press.

Thomas, A., Bax, M., Coombes, K., Goldson, E., Smyth, D., & Whitmore, K. (1984). The Health and Social Needs of Physically Handicapped Young Adults: Are They being Met by Statutory Services. Report of the Community Paediatric Research Unit. London: St. Mary's Hospital Medical School.

Tomlinson, S. (1981). Professionals and ESN(M) education. In W. Swann (Ed.), *The Practice of Special Education*. Oxford: Basil Blackwell in association with The Open University Press.

Warnock Report (1978). Special Educational Needs. Report of the Committee of Enquiry into the Education of Handicapped Children and Young People. DES (Department of Education and Science). London: HMSO.

Wolfendale, S. (1986). Ways of increasing parental involvement in children's development and education. In J. Harris (Ed.), *Child Psychology in Action*. Beckenham: Croom Helm.

Woolgar, S. (1988). *Science: The Very Idea*. London: Tavistock.

# 11    The collective construction of scientific genius*

*Chandra Mukerji*

Issues of mind and rationality in science are routinely discussed by philosophers of science but not so often by social scientists studying the practice of scientists.[1] There are obvious reasons for this. Mind and rationality as individual attributes seem particularly asocial, perhaps understandable through the tools of individualist psychology but not techniques developed for understanding the collective qualities of human life. Leigh Star[2] has made an effort to look at how the construction of the brain as a site of mental activity is structured collectively by brain researchers, and students of cognition have considered how thought enters into the social processes of problem solving,[3] but most work by social scientists has given secondary importance to mind and rationality as elements of science. Their work instead has focused on the social nature of knowledge, its character as part of the culture of human groups, not individual minds. Thinking that is not communicated to others cannot be science; it can be smart and observant about the natural world, but it cannot be part of science unless it enters the social world of scientists through some collectively understood medium. Similarly, the processes of determining the differences between good and bad science, whether the decision-making structures for making these assessments are rational or not, are fundamentally social activities; scientists will not usually begin to consider the epistemological standing of a scientific claim until is is claimed as scientific. There is obviously much work for students of the social to do in teasing out how forms of association become central to the establishment and power of scientific knowledge, focusing on the social nature of science both as an activity system and a tradition of knowledge.[4]

This tradition leaves out something in the practice of science, however, that will be addressed in this chapter: how mental acuity (and to a lesser extent, individual rationality) are made into social attributes of chief scientists through the activities of laboratory workers. Part of what research teams do is collectively produce a "scientific knower" at the same time that they produce scientific

*An earlier version of the chapter was presented at the University of Bielefeld.

knowledge. They give authority to the knowledge they collectively produce by making it the brain-child of a "great man" (almost always gendered as male) – someone who can think better than ordinary people because he is in fact expressing the thoughts of a group. They organize their group life to construct an authorship that makes the results of their work socially more authoritative; they give their collective actions a singular identity, centered around the chief-scientist-knower. It is this scientist's mind that is said to govern the construction of the research, making the reading of nature done in the laboratory objective; it is this scientist's mind that reviews research results and imposes strict rationality on the arguments used to explain it. The chief scientist orders nature and culture at the same time to set up a laboratory structure that renders nature "objectively," producing models of the world that seem true enough to be considered part of reality. This is the chief-scientist-knower that the group makes an active part of their work lives, helping realize this ideal through their own chief scientist.

Louis Marin argues that the 17th-century sovereign, whose authority was central to life in this period, had two bodies: the corporeal one that was mortal and an ideal one that carried the authority of monarchy, which was constructed through art and collective performances.[5] One can argue that there are two minds of the great scientist: the human one that works with others to solve problems and the ideal one that may use the work of others to manipulate nature in new ways but does not need them to know truths. The first is a learner; the second a maker and authorizer of knowledge. The first lives and dies, while the second gains immortality in a permanent genealogy of scientific minds. The first step is created mostly by the scientist himself, while the latter is in large part the construct of group process made through publications and public performances.

Mind, in this cultural context, is essential to science, not as a personal attribute as much as a social one. Pursuing scientific greatness and locating it in the individual mind together help to construct a social script used by research groups to do their work and reproduce the social power of science. Scientists generally take their thinking seriously, and expect members of the wider social world to respect their work in large part because of its thoughtfulness and accuracy. Philosophers turn to scientists for considering how minds work and how they can achieve rationality because the culture as a whole defines scientists as repositories of mental superiority. Cognitive scientists like Ed Hutchins[6] may study sailors navigating large military vessels into harbors in order to understand cognition, but philosophers tend to pay more attention to DNA researchers.[7] Mind is at work in both contexts, rationality is at stake in each domain, but the routines of scientists get a lot more attention from those who want to speculate about thought-as-mind rather than thought-as-process. This is because of where the culture locates mind.

Recent studies in the sociology of science have made clear how scientific researchers work collectively to constitute scientific "facts" from the everyday activities within the laboratory. Working toward a sociology of scientific knowledge, students of laboratory practice pay attention to the techniques used by scientists to transform social activity into "knowledge." The great virtue of these laboratory studies is that they do not take the facticity of findings for granted, and they see research results as deeply social constructs. They see "scientific knowledge" as a social object that develops collectively from group relations and patterns of communication. This same literature draws attention to the social nature of authoritative knowledge, and points out techniques by which groups make only some knowledge authoritative.[8]

This new literature is extremely useful, and has advanced social studies of science no end, but it does leave some things out. By focusing on the local production of scientific knowledge, and the collective evaluative systems used to assess the quality of scientific knowledge, most ethnographers of science ignore how the cultural authority of science is produced in the laboratory through the collective and self-conscious construction of the chief scientist's mind.

Bruno Latour, in his book on Pasteur, comes close to this project.[9] Latour shows how Pasteur acted as an intellectual entrepreneur who staged public experiments to empower his science and secure resources for his own research program. Pasteur turned laboratory work into a public spectacle where he could make his power as a knower culturally visible, contributing to the standing of science generally and elevating (most of all) the stature of his particular approach to science. Pasteur remains in Latour's book, however, very much the individual author of this narrative of power.

There is an irony in the silence among sociologists of science about the reproduction of "great minds" in the work life of the sciences because the new laboratory-based research in this field has gained much of its distinctiveness from applying to the activities of scientists ethnographic methods developed in anthropology for understanding the mythologies and methods of cultures.[10] While many sociologists of science have been struggling directly with some of the troublesome veils of cultural illusion shrouding science, trying to tear them aside and see the real science in action, few have thought to study the cultural veils themselves to see how they are woven in the daily routines of research. Scientists clearly make sense of what they do using cultural assumptions about the importance of science, the scientific method, and scientific minds; they use cultural illusions about greatness to spur their studies, and organize their social worlds. To think that we can render their world with any accuracy without attention to the dreams, the structures of virtue and desire, that make it attractive to participants is a strange kind of pseudoscientific hubris in social studies of science that it does not make sense to sustain. Philosophers of science have insistently drawn attention to the centrality of mind in science, but we in social studies of science have all too often just argued with them, and not recognized that they have been pointing to the powerful cultural systems that have authorized scientific work and lured scientists to it. Scientists, on the whole, share the philosophers' concerns about mind and rationality because they need to mobilize these cultural constructs in their work. Studying these cultural ideals and their working out in the social lives of scientists ought to be at the heart of social studies of science.[11]

As a move in this direction, I examine in this chapter observations and interview data from my research on oceanography that show how the collective cognitive work done in labs comes to be attributed to chief scientists, giving them apparent mental powers beyond those of normal individuals. In this process, the intellectual life of the laboratory is made to reproduce the "scientific knower" as a cultural type. A mind is made along with a body of knowledge, and both are disseminated together as a science of rational knowers, populated by larger-than-life characters who develop breathtakingly clever solutions to technical problems in their daily lives, using the skills of the groups in their labs.

It is conventional in analyzing the role of science in modern societies to study well-established physicists or biologists (i.e., elite members of traditional and prestigious sciences), and use them as models for the rest of science, even though they are exceptional cases. Instead, I have studied one of the less prestigious sciences, oceanography, one that has not traditionally been a great source of great men for scientific textbooks. Nonetheless, notions of scientific genius and individual mental ability remain part of this world. Oceanography tends to be technologically complex and hence expensive work, which has been funded and shaped by military needs during the Cold War into a domain of mostly big science. This area of research is not generally a site of lone thinkers; there are few of the itinerant theorists of physics. Oceanographers rarely have the freedom simply to follow their instincts and hone their analytic gifts independently, so their field seems an unlikely site for producing individual genius. Nonetheless, dreams of this sort remain powerful. Major new work in the deep ocean, the revitalization and reformulations of plate tectonics, and (on a smaller scale) the discovery of the hydrothermal vents on the seafloor, have refueled the ambitions of researchers and kept alive the sense that path-breaking thinkers could indeed be among them.

I use the writings of Erving Goffman on teamwork and public behavior to analyze the collective activities that help reproduce the culturally prescribed, individualized scientific knower among oceanographers. Many years ago, Goffman drew attention to the scripting and improvising of collective, public performances as part of everyday interaction. Goffman made clear that groups routinely act in concert in order to project a definition of reality to wider social groups.[12] Scientific research teams are no exception. They quite self-consciously rehearse how they will present new findings at scientific meetings; they prepare for site visits from the National Science Foundation or other funding agencies; they ready themselves before visits from administrators, who come to evaluate their progress and needs; and, most importantly, they craft a single voice for publications in which they present their work to their peers, using a naturalistic discourse that evokes images of scientific research as a seamless and rational activity. These collective performances help to forge the social group into a cognitive unit, and make their work credible as a singular, rational site of thought that can be attributed to the chief scientist.

Part of my analytic purpose in this work is to indicate how this kind of performance analysis could be combined with the laboratory study tradition of the sociology of science through a communication approach to scientific practice.[13] Students of the laboratory have already shown the importance of communication in laboratory practice. "Talk" in the laboratory is the site of much scientific thinking. People develop interpretations of experimental phenomena with each other, and talk about their analyses before and while writing them up. "Information" is both distinguished from experimental error and retrieved from experimental practice through group work, and it is shaped by groups into journal articles and conference papers that present the lab's work to the public. This social activity is organized around and coordinated through different media of communication – from computers and telephones to public forums and print media. Communication is at the heart of science, since public information about the natural world is the avowed purpose of research.[14] The point is that communication does not end with the exchange of information. Information only makes sense in cultural context and this context must be conveyed in the same activities that generate information. The results of an experiment (changes in cleaning fluid set deep in a mountain) only make sense in terms of a tradition of particle physics that would explain what particle would go through so much rock and be able to affect the fluid set out there. Moreover, the study of particles among physicist cannot be understood without reference to the importance of the cultural celebration of scientific genius as a means of attracting participants to this difficult domain of social life. Underlying belief in the value of science and the greatness of scientists is an underpinning of the everyday life of laboratories, a place where the political power of science enters into its practice.

Much of the precedent for this kind of analysis comes from feminist studies of science, which have asked questions about the political and cultural status of the scientific knower and the construction of scientific knowledge. Attention to the power of gender politics in the world of science provides precedent for thinking about the political construction of the scientific knower and knowledge.[15] The study here does not focus much on gender, per se, but it does show how scientific knowledge, the practice of science, and accounts of nature are coconstructed in laboratory work as part of a system of politics that stratifies participants, making the chief scientist the repository of the gifts of the group and relegating others in the lab to bit parts in the drama of discovery. It turns out that this stratification system does indeed map onto gender differences. As laboratories glorify their head scientists, they move authority away from technicians (who are often women) to chief scientists (who are usually men). How this pattern of gender relations and the cult of genius interact is not clear enough from my data to be pursued much farther here. Still, there is clearly something gendered about ideal images of scientific brilliance that helps tailor the celebration of genius to the gender stratification of science. No wonder analytic strategies from feminist studies of science prove useful in this kind of analysis.

The making and remaking of "great thinkers" among chief scientists in the everyday conduct of research is, in sum, a central and consequential way in which the cultural power of science and the image of scientists are aligned through social relations and the layered patterns of communication that coconstruct them. The result is a stratified world of science, shaped in part by gender relations and organized to reproduce a particular vision of personal (and masculine) virtue that drives the everyday activities of those who work in science.[16]

## The inheritance of greatness

Science gains its authority not only because it can solve problems (as people like to say), but also because scientists are supposed to be smart and are thought to tackle successfully the most recalcitrant of problems with their minds and methods. Scientists are drawn to their work in part because they like these images of science and scientists. Many want to participate in the culture of genius and help construct its next incarnations. They have stakes in this cultural stream, so as they work on their research, they also work on reproducing a social image of science that prizes rationality and genius. They aspire to Nobel prizes and they take them very seriously, supporting the notion of genius through the culture of its reward. They learn a naturalistic discourse in which to couch and promote their ideas in order to impress on their listeners the rationality of their work. They translate the frequent confusions of laboratory life into a clear voice of truth. They masculinize the scientist-knower in order to mark him as objective and authoritative, or locate any woman in that position as unusual enough to be able to occupy this masculinized space.

The procedures laboratory workers use to arrive at scientific explanation of the world are complex patterns of social interaction that, while getting cognitive work done, also assume and elaborate a culture of authority for science defined as deriving from a genealogy of great minds invested in a tradition of rational thought. The genealogical strain in scientific culture comes out not only in the textbook stories of the history of science, in which Newton, Galileo, and Einstein are featured, but also in the everyday language of scientists. It is not that they are so arrogant that they routinely talk about being like these men. In fact, quite the contrary, they are more likely to say in a rather disappointed or disparaging tone that they could never have that kind of genius. But even in suggesting that there is no genius in themselves, these speakers point to the importance of the inhumanly smart scientific knower still alive in their world.

Scientific genealogies are also commonly drawn among researchers, not so much back to Newton or Bohr but to living but important scientists. Young scientists do this most frequently. They tend to locate themselves intellectually as someone's student or a follower of a "thinker" whose work has influenced them deeply. Sometimes they describe themselves as members of a cohort that has broken away from its intellectual inheritance to forge a new kind of science, but even in these cases the cohort is defined in terms of a generation that fits within a system of descent. The genealogies that scientists use to describe themselves can vary from one occasion to the next, depending on the audience and context. When speaking to those who know little about science, they may refer to some great scientist in the past just because they assume this is all their audience will know. On other occasions, they may use more current scientists and scientific work to lay out their sense of familial ties. In all these cases, however, there is little question that they locate themselves within a stream of history defined in terms of generations of thinkers passing on their wisdom and skills to the next generation.

These genealogies are, importantly, ways to claim more than mere intellectual heritage; they are ways of claiming credentials and acquiring status by association. One young man traced two generations in his line of descent to explain why he was doing the kind of work he did – in large part because his intellectual "grandparent" was better known than his mentor. Sometimes, this kind of talk placed the speaker within a pattern of normal science, describing social networks and patterns of intellectual interests that were well known and well respected. Other times, the genealogies placed the speaker in a world of changing paradigms; the young scientist was located in a history of men of science, who were working at the cutting edge of a field.

This view of historical legacy is clearly tied to the pursuit of scientific greatness. Each claim of lineage shows the value of the speaker, either by association with greatness or in contrast to a discredited heritage. This kind of claim may be most evident in the young, who have not yet determined how great or ordinary they will be as scientists, but it is also present among the most advanced cohorts of scientists. They may, however, define their familial ties less through associations by training and more through relationships developed during their careers. One quite old oceanographer talked at length about the highlight of his career: working with a man who he saw as the greatest in his field. The interviewee was certainly among the notables in the field himself, but he could not stop repeating his delight in the wit and wisdom of his idol. This kind of genuine respect and delight in the gifts of others could only occur because this man saw his world in terms of scientific genius. Getting near to this genius and learning from and with him was enough to define his career as valuable and exciting.

The respect scientists generally hold for Nobel prizes is also a marker of this culture of greatness. They may grumble about who the winners have been, and discuss who else might have won, but the association of the prize with greatness goes unquestioned. There is thought to be a possibility of genius in science, politics, and literature that makes sense of Nobel prizes in these areas, and scientists subscribe to this view.[17]

The excitement that technicians can gain from working in well-known laboratories also has some roots in this culture of greatness. To see themselves as part of something that might be historically significant, that might lead to a Nobel prize, or at least a lasting entry in histories of science, adds to the reward structure of being an assistant. One man transferred from industry into a laboratory in a research institution to work under a man he felt was making massive contributions to his field. He did not want to leave industry because the pay was so good, but he wanted to work with the man who ran this lab because it would give him the sense of adventure he lacked in industry.

The legacy of greatness in science, then, leaks into the world of everyday scientific practice even for those who are not singled out as geniuses. This influence shows not so much in the ways scientists talk to each other about their experiments but in the ways they develop careers and discuss their sense of personal accomplishment. Many turn to science to develop or at least be near a great scientific "mind," and they find themselves willing to help construct one, if one is not at hand. What is striking is their willingness to bring this greatness to life in others, just to keep it part of their social world. They seem to want to have genius in science, even if it is not their own.

### Laboratory signatures and corporate identity in labs

The linchpin in the process of collective "mind" building in science is what I call laboratory signatures. Different laboratories develop and use peculiar combinations of research techniques, theoretical allegiances, and empirical goals that constitute signatory attributes of the labs. The signature of a research group is (by convention) assumed to be "written" in the hand of the chief scientist, and the question of whether it really is or is not a personal construct does not enter the public life of science. A signature both gives a laboratory a distinctive position in the world of science and simultaneously structures the work life within labs; it sets out the analytical strategy for the group. Signatures give laboratories identities on which to hinge claims for fame and requests for funds. One oceanographer put it this way: "There are an awful lot of people out there trying to do the same thing, and if you've got a tool that can set you apart, you know, a machine that allows you to do something that nobody else can do, it just makes it a lot easier to get funding." The signatory technique is a useful tool for managing the laboratory's finances because it provides a way of distinguishing one research group from other labs; it locates the lab's choice of problems and techniques for solving them so that its success can be anticipated for funding purposes and assessed when their results are published.

There are many interesting characteristics of signatures, but the one that concerns us here is the ways they help promote the lab's work through the reputation of the chief-scientist-knower. On one hand, the signatory techniques of a lab are developed and used by a group consisting of not just the chief scientist, but also the technicians, graduate students, and post-docs who execute most of the research protocols in labs. On the other hand, the design and success of the signatures are attributed to the chief scientist as a kind of author of the group's work. Laboratory workers of all categories, who are loyal members of the group, present themselves as merely acting out research scripts written by their chief scientist. In laboratories where the support personnel are unhappy, they often see this system of scientific credit as unfair. They claim they do most of the real work in the lab and get little reward or recognition for it. In more contented groups, the laboratory workers see the chief scientists as providing them with opportunities for interesting research that they would not have on their own. They see themselves as gaining from the success of the chief scientists, so they readily serve their careers.

In fact, many of the fascinating, imaginative, and subtle thinkers who contribute to science are not the named leaders of the field, but the graduate students, post-docs, and technicians who help to make the careers of chief scientists. Chief scientists often know and acknowledge this in private, saying that the members of their groups make their work what it is. They know they are too busy to exercise the kind of control over their labs that would make all the work done there properly attributable to them. Participants in the group know this, too. One man I interviewed said that the head engineer in his lab, not the chief scientists, was the one who really mobilized and disciplined the lab employees. In a large lab like his one, the chief scientist could never develop and oversee all the projects that went on in the lab. Chief scientists cannot even tell technicians what they want done in the laboratory when they hire the technicians for skills that they do not have. Instead, they ask these assistants to tell the group what they *could* do with equipment or techniques. Heads of labs also cannot be directly acquainted with all the patterns of in the data that end up in the papers written by their groups. Often they are not at the bench when new phenomena are seen, and must rely on descriptions and data logs by others to bring them "up to speed." On these occasions, the laboratory workers exchange their experience at the bench for the authorization of their "findings" by the scientist-knower. They make the chief scientist the new owner of the laboratory activity and, in return, make what they learn part of the collective thought of the group.

Some lab members resent this exchange system, but it is a rare person who does not try to sustain it in public. Most stories about the problems with the system are told by young scientists who have recently broken out of a lab of a major scientist. They are free to speak. Most laboratory workers are not. Without openly articulating or questioning the logic of it, they present their head scientists as running shops in which all products (discoveries) belong in some sense to the owner. When pressed about unfair attribution, they point out that scientific journal articles from the lab usually contain a long list of authors, showing who worked on the project: the first author did most of real work, and the last author was the chief scientist. But on some occasions, junior scientists or graduate students ask their famous chief scientists to take a more prominent place on the list to help their paper get published. In some scandals, when papers were found to be based on falsified data, it has turned out that the chief scientists who had put their names on the pieces had never really checked the data. This was particularly scandalous because members of the world of science *wanted to assume* that the senior author of a piece was prepared to stand behind its quality and be the objective knower, overseeing the collective enterprise. The chief scientific knower turned out to look like a naked emperor.

Knowledgable readers, of course, realize that senior authors may not always have much to do with the work they legitimate with their names, but they nonetheless persist in treating the work as a product of the chief scientist's lab. A current article is often called by a chief scientist's name if it comes from his or her lab, even if a graduate student is first author on the publication.[18] Unknown names become as invisible as the unnamed bodies of laboratory workers. Junior people become hidden behind their chief scientists unless or until a pattern of coauthorship is socially recognized, and the new scientist can take on a separate identity and set up a new lab. Managing this subordination and struggling to become visible in this system constitutes one of the first problems of young scientists; they are particularly aware of the difference between knowing some science and being a scientific knower. Constructing scientific knowers as laboratory workers is both good training for becoming such a scientist some day and a difficult place from which to start.

Does this mean that lab assistants and technicians are simply exploited by chief scientists who use their skills and reap the rewards of their work, getting big reputations and big heads? Some technicians think so, but most do not. Members of research groups often desire and gain benefits from the collective construction of a "great scientist." Even if they have reservations about this system, they still adhere to it. A technician who has no alternative way of making a living or a postdoc who has failed to secure an independent identity and job are both linked in their careers to the success of the chief scientist. If the work is exciting in their lab and they have a happy relationship with their coworkers, they have more to gain from promoting the chief scientist than trying to get attention for themselves and their own science. That is why they are willing to work together (and subordinate themselves explicitly) to constitute through their research contributions a public and fictional scientist – someone who can indeed think better than mere mortals because the thinking body for this creature, the "scientific genius," is a group.

## Laboratory signatures and technique in oceanography

Oceanographers, because they often need to use elaborate equipment to get data from the ocean, tend to organize laboratory signatures around particular pieces of equipment. In this, they are not unusual. Physicists using particle accelerators and astronomers using observatories are much like oceanographers who go to sea in ships; they all use common equipment and often define differences in terms of the particular equipment they bring to the common core set.[19]

If a laboratory signature consists of a set of technical protocols designed to address a particular scientific problem, then it is realized, not in the chief scientist's quiet office, but in work stations scattered around the laboratory, or at sea. Technical protocols may be discussed and defended in an office, but they are tried, revised, abandoned, or improved in the laboratory (or ocean) itself. The most noticeable aspect of the work is that it is located where machines are manipulated. Thinking in this kind of collective yet technically distributed setting consists not of abstract contemplation, but structured patterns of interaction with equipment and patterned interactions for transferring the encounters with machines over to the chief scientist. We will turn later to the way the chief scientist is made the beneficiary of this structure. For now, we will turn to the relations with equipment by laboratory workers, which constitute the backbone of the research process.

The spatially decentralized work of most laboratories sets up a pattern of distributed cognition. Not only the work but the *thinking* of a lab is scattered about the laboratory at different work stations or stretched from land to sea. Technicians using the equipment are also generally responsible for what they do on their own, particularly when they go on board a ship without the chief scientist. The analysis of an experiment goes on intermittently and socially among those responsible for different parts of the work. It is the combination of the social interaction integrating different parts of a signatory technique and the decentralized interaction with machinery that form the basis for the coordination of laboratory work that gives it a distinctive character.[20]

One cannot begin to understand the collective cultural work of labs without looking closely at what lab personnel do at their work stations. As Ian Hacking argues,[21] experiments are not just events in which hypotheses are checked, but structured opportunities for thinking about nature while messing about with it. Researchers generate scientific ideas, not just data, as they manipulate samples (that they think of as nature under study) or devices that measure some phenomenon not directly observable.[22] This kind of manipulation is not mindless drudgery, but rather depends upon ongoing interpretation of results and decision making about how to alter the equipment or fiddle with the research design. Each change in equipment or its use allows researchers new opportunities for manipulation, and yet also challenges them to discover the limits to the equipment and the generalizations the group might make from its use. Hence, technicians at the workbench, even while doing superficially boring and repetitious work, have to think continuously about the research process.

Shapin and Schaffer make clear that this kind of work with machines is and has been at the heart of modern experimental science since its inception. Steve Shapin has also continued to investigate the role of technicians in making experimental science possible, demonstrating that much of the thinking that Hacking thinks *scientists* do in the laboratory is in fact done by their assistants, and constitutes not support work (although it is seen this way) but the heart of learning by experiment.[23]

What is it that technicians or research assistants do when they are at the workbench using equipment? David Sudnow provides an interesting model for thinking about the social psychology of this kind of play with machines in his book, *Ways of the Hand.*[24] The usefulness of the model may not be immediately apparent to students of science because this book is substantively about playing jazz piano, but in it Sudnow describes how people learn to improvise on an instrument. One can use his analysis to consider how people in other areas learn to think and act with other kinds of instruments, including ones for making scientific analyses. Sudnow himself invites this kind of extrapolation when he compares the process of solo jazz improvisation on piano to writing on a typewriter or driving a car. In all these cases, he argues, manipulation of equipment is most successful and fluid when it becomes only semiconscious, almost automatic. Trying to think about how you shift gears can almost destroy your ability to drive a car. There is a kind of kinesthetic logic to the touch of hands on machines that "takes over" when machine use is going well. This is when musicians begin to improvise well or drivers lose consciousness of their actions at the wheel and simply feel themselves move as vehicles on the road. At this point, Sudnow says pianists can think with their hands. Similarly, in scientific labs, researchers running their machines think through the machines and their hands. They compensate for problems in the apparatus. They add to the protocols activities that will make the work scientifically more reliable or convincing. They "play" their instruments to see what they can do with it. Even in routine work, there is room for improvisation. As Phil Agre has pointed out, an office worker faced with a large xeroxing job will build up a rhythm and style of work to make her (in his study) interactions with the machine more and more efficient over time. For the office worker, this may only lead to faster xeroxing, but in a scientific lab, this may lead to increased awareness of aberrations in the data that break this flow, either bringing errors to the attention of the lab or making obvious the discovery of some new pattern in the data.[25]

One marine scientist frequently praised by his peers was said to run a model laboratory. What made it model was the way his technicians could develop machinery and array it smoothly around the problems they were supposed to solve. The chief scientist was known as the consummate technical researcher, but he got that reputation by surrounding himself with the kinds of people who could translate desired measurements into working machinery. The point was not just that he enjoyed translating problems into measurement systems (as the model of the talented chief scientist required), but that the working measurement systems were refined long enough to allow sustained studies in which the technicians could explore the possibilities of the equipment until they had it fine-tuned.

The importance of thinking while making measurements with machinery was made clear to a young geologist who could have been but was not the first discoverer of hydrothermal vents on the seafloor. He was taking pictures of the seafloor for a geological survey, working for a distinguished senior scientist, when he found in the pictures images of colonies of clams, crabs, and tube worms. As a geologist, he did not think about whether or not these were routine objects or unusual ones, so he did not think any more about it or bring it to the attention of his chief scientist. Only after the hydrothermal vents had been formally discovered by others did he realize what he had missed. An opportunity for this young man, his chief scientist, and their laboratory was missed in large part because of the decentralized process of data analysis in the group and the isolation of scientific specialties in the institution where this group was located.

Distributed cognition among specialists like this can lead to this kind of narrowness of vision, but it does not preclude making important contributions to the group.[26] In these technically complex research projects, different group members learn a limited repertoire of techniques and ways of thinking about their uses. There is a submission by the technician to the limited range of human senses and capacities that are addressed by the machinery. There is a concentration of energies in a certain direction achieved through the sacrifice of other faculties. A researcher at a microscope concentrates on the sense impressions gathered from the microscope rather than what she or he could smell or hear. At the same time, the microscope narrows the field of vision to a small area in order to make it larger. Both machine and its user contribute to a kind of "tunnel vision." Something similar happens in a research submarine as well, although it is less obvious at first. In the dark and murky waters near the seafloor in most areas of the deep ocean, scientists can see very little. There are small pools of light created by the submarine's exterior floodlights, but even they do not pierce the murk very effectively. Scientists in such a submarine concentrate attentively on what they can see, what their equipment is doing, what kinds of readings they are getting from it, and where the submarine is or is not going. The result is that the researchers get a relatively intimate look at very small portions of the seafloor, blind to what goes on beyond their field of vision, the capacities of their instruments, and the input from the senses that they are not treating as significant. The capacity to think is restricted by machinery while it is also stimulated by it.

Whereas the narrowness of their tasks is often thought to hamper the ability of assistants in the lab to think independently of the chief scientist, who is supposed to have "perspective" on the whole project, much is actually located in the details of everyday lab practices. Sometimes playing with the machines opens new technical or analytic possibilities that only a technician is in a position to recognize. In labs, machines and their tenders can become (at least cognitively) a kind of corporate entity. The end of one and the beginning of the other may be physically obvious; one can see where the hands hit the typewriter. But the activity of making music, conducting an experiment, or writing a line of prose is the act of the corporate entity, not its constituent parts. The violin and violinist both need each other to make music; the musician is really the amalgam of both. Laboratory workers can begin to think through machines in just the way musicians can play through their instruments, feeling how to make something they want. They submit their activities and understanding of these activities to the restricted properties of the equipment, and in the use of those properties learn what research possibilities may be located in them. They do not think about what a microscope is doing to their perception as much as they "see" through their understanding of the microscope and what it does. Much of this understanding is never verbalized; it comes from experience with the machines themselves. Once they can think "through" their instruments, scientists are able to design more successful research projects because they can structure experiments to yield new kinds of results.[27]

> What I've been doing to count the colonies [of bacteria] and the distributions of them in tubes is to count them with an image analyzer. Part of that was just to develop the technology to see what the image analyzer was good for and it's a really sophisticated piece of equipment. It's fantastic . . . . [The chief scientist in the lab] has this device which is a temperature-gradient block; it sets up a temperature gradient from like 0–50° in pressure chambers. So you put a bunch of bacterial cells in a long glass tube in agar, which is a solidifying agent, and so they're distributed along the whole length of the tube. You shove them into a temperature gradient from 0–50° and pressurize them. And I had like eight of these chambers and you put them at all different pressures at the same gradients, then you leave them for a period of time, take them out and then you look to see in what temperature range the colonies formed. Well that's fine and [the chief scientist] had used this device for a long time. You'd mark the extremes and then you'd find that at higher and higher pressures the extremes get narrower and narrower. That's fine but there were some subtleties going on that were really hard to resolve. Like there were areas where the numbers of colonies were different in the tubes and so I wanted to be able to quantify the numbers of colonies and it was really hard. I mean [if] you sit at a microscope and try to count these things you go nuts. So I sat down with [the lab technician] who is our programmer and I said, you know, we have this image analyzer and I . . . and the two of us worked out a program. Basically I was dictating the criteria for the program and he was writing the code and it works great. It's really a nice

> program. In fact I just finished the paper on it . . . . The image analyzer looks
> through a microscope and it photographs an area . . . a small area of the tube;
> then it transforms it to high contrast and then it circles and counts each of the
> colonies . . . . You have to have something that's fairly uniform and the world is-
> n't uniform . . . . The only reason I had any success I think is because the system
> I was dealing with was fairly uniform and the processing that I was doing were
> relative measurements, so that because it was uniform I could say, "Well, even
> though I'm not counting a hundred percent of what's in this tube, I'm doing the
> same thing all along the tube so that the relative numbers are going to be valid
> even if the absolute values aren't." And the image analyzer was great for doing
> that. It generated some data that it would have taken me ages to be able to get by
> eye.

This experimental design was a moment of virtuosity in the play with machines. Like all collective work, laboratory work depends on convention, but it also grows through innovations made within groups.[28] At the workbench, this young man began to play with techniques and machines that he did not know would work. He simply wanted to try the image analyzer, in large part because he was sick of counting colonies by eye. The image analyzer had been in the laboratory, sitting on a shelf, when he noticed it, and asked why it was not being used. He learned that the machine had been abandoned because it was not good at distinguishing overlapping colonies. Absolute counts were inaccurate. But this postdoc realized that you could compare the counts at different parts of the gradient, and the errors would cancel each other out. With this comparative strategy and the computer program to analyze the counts, he and the computer expert in the lab were able to integrate this machine into the repertoire of the lab. The two of them added a new technique for studying variations within the temperature-gradient block to the signatory possibilities of the lab.

## Laboratory technicians and the performance of invisibility

If you enter scientific labs as a visiting interviewer (as I frequently did during this research), you see a very interesting phenomenon that tells a great deal about the structure of labs. When you first appear, most of the technicians first check to see if they know who you are and then, if they do not, get very busy, even if they were not so busy before. They often wait before asking who you are or what you want. They avoid eye contact and concentrate on their tasks. They treat themselves as socially invisible and wait to see what you do or what the chief scientist will do with you.

Steve Shapin has pointed out that 17th- and 18th-century lab technicians were easy to make invisible because they were already members of a group trained to fade into the background: servants. They might have done much of the lab work, but they were hardly able to develop real reputations as independent scientists in the age of the gentleman scientist.[29] Today's lab technicians work in this tradition, reproducing comparable levels of displayed deference without holding the same social position as servants. Their autonomy has officially increased over time, but their investment in subordination has been sustained. They are now meant to disappear and appear on the laboratory stage as commanded and needed by the chief scientist, making their contribution to the group effort sometimes quite visible but other times quite obscure.

Strangers frequently enter labs. They come as members of site visit committees from NSF, and as visiting scientists wanting to learn about the lab's work. They generally come to learn about the signatory techniques of the lab, assuming them to be the outward manifestations of the chief scientist's thinking. This is what they want, and this is what they are shown. If the group is to benefit from such a visit, lab workers usually need to make themselves socially unimportant and intellectually subservient. They will drop the pretense if the chief scientist tells them they should, and restore the ordinary backstage informality of the lab, where more egalitarian interactions shape the research process. If they learn that a visiting scientist is a friend of the chief scientist, for instance, then the need for pretense will be diminished. If a visitor has worked with members of the lab on a cruise, the pretense would seem disingenuous, and hence never fully begins. On the other hand, sometimes the chief scientist wants to be treated as a kind of stranger to the group of lab workers because he believes he is much better than them. In this case, the unhappy assistants will be subservient in his presence, but will drop much of the hierarchical pretense that the chief scientist expects once he leaves the room.

The management of backstage and frontstage performances and the contrast between the two is the most blatant and yet rudimentary evidence of the collective construction of the superior scientist. It explains much about how it is accomplished and why it is valued by those who must become invisible. The scientist is socially forefronted, put on stage while the rest of the laboratory disappears, not usually for insiders or near neighbors, but for strangers who affect the distribution of rewards in science. The laboratory space (separate from the chief scientist's office) constitutes a physical backstage, where the collective cognition of the group is hidden, until this space is "invaded" by important strangers. Then physical separation of researchers from outsiders is replaced by a social separation that (through avoidance) erects a barrier between strangers and the laboratory's routine social processes.

Machines are sometimes used not only to do research but help lab workers socially disappear, too. Many people think lab technicians do mindless and repetitious work that is too alienating to be cognitively significant. This view is derived in part from the deskilling thesis: the idea that workers using machinery become deskilled.[30] There are indeed repetitious machine manipulations inherent in doing scientific experiments: the numerous runs of an experiment needed to show that a particular outcome is not a fluke but will hold up over time, or the laborious counting techniques required to determine what the outcome of an experiment really is. It is easy to see this work as routine machine-tending, but much of it is not. More importantly, many strangers will not know at a glance which is which. The cultural predisposition to see machine tending as mindless makes it easy for an outsider entering a lab to assume that someone hunched over a piece of equipment is not really thinking. Hence it is easier to discount the importance of that person to the process of scientific discovery and to assume that the scientist reading or writing in a separate office is the "true thinker" in this social sense.

Whatever the social threads that buttress the system of attribution, in the end, the chief scientist in a lab is treated like the director of a film. This person "uses" assistants, but has final authority and responsibility for the outcome of their group work. This kind of attribution is, according to Howard Becker, fundamentally arbitrary. There is a lovely contrast he draws between poetry readings and political speeches that points to the arbitrariness of attributions. Political speech writers write words that "belong" to the politicians who utter them in public, while poets write lines that "belong" to the poet, no matter who reads them. There is no essential authorial relationship; only one determined by convention and legal precedent.[31]

The extent to which junior researchers run laboratories in the name of chief scientists may be indicated by a bitter comment from one chief scientist I interviewed. When I asked him what it would be like for him if he lost all his funds, he said it would be an opportunity to get back to doing some science. It was a bad day for him, when he said this, because he was facing a massive cut in funds, but the sour remark is still revealing. It suggests the extent to which chief scientists rather than laboratory personnel may be deskilled by the division of labor in science. A large laboratory establishment can make administrators of chief scientists.

Chief scientists are often particularly dependent on younger colleagues in their lab to keep them up-to-date technologically. The junior people who fulfill this function are often so important to the lab that if they leave, they are sorely missed.

> [After I took a job of my own] amazingly, you know, I still had access to the machine, to the lab and the mass spectrometers and stuff at [Big Lab], so I could go down there and still analyze samples. . . . I think that [arrangement] was sort of mutually beneficial because [my former boss at Big Lab] was, I mean I was the guy that kept all the equipment running and everything else. So, it was fine if I wanted to come back because if they had some problems they could ask me about it, so . . . . I mean one of the things I'm good at is building and operating complicated equipment and getting it to work right, and stuff like that. I mean not every earth scientists is, takes an interest in that or is as good at doing it.

It was not sentimental feeling that tied this former technician to his old boss. It was his importance to the laboratory. The fact that he was able to get his own position testifies to his ability to make himself a visible as well as useful member of the lab. He could use his skill with the equipment to articulate a separate signature for his work. This does not mean, however, that other researchers at his or other labs who became permanent parts of their labs were necessarily any less valuable to their research groups. Some might be and some might not.

One of the not-too-hidden secrets of scientific life is that many of the most talented scientists do not become the scientific knowers of their fields. One version of the genius myth in science is used to explain this. Some people, we are told, are just too bright, too sensitive and too talented to do the political work necessary for a career. These "real geniuses" cannot shake hands at NSF and exchange pleasantries at scientific meetings, so they cannot become the movers and shakers of their disciplines. But (the story goes) they still make the science better. Many young men (but only one woman) in big labs were introduced to me as the real brains of the laboratory. Some were said to have developed ideas or research strategies that had made the lab famous. Others did less work on the central problems of the group but were able to do dazzling technical work on one aspect of the lab's methodology that allowed the group to gather or analyze data better than anyone dreamed possible. Some labs had a handful of these people in them, most described by the chief scientist as just beginning their careers there. The ones who were good at doing the social work of organizing and leading groups in the lab were distinguished by the chief scientist and other technicians as ones who would someday strike out on their own. The others, who were easily distracted and always obsessed by the intellectual problems at hand, were said to be too withdrawn from social life to manage a career. They were often avoided or hidden because of their odd mannerisms or ways of talking. Some of these lab members even explicitly said that they felt protected by their anonymity in the group, and sought it out. These were the sad but wonderful geniuses, whose abilities were to remain hidden inside the lab, but were still made available to science. They worked, and they published. They might even get a lab of their own some day, but their delicacy and brilliance were socially linked, so that they had good reason to remain too good for the public life of science, and hence part of the hidden rather than public world of scientific genius.

Over time and if they do not strike out on their own, these people may become increasingly identified as extensions of their chief scientists, just as their equipment is treated as extentions of their senses and manual abilities. The chief scientist will be praised for locating and making room for the talented assistants. In this move, the gifts of the support personnel will be absorbed into the greatness of the chief scientist.

The scientist with the right lab, filled with this kind of help, can indeed become larger than life, more brilliant than any individual could be, but not as an individual knower. The scientists who knows how to use this kind of assistance can better fit the inflated image of the scientist-knower in modern societies, but only through cooperative work.

It is possible to argue that this system actually makes the chief scientist a better thinker. Given a talented group of helpers, the chief scientist becomes a superior student of the natural world. In a kind of self-fulfilling prophecy, the social desire for mental greatness produces a social system for making some people better thinkers than others. The lab workers learn from the research; they pass along their observations to the chief scientist who makes sense of the results. A cognitive hierarchy results from a social one.

The trouble with this model is that it leaves out all the shop talk described by Knorr-Cetina and the collective construction of novelty observed by Garfinkel, Lynch, and Livingston.[32] Laboratory discussions caught in transcripts simply do not show information passing up along a chain of command, and analytical insight passing down along the same chain. The system is much more complex, and much more a distributed system of learning, where different technical skills and analytic abilities are arrayed around a joint project. Distributed cognition is masked behind a system of social performance, developed to reinforce the social power of science by giving to groups the problems that individuals could not solve on their own, and attributing the solutions to select individuals.

**Implications**

Scientists, when they do research, do not simply want to find or construct new theories or data about the world. They also want (to a greater or lesser extent) to empower themselves and the social world in which they live.[33] They are not dispassionate observers of their own lives and work. They do not keep their laboratories thoroughly and pragmatically attached to the pursuit of pure knowledge. They would be lucky if they had lives simple enough to permit them that purity of vision and motive. But they are part of a culture that glorifies (albeit also criticizes) science, and most of them chose to be scientists because they like *to think of themselves as* scientists. The intellectual and cultural forces at work behind choosing a life of science cannot be properly separated from the other, since the meaning of the work for most scientists contains both elements. How their pursuit of knowledge is affected by these cultural currents is only just indicated but not thoroughly studied here.

Noticing the ways in which scientific work is organized to serve cultural as well as practical goals not only can tell us more about science; it can help us to think more about work places as sites of culture production and reproduction. The day-to-day activities that make up the daily lives of school teachers, physicists, garbage collectors, nurses, and pilots partake of cultural images and scripts. The interactions people have in their own work worlds, and the ways they interact with people from other social worlds depend upon shared (or, during periods of mobility, contested) bits of culture that define their occupations and those who perform its functions. Just as we cannot explain how labs "make science" without reference to these cultural systems, we should not assume we know why teachers act the ways they do in the classroom simply on the basis of their perceptions of students and of teaching techniques without reference to "the teacher" as an historical figure. How they teach and work with other teachers must necessarily be deeply saturated with dreams (or nightmares) of schools and teachers, past and future. The study of work and communication through culture provides one means of trying to tap these patterns, and recover the side of work that too many analysts have forgotten.

## Notes

1  For a few examples from philosophy, see Philip Kitcher, *The Advancement of Science,* New York: Oxford University Press. *Progress and Its Problems,* Berkeley: University of California Press, 1977.

2  Leigh Star, S. (1989). *Regions of the Mind.* Stanford: Stanford University Press.

3  Agre, P. and Shrager, J. "Routine evolution as the microgenetic basis of skill acquisition" *Proceedings of the Cognitive Science Conference,* pp. 694–670. Boston, MA; Engeström, (1984). *Learning and Teaching on a Scientific Basis.* Aarhus Universitet, psykologisk institut; Cole, M. & Scribner, S. (1974). *Culture and Thought.* New York: Wiley. Vygotsky, *Mind in Society.* Cole (Ed.) (1978), Cambridge, MA: Harvard University Press. And see the chapter by Ed Hutchins in this volume.

4  See Star, ibid.; Knorr-Cetina, K. (1981). *The Manufacture of Knowledge,* New York: Pergamon; Latour, B. & Woolgar, S. (1979). *Laboratory Life,* Beverly Hills: Sage; Latour, B. (1987). *Science in Action,* Cambridge, MA: Harvard University Press; Lynch, M. (1985). *Art and Artifact in Laboratory Science,* London: Routledge and Kegan Paul; Leigh Star, S. (1988). "The Structure of Ill-Structured Solutions, *Proceedings* of 8th Annual AAAI workshop on Distributed Artificial Intelligence, Lake Arrowhead, CA; Latour, B. (1988). *The Pasteurization of France,* A. Sheridan and J. Law (trans.), Cambridge, MA: Harvard University Press; Shapin, S. & Schaffer, S. (1985). *Leviathan and the Airpump,* Princeton, NJ: Princeton University Press; Traweek, S. (1988). *Beamtimes and Lifetimes,* Cambridge, MA: Harvard University Press; Pickering, A. (1992). *Science as Practice and Culture,* Chicago: University of Chicago Press; Collins, H. M. (1985). *Changing Order,* London: Sage; Gilbert, N. & Mulkay, M. (1984). *Opening Pandora's Box,* Cambridge: Cambridge University Press.

   Critical sociology of science (derived from critical theory) also focuses on the social to the exclusion of mind (much like most laboratory ethnographies), but it is centrally concerned about rationality at the level of the social – the rationalization of social relations deemed so often detrimental to human life. In this tradition, rationality is not so much a matter of individual thought or the peculiar attribute of unusual scientists, but a ubiquitous cultural formation that is fundamentally historical, not contained in scientific practices or individual problem solving, and hence not a particular attribute of laboratories (although these are central sites of its production). Science and technology are important ways of spreading rationalization through more of the culture, but individual minds of scientists and their rationality have little importance to this historical process. See Leiss, W. (1972). *The Domination of Nature,* New York: George Braziller; Aronowitz, S. (1988). *Science as Power,* Minneapolis: University of Minnesota Press.

5  Marin, L. (1981). *Le Portrait du Roi.* Paris: Les Éditions de Minuit.

6  See the Hutchins, E. (1995). Cognition in the Wild. Cambridge, MA: The MIT Press.

7  Kitcher, ibid.

8   See, for example, Knorr-Cetina (1981); Latour & Woolgar, ibid.; Latour (1987); Lynch (1985); Leigh Star (1988).

9   Latour (1988).

10  For essays on the tradition of ethnography in anthropology, see Marcus, G. & Fisher, M. (1986). *Anthropology as Cultural Critique,* Chicago: University of Chicago Press. For some of the books that use ethnography to study scientific practice, see Latour & Woolgar, ibid.; Knorr-Cetina, K., ibid.; Lynch, M., ibid.; Mulkay, G.

11  See Berger, B. (1981). *The Survival of a Counterculture,* Berkeley: University of California Press, for a discussion of the kinds of ideological work people will do to try to rationalize their actions in terms of the cultural scripts that they hold dear.

12  Goffman, E. (1959). *Presentation of Self in Everyday Life,* New York: Doubleday; (1963). *Behavior in Public Places,* New York: Free Press; (1963). *Encounters,* Indianapolis: Bobbs-Merrill.

13  More scholars of the culture of science have more clearly linked the culture of science to issues of power. Paul Starr, in his study of the rise of medicine, has examined how medicine was able to gain social legitimacy and cultural authority in the United States. He has not taken as his job justifying the special place of medicine in American society or attributing special characteristics to doctors. To him, the important thing is the historical process for gaining cultural authority. Similarly, other recent scholars working have been interested in science not so much as a knowledge system as a cultural one participating in a political environment. This tradition (derived in an early form from the Frankfurt school and now, surprisingly, also attached to the U.S. production of culture school), takes the institution of science and its social career as central to any understanding of scientific knowledge systems. See, for example, the paper by Michael Useem in Richard Peterson (Ed.), *The Production of Culture,* Beverly Hills, Sage, 1976, and the discussion of science by Paul Starr in *The Social Transformation of American Medicine,* New York: Basic Books, 1982. To some extent this tradition is tied to the work on science by critical theorists. See Jürgen Habermas, *Toward a Rational Society* (trans. J. Shapiro), Boston: Beacon Press, 1970; *The Theory of Communicative Action,* vol. I; *Reason and Rationalization of Society,* Boston: Beacon Press, 1981; and Leiss, ibid. But the production of culture school has become increasingly tied to the ethnographic tradition within sociology, turning attention to the everyday activities of culture makers. This has kept it in tension with the Mertonian school of sociology of science, while reintroducing the possibility of institutional analysis. See Robert Merton, *The Sociology of Science,* Chicago: University of Chicago Press, 1973.

14  Knorr-Cetina, ibid.; Latour & Woolgar, ibid.; Lynch; Gilbert and Mulkay, ibid.

15  See Haraway, D. (1989). *Primate Visions,* New York: Routledge; *Simians, Cyborgs and Women,* New York: Routledge; Hartouni, V. (1992). Reproductive Technologies and the Negotiation of Public Meanings, in *Provoking Agents,* J. K. Gardiner (Ed.), Urbana: University of Illinois Press; Reproductive Discourses in the 1980s, in *Technoculture,* C. Penley and A. Ross (Eds.), Minneapolis: University of Minnesota Press, 1991; Brave New World in the Discourses of Reproductive and Genetic Technologies, in *Nature/Discourse,* J. Bennet and W. Chapoupka (Eds.), Minneapolis: University of Minnesota Press, 1992; Namoi Oreskes, "Objectivity or Herois? On the Invisibility of Women in Science, to appear in *Osiris.*

16  Traweek, S. (1994). VisEd. Paper presented at the Conference on Visualization in Science, Galveston, Texas.

17  Friedman, R. M. (1989). Text, context, and quicksand, *HSPS, 20,* 63–77; Zuckerman, H., *The Scientific Elite,* New York: Free Press, 1977.

18  See Latour (1987) for an early discussion of networks in science.

19  To highlight the technological dependence of the scientists I studied, I focused on deep-ocean researchers. Oceanographers distinguish between blue-water and white-water researchers, those who work far offshore and those who work close to land. I interviewed exclusively blue-water scientists, but I was more selective than that. With a few exceptions, I talked to scientists who did work on or near the seafloor off the continental shelves. Just getting to their research sites

was necessarily a difficult task; using equipment there to conduct experiments or collect samples was also a technological challenge.

In the course of my research I conducted 74 interviews with 63 ocean researchers and/or science policy experts located in nine institutions around the country. I used snowball sampling to generate a list of the scientists, engineers, technicians, and graduate students to interview. I spent a short time in institutions far from my own, but greater time in nearby sites where oceanography was being practiced.

20   Lave, J. (1988). *Cognition in Practice,* Cambridge: Cambridge University Press; Knorr-Cetina, ibid.; Lynch, ibid.
21   Hacking, ibid.
22   Latour, Latour & Woolgar, ibid.
23   Shapin and Schaffer, ibid.; Steve Shapin, *A Social History of Truth,* Chicago: University of Chicago Press, 1994, ch. 8; Hacking, ibid.
24   Sudnow, D. (1978). *Ways of the Hand.* Cambridge, MA: Harvard University Press.
25   Agre, ibid. The relationship between expectations and innovations is discussed by Becker for the arts. See *Artworlds,* Berkeley: University of California Press, 1982.
26   Compare Jacques Ellul, *The Technological Society* (J. Wilkinson, trans.), New York: Vintage, 1964, to Sudnow, ibid.
27   Sudnow, ibid.; Latour (1987, 1985).
28   Becker (1982). *Outsiders.* Glencoe, IL: Free Press, 1963.
29   Shapin (1990).
30   Braverman, H. (1974). *Labor and Monopoly Capitalism.* New York: Monthly Review Press.
31   Becker, ibid.
32   Knorr-Cetina, ibid.; Garfinkel, H., Lynch, M., and Livingston, E. (1981). The Work of Discovering Science Construed with Materials from the Optically Discovered Pulsar, *Philosophy of the Social Sciences,* 11:131–158.
33   See Friedman, R. M. (1989). *Appropriating the Weather.* Ithaca: Cornell University Press.

# 12    Experience and the collective nature of skill

*Harley Shaiken*

## Introduction

As information technology diffuses through manufacturing, an increasingly important question concerns the ways in which workers acquire and use skills in
high-tech production (Cole, 1989; Brown, Reich, & Stern, 1991). In this chapter
I explore skill formation in two advanced auto plants in Mexico: an engine plant
and an assembly and stamping complex. The plants – at the cutting edge of a new
international division of labor – provide an excellent context to observe the ways
in which skills are formed and used. At their launch in the 1980s, the two factories brought together inexperienced though well-educated workers with some of
the most advanced manufacturing technologies used anywhere in the world. People who had never been in a factory before had to grapple with operating and
maintaining robots, computer-controlled machining lines, laser measuring systems, and a host of other advanced machines and computerized systems. Surprisingly, both plants enjoyed impressive success: in the space of several years they
matched or surpassed the performance of comparable U.S. and even Japanese
plants in critical areas such as quality.

My original purpose in undertaking these studies was to better define the mobility of advanced manufacturing in an age of computers and telecommunica-
tions, focusing on the tradeoffs between siting production in advanced industrial
economies or newly industrializing countries (Shaiken & Herzenberg, 1987;
Shaiken, 1990). I soon found, however, that this mobility was heavily dependent
on the effectiveness with which workers could acquire new skills, especially the
ability to maintain and quickly repair complex equipment. The critical macro
question, then, of where high-tech manufacturing might be located is ultimately
shaped by the decidedly micro interactions of workers and machines on the shop
floor.

In this chapter, I probe these interactions, focusing on the relationship of training, experience, and skill. The operation of these Mexican auto factories poses
two central questions about skill formation: first, what is the role of experience

in advanced manufacturing and, second, to what extent is skill collaborative? Based on the data from these sites, I argue that experience remains vital in operating a high-tech plant. A broad frame of reference – know-how acquired and honed over time – proved essential in debugging and maintaining advanced forms of automation at the core of the manufacturing process. Since these plants are staffed by workers new to manufacturing, this expertise was initially provided by a small cadre of managers and engineers imported from around the world. I term this organizational form "transitional Taylorism" because it temporarily separates conception (diagnosing problems and planning solutions) from the execution of carrying out repairs. It is transitional because the consequence of moving decision making off the shop floor is slowing the repair of equipment on it, underscoring a contradiction between a key element of classical Taylorism and the demands of automated production. Consequently, as workers gain experience, managers themselves seek to return certain kinds of decision making to the shop floor.

The performance of these plants also indicates that skill is a collective phenomenon as well as an individual attribute. To an unusual degree, workers shared their insights and emerging expertise in operating these factories in "communities of practice." The collective memory of groups of workers – formally organized into teams in one plant or informally collaborating in the other – proved decisive in many critical situations. The shared aspects of skill are highlighted because the pressures of production left novice workers few alternatives but to work together to diagnose problems and plan solutions. The fact that the cooperative dimension of skill is especially visible here, however, does not mean it is absent in more conventional circumstances but rather that it is exercised in different ways.

An important related debate I do not directly address concerns the qualitative impact of information technology on work; that is, whether there is a broad trend towards upgrading or deskilling (Braverman, 1974; Noble, 1984; Shaiken, 1984; Piore & Sabel, 1984; Zuboff, 1988). The finding that skill is vital to sophisticated forms of mass production in these cases does not, in and of itself, define the overall distribution of skill in the factory. Access to an extensive pool of experience, for example, may prove critical at the same time that jobs become more polarized. In a study of an automobile assembly plant in the U.S. that went through a major technological change, Milkman and Pullman concluded that "skilled-trades workers experienced skill upgrading and gained enhanced responsibilities, while production workers underwent deskilling and became increasingly subordinated to the new technology" (Milkman & Pullman, 1991, p. 123). These issues are vital but largely beyond the scope of this inquiry.

I seek to locate the discussion of skill formation in the production realities of these two plants. Skill is not acquired nor does it exist in a vacuum in the real world. Instead, skill is shaped by cultural, organizational, and technological specifics that are an important part of this discussion. As Lave and Wagner put it, "activities, tasks, functions, and understandings do not exist in isolation: they are part of broader systems of relations in which they have meaning" (Lave & Wenger, 1991, p. 53). I begin with an overview of the two factories, address technology and worker selection strategies, and then explore the ways in which skill is acquired. Within this context, I examine the role of experience, transitional Taylorism, collective skill, and work teams. I conclude with a brief discussion of manufacturing performance.

## The two plants

The two plants in the study are owned and operated by a U.S. automaker. I call the automaker Universal Motors and I refer to the engine plant as Verde and the assembly and stamping plant as Azul. Although the plants produce very different final products – four-cylinder auto engines in one case and finished compact autos in the other – they share a number of similarities. They both are state-of-the-art facilities that represent considerable initial investments. Verde, which went on line in 1983, required an investment of $250 million and has an annual capacity of over 400,000 engines. Azul was launched in 1986 at a cost of $500 million and can product 135,000 cars a year. Almost the entire production of both plants – 90% at Verde and 100% at Azul – is exported to the U.S. The plant manager of Verde described essential characteristics of the two facilities when he commented that the engine plant brings together "U.S. managers, European technology, Japanese manufacturing systems, and Mexican workers" (see Table 1).

The two sites are located in different cities in northern Mexico, both somewhat over 150 miles from the U.S. border. The plants are among the most advanced manufacturing facilities in Mexico and by far the most sophisticated factories in the states in which they are located. Universal chose to locate them near agricultural and administrative centers rather than industrial hubs, seeking highly educated, motivated workers with no previous automotive experience. Instead, Verde and Azul endeavored to develop skills through their own extensive training programs. Both facilities are unionized by the Confederacion de Trabajadores de Mexico (CTM) – but the union has little presence on the shop floor. The unions do, on occasion, bargain aggressively over wages, sparking periods of intense la-

Table 1

| Plant | Product | Annual capacity | Initial investment (millions) | Date launched | Hourly workers |
|-------|---------|-----------------|-------------------------------|---------------|----------------|
| Verde | Engines | 400,000 | $250 | 1983 | 800 |
| Azul | Autos | 135,000 | $500 | 1986 | 1,800 |

bor–management conflict, particularly at Azul. Surprisingly, however, quality has remained high even when industrial relations have been decidedly rocky.

Verde and Azul share a common emphasis on extensive managerial flexibility – manifested in labor agreements that provide few restrictions – but differ extensively beyond that. The most striking difference between them, other than the obvious ones of product and technology, is the way work is organized. Verde has a traditional form of work organization featuring two skilled and three production classifications, whereas Azul employs work teams and a single classification for all workers. Moreover, Azul has eliminated separate groups of skilled workers in key areas such as the body shop. Instead, production work teams elect one or two people to do maintenance and repair for a nine-month stint after which they return to the line.

Data was collected at Verde from six months after the first engine was produced at the end of 1983 through the beginning of 1986. At Azul, the research began in mid-1988 and continued through the beginning of 1991. I made follow-up visits to both plants in early 1992. Staff and operating managers – both Mexican nationals and international visitors, primarily from the U.S. and Canada – were interviewed in virtually every area from the plant managers to shop floor supervisors. In addition, I and several research assistants spoke with union representatives and interviewed over 30 workers at Verde and more than 200 at Azul. In well over a dozen visits, we spent a considerable amount of time on the shop floor, informally speaking with workers, observing machines repaired, and watching engines being machined and cars assembled.

**The context: Technology and worker selection**

The process of skill formation took place in a context of two seemingly contradictory decisions: Universal chose to deploy some of the most advanced auto technologies used anywhere in the world at the same time it opted to hire a totally inexperienced work force. The company selected a high-tech approach because, although the plants are geographically in Mexico, Universal perceives them as part of a world-wide production system and is targeting the most advanced global standards of quality and productivity. As a result, Universal made few concessions technologically to the inexperience of its workers or the problematic industrial infrastructure. This high-tech route, however, meant expanded training requirements and more complex issues to deal with once the plants were operating.

Consider the technologies employed. The two sites utilize extensive amounts of advanced, highly automated computer technology. Verde, the engine plant, relies on state-of-the-art transfer lines that tie together dozens of individual machines into complex automated networks. A part such as the raw casting for an engine block is inserted on one end and comes out the other end machined to tolerances as close as .001 of an inch, about one-third the size of a human hair. Just 16 operators supervise the production of 150 precision-machined blocks an hour, or one every 24 seconds. These operators each oversee 50 to 100 feet of fast-moving and sophisticated equipment. Given the tight tolerances and the highly integrated nature of the machinery, there is a critical premium on operators anticipating problems before they happen. A slight change in the sound of a hydraulic pump, for example, can indicate erratic movement on a machining head and the possibility of scrap parts. In this kind of operation, as Koike points out, "minor changes and problems are inevitable, and unusual or even unforeseen operations are repeatedly necessary in order to maintain the steady flow of production" (1990, p. 8).

The assembly plant produces to less-exacting manufacturing tolerances but must meet exacting fit-and-finish standards. To do this, Azul employs state-of-the-art computerized equipment, especially in the capital-intensive body shop and stamping areas. In the body shop 96 robots – linked to larger automated systems – weld the car bodies. In the stamping area, a transfer press – combining the functions of three or four conventional presses – stamps out major sheet-metal parts such as doors. Even minor defects in quality in an assembly plant can prove disastrous, which puts a heavy burden on coordinating the fast-moving and disparate parts of the system.

Universal did hedge its technological bets in one important way: the types of production processes installed at both Verde and Azul were first deployed and debugged elsewhere.[1] Verde was patterned after a Universal plant making the same engine and using similar technology that went on-line six months earlier in the U.S. Azul was largely cloned from the operations of a Universal affiliate in Japan that produced a nearly identical model with many of the same types of machines and systems.

Although Universal had learned much from these earlier efforts, production requirements in the new facilities were extremely demanding. Why, then, did the company opt to hire an inexperienced work force? Part of the decision was based on the obvious fact that the local labor pool included few workers with previous industrial experience. Universal, however, made no effort to recruit skilled workers from other areas of Mexico, including its existing operations near Mexico City. The company's training manual for Verde explained why. "Transfers of hourly personnel and their supervisors from [Universal's] Mexico operations were not allowed, in order to avoid inflated wages/benefits and old work practices." In fact, the goal of insuring managerial flexibility influenced a choice of sites that would have little comparable industry nearby whose work practices might influence Universal's workers.

Selecting from a pool of inexperienced candidates, Universal went to great pains to find highly motivated and well-educated workers. In both cities, jobs in the plants were initially perceived as stepping stones into a high-tech career and thousands applied for the hundreds of available jobs. The applicants went through an exhaustive selection process, often taking over a day. Most of the young workers who were hired – average age 21 at Verde and 23 at Azul – had the equivalent of a high school education and many had more advanced training. At Azul, about one-third of the initial cohort had some university or professional schooling beyond high school and at Verde many were graduates of the local technologico or technical school.

Recruiting novice workers to do assembly work in the auto industry is hardly a unique strategy. Almost all the transplanted, Japanese-owned auto factories in the U.S. have hired inexperienced production workers (Kenney & Florida, 1991). One industry training consultant observes that "the Japanese, believing in the efficacy of training, traditionally set minimum experience criteria" (Henry, 1989). The challenge, however, is much greater for taking on unseasoned skilled workers, responsible for maintaining and repairing sophisticated computerized systems. Here the transplants sought workers with previous experience in skilled trades, such as electricians, if not experience in the auto industry (Shaiken, 1992). In contrast, Universal's Mexican plants recruited novices in this area as well. It is to this critical bottleneck – skill formation for maintenance workers – that we now turn.

**Transitional Taylorism**

Skill is easy to observe on the job but difficult to define (Vallas, 1990; Spenner, 1990; Attewell, 1990). A rough definition for our purposes is a creative response to uncertainty based on theoretical knowledge, experience, and technique. Koike, Zuboff, and others emphasize the intellectual component of skill, particularly in environments that heavily rely on information technology (Koike, 1990, 1991; Zuboff, 1988). Koike argues that "diagnosis and rectification of problems imply knowledge of the structures, functions, and mechanisms of equipment, products, and the production process itself" and that this aspect of skill is largely intellectual in character (1990, p. 9). Theoretical knowledge must be combined with experience, the second aspect of skill, to provide a framework for diagnosing problems on the job, particularly with the pressures of high-speed production. Finally, the third and most visible part of skill is technique, the ability to perform those tasks or "tricks of the trade" that allow a skilled worker to carry out a repair. An important part of theoretical knowledge can be learned in the classroom but experience and technique are largely acquired on the job. Koike points out that "the knowledge-content of a skill is . . . largely indefinable and only partially communicated through words. There exists no way to acquire these skills other than by following the teacher's pattern, which is precisely the content of OJT on the job floor" (1990, p. 10).

In the U.S., workers generally acquire maintenance skills through an apprenticeship. Although there isn't a clear divide concerning where the various aspects of skill are acquired, intellectual skills are often enhanced in off-the-job training that can range from several hundred to several thousand hours. In these classes, an apprentice learns broad principles: how to read blueprints, the way hydraulic systems operate, or the fundamentals of electronics, among others. At the core of the program, however, is on-the-job training with seasoned journeyman, generally for about four years. An apprentice is usually rotated through all the principal areas of the plant, learning how to troubleshoot machines and acquiring the ability to use tools along the way.

The most important and most complex part of an apprenticeship is learning how to diagnose a machine problem or breakdown. This diagnosis builds on a base of theoretical knowledge and practical technique but can be greatly facilitated by having an experienced guide to avoid countlessly reinventing the wheel. A sluggishness in a hydraulic arm, for example, can instantly be linked to a particular type of valve if the skilled worker understands the way a hydraulic system works. Once this initial evaluation is made, however, the path divides: a seasoned worker, who has seen this type of problem before, might simply flush a piece of dirt from the valve but a novice could very well rebuild the entire unit, a far more time-consuming process.

An apprentice also learns technique on the shop floor by observing and emulating a journeyman. The best journeymen to work with are those who turn over the tools to the apprentice, observing and instructing rather than actually doing the job. The apprentice gains a hands-on feel for the job while the journeyman can immediately provide input. Consider the installation of a hydraulic pump. The apprentice might put the pump on a manifold and then begin to tighten the bolts. If the bolts are too loose the pump may leak; if they are too tight the pump body might distort. A journeyman can pick up the wrench and demonstrate how tight a bolt should be, after which the apprentice completes the job.

The knowledge of past repairs that worked, short-cuts that saved the day, and jobs that became fiascoes become part of a collective memory. This memory is shared among skilled workers and represents a source of their power as well as part of their technical knowledge. Skilled workers might discuss these experiences over a cup of coffee, talk about them at lunch, or consult with one another on the job. Journeymen relate these events to apprentices, who integrate them into their own frame of reference. In fact, part of becoming a journeyman is learning to pass on as well as receive these tales.

Apprentices, however, learn more than technical skills: they develop the world view of the journeymen and the community into which they are being initiated. "Apprentices gradually assemble a general idea of what constitutes the practice of the community," Lave and Wenger observe about a broad range of apprentice situations. This knowledge "includes an increasing understanding of how, when, and about what old-timers collaborate, collude, and collide, and what they enjoy, dislike, respect, and admire" (1991, p. 95). In unionized plants in the U.S. and Mexico, the understanding apprentices develop includes a sense of independence and cohesiveness based on their knowledge and critical position in the production process. As apprentices are brought into the community of journeymen, these qualities easily translate into militance on the job.

To avoid this consciousness, as we have seen, Universal chose not to hire experienced workers. This decision precluded apprenticeship as a means of skill formation. Instead, the basic training strategy for skilled workers at Universal's Mexican plants was front loaded: new hires received intensive off-the-job training before ever entering the shop floor. This training was meant to lay the basis for a strong intellectual understanding of the manufacturing process through classes and to provide some familiarity with repair techniques through laboratory simulations. The expectation was that this background would allow highly motivated workers to more quickly learn repair techniques once production began.

The initial training for skilled workers at Verde was intense. It began with a six-month program at the local technical college, where the trainees first took classes in basic subjects such as math and in specific areas such as machine controls. The last five weeks were spent tearing down and rebuilding on old piece of transfer-line equipment brought from the U.S. After this introduction, about one-fourth of the trainees went to machine tool shops in the U.S. for up to three months to familiarize themselves with machinery that was being made for the plant. Once the trainees arrived at the plant, they installed equipment and, in general, prepared for production.[2] The skilled workers had on average about six months before the first engines would come down the line and several months after that until high volumes would be reached. This 15–18 months, however, is far short of a traditional apprenticeship. Machine operators – the workers responsible for the intricate transfer machines – received eight weeks of training, split between theoretical classes and operating simulated machining lines.

At Azul all new hires, whether they ultimately work on the assembly line or repair robots, receive the same four months of initial training, largely in the classroom. "We don't want to emphasize differences in job," the training manager commented. "We want to emphasize the commonness of the problem-solving techniques." After this introduction, workers receive from several weeks to several months of additional training in the department where they are assigned. The first 300 or so workers who were hired spent from one to four months in Japan, working in a factory similar to Azul. As we will see, this initial training is the basis for the style of work organization that the plant employs.

The ability to run sophisticated, capital-intensive plants such as Verde or Azul with novice workers at first glance may seem to indicate that high levels of skill are no longer needed in automated production. While the jobs of many production workers may in fact have been deskilled, maintenance and repair workers as well as some machine operators have new, more-complex diagnostic and repair skills to master.[3] These skills require a broad frame of reference that can only be acquired over time. "You can't take a book and tell somebody, 'these are the things you do on a grinder to solve this problem,' " a senior manufacturing manager at Verde emphasized. "It's purely experience, nothing else."

Universal was to provide this missing knowledge base through a cadre of highly experienced managers recruited from the company's world-wide operations. A number of these managers – many formerly skilled workers themselves – had made a career as service employees in Universal's overseas plants, setting up plants in Brazil, Portugal, Germany, England, and elsewhere. Also central would be a group of Mexican managers and engineers from the company's Mexico City operations. And the final component would be service people from machine-tool builders who could instruct workers about the intricacies of their equipment. In the Verde plant, foreign service employees numbered about 60 people at peak and by the beginning of 1986 only few remained on the shop floor. At Azul, the number of foreign service people reached 80, although fewer were on the shop floor than at Verde.

These managers were central to a strategy of transitional Taylorism, raising the site of decision making off the shop floor. Managers routinely made decisions that would normally be the province of machine operators, skilled workers or first-line supervisors. In the short run, "problems [were] all elevated to higher management," a manufacturing manager at Verde observed. Moreover, these managers also play the role of surrogate journeymen. When there is a particularly involved or sensitive job, a manager might grab the tools and show the worker what to do.

In highly automated manufacturing, the price of removing decision making from the shop floor can be considerable: inexperienced workers are slow to anticipate troubles, hampering the repair of complex, often fast-moving machines. "If you take an experienced machine operator up north," a manufacturing manager at Verde related, "he can hear a drill squeal . . . he reacts to that, he knows something is wrong." Moreover, an experienced operator is likely to make a minor adjustment to a malfunctioning machine while a novice will call for a repair person. "Maybe it's only a matter of going click and flicking the limit switch," the Verde manager elaborated. As a result, another manager at Verde pointed out, "sometimes we go to meetings and when we come back the line is stopped. [In an older plant] the operator would change a bushing or change a drill but here someone has to make the decision."

Incidents such as this underscore the value of experience and the limits of Taylorism in advanced manufacturing. Rather than viewing an extreme separation of planning from doing as a benefit, managers viewed it as a liability. A senior manufacturing manager at Verde summarized the feelings of managers in both plants.

> It's important that we force the decision making to the lower level. You can't run an operation where the managers have to make every decision. It's important to let the lower levels make the decisions so they see the results of their actions.

Over time, of course, the workers at Verde and Azul will establish their own collective memory. A maintenance manager at Azul described how the process was unfolding.

> [The skilled workers] are always talking among themselves and they're learning. "Oh yeah, you've really got to be careful if you're going to do this, this, and this. This is how you've got to do it." We're building a memory within the groups . . . . We're getting a history, getting spread out among the people because of the rotation and because of the fact that they do talk a lot.

"As the experience level builds," a manager at Verde predicted, "the level of decision making will come down" and this, in fact, has taken place to date.

### Work teams at Azul

Verde and Azul both emphasize multiskilling, though in different ways. A conventional plant might have skilled workers divided into machine repairmen, electricians, millwrights, pipefitters, hydraulic repairmen, and toolmakers, among others, and production workers split into more than 100 classifications. Verde has combined the 10–15 major skilled trades found in a conventional plant into two maintenance crafts – mechanical and electrical – and compressed dozens of production classifications into three broad groups. Azul, however, goes much further: it has consolidated all maintenance and production divisions into a single classification and a single pay rate.

The collective nature of skill is further underscored by the organization of work at Azul. In contrast to Verde's flexible, though conventional, organization of work, workers at Azul are organized into teams of from 10 to 25 people. Workers still assemble cars on the line and the tasks each person carries out are the same as in a more conventional plant, but the teams integrate workers into the plant's operations in a significantly different way. Each team elects a facilitator to coordinate production and workers are expected to learn all the jobs on their team, generally through rotation. The teams meet at least once a week for 30 minutes and, if there are problems, more often and longer. The typical team meeting generally is dominated by discussions of ways to improve quality or productivity.

Work teams are most often associated with a range of production techniques pioneered and popularized by Japanese manufacturing firms. These techniques include just-in-time inventory, kaizen or continuous improvement, multiskilling, and job rotation. Some observers such as the authors of *The Machine That Changed The World* ascribe almost magical qualities to teams and the manufacturing approach they dub "lean production" (Womack, Jones & Roos, 1990). Others have emphasized the pressured nature of the system, which has been termed "management by stress" (Parker & Slaughter, 1994). While this is a critical debate, this chapter focuses on the relation of the team to skill formation rather than the implications of teams themselves for workers or the structure of work.

The team provides the context in which skill formation takes place at Azul. Robertson, Rinehart, and Huxley explore elements of this context in a study of the team concept in a unionized Canadian auto assembly plant, a joint venture of General Motors and Suzuki. The authors summarize four key functions of work teams.

> First, the team provides a vehicle for job rotation, training and productivity improvement activities. Second, it provides a supervisory system in which peer pressure is combined with more traditional supervision. Third, the team (by its very existence and dynamic) will serve both a social function and as a vehicle for communicating management values. Finally, the team serves a production function with the expectation that people are not performing an exclusive job. (p. 10)

The team plays a central role in training. Production workers master new jobs primarily through job rotation, switching jobs as often as every two hours in strenuous areas such as the body shop. The facilitators – who coordinate production and fill in for workers when they have to leave the line – themselves rotate back onto the line after two months. This rotation, in addition to relieving boredom and limiting exposure to the worst jobs, provides workers with a broader overview of the labor process in a given area. "Since we rotate and many of us have been in each other's stations," one worker noted, "we all try to pitch in so that problems can be resolved quickly and efficiently. We give each other feedback." When there are significant problems on the line or when absenteeism is high, managers halt rotation, despite the fact that this prohibition is unpopular with workers. The managers are willing to pay for the benefits of specialization in the present – workers remaining on the jobs they know best – with less flexibility for the future. In addition, the team selects those workers who will receive additional technical training, a prerequisite for coveted maintenance jobs.

Many decisions made by managers in a conventional plant are made by the team at Azul. In some areas, for example, the team decides the penalties for absenteeism. Work is organized so that when someone is absent it puts the burden on the remaining team members. Absenteeism can result in the facilitator having to work a single job on the line or, if it is extensive enough, provoke the cancellation of training classes. Not surprisingly, this approach lays the basis for considerable informal peer pressure or even formal team-meted discipline on those who don't come. "When somebody is absent in the group the work gets very over-loaded," one worker complained, "and we ask him why he was absent and we put it in writing and he signs it so that he doesn't forget." In some cases, however, team solidarity with absent workers occurred instead of team pressure. When this happened, managers resumed dealing with absenteeism-related discipline.

The formal work teams overlap informal work groups, capturing some of the elan and loyalty of people who work together. "What I like best is that we are all companeros [friends]," one worker remarked. "There's unity, and when there's a problem we all have to solve it." Another worker commented that "we get along really well, there is a lot of trust. We also help each other on the job, and we do things together outside the plant." This same setting is the primary communication channel from managers to the work force. Supervisors, who conduct the team meetings, lay out issues from Universal's position in the global marketplace to a quality problem on the previous shift. Workers are then expected to contribute to improving quality and enhancing productivity, and to a great extent they do.

The most unusual aspect of the organization of work at Azul is the combining of production and skilled maintenance functions in the same work teams. In fact, several key departments such as the body shop have eliminated the permanent assignment of workers to skilled maintenance jobs. Instead, team members elect several production workers to carry out maintenance tasks, such as repairing the sophisticated robotic systems, for nine month stints, after which they return to the line. The team selects its maintenance specialists from a group of volunteers, who generally have taken optional maintenance classes. "The group decides who the equipment technician should be because the group knows its members best," a maintenance worker commented. Workers view these repair positions as highly desirable, even though they pay the same as working on the line, because they provide a break from the grueling pace and they open up the possibility of learning valued technology skills. "That position is something like a prize that someone wins with his effort," another maintenance worker maintained.

Ironically, this egalitarian restructuring of work stems from two consuming managerial fears. First, managers were apprehensive that they would be vulnerable to the desires of a small group of skilled workers because few replacements would be available in the local labor market. "We cannot rely on experts in one field," a maintenance superintendent related. "We've got to try to develop everybody so that we don't get stuck with a shortage of people who know what the hell is going on." Second, the primarily U.S. managers who set up the plant disliked the power of skilled workers in conventional factories. "Managers in this plant hate the [old] skilled trades," an industrial relations manager stressed. "To them, the very mention of the term is like running your nails down a blackboard." A maintenance superintendent elaborated on the potential benefits of this new approach by commenting that "The absolute number one biggest benefit is you do not develop any prima donnas. Everybody is the same."

Despite its origins as a vehicle to weaken the power of skilled workers, Azul's form of work organization integrates skilled and production work in unprecedented ways, underscoring the collaborative dimension of skill. In the short term, experience is provided through transitional Taylorism, shifting diagnostic decision making off the shop floor in a new vertical distribution of knowledge. At Azul, however, the way work is organized lays the basis for more extensive cooperation between workers performing production and skilled jobs. The result is the development of a broadly distributed collective memory, based on a horizontal distribution of knowledge on the shop floor. The lack of experience pushes everyone into a closer reliance on their colleagues: workers seek all knowledge possible when there is a breakdown and information is forthcoming. "If you have a technician who has a high level of expertise with some of this equipment," a production manager related, "he is more than willing to teach somebody else. And he shares that experience within the work groups."

When a machine breaks down in a conventional plant, managers and skilled workers know that production workers are vital for diagnosing breakdowns. Consider a malfunctioning robot. The first thing a seasoned maintenance worker will likely do after arriving on the scene is talk to the operator. The production worker, stationed near the robot all day long and attuned to its nuances, might say the robot is missing every third weld on the door pillar because its wrist is sticking. That information can save the maintenance worker from slowly testing out a host of other possibilities. "There's open lines between the maintenance people and the production people [at Azul]," according to a maintenance superintendent, "because they're the same people." Moreover, this rotation makes production workers unusually adept at minor repairs that would normally require a maintenance worker or stop the line.

When a repair person rotates back on the line after nine months, expertise is reintegrated into the work group rather than lost. On breakdowns, production workers often pitch in with maintenance workers and, if they have previous experience, can be taken off the line to work on critical repairs. "If I've got a breakdown during the day," a maintenance superintendent commented, "and he's the most qualified guy out of the production line that's down to fix that breakdown, here he comes." The result is an unusual depth of expertise when it comes to maintenance and repair.

While skilled workers and production operators in a conventional plant are generally cooperative, skilled trades draw a strong line over others doing their work. A skilled worker in a stamping plant underscored the point. "I had a guy ask me how I repaired something, I'd say, 'Does K-Mart tell Meijers where they buy their product? If fixed it, you forget it' " (*Guide,* 1991, p. 13). Another skilled worker in a Japanese transplant added "Production members have to realize that by doing our work, they're cheating themselves. A lot of people would like to get in on the apprenticeship program at Mazda. . . . The company won't feel the need to add any more apprentices" (*Guide,* 1991, p. 13).

When a complex new model was introduced in 1990, rotation of production workers through skilled positions was halted, supposedly temporarily. Although whether or not the rotation resumes is an open question, the fact that it was successfully carried out for a three year period – during the critical launch of the plant and the entire run of its first model – demonstrates the technical feasibility of this integration and redistribution of skills. In particular, this job rotation underscores the collective nature of skill.

This innovative structuring of work takes place against a backdrop of a production process that remains decidedly Fordist. Ultimately, these new organizational forms refigure but do not transcend the dominant, rationalized form of work organization. Typical of more conventional plants, the assembly line jobs at Azul are minutely sub-divided, fast paced, heavily loaded, and often grueling. "Work loads here are comparable to those in the States," an assembly manager admitted who had broad experience in the U.S., "[and] in some cases exceed [the States]." A body shop worker summarized the feelings of many when he complained that "there are times when you have constant work to do that is really heavy. If you do it once or twice, then you don't mind, but doing it constantly takes a toll on your body." The strains of the job are alleviated, though hardly eliminated, through group camaraderie, job rotation, and the ability to move into skilled positions.

**Plant performance**

Universal utilizes a wide variety of measures to judge the performance of its manufacturing and assembly plants. Four critical areas are product quality, machine uptime, labor productivity, and performance to budget. Verde and Azul have performed extremely well by these measures and, while all are important, I will focus on machine uptime at Verde and product quality at Azul as rough indicators of the effectiveness with which skill acquisition took place.

The four major transfer lines at Verde – the engine block, engine head, camshaft, and crankshaft – are very capital intensive, each costing between $10 and $20 million. Consequently, maintaining high machine uptime is central to the plant's operation. Given the complexity and highly integrated nature of the machinery, transfer lines generally only reach 60–70% machine uptime with a highly skilled work force and optimal infrastructure in the U.S. I compared the performance of Verde to a Universal plant in the U.S. producing the same engine with nearly identical transfer lines in two key areas – the engine block and engine head. Verde achieved 115% of the U.S. plant's machine yield on the head line, the area where the two plants had the most comparable technology, and reached 94% on the block line about 18 months after the Mexican plant was launched. Comparing the monthly performance of Verde with the U.S. plant, the Mexican facility matched the performance of the U.S. head line about 11 months after the plant was launched, sustained a comparable level until about 17 months, and then surpassed the U.S. plant. Overall, Verde achieved about 85% of the machine yield of the U.S. plant on the four major machining lines.

The key performance measure at Azul is product quality, since the finished car is sold in the highly competitive U.S. auto market. In one important quality measure, Universal compares the cars produced at Azul with all competitive makes sold in the U.S. market. The measure is based on a consumer survey after the cars have been driven for three months and compares "things gone wrong" (TGW) per thousand vehicles. The vehicle produced at Azul sprinted from a strong tenth-place showing among small cars in 1988 to a virtual tie for first place for the 1989 model year, improving its quality by 27% and outdistancing many better-known rivals assembled in Japan.

## Conclusion

On one level, the very success of these two plants seems to devalue the importance of skill. After all, if Verde matches the machine uptime of a U.S. plant on a critical machining line after 11 months and if Azul assembles higher quality cars than competing Japanese nameplates after several years, then how important can skill and experience be? What took place in the Mexican plants is very impressive, but managers almost universally agreed that the young workers at Verde and Azul were a long way from the overall know-how of their veteran counterparts. The key difference manifests itself in an area difficult to measure quantitatively: the ability to debug and maintain a new manufacturing process rather than operate an advanced technology first employed elsewhere. Ultimately, the workers at Azul and Verde will have developed the capability to handle any kind of technology but it will take a frame of reference developed over time.

The highly motivated workers at Azul acquired skills rapidly through a combination of continuing training, transitional Taylorism, and the integrated nature of the work group. The approach, however, still falls short of the type of instruction possible through an apprenticeship, wherein hands-on-training takes place with the direct supervision of a skilled worker on the shop floor. Apprenticeship is hardly incompatible with teams but does require the presence of seasoned workers on the shop floor. In these cases, the ideological bias against skilled workers hampered the process of skill acquisition. As Lave and Wenger suggest, "the mastery of knowledge and skill requires newcomers to move toward full participation in the sociocultural practices of a community" (1991, p. 29). Universal sought to separate the development of skill from the acquisition of the worldview of unionized skilled workers. The result was described by a maintenance superintendent at Azul who admitted that "we have a plant full of three-year apprentices running this joint." Underscoring the importance of direct experience, he estimates that it will be about 10 years before skilled workers at Azul are fully comparable to those in the U.S.

Although maintaining a Fordist framework for production, the operation of both plants indicated the incompatibility of core aspects of Taylorism with advanced automation. In traditional labor-intensive production, if a single machine or operation is halted, it does not necessarily paralyze the entire area. Often, a number of machines perform the same job and heavy stores of parts between machines buffer the disruption. Separating planning from doing, even if it slows repairs, has a limited impact. In highly integrated, capital-intensive manufacturing – particularly with an emphasis on low inventory levels – breakdowns can quickly cripple large sections of a plant. If a key computerized fixture in the body shop at Azul goes down, for example, the entire plant could grind to a stop within an hour or two. To avoid these dislocations, workers must anticipate problems as well as respond to them rapidly.

Overall, the data from Verde and Azul emphasize the importance of experience and the collective nature of skill in high-tech production. Although the plants are unusual in that they initially combined high technology with novice workers, the conclusions highlight important aspects of skill that have a broader relevance to the industrial workplace.

## Notes

1   Although most of its technologies were first used elsewhere, the engine plant did introduce several processes not yet employed in most comparable plants in the U.S. Near the start of the crankshaft line, for example, lasers guide automatic tools in drilling precisely located centers in crankshaft ends.

2   At this point, motivation and learning, on the one hand, clashed with production needs on the other. Managers complained that workers dismantled new machinery to familiarize themselves with it and, when they went to reassemble it, realized they needed more experience.

3   New machinery would provide a bridge of reliability while workers gained experience. A maintenance manager at Azul observed "[there is a] time buffer between the time the equipment does need a lot of maintenance and the guys have finally gotten to the skill level where they can give the equipment that maintenance."

## References

Attewell, P. (1990). "What is Skill?" *Work and Occupations, 17*(4).

Braverman, H. (1974). *Labor and Monopoly Capital.* New York: Monthly Review Press.

Brown, C., Reich, M., & Stern, D. (1992). *Innovative Labor-Management Practices: The role of Security, Employee Involvement, and Training.* Institute of Industrial Relations, University of California at Berkeley.

Cole, R. E. (1989). *Strategies for Learning.* Berkeley, CA: University of California Press.

*Guide* (1991). Official Publication of Local 3000 UAW. Vol. 3, no. 3.

Henry, S. (1989). The Humanware Dimension of Production: Selecting and Creating High-Performing Work Teams. Unpublished paper. Towers Perrin.

Kenney, M. & Florida, R. (1991). "How Japanese Industry is Rebuilding the Rust Belt." *Technology Review, 94*(2).

Koike, K. (1991). Learning and Incentive Systems in Japanese Industry. Unpublished paper.

Koike, K. & Inoki, T. (1990). *Skill Formation in Japan and Southeast Asia.* Tokyo: University of Tokyo Press.

Lave, J. & Wenger, E. (1991). *Situated Learning: Legitimate Peripheral Participation.* New York: Cambridge University Press.

Milkman, R. & Pullman, C. (1991). Technological change in an auto assembly plant: The impact on workers' tasks and skills. *Work and Occupations, 18*(2).

Noble, D. (1984). *Forces of Production.* New York: Alfred A. Knopf.

Parker, M. & Slaughter, J. (1994). *Working Smart: A Union Guide to Participation Programs and Reengineering.* Detroit: Labor Notes.

Piore, M. & Sabel, C. (1984). *The Second Industrial Divide.* New York: Basic Books.

Robertson, D., Rinehart, J., & Huxley, C. (1991). Team Concept: A Case Study of Japanese Production Management in a Unionized Canadian Auto Plant. Unpublished paper.

Shaiken, H. (1984). *Work Transformed: Automation and Labor in the Computer Age.* New York: Holt, Rinehart, and Winston.

Shaiken, H. (1990). *Mexico in the Global Economy: High Technology and Work Organization in Export Industries.* San Diego: Center for U.S.-Mexican Studies, University of California.

Shaiken, H. (1992). Skill Formation and Work Organization in High Technology Manufacturing: A Case Study of Saturn, Mazda, Nissan, and Toyota. Unpublished paper.

Shaiken, H. & Herzenberg, S. (1987). *Automation and Global Production: Automobile Engine Production in Mexico, the United States, and Canada.* San Diego: Center for U.S.-Mexican Studies, University of California.

Spenner, K. I. (1990). Skill: Meanings, methods and measures. *Work and Occupations, 17*(4).

Vallas, S. (1990). The concept of skill: A critical review. *Work and Occupations, 17*(4).

Womack, J., Jones, D., & Roos, D. (1990). *The Machine That Changed The World.* New York: Rawson Associates.

Zuboff, S. (1988). *In the Age of the Smart Machine.* New York: Basic Books.

# 13    Working together: Symbolic interactionism, activity theory, and information systems

*Susan Leigh Star*

## Introduction

> There can be no doubt that in 1896 John Dewey was anticipating important aspects of what we now know as activity theory. (Tolman & Pikkola, 1989, p. 46)

I find myself these days as a point in a dialogue between three voices: activity theory, American symbolic interactionism (pragmatism), and the development of large-scale information systems. I write this chapter in order to enliven that dialogue. It might simply be a Whiggish[1] exercise or a history of ideas-in-common, such are the density of the threads that unite their founders and practitioners. But my concern here is not whether both Mead and Vygotsky both read Pavlov (of course they did), or whether their students read and taught each other (some did and do), nor simply about drawing structural analogies between lines of inquiry (although they are striking).

I'm more concerned here to make a tool that will extend the usefulness of symbolic interactionism to the communities of practice (Wenger, 1990; Lave & Wenger, 1992) of activity theory and information-systems research. The three approaches *afford* each other—a word used mostly in this context by activity theorists, drawn from Gibson's ecological psychology (Gibson, 1979).[2] Symbolic interactionism affords information-systems research a body of empirical studies of work and interaction, in the context of an elaborated philosophical framework that emphasizes collectivities and consequences. For activity theory, it is rich in understanding the subtle differences between types of work and practice, and how those are realized within and between communities. Activity theory offers the most sophisticated approach I have found toward understanding the historical and material specificity of cognition, and a way to do away with arguments about perception and cognition that are either idealist or determinist. Finally, much of the cutting-edge research in information systems (especially that in distributed artificial intelligence and computer-supported cooperative work) critiques the dominant metaphors of computer science as either too closed (and therefore ir-

296

relevant to the real world), or too much based on a priori, hyperrational assumptions about human behavior that do not hold up to investigation, especially investigation of collective or organizational phenomena.

In her study of the ways in which people learn and use mathematics in everyday life (as opposed to in formal testing situations and the classroom), Jean Lave writes of cognition that:

> There is reason to suspect that what we call cognition is in fact a complex social phenomenon. The point is not so much that arrangements of knowledge in the head correspond in a complicated way to the social world outside the head, but that they are socially organized in such a fashion as to be indivisible. "Cognition" observed in everyday practice is distributed – stretched over, not divided among – mind, body, activity and culturally organized settings (which include other actors). (1988, p. 1)

Activity theory, interactionism and information systems research [again, especially distributed artificial intelligence and computer-supported cooperative work (CSCW)] are all concerned with the meaning of "stretched over." The former two, being antiidealist, broach no concept of social cling-film[3] stretching without substance between people or situations. Information-systems research, being in the end coupled with computing, is equally concerned with the pragmatics of the stretch – how to make heterogeneous data bases, organizations, and machines talk to each other in a timely and coherent fashion.

The affordances offered to each other by symbolic interactionism, activity theory, and information-systems research are large. Some are political, some aesthetic. Interactionism and activity theory are among the very few traditions that have survived in the West with an unbroken record of antiidealism, antiindividualism, and a dialectical model of development.[4] Symbolic interactionism and activity theory share a fundamental nondeterminism, often quite formally worked out. Both are interested in the puzzles and mysteries of workplaces and of organizations. In the West, each has been a stronghold of mavericks challenging the dominant ideologies of their disciplines.

I believe that really adhering to pragmatic dialectical representations and technologies is a fiercely delicate job and a dangerous one. We're subverted all the time in the enterprise. We often feel isolated, except for temporary islands in time and space that manage to survive by a series of administrative miracles, unnamed clusters of colleagues meeting in hallways outside of conferences, talking feverishly, sending each other messages of hope.

I want this chapter to be such a message. I "grew up" as a symbolic interactionist, learned about distributed artificial intelligence, and became interested in its heuristics for understanding knowledge that is spread out over space and time. Only latterly did I begin learning about activity theory.[5] Thus, this chapter is primarily written in my "native" language of interactionism, and uses that as a vantage point for drawing together some threads from activity theory. The application of these theories to information-systems development has appeared most prominently in the fields of participatory design (Bødker, 1991; Greenbaum & Kyng, 1991) and computer-supported cooperative work (Star and Ruhleder, 1994; Kuuti, 1991; Rogers, 1993).

I've chosen to present my points through an exegesis of several classic articles from 1950s interactionist studies of work and workplace culture: several pieces by Howard S. Becker on the cultural and work worlds of jazz musicians (1951; 1953; 1953–1954) and "Banana Time': Job Satisfaction and Informal Interaction," by Donald F. Roy (1959). Classics are like great aunts and uncles – often forgotten save at family reunions, but there well remembered for the smile, the advice, and the pumpkin pie. But every time I read these two, I recognize them as closer relations.

I begin by analyzing how these articles might be read from the point of view of activity theory, and conclude with a general discussion of the points from information-systems development.

### Synopsis of the articles

These articles were written during an era in symbolic interactionism in which researchers were creatively weaving together the Pragmatism of Mead, Dewey, and Blumer with that of the community and occupational studies of Park and, later, Hughes (Fisher & Strauss, 1978a,b). While the two approaches had been intertwined and taught to students throughout the history of the Chicago school, they had somewhat different foci. Very simply, Mead, Dewey, and Blumer worked out an approach to identity, self, becoming, and awareness that emphasized the collective, the ways we constitute each others' ontologies and epistemologies. Park and Hughes concerned themselves with the unique character and dynamics of collectivities in an ecological space: first, the city; later the workplace. They borrowed metaphors from field ecology and evolutionary biology, talking of succession, the dominance of institutions, and arrangements in shared space.

During the 1950s, these foci appeared simultaneously in the work of Blumer and Hughes' students, notably Strauss, Becker, and Shibutani. Here the question became: given that we inhabit these unique collectivities (often more than one at once), and that selves and identities are collective, how can we understand the being-and-becoming interactionally? The *tension* between the conventions of the collective and the process of development, all in an ecology of other collectivities, became the unit of analysis. The venues of studies were varied: schools, hospitals, nightclubs, army bases, art studios, disaster sites. Many continued the Hughes tradition of looking at devalued or understudied occupations, such as nursing, jazz musicians, taxi drivers, and janitors. The Becker and the Roy work should be read as part of the "workplace studies" tradition that goes back to the 1920s in Chicago.[6] Roy's article also came in part from the vigorous "human relations" studies of workplaces that had their parentage both in the Chicago school and in other antirationalist approaches to work and management, many of which were published in the journal *Human Organization*. These were in important ways forerunners to today's industrial anthropology, and in fact many were conducted by anthropologists.

### Jazz musicians and workplace learning

These articles report a participant-observation study of the occupational culture of jazz musicians. They examine several issues: the nature of careers in the world of professional dance music; the relationship between the audience and the musicians, viewed from the point of view of workplace and occupations; and the process of learning to get high on marijuana, in the context of friends and colleagues who act as coaches. (Although this last article is not limited to musicians, it draws on the use of marijuana within the context of the musician's world, where it was common, and was, as well, an important part of the workplace culture.)

### The professional dance musician's audience (Becker, 1951)

The relationship between the jazz musician and the audience is a troubled one. Musicians define audiences as more and less "square." At the time of this research, Chicago sociologists were concerned with the nature of solidarity and collectivity in occupational groups. For example, Hughes spoke of "spreading the risk" in occupations: the ways that different occupational groups share blame, mistakes, and risks. Later research by his student, Freidson, would tie this in with professional control, and how, for example, doctors define and control the concept of error in medical work (1970). Becker illuminates several of the dynamics of group identity: how musicians bond together against their audiences, or play popular "square" tunes with a sense of irony, or how they negotiate for a space of autonomy within the job where they can play the sort of jazz *they* like. "The musician feels that under no circumstances should any outsider be allowed to tell him what to play or how to play it" (Becker, 1953, p. 137).

The "insiders" and "outsiders" division permeates more than the actual workplace – musicians come to form cultures they see as set apart from other straight worlds. This sometimes takes the form of physical barriers between musicians and audiences at work: the dais, or a row of chairs between performers and listeners. Becker concludes the article by noting that the self-segregation of musicians is similar to that found in many of the service occupations and, in fact, is the central tension in the client–provider relationship. This in turn has links with the ongoing discussion of professional autonomy within sociology (e.g., Freidson, 1970; Abbott, 1988).

*The musician's career* (Becker, 1953)

This article begins with the observation that "the nature of careers within any particular occupation is shaped by problems peculiar to that occupation, which in turn are a function of its position in a larger institutional arrangement" (p. 22). Again, Becker sees the musician's career as an example of the problems found in any service occupation. Drawing on the audience work, he notes that careers are influenced by the insiders/outsiders problems developed in the workplace culture. Specifically, success in the career sense becomes problematic as outsiders try to influence or control the nature of work; and family life exerts pressures on musicians to become more like outsiders.

Musicians are faced with a direct tradeoff: play square music and make money, or play music other musicians consider cool and make less. There are a few successful "pure" jazz musicians who become both monetarily successful and continue to play autonomously, but they are rare. Often, careers are structured by a series of juggling acts between safe, boring gigs and creative, autonomous ones that are less secure or less well-paying.

Careers are furthermore structured by "a network of informal interlocking cliques" (p. 22) – colleagues who learn about jobs and then recommend each other for bands and gigs. "In addition to providing some measure of job security for their members, these cliques also provide routes by which one can move up through the levels of jobs" (p. 23). So the tension between insider/outsider (or musician/client) is a permanent one – one needs other musicians for recommendations, but also needs clients who pay. Having a spouse and children exacerbates the tension between autonomy and financial need in a similar way – will it be security or creativity that wins out?

*Becoming a marijuana user* (Becker, 1953–1954)

The article is an explicit statement against the search, prevalent then and now in social psychology and social work, for those individuals carrying "traits" that predispose them to marijuana or other drug use. Instead, the workplace and group culture are the primary explanandum. Becker studies the process of getting high on marijuana as a group process, one common to the world of jazz musicians, and an extension in many ways of the division between insiders and outsiders. Becoming a marijuana user is part of becoming an insider. In his antireductionist approach, Becker follows the earlier work of Chicago school sociologist Alfred Lindesmith (1947) on narcotic addiction. Lindesmith was as well concerned with the question of why some people become addicts and some do not. Lindesmith found that mere use of the drug was not enough. Some people, for example, those severely injured in battle, would be given morphine or heroin for long periods of time, yet not become addicted. He found that you needed an interactional process to become addicted. First, you must take the drug long enough so that stopping it produces physical symptoms. Second, you must be *taught"* that your physical withdrawal discomfort can be eased by the administration of more of the drug. Without this second process, which is so-cial/interactional, you cannot become the sociophysiological entity, an addict.

Becker, like Lindesmith, found that physiology alone could not explain either the use of the drug or the guaranteed experience of getting high. In his words:

> The presence of a given kind of behavior is the result of a sequence of social ex-periences during which the person acquires a conception of the meaning of the behavior, and perceptions and judgments of objects and situations, all of which make the activity possible and desirable. Thus, the motivation or disposition to engage in the activity is built up in the course of learning to engage in it and does not antedate this learning process. (Becker, 1953–1954, p. 235)

There are several components to the coaching process Becker describes, and if any one of them is absent, the person will not become a marijuana user. The steps are: 1) learning to smoke the drug properly (right amount of air around the joint, how long to hold it in the lungs); 2) learning to connect bodily sensations with the use of the drug (Becker calls this "learning to get high"); and 3) learning how to enjoy those sensations (it is by no means obvious to a novice why extremes of hunger and wobbly legs are sensations to be sought after!). Both recognition and redefinition are part of the situation of learning – the one cannot be extracted from the other.

### "Banana Time": What is a routine?

Donald Roy's article is based on participant observation in a factory. He joined a small work group whose job, six days a week, twelve hours a day, was to put fas-teners in the material that would then go to make up raincoats. In addition to be-ing boring, the work group was isolated from the rest of the factory, shut into a small room away from the larger machinery of the factory. This room was called the "clicking room," after the noise made by the semiautomatic press that squeezed the metal down into the fabric. Nor was the work enlivened by the local competitiveness or games of piecework or sabotage of management. Workers here rarely even saw management, and they were paid by the hour.

Roy's problem in the article is to explain how these people survived such mon-umental boredom without going mad. In an era when many management-orient-ed texts were becoming increasingly rationalist, and where phrases like "happy robots" could be unblushingly applied to workers, Roy's discoveries are a breath of fresh air.

At first, Roy is simply led to his work bench, given minimal instructions, and told to start clicking. He pays little attention to his coworkers, and soon finds that:

> My clicking career was going to be a grim process of fighting the clock . . . . I had struggled through many dreary rounds with the minutes and hours during

the various phases of my industrial experience, but never had I been confronted
with such a dismal combination of working conditions as the extra-long workday, the infinitesimal cerebral excitation, and the extreme limitation of physical
movement. (Roy, 1959, p. 160)

In desperation, Roy begins to make a game of varying colors of material and
shapes of fabric strips. This allows him to get through the first week, but barely.
Then he begins to pay attention to what people around him are saying and doing.
"What I heard at first, before I started to listen, was a stream of disconnected bits
of communication which did not make much sense. Foreign accents were strong
and referents were not joined to coherent contexts of meaning. It was just 'jab-
bering' " (p. 161).

He notices what at first he thought was random, childish horseplay – turning
someone's machine off when he went to the toilet, throwing bits of each others'
lunches in the air. Roy begins to realize that the operators have names for each of
these kinds of breaks: the article's title is taken from one where the daily banana
in Sammy's lunch bucket is stolen and eaten by Ike. Similarly, there is window
time, pickup time, fish time.

The group also develops an elaborate set of verbal games, which are interspersed seemingly at random with serious conversations about pay, retirement,
death benefits, etc. Some of the kidding is repetitive and childlike in nature: "Ike
is a bad man, a very bad man! George is a good daddy, a very fine man!" (p.
163), which could go on for ten minutes. Other kidding is more elaborated:
imagining furnishing a farm for Roy, or sexual ribbing. There are also tales of
Nazi invasion precipitating Sammy's emigration to America, and stories of
George's daughter, whom he says is married to a "professor."

As Roy becomes involved in the kidding and story telling, "the 'beast of boredom' was gentled to the harmlessness of a kitten" (p. 164). However, the story
does not end there. One Friday (Roy calls it "Black Friday") Roy decides, imp-
ishly, to suggest to Sammy that George's daughter is in fact only married to an
instructor in the local barber college. "Then came a succession of dismal work-
days devoid of times and barren of themes" (p. 164). This goes on for thirteen
days, in which George refuses to participate in the times or games, and insists on
"businesslike" interaction. Gradually, the morale and moral order is restored, but
at the cost of never mentioning the "professor" stories again. Roy analyzes several stages in the restoration of social order and stresses that these are not prefixed
or necessary.

This collection of articles contain several important threads common to interactionism and activity theory. These are explicated below.

### 1. Antideterminism: "Matter means conditions"

It thus turns out that the old, old dread and dislike of matter as something opposed to mind and threatening it, to be kept within the narrowest bounds of

> recognition; something to be denied so far as possible lest it encroach upon ideal purposes and finally exclude them from the real world, is as absurd practically as it was impotent intellectually. Judged from the only scientific standpoint, what it does and how it functions, matter means conditions. (Dewey, 1920, p. 72)

> If [people] define situations as real, they are real in their consequences. (Thomas & Thomas, 1928, p. 572)

In critiquing either individualist, functionalist, or closed-world accounts of science and knowledge, various writers from these perspectives have suggested several types of indeterminacy. First, Dewey and Bentley, among other pragmatist writers, suggest that knowledge itself is indeterminate (Dewey & Bentley, 1949). This indeterminacy arises because *the meaning of knowledge is given in its consequences,* in a community of listeners, not in its a priori analytic specification. This is both formally and empirically the case. Becker later translated this idea into a critique of static, overly structural accounts of commitments (1960). He argued that we construct the commitments of our world out of joint practice, and that at any one time we are participants in a number of activities. We therefore run multiple "side-bets" all the time, and the structure of our commitments is determined by their fate in the multiple communities of which we are all a part.

"Banana Time" describes a situation where social order, temporary and local though it is, becomes disrupted, and only gradually, through a series of steps, is restored to a semblance of its former existence. Yet Roy denies that this can be understood by any simple "stage theory" or homeostatic functional model:

> To point out that George played a key role in this particular case of re-equilibration is not to suggest that the homeostatic controls of a social system may be located in a type of role or in a patterning of role relationships. Such controls could be but partially described in terms of human interaction; they would be functional to the total configuration of conditions within the field of influence. The automatic controls of a mechanical system operate as such only under certain achieved and controlled conditions . . . . The clicking-room group regained equilibrium under certain undetermined conditions. (Roy, 1959, p. 168)

These conditions were undetermined in the sense that they followed no logical or previously set developmental sequence. Rather, they were neither random nor determined – one aspect of the breach would heal, that in turn mediating the next, and so on.

The concept of undetermined conditions has become important for recent symbolic interactionists writing about science and technology. In my own work, I present a model of robustness of knowledge, which, following biologist Richard Levins, is seen as "the intersection of independent lies." That is, each local truth is partial and flawed; no a priori specification can encompass any global truth, but when scientists and other actors join local truths they create a robust, emergent negotiated order (Star, 1989). Fujimura (1991) and Clarke (1990, 1991) have written about the indeterminacy of perspectives arising from interactionist approaches to science, and compare this with postmodern interpretations of ethnographies. Because we interactionists premise our findings on multiple perspectives and negotiations, we refuse the omniscient monovocal narrative of scientific authority. In this there is a kinship with voices often absent from those narratives: third-world peoples, women of all colors, behind-the-scenes workers such as lab technicians and janitors, and animals. The jazz musicians and their audiences, as well as their families, are in a permanent, unresolvable conflict, where each perspective is equally valid. Bowers (1991) in a recent critique of cognitive psychology, makes much the same claim about indeterminacy of time – once true pluralism is admitted, even such taken-for-granted constants as time relativize. In all this, we lose the illusion of control so important to rationalist science.

Loss of control of a slightly different sort is important in the theoretical foundations of distributed artificial intelligence (DAI). Hewitt (1985) speaks of "unbounded nondeterminism" as critical for the design of DAI systems. He calls these "open systems" – those which occur in the real world, which include both people and machines, and which are distributed over time and space. Such systems, he postulates, have the characteristics of openness due to certain formal properties, partially inhering in their distributed nature. Updates are asynchronous; components have arms' length relationships, and thus must negotiate with each other; systems are continually evolving; and there is no centralized control or overview. Systems semantics, therefore, must be approached locally (through what he calls "micro-theories"), and the outcome of a contest between two theories is formally indeterminate. Suchman (1987) and Agre (1988), both arguing with the concept of plans and goals in traditional artificial intelligence, demonstrate that planning cannot be understood as other than locally contingent. For them, local means an entire situation of activities and material conditions – bodies, other people, machines, as well as documents, formal organizational arrangements, and previous interactions. They are furthermore composed of the categories of members, not pregiven logically or structurally from outside. Because of the contingent nature of planning and action, there is a fundamental nondeterminism to plans and goals themselves.

*Contingencies become conditions; conditions mediate.* Antideterminism alone could not form the core of a community of practice. While necessary, it is not sufficient to account for regularities in behavior, for structure, and for the ways in which human behavior is clearly not a series of simple physical (or stimulus–response) reactions. Both activity theory and interactionism developed accounts of the ways in which actions (or gestures, or signs) acquire symbolic meaning in a community and may subsequently come to have the force of mediating conditions.

Central to much activity theory, particularly that of Vygotsky and Ilyenkov (Bakhurst, 1990), is the idea that contingencies becomes conditions in light of community or joint activity, and subsequently mediate action. Bakhurst says of Vygotsky's position:

> We now stand in relation not just to a brute, physical world, but to an *interpreted* environment, an environment conceived as being *of a certain kind.* This being so, our behaviour can never be simply "called forth" by the world in itself. Rather, we act in the light of some reading of reality, a reading that renders our behaviour an appropriate response to the perceived situation. On this view, our actions are more like conclusions to arguments than effects of physical causes. (Bakhurst, 1990, p. 208)

Similarly, George Herbert Mead's theory of the development of the collective "other" as object, and especially of what he called "the objective reality of perspectives," emphasized a progressive elaboration and revision of conditions, which were simultaneously symbolic and physical:

> The existence of motion in the passage of events depends not upon what is taking place in an absolute space and time, but upon the relation of a consentient set to a percipient event. Such a relation stratifies nature. These stratifications are not only there in nature but they are the only forms of nature that are there. (Mead, 1964 [1927], p. 315)

A consentient set – a community jointly imbuing meaning – and a percipient event together form a unit of mediated activity, in precisely the way both Vygotsky and Ilyenkov intended. Compare this notion with Becker's analysis of how the marijuana user continues to learn to use the drug: "He examines succeeding experiences closely, looking for new effects, making sure the old ones are still there. Out of this there grows a stable set of categories for experiencing the drug's effects whose presence enables the user to get high with ease" (Becker, 1953–1954, p. 239); and "In no case will use continue without such a redefinition of the effects as enjoyable. This redefinition occurs, typically, in interaction with more experienced users who, in a number of ways teach the novice to find pleasure in this experience which is at first so frightening" (p. 240).

Similarly, the musician's career is a series of negotiated events, whose stability is only found in collectivity:

> These cliques are bound together by ties of mutual obligation, the members sponsoring each other for jobs, either hiring one another when they have that power or recommending one another to those who do the hiring for an orchestra . . . the person who is unknown will not be hired. (Becker, 1953, p. 23)

Again, this is within the context of a workplace culture where use of the drug has a jointly construed and learnt meaning. A similar kind of analysis grows as Roy attempts to account for the meaning of informal interactions in the workplace. These actions are so meaningless to an outsider that they resist functional definition:

> This emerging awareness of structure and meaning included recognition that the long day's grind was broken by interruptions of a kind other than the formally instituted or idiosyncratically developed disjunctions in work routine previously described. These additional interruptions appeared in daily repetition in an ordered series of informal interactions. . . . Their significance lay not so much in their function as rest pauses . . . nor did their chief importance lie in the accentuation of progress points in the passage of time, although they could perform that function far more strikingly than the hour hand on the full face of George's alarm clock. (Roy, 1959)

Rather, Roy develops a metaphor of a "special kind of cuckoo clock" – one with a cumulative, negotiated, and mediating function:

> If the daily series of interruptions be likened to a clock, then the comparison might best be made with a special kind of cuckoo clock, one with a cuckoo which can provide variation in its announcements and can create such an interest in them that the intervening minutes become filled with intellectual content. The major significance of the interactional interruptions lay in such a carryover of interest. The physical interplay which momentarily halted work activity would initiate verbal exchanges and thought processes to occupy group members until the next interruption. The group interactions thus not only marked off the time; they gave it content and hurried it along. (Roy, 1959, pp. 161–162)

What was at first contingency and informal play then in fact becomes a set of workplace conditions. The earlier ones give rise to later ones, as becomes evident when the situation is disrupted and then gradually repaired:

> My purpose in discriminating the seven changes is primarily to suggest that re-equilibration, when it does occur, may be described in observable phases and that the emergence of each succeeding phase should be dependent upon the configuration of conditions of the preceding one. Alternative eventual outcomes may change in their probabilities, as the phases succeed each other. (Roy, 1959, p. 168)

Engeström's discussion of the nature of tools also gives a contingent and situated meaning to artifacts, which then mediate experience. Consider the evolution of marijuana as a tool in Becker's article, from the point of view of Engeström's analysis of medical computing:

> Tools are dependent on the object of actions. The object is a transitional being. It is both "anything presented to the mind or senses" and "an end or aim." In other words, the object is both something given and something anticipated, projected, transformed, and achieved. In the transformation of the object, also the tools, or mediating artifacts, are transformed. (Engeström, 1990, p. 9)

Cole's discussion of "cultural co-evolution" calls forth a similar image from the point of view of activity theory. He says that historical, cultural, and biological contexts are thoroughly intermingled, and that constraints and innovation are two aspects of one process. He notes that stages are not, in this sense, linear, or even stages as normally understood within psychology, but a situated evolution, where mediated become mediator in inseparable fashion (1991a). Raeithel (1991) calls this the "dialectic of means and forms," and says that "Societal forms can be, and usually are, transformed into operative means." Drawing on activity theory to discuss software development and design, he also notes the historical and philosophical links between several of the early pragmatists and the activity theorists.

## 2. Antiindividualism and the primacy of the dialectic and the collective

In a recent collection of articles about collective remembering and memory, several authors attempt to stretch the boundaries of these concepts, traditionally located within an individual skin (Middleton & Edwards, 1990). Engeström et al. (1990) discuss collective remembering as an act mediated by one's own experience, material traces such as records, and the experience and communication of others. Forgetting is thus a breach or rupture between features of the collective, including material culture, and one's own experience; it is *not* a failure of retrieval or of the individual simply to "perform" a memory task.

Roy's discussion of the creation of a stable activity in the clicker group also discusses the ways in which others build experiences:

> In both the cultural content and the social structure of clicker group interaction could be seen the permeation of influences which slowed from the various multiple group memberships of the participants. Past and present "other-group" experiences or anticipated "outside" social connections provided significant materials for the building of themes and for the establishment and maintenance of status and role relationships. (Roy, 1959, p. 167)

The local culture of the room is built up as series of activities mediated by outside membership, the material conditions of the workroom, and dynamic interpretations of action in the site. Rupture occurs when Roy disrupts the relationship between the self-in-the-room and George's membership in the outside collectivity (the world of academia). Similarly, Becker holds that one *cannot* learn to experience pleasure from the use of marijuana without collective mediation: "Enjoyment is introduced by the favorable definition of the experience that one acquires from others. Without this, use will not continue, for marijuana will not be for the user an object that he can use for pleasure" (Becker, 1953–1954, p. 241). For Roy, leaving the jointly created zone of mutual culture casts him into solitude and despair. After Black Friday, he says:

> With the return of boredom, came a return of fatigue. My legs tired as the afternoons dragged on, and I became engaged in conscious efforts to rest one by shifting my weight to the other. I would pause in my work to stare through the barred windows at the grimy brick wall across the alley; and, turning my head, I would notice that Ike was staring at the wall, too. (Roy, 1959, p. 165)

In exploding individualist explanations for activities such as cognition, feeling, and remembering, both interactionists and activity theorists created new units of analysis powerful enough to explicate how we are coimplicated in each others' actions, including those actions usually thought private and individual. Cole's (1991b) analysis of socially shared cognition makes it clear that this approach is both culturally specific and embedded in ongoing organizations. This accords with Becker's (1953) analysis of careers: "The successful career may be viewed as a series of such steps, each one a sequence of such sponsorship, successful performance, and the building up of relationships at each new level" (p. 23).

For Vygotsky, one such important conceptual tool was the *zone of proximal development*. In contradistinction to theories of child development which relied on a priori, innate, and individualist schemes of development, he saw children as having "buds" of potential which would only be actualized collectively, within a shared zone of development. This he defined as:

> The distance between the actual developmental level as determined by independent problem solving and the level of potential development as determined through problem solving under adult guidance or in collaboration with more capable peers. (Vygotsky, 1978, p. 86)

Zones may be populated by tools, physical and cultural, as well as other people. But outside such a zone, there is no realization of the tool or the experience. This concept can directly be applied to learning to use the tool of marijuana in order to get stoned – something which occurs only in the presence of a knowledgeable community: "Many new users are ashamed to admit ignorance and, pretending to know already, must learn through the more indirect means of observation and imitation," says Becker (1953–1954, p. 237), and he goes on to describe first imitation, then "contact high." He describes a person not feeling anything, then another person telling him to sit on a bar stool and notice that his feet are cold. "And I started feeling it, you know. That was the first time" (p. 238). Here we have all the elements of a Vygotskyian triangle, as elucidated by Engeström (1987): the body/tool, the community, and the individual experience, located within a zone of proximal development.

## 3. The pragmatic theory of action: Situated actions and the definition of the situation

The theories of knowledge of both activity theory and symbolic interactionism are nondichotomous. It is not a question of the interaction of organism and environment that create the individual; rather, it is a question of what Rogers Hall (1990) has called "ecologies of representations": people, symbols, machines, things producing understandings that are *simultaneously* structured and novel.

This means that understanding is both dynamic and local. As Yrjö Engeström (1987) writes, this means that objects and situations develop together: "We are not talking of an eternal and content-indifferent logic but of a developmental logic of the object itself. This logic is stored nowhere in the form of ready-made formulas to be imposed upon the object" (p. 242). He goes on to discuss Ilyenkov's notion that objects must be considered historically, and concludes that "in dialectical logic, the concrete is an interconnected systemic whole. But the interconnections are not of any arbitrary kind. At the core of the interconnections there are *internal contradictions*" (p. 242). The contradictions arise as a tension between the situated connections of the concrete, which allows for interconnectedness, and the experience of wholeness, and the abstractions which are imported (synchronic) or a priori (diachronic). As one is (necessarily) open to novel experience, the kind of consistency associated with unified, top-down, or dichotomous models becomes impossible.[7]

I have already discussed some of the contradictions in this sense involved for someone learning to use marijuana: an experience entered into for pleasure is unpleasant until others help interpret it, or one feels isolated, unable to experience much of anything until others join in and make the feeling possible, make the connections to make the action whole. This concept is also key to the definition of insider or outsider in the musician's world:

> The whole system of beliefs about what musicians are and what audiences are is summed up in a word used by musicians to refer to outsiders – "square." It is used as a noun and as an adjective, denoting both a kind of person and a quality of behavior and objects . . . a way of thinking, feeling and behaving (with its expression in material objects) which is the opposite of that valued by musicians . . . the musician is conceived of by the professional group as an artist who possesses a mysterious artistic gift setting him apart from all other people. . . . The gift is something which cannot be acquired through education; the outsider, therefore, can never become a member of the group. (Becker, 1951, p. 137)

Similarly, Roy's experience of the meaningless babble of the workplace, and his attempts to find rational function in the situational workplace culture, are unintelligible until he gives up and allows himself to become part of the concrete work process. The contradictions become temporarily resolved with understanding, but in all cases, new understanding and developments also lead to new contradictions.

Engeström's definition of the concrete as connected wholeness is echoed in Becker's description of the development of pleasure in marijuana use:

> The evidence makes it clear that marijuana use for pleasure can occur only when the process described above is undergone and cannot occur without it. This is apparently so without reference to the nature of the individual's personal makeup or psychic problems. Such theories assume that people have sta-

ble modes of response which predetermine the way they will act in relation to any particular situation or object and that, when they come in contact with the given object or situation, they act in the way in which their makeup predisposes them. . . . This analysis of the genesis of marijuana use shows that the individuals who come in contact with a given object may respond to it at first in a great variety of ways. If a stable form of new behavior toward the object is to emerge, a transformation of meanings must occur, in which the person develops a new conception of the nature of the object. This happens in a series of communicative acts in which others point out new aspects of his experience to him, present him with new interpretations of events, and help him achieve a new conceptual organization of his world, without which the new behavior is not possible." (Becker, 1953–1954, p. 242)

*"Without which the new behavior is not possible."* One of the powerful messages in this piece is the refusal to accept the term "behavior" except as a web, a situated package occurring in a situation. Behavior emerges as novel. Music might be taught, but being a musician cannot be. "This suggests that behavior of any kind might fruitfully be studied developmentally, in terms of changes in meanings and concepts, their organization and reorganization, and the way they channel behavior, making some acts possible while excluding others" (Becker, 1953–1954, p. 242).

Interactionist Strauss, following Dewey (1920), analyzed the ways in which identities are constantly renegotiated in light of new conditions (1959). Continuity of identity, and thus of human development itself, is problematized and, as above, contingencies form new conditions of evaluation. Biography is taken from the static nature of stage theory, and made dynamic and historically situated. Strauss's recent book, *Continual Permutations of Action* (1993), extends this complex modelling of time, work-practice and action nested across different scales.[8]

### Summary and conclusions: Why is this important now?

At the beginning of this chapter, I quoted Jean Lave on the importance of understanding how cognition is stretched over individuals in situations. I would like to conclude by stating why I think it is important to bring the insights of activity theory and interactionism together, and the role that might be played by information-systems development.

Two things are occurring quite rapidly in the modern world. The first is the failure of rationalism to account for or to prescribe people's behavior (which is not new), and what *is* new, a large interdisciplinary movement in the academy and in the sciences that is documenting this state of affairs. The second is the rapid rise of information technologies, which are insinuating themselves into the conduct of work, being integrated with each other in new kinds of international networks, and also being embedded within each other to produce a newly complex state of what Etienne Wenger (1990) has called "the black box syndrome."

*Documenting the failure of rationalism*

Many recent studies have shown that what we take to be the simplest of rational practices, in organizations and in everyday life, are in fact extremely problematic, negotiated, and situated. I will adumbrate several here to make the point; this list is in no way exhaustive.

Practices of measurement and accounting show that there is no such thing as a simple "number." Harper's careful ethnography of accounting in a scientific laboratory, for example, shows that people check the behavior of calculators and other accountants by developing a qualitative sense of the "right numbers" at the right time (Harper, 1988). Lynch's analysis of measurement by social scientists shows a similar pattern of accounting practices; the numbers are not pregiven (Lynch, 1993). Similarly, Lave's work on everyday use of mathematics shows that people have qualitatively different ways of using numbers depending on the situation of the activity – in supermarkets and Weight Watchers meetings, they are inventive and sufficient; in testing situations and classrooms, those same people appear to be dullards and incompetent. Hall's work on algebra problem solving (1989, 1990) similarly shows both students and teachers who, working informally with the materials at hand, produce novel and adequate-to-the-purpose solutions, many of which go unrepresented in final reports. Restivo's (1992) historical and larger-scale investigations of mathematics practices similarly undermine the claims to transcendent rationalism of much mathematics.

Much of the work of the "new" sociology of science has been aimed at a similar deconstruction of scientific practice in light of overly rational published reports. Study after study (e.g., Latour & Woolgar, 1979; Latour, 1988; Star, 1989, 1995b); Clarke, 1990; Fujimura, 1992) has documented the gradual erasure of disclaimers, uncertainties, local practices, and modifiers from the pages of scientific reports. Yet these are abundantly clear by observation in the laboratory, once certain preconceptions about science are dispensed with.

The work of Suchman and of Agre on the failure of the rational model of plans and goals in artificial intelligence has already been discussed, above. They are joined by a number of other researchers in and around information systems research who emphasize the contingent, continually renegotiated nature of planning in organizations. Gasser's work (1986) tells the story of the impossibility of capturing routine computing, since workers are always tailoring and fitting what is supposed to be routine and standard to local contingencies. Wieckert (1990) notes that expert systems are in fact good occasions for people in a workplace to discuss their work and make it explicit, but there is nothing rational about either the design or use of the system. Forsythe (1993; Forsythe & Buchanan, 1989) finds a similar situation in the design of medical expert systems.

Finally, a few studies are coming out that show that even tasks that many would call very low-level, such as filling out insurance claim forms and processing claims, develop in conjunction with complex workplace cultures (Wenger, 1990) and issues of justice and distribution (Gerson & Star, 1986; Star, 1991). Orr's work on photocopier repair technicians and their cultural remembering and situated practices displays a rich interweaving of technology, bodies, interaction, and locale (1990a,b). We cannot find a rational, reliable resting place in the old way by falling back on ideas of routine, standards, and universal reliability – we are in the processing of discovering that it's local all the way down, including the work of transporting it across locales.

*New developments in integration and embeddedness*
*in information systems*

At the same time as these developments are occurring across a range of social and natural sciences, the number and density of information technologies are growing. They are rapidly integrating; that is, they both plug into each other more easily and are more easily translated and linked. Consider the amount of integration in a fairly common activity, banking from home with a personal computer, which requires translation across several electronic media, software packages, and accounting conventions. They are also becoming more embedded in each other, layered, or nested. For instance, there are medical imaging systems that take a picture from a laboratory slide, automatically process it, and compare the image with information in an internal database of similar cases, adjudging the slide's normalcy given the patient's age and sex. There are as well medical classification and software systems that link global epidemiology, local clinical practice, and insurance reimbursement (Bowker & Star, 1994).

From the point of view of the studies discussed in the previous section, such developments could be nightmarish were they themselves embedded in a rationalist perspective – and they often are. For example, who put together the medical database, and with whose knowledge? We know now that all knowledge, including scientific, comes in many voices, and that normalcy is a negotiated, contested phenomenon. What then of the invisible database embedded out of reach, built on an old-fashioned idea of medical rational knowledge? We know from our studies of data entry and accounting that local knowledge, as well as local error, partly determine the nature of all information, including the numerical. What then of credit reports, statistical safety assessments, and other sorts of important judgments that are linked together in integrated electronic systems (see Perrow, 1984 for a partial discussion of the negative aspects of this answer).

Several recent studies in the joint region of organization theory, artificial intelligence, computer-supported cooperative work and/or sociology join the other voices in this chapter in calling for analyses of this stage of affairs that are both situated and structural. Clarke (1991) joins the idea of organizational "environments" with the interactionist concept of social worlds[9] to analyze tools, medication, and social change. Kling and Scacchi (1982), also joining interactionism with organizational analysis and computer science, call for analyses of the "web of computing" – people, machines, and situations. Star (1995a) analyzes the role of formal representations in the design of computer architecture. Brown and Duguid (1989, 1990) argue for a wholistic view of organizations, learning and work – again, both situated and mediated by technology and other tools. Arne Raeithel's thoughtful philosophical examination of activity theory and software development calls for an eclectic, multivoiced approach to design and use (Raeithel, 1991). Bannon (1990) and Schmidt (Schmidt, 1990; Schmidt & Bannon, 1992), Bødker, et al. (1988, 1991; Bødker, 1991), Sharrock and Anderson (1994), Greenbaum and Kyng (1991), Rogers (1993), Harper et al. (in press), Starr (1995c), and Jirotka, Gilbert, and Luff (1992), among others, are bringing social theory into the realm of computer-supported cooperative work to challenge both traditional ideas of management and organizations and in the process, technocratic determinism.

## Conclusion

I believe that jointly activity theory, interactionism, and information-systems research have some important insights to offer scholarship and development. We know that, in spite of the failure of rationalism, the world does not fall apart. We've begun to understand that the absence of a monolithic voice does not mean chaos or babble, but pluralism, and that requiring translation. Having walked away from several important dichotomies (including organism/environment, individual/collectivity, mind/body, formal learning/everyday practice), we've learned not to replace them with mysticism, but with an analysis of novelty as it arises in communities and other collectivities (Starr, 1995). In spite of social science and philosophical establishments in the West that were intolerant of these perspectives, we relied on empirical work and ethnography, and have come away with a valuable bank of studies and findings about how people think together.

Together with some of the tools of information systems research, activity theory and interactionism offer a rich theory of the interpersonal "stretch" of cognition and work. I hope this chapter will help strengthen the already flourishing three-way dialogue.

## Glossary

This glossary defines some terms used in this chapter: activity theory, symbolic interactionism, distributed artificial intelligence, and CSCW.

**Activity theory,** originally associated with the work of Soviet psychologists and philosophers (especially Vygotsky, Leontiev, and Ilyenkov), has extended beyond the former Soviet Union, and claims adherents in many countries. It is particularly concerned with the ways in which tools, collectivities, and historical and material conditions together form actions and contexts of problem solving and knowing. It is also known as sociocultural analysis, sociohistorical and cultural-historical psychology. For a review, see Cole (1991a).

**Symbolic interactionism** is a community of practice that also has several different names, not all of which mean exactly the same thing. "Chicago school sociology" refers to a body of work originally coming out of the sociology department at the University of Chicago, between roughly 1915 and 1955. Together with the pragmatist philosophy of Dewey, James, Mead, and Bentley, and the social psychology of Herbert Blumer, it came to form a movement in American sociology distinct from, and antithetical to, the functionalism of Parsons and Merton. Many attempts at new names have been made for this movement, including pragmatic interactionism, negotiated-order theory, and pragmatist sociology. Because many of the studies relied on ethnographic methods during a period of quantitative dominance, and also because of the popularity of Glaser and Strauss' *The Discovery of Grounded Theory: Strategies for a Qualitative Sociology,* the approach is also sometimes just called "qualitative sociology." Yet there are, of course, qualitative sociologists who are not interactionists and many interactionists who do quantitative research. In this chapter it is called "interactionism." For a review see Fisher and Strauss, 1978a,b.

The term **distributed artificial intelligence,** includes human/organizational concerns, and can be ecological/situational in orientation. Its subject matter is how to best represent knowing and problem solving as distributed over actors (sometimes human, sometimes not) or situations. It "lives" in computer science, cognitive science, sociology, and anthropology. A review can be found in Huhns and Gasser (1989).

**Computer-Supported Cooperative Work (CSCW)** is a new, interdisciplinary field with participants from software engineering, systems design, human–computer interaction, management, and sociology. It is the study and design of computer systems to support the work of large and small groups, and theory arising from this endeavor. Research can be found in a journal, *Computer-Supported Cooperative Work (CSCW): An International Journal.*

### Acknowledgments

Geof Bowker, Erik Axel, Joan Fujimura, David Middleton, and Arne Raeithel made detailed and very helpful comments on an earlier draft of this chapter. The electronic conversations over "XLCHC" are an extraordinarily rich source of stimulation and open-minded discussion of these issues. Rogers Hall, Etienne Wenger, Mike Cole, Phil Agre, Danny Bobrow, Anselm Strauss, and other Institute for Research on Learning members helped collectively to clarify many of these issues at a seminar hosted by the Institute in Palo Alto, California in January, 1991. This chapter is dedicated to Jean Lave.

## Notes

1  That is, all previous events inevitably leading up to the present state of affairs/status quo.
2  For a tool to afford means that in another's presence, and for a given situation, and in action itself, something can be done or known. So, for example, from an ecological point of view, the suffering and experimentation of many other women and healers, in their presence or with their technologies, affords me the capacity to give birth in a particular fashion – with anaesthesia, perhaps, or with special breathing technologies, or with touches that will coach and guide me through the experience (Jordan, 1989). The capacity does not inhere in me alone, is not innate in my body alone, and it makes no sense to speak of it that way.
3  Or Saran Wrap in American (not to be confused with English).
4  Of course, activity theory was born and survived in the East, as well, but I wish here to address the circumstances it faced in the West in common with interactionism.
5  I have greatly benefitted from a remarkable electronic mail conversation known as "xlchc," in which activity theory is often discussed, from the Laboratory for Comparative Human Development, Department of Communication, University of California, San Diego.
6  Everett Hughes' 1928 study of the Chicago Real Estate Board forms a bridge between the earlier community studies and the studies of occupations that began in the 1920s (republished as Hughes, 1979).
7  This is formally the same as Hewitt's (1985) basis for claiming "necessary inconsistency" in open systems.
8  A summary of this book, and its links with activity theory, can be found in a special issue of the journal *Mind, Culture and Activity,* with commentaries by several interactionists (Vol. 2, No. 1: 1995).
9  This is the same concept as that of "community of practice" (Lave & Wenger, 1992; Wenger, 1990, private communication).

## References

Abbott, A. (1988). *The System of Professions: An Essay on the Division of Expert Labor.* Chicago: University of Chicago Press.
Agre, P. (1988). The Dynamic Structure of Everyday Life, Technical Report 1085, Artificial Intelligence Laboratory, MIT, 1988.
Bakhurst, D. (1990). Social memory in Soviet thought. In D. Middleton & D. Edwards (Eds.), *Collective Remembering,* pp. 203–226. London: Sage.
Bannon, L. (1990). A pilgrim's progress: From cognitive science to cooperative design. *AI and Society, 4,* 259–275.
Becker, H. S. (1960). Notes on the Concept of Commitment. *American Journal of Sociology, 59,* 235–242.
Becker, H. S. (1953–1954). Becoming a marihuana user. *American Journal of Sociology, 59,* 235–242.
Becker, H. S. (1953). Some contingencies of the professional dance musician's career. *Human Organization, 12,* 22–26.
Becker, H. S. (1951). The professional dance musician and his audience. *American Journal of Sociology, 57,* 136–144.
Bødker, S. (1991). *Through the Interface.* Hillside, NJ: Erlbaum.
Bødker, S., Ehn, P., Knudsen, J., Kyng, M., & Madsen, K. (1988). Computer support for cooperative

design, pp. 377–394 in *Proceedings of the Conference on Computer-Supported Cooperative Work, September 26–28, 1988, Portland Oregon.* New York: ACM.

Bødker, S., et al. (1991). Computers in context: Report from the AT project in Progress: Report of the 1991 NES-SAM conference, Ebeltoft, Denmark.

Bowers, J. M. (1991). Time, representation and power/knowledge: Towards a critique of cognitive science as a knowledge producing practice. *Theory and Psychology.* Vol. 1, pp. 543–569.

Bowker, G. & Star, S. L. (1994). Knowledge and Infrastructure in International Information Management: Problems of Classification and Coding. In L. Bud (Ed.), *Information Acumen: the Understanding and Use of Knowledge in Modern Business,* pp. 187–213. London: Routledge.

Brown, J. S. & Duguid, P. (1990). Toward a unified view of working and learning, and innovating. *Organization Science, 2,* 40–57.

Brown, J. S. & Duguid, P. (1989). Learning and Improvisation: Local Sources of Global Innovation. Institute for Research on Learning, Working Paper, September.

Clarke, A. E. (in press). Modernity, Postmodernity and Reproduction, 1890–1993, or Mommy, where do cyborgs come from anyway? To appear in, Dugdale, A. & Fujimura J. (Eds.), *Making Sex, Fabricating Bodies: Gender and the Construction of Knowledge in the Biomedical Sciences.*

Clarke, A. E. (1991). Social worlds/arenas theory as organizational theory. In D. R. Maines (Ed.), *Social Organization and Social Process: Essays in Honor of Anselm Strauss,* pp. 119–158. New York: Aldine de Gruyter.

Clarke, A. E. (1990). Controversy and the development of reproductive sciences, *Social Problems, 37,* 18–37.

Cole, M. (1991a). On cultural psychology: A review article. *American Anthropologist, 93,* 435–439.

Cole, M. (1991b). On socially shared cognition. In L. B. Resnick, J. M. Levine, & S. D. Teasley (Eds.), *Perspectives on Socially Shared Cognition.* Washington, DC: American Psychological Association.

Dewey, J. (1920). *Reconstruction in Philosophy.* New York: Henry Holt.

Dewey, J. & Bentley, A. F. (1949). *Knowing and the Known.* Boston: Beacon.

Engeström, Y. (1987). *Learning by Expanding: An Activity-Theoretical Approach to Developmental Research.* Helsinki: Orienta-Konsultit Oy.

Engeström, Y. (1990). When is a tool? Multiple Meanings of Artifacts In Human Activity. In *Learning, Working and Imagining,* pp. 171–195. Helsinki: Orienta-Konsultit Oy.

Engeström, Y., Brown, K., Engeström, R., & Koistinen, K. (1990). Organizational forgetting: An activity-theoretical perspective. In D. Middleton and D. Edwards (Eds.), *Collective Remembering,* pp. 139–168. London: SAGE.

Fisher, B. & Strauss, A. (1978a). The Chicago tradition and social change: Thomas, Park and their successors. *Symbolic Interaction, 1,* 5–23.

Fisher, B. & Strauss, A. (1978b). Interactionism. In T. Bottomore and R. Nisbet (Eds.), *A History of Sociological Analysis,* pp. 457–498. New York: Basic Books.

Forsythe, D. (1993). Engineering knowledge: The construction of knowledge in artificial intelligence. *Social Studies of Science, 23,* 445–477.

Forsythe, D. & Buchanan, B. (1989). Knowledge acquisition for expert systems: Some pitfalls and suggestions. *IEEE Transactions on Systems, Man and Cybernetics, 19,* 435–442.

Freidson, E. (1970). *The Profession of Medicine.* New York: Harper and Row.

Fujimura, J. H. (1992). Crafting science: Standardized packages, boundary objects, and translation. In A. Pickering (Ed.), *Science as Practice and Culture,* pp. 168–214. Chicago: University of Chicago.

Fujimura, J. H. (1991). On Methods, ontologies, and representation in the sociology of science: Where do we stand? In D. Maines (Ed.), *Social Organization and Social Process: Essays in Honor of Anselm L. Strauss.* Hawthorne, NY: Aldine de Gruyter.

Gasser, L. (1986). The integration of computing and routine work. *ACM Transactions on Office Information Systems, 4,* 205–225.

Gerson, E. & Star, S. L. (1986). Analyzing due process in the workplace. *ACM Transactions on Office Information Systems, 4,* 257–270.

Gibson, J. (1979). *The Ecological Approach to Visual Perception.* Boston: Houghton-Mifflin.

Greenbaum, J. & Kyng, M. (Eds.). (1991). *Design at Work: Cooperative Design of Computer Systems.* Hillsdale, NJ: Erlbaum.

Hall, R. (1990). Making Math on Paper: Representational Ecologies. Ph.D. Dissertation, Department of Information and Computer Science, University of California, Irvine.

Hall, R. (1989). Computational approaches to analogical reasoning: A comparative analysis. *Artificial Intelligence, 39,* 39–120.

Harper, R. (1988). Not Any Old Numbers: An Examination of Practical Reasoning in an Accountancy Environment. *The Journal of Interdisciplinary Economics, 2,* 297–306.

Harper, R., Hughes, J., Randall, D., Shapiro, D., & Sharrock, W. (in press). *Order in the Skies: Air Traffic Controllers and CSCW.* London: Routledge.

Hewitt, C. (1985). The Challenge of Open Systems. *BYTE, 10,* 223–242.

Hughes, E. (1979) [1982]. *The Chicago Real Estate Board: The Growth of an Institution.* New York: Arno Press.

Huhns, M. & Gasser, L. (Eds). (1989). *Distributed Artificial Intelligence 2.* Menlo Park, CA: Morgan Kauffmann.

Jirotka, M., Gilbert, N. & Luff, P. (1992). On the Social Organization of Organizations. *Computer Supported Cooperative Work, 1*(1–2), 95–112.

Jordan, B. (1989). Cosmopolitical obstetrics: Some insights from the training of traditional midwives. *Social Science and Medicine, 28,* 925–944.

Kling, R. & Scacchi, W. (1982). The web of computing: Computing technology as social organization. *Advances in Computers, 21,* 3–78.

Kuutti, K. (1991). The concept of activity as a basic unit of analysis for CSCW research. Proceedings of the Second European Conference on Computer-Supported Cooperative Work, Amsterdam.

Latour, B. (1988). *Science in Action.* Cambridge, MA: Harvard University Press.

Latour, B. & Woolgar, S. (1979). *Laboratory Life.* Beverly Hills, CA: Sage.

Lave, J. (1988). *Cognition in Practice.* Cambridge, England: Cambridge University Press.

Lave, J. & Wenger, E. (1992). *Situated Learning: Legitimate Peripheral Participation.* Cambridge: Cambridge University Press.

Lindesmith, A. (1947). *Opiate Addiction.* Bloomington, IN: Principia Press.

Lynch, M. (1993). Ordinary and Scientific Measurement as Ethnomethodological Phenomena. In G. Button (Ed.), *Ethnomethodology and the Human Sciences: A Foundational Reconstruction.* Cambridge: Cambridge University Press.

Mead, G. H. (1964) [1927]. The Objective Reality of Perspectives. In A. J. Reck (Ed.), *Selected Writings,* pp. 306–319. Chicago: University of Chicago Press.

Middleton, D. & Edwards, D. (Eds.). (1990). *Collective Remembering.* London: SAGE.

Orr, J. (1990a). Sharing Knowledge, Celebrating Identity: Community Memory in a Service Culture. In D. Middleton and D. Edwards (Eds.), *Collective Remembering,* pp. 169–189. London: Sage.

Orr, J. (1990b). Talking about Machines: An Ethnography of a Modern Job, Ph.D. Thesis, Department of Anthropology, Cornell University.

Perrow, C. (1984). *Normal Accidents: Living with High-Risk Technologies.* New York: Basic Books.

Raeithel, A. (1991). Semiotic Self-Regulation and Work: An Activity Theoretical Foundation for Design. In R. Budde, C. Flloyd, R. Keil-Slawik & H. Züllighoven (Eds.), *Software Development and Reality Construction.* Berlin: Springer.

Restivo, S. (1992). *Mathematics in Society and History: Sociological Inquiries.* Dordrecht: Kluwer Academic Publishers.

Rogers, Y. (1993). Coordinating Computer-Mediated Work. *Computer-Supported Cooperative Work, 1,* 295–315.

Roy, D. (1959). Banana Time: Job Satisfaction and Informal Interaction. *Human Organization, 18,* 158–168.

Schmidt, K. (1990). Analysis of Cooperative Work: A Conceptual Framework. Technical Report, Risø National Laboratory, Risø-M-2890, June.

Schmidt, K. & Bannon, L. (1992). Taking CSCW Seriously: Supporting Articulation Work. *Computer Supported Cooperative Work (CSCW): An International Journal, 1*, 7–40.

Sharrock, W. & Anderson, R. (1994). The User as a Scenic Feature of the Design Space (How the User Becomes A Factor in the Design Process). *Design Studies, 15*, 5–18.

Star, S. L. (1995a). The Politics of Formal Representations: Wizards, Gurus and Organizational Complexity. In S. L. Star (Ed.), *Ecologies of Knowledge: Work and Politics in Science and Technology*, pp. 88–118. Albany: SUNY Press.

Star, S. L. (Ed.) (1995b). *Ecologies of Knowledge: Work and Politics in Science and Technology*. Albany, NY: SUNY Press.

Star, S. L. (Ed.) (1995c). *The Cultures of Computing*. Oxford: Basil Blackwell.

Star, S. L. (1991). Power, technology and the phenomenology of conventions: on being allergic to onions. In J. Law (Ed.), *A Sociology of Monsters: Essays on Power, Technology and Domination*, pp. 26–56. London: Routledge.

Star, S. L. (1989). *Regions of the Mind: Brain Research and the Quest for Scientific Certainty*. Stanford, CA: Stanford University Press.

Star, S. L. & Ruhleder, K. (1994). Steps toward an Ecology of Infrastructure. In *Proceedings of CSCW 94*, pp. 253–264. New York: ACM Press.

Strauss, A. (1975) [1959]. *Mirrors and Masks: Notes on the Concept of Identity*. San Francisco: Sociology Press.

Strauss, A. (1995). *Continual Permutations of Action*. Hawthorne, NY: Aldine de Gruyter.

Suchman, L. A. (1987). *Plans and Situated Actions: The Problem of Human-Machine Communication*. Cambridge: Cambridge University Press.

Thomas, W. I. & Thomas, D. S. (1928). *The Child in America: Behavior Problems and Programs*. New York: Alfred A. Knopf.

Tolman, C. W. & Pickkola, B. (1989). John Dewey and dialectical materialism: Anticipations of activity theory in the critique of the reflex arc concept. *Activity Theory, 1*, 43–46.

Vygotsky, L. S. (1978). *Mind in Society: The Development of Higher Psychological Processes*. M. Cole, V. John-Steiner, S. Scribner, and E. Souberman (Eds.). Cambridge, MA: Harvard University Press.

Wenger, E. (1990). Toward a Theory of Cultural Transparency: Elements of a Social Discourse of the Visible and the Invisible. Ph.D. Dissertation, Department of Information and Computer Science, University of California, Irvine.

Wieckert, K. (1990). The Case of the Fickle Expert System, Paper presented to Conference on Computers and the Quality of Life.

# 14    On the ethnography of cooperative work

*Arne Raeithel*

Psychological research into cooperative work is still in its infancy as far as the emergence, usage, and extension of shared forms of thinking, special languages, and group-specific forms of action are concerned. What we have at present is a multitude of laboratory studies of small groups, and a growing number of field research reports like those in the other chapters of this book. Nearly all ethnographic studies that I am aware of have been done in the United States, Great Britain, or Scandinavia. I will not attempt a complete review of those studies here. Rather I shall aim first at explaining why this recent research looks new and exciting for many German readers, concentrating on the reasons for and the results of using qualitative methods, which is still quite unusual in German industrial psychology (but see Haug et al., 1987; Senghaas-Knobloch & Volmerg, 1990). Then I will go on to present a sketch of the concept of "semiotic self-regulation of groups." After analyzing two paradigm cases for ethnographic work research, I offer some closing remarks about historical and possible future links between developmental work research (see Engeström, 1987, and chapters by Engeström and Norros, this volume) and the traditions variously called "naturalistic research," "symbolic interactionism," or "cognitive ethnography" (see Hammersley, 1989 for a short history).

## A first view of the ethnographic approach

My first theme is to examine the applications of methods widely used in ethnology and cultural anthropology in *psychological* studies of the social regulation of work practices. My aim is to demonstrate that this affords a sounder methodological grounding for domain-specific theories of the cognition and communication patterns in the joint activity of working teams. I want to advocate the more widespread use of ethnographic methods to investigate group workplaces and the reproduction of social coherence of the persons working there.

Cultural anthropology assumes that different peoples and cultural communities each have their own system of world-explanation, which are taken as the basis for their practices (Sahlins, 1976). Any firmly established theory of the social world in the heads of the researchers would prove a hindrance to understanding participants' or members' views and positions. This is particularly pertinent to the psychologist's standard repertoire of methods, in which it is customary to define and measure variables without having to show that these represent the essential elements of some, let alone *alien,* culture (cf. Oesterreich & Volpert, 1983; Holzkamp, 1991). Ethnographers, on the other hand, try as far as possible to put aside their own familiar perspectives in order to gain an awareness of that which is alien to them.

This calls for "qualitative methods" (Lofland & Lofland, 1984; Strauss, 1987). In a rapid, cyclical succession of assumption-driven observations – including conversations and interviews – and detailed analysis of documents and dialogue transcripts found or generated during this process, the attempt is made to recast the salient and action-governing distinctions of the alien life-world in the researcher's own language and to describe the corresponding practices in such precise terms that they can be reconstructed from those distinctions.

Another feature of the qualitative, ethnographic, or "naturalistic" (cf. Hammersley, 1989, Chapter 7) research strategy is the systematic endeavour to seek out in the field individual cases that vary as widely as possible in order to be able to cover all typical perspectives of the actors ("theoretical sampling," Glaser & Strauss, 1967). There is no room for the random-sample method here. For what appears to the experimental methodologist as an interference factor – as "unwanted noise" – that must be identified as such, is, in the qualitative method, the central signal: contextual distinctions that explain the "situated action" of the actors and are congruent with or at least linked to the terms and categories deployed by the group members (Suchman, 1987). I shall come back to this point later on.

Finally, the ethnographic reports usually show a distinct style of presentation: commentaries on the structure and function of cultural elements alternate with lengthy, typographically contrasted excerpts taken from the documents or transcripts. The references are selected for their *exemplary and prototypal nature* and are intended to give a "thick description" (Geertz, 1973, a term borrowed from Gilbert Ryle) of life in the field by treating it as a sort of text and translating it into the language of the ethnographer. This can be done using the observer's understanding only, or indeed as an examination and appropriation of the formulations of work practices adopted and used by participants in the organization and change of their cooperative work practices (see Heath & Luff; Middleton; Suchman, all this volume).

The application of ethnographic methods to work research, then, begins by our viewing each work group or organization as a culturally alien community whose world-model and practices we must reconstruct from the utterances and situated actions of the working persons.

## The concept of semiotic self-regulation of groups

Now that we have named a suitable method, I must say more clearly what the principal object domain of ethnographic work research should consist of. To do this, I shall take a short historical digression. Much of my argument draws upon insights derived by Marxist social philosophers and psychologists. The chapter is not, however, intended to be a contribution to the Marxist analysis of communication (see Habermas, 1984; Krüger, 1990). I attempt instead a sort of politicophilosophical backtracking to one of several common roots of current theories of communication and cooperation. An apt metaphor might be: the "node in the web of discourses" in which many earlier threads converged and from which they fanned out again. This nodal phase in historical thinking was German Idealism – a peculiar mixture of rational enlightenment, romantic subjectivism, idolization of nature, criticism of religion, and economic analysis of the emerging industrial societies, which names like Kant, Goethe, Fichte, Schelling, Humboldt, Hegel, Feuerbach, and Marx might help to evoke.

At the dawn of the 19th century, many western thinkers and writers saw their work as contributing to the development of the universality of the human mind. Hegel thought that humankind would eventually develop to live inside one vast and all-encompassing consciousness. The grandiose and – by today's standards – fantastic and weird idea of a world-spirit (*Weltgeist*) speaking to us through the writings of these authors is still present today, as many early science fiction novels about telepathic world communication, and also the postmodern epics à la William Gibson's "Cyber-space" trilogy, clearly show.

But the idea of "social mind" or "social spirit" has also been secularized and refined into humanistic and scientific traditions, mostly taking a linguistic or semiotic turn in explaining the reality and apparent power of socially and societally distributed ideas. Three very famous examples are symbolic interactionism (Blumer, 1969), the theory of the social construction of reality (Berger & Luckmann, 1963) and interpreter-centred semiotics (Eco, 1990). There is a wealth of studies from cultural anthropology, sociology, and other humanities that show how national, regional, municipal, or small-group communities do indeed produce common ideas and ways of grasping their life-world. However, this line of enquiry has not yet gained a comparable strength in psychology (but see Cole, 1978, 1990; Lang & Fuhrer, 1993).

Today, there could be general agreement among psychologists, cognitive scientists, semioticians, and most cultural researchers that human beings are able to create for themselves *new possibilities of action* by operating on semiotic representations – including dramatic media and daydreams, language, and writing as well as all types of formal sign systems, using the *forms* (syntax) of their actions and the (content-related) *similarities* between old and new possibilities. The main disagreement seems to be whether those signs are to be interpreted as absolutely internal to the epistemic subject – as, e.g., the "physical symbol systems hypothesis" of Newell and Simon states very clearly (Newell, 1980) – or whether such a computer-oriented constriction of the category of the mental should not be accepted, because signs are judged inherently social and much more "between" persons than "somehow inside them." Early in this century Bartlett (1932) argued along similar lines. Two decades ago this was still a minority position (see Hinkle, 1970; Leman, 1970; Shotter, 1970). Recently Lang (1991) has presented a fresh formulation, starting from ecological psychology.

If we analyze the signs and signals produced and used by cooperating persons – their semiotic means – as environmental, physical, replicated presentations of their common social mind and practices, we find a starting point for understanding how the regularities and functional patterns of action may become the objects of a special mode of work that is anticipatory and rule-related in nature. What is meant here is the planning and control of production, the search for the causes of miscarried intentions, the communicative reaching of agreement on realizable possibilities, and the disputation and resolution of arguments. It follows then that the "historical self-transformation of human activity" – Karl Marx coined this phrase in his "Theses on Feuerbach" (1844) – demands communicative reflection of the signs of the actions of a "Generalized Order" (adopting Mead terminology) if it is to be realized with awareness, presight, and consciousness.

Marx himself and the orthodox Marxists never expanded much on this *symbolic construction of possibilities.* The insight that language and other systems of signals or symbols function in exactly the same way as all other means of activity has been explored, in the materialist tradition, in particular by Lev Semyonovich Vygotsky (1978). His analysis comes to much the same conclusions as the semiotic philosophy of Charles Sanders Peirce (1931; Houser & Kloesel, 1992). The substantial equivalence of their results can be explained in terms of their realistic interpretation of the objectivity of ideas: As signs, general concepts and possibilities have a real, physical existence in the presence of the actor (Peirce), and also a definite (range of) interpretation(s). And because of this, those signs may be practically used to control one's own action: they are, from a practical point of view, the tools of the actor's will (Vygotsky).[1]

The main rule used by Vygotsky to express the difference between productive and communicative means runs as follows: Tools and machines have "external effects" while language and other sign systems are directed "internally." This topographic metaphor provides us with a common exterior for individuals and groups – their physical environment. The partners in a cooperative activity are not seen as part of the respective environment of each "individual," but rather as coactors in a common interior space. What I mean here might become clearer by employing an analogy: A family's dwelling is the common interior space. The part of town in which the family lives constitutes its common exterior space. This applies to every member of the family, although there are other – mutually nested and intersecting – more intimate "interior zones" inside the dwelling and also "inside their heads." Other formulations of the topologies of "external" and "internal" action spaces exist (see, e.g., Csikszentmihalyi & Rochberg-Halton, 1981; Busse & Lampe, 1987; Lang, 1993), but I cannot review them here for lack of space.

We can distinguish two forms of "internal" effects and at the same time subsume them under the notion of *semiotic self-regulation* (of an individual or group): speech and other semiotic action has effects "inside the head," thus changing thinking, perception, and regulation of action. But speech also has effects "inside social groups," thus changing shared ways of thinking, traditionally accepted world views, and the culturally patterned actions themselves. Captured in a simple phrase, the dual interpretation reads: "The regulative effort may be directed at myself or at ourselves."

Thus, the problem of "semiotic self-regulation" is concerned with the way in which the actors coordinate their activities in cooperative work by the exchange or shared use of signs in the broadest sense. My second theme then is: cooperative work is constituted by communicative transactions, and these may be functionally analyzed as a complex process of semiotic self-regulation.

It now, of course, becomes necessary to transfer the insights arrived at by semiotics and other cultural sciences to psychology, but the new prospects offered by a psychological investigation of cooperation are no doubt worth the effort entailed, as I intend to show in the following sections. I should now like to use two examples to, first of all, illustrate the ethnographic strategy and, at the same time, to gradually highlight the sort of insights that can be derived by applying it to the problem of understanding semiotic self-regulation.

## A physicist tries to make a working copy of a TEA laser

> Knowledge is like a [bottle-] ship because once it is in the bottle of truth it looks as though it must always have been there and it looks as though it could never get out again. (Collins, 1985, p. vii)

The field worker in the first example is a sociologist of science who sees himself as a cultural scientist. His field is in the enemy camp of the "two cultures" – he is observing a laser specialist at work in a scientific laboratory (Collins, 1985, Chapter 3). This physicist is engaged in the attempt to technically reproduce a newly developed variant of the laser and is encountering great difficulties. What Collins observes is someone pottering about with the apparatus, trying to puzzle out what is wrong – a far cry from the textbook ideal of the scientific experiment conducted along the lines of an underlying theory. When questioned, the physicist is forced to admit that his understanding of laser technology only extends to the various separate components – the electrodes, the capacitors, the gas-filled chamber – taken on their own. But this particular new configuration keeps him guessing the whole time, producing as it does unwanted flashes between just about all the various parts of the apparatus instead of the desired laser pulses. For nearly six whole months, he does not even succeed in getting the gas molecules in the chamber to radiate – a prerequisite for producing the coherent light of the laser pulse.

During this period, the physicist questions almost every aspect of his knowledge and explains to the sociologist the – so far undecidable – alternative approaches. Being aware that experience and intuition are essential if an engineer is to master the application of high-voltage technology in conjunction with ultrashort pulses, he revisits the laboratory in which the TEA laser was first developed. There he discovers that he has previously overlooked a number of details concerning the way the apparatus is set up, and he returns with some new ideas about the possible reasons for its failure to function. He follows these up, modifying his own apparatus to make it resemble the other laser more closely, but the desired radiation still refuses to materialize. When, by now pretty much at the end of his tether, he mentions on the phone to the specialist in the other laboratory some spark traces he has noticed in the anode, the other man suspects that the polarity of anode and cathode may have been reversed. The physicist thinks this highly unlikely, but he agrees to check on it all the same and discovers that the specialist's hunch was correct. Once the polarity has been reversed, the long awaited glow discharge finally occurs, and soon afterwards the laser pulse is produced as well. The physicist feels rather a fool and immediately forgets the doubts he had begun to entertain about his knowledge of physics, which, in the end, turned out to be sound, as shown by the effect.

But, for the field worker Collins, natural scientific practice was sufficiently unfamiliar to lead him to consider the interim period of doubt to be more important than the textbook ideal reattained in the end. He concludes that a physicist's practical experience is evidently a question of separating the important differences between two sets of apparatus from the unimportant ones, a skill that finds no mention in the literature and cannot be learned from it, but one which is, instead, reproduced invisibly in social intercourse between specialists.

Five years later, Collins has the opportunity to watch the same physicist trying to get a duplicate of his own laser apparatus – which has, in the meantime, functioned perfectly – to work. Again, the familiar difficulties are encountered. The occurrence of high-voltage flashovers instead of the desired glow discharge indicates that something is wrong. The physicist again questions his knowledge, but not at the same points as last time. The fact that there is once again evidence of spark traces in the anode is, this time, not taken by him to be an indication of incorrect polarity, and he carries out a quick measurement to convince the sociologist.

During the two days available to Collins for this observations, it does not prove possible to find the cause of the laser's failure to work. Early the following week, however, the physicist is, after working on the apparatus for an hour, able to inform the sociologist that the laser is working. This time it was the gas pumps that were not working as they should have done in theory. Again, the physicist feels that he has made a silly mistake, whereas the sociologist takes the doubting phase as evidence of the learning process in which the specialist's professional know-how, his "tacit knowledge" (Polanyi, 1967) emerges:

> One might say that learning tacit knowledge, or acquiring culture, is a matter of learning this indefinitely long list of what is insignificant and, inter alia, learning what is significant. It entails learning that what might seem to the unskilled, or the uncultured, as going on in a different way is in fact going on in the same way and that what might seem to the uncultured as going on in the same way is in fact going on in a different way. (Collins, 1985, p. 71)

The ability to swiftly and effortlessly identify the essential features of a situation and, at the same time, to overlook irrelevant differences appears to be a special and astounding achievement only to those who are unfamiliar with a particular field; for those native to the field, it is something quite normal and taken for granted. In contrast, the phases of instability of their previously acquired knowledge – in which the typical result refuses to appear, and thus the "effectual signs" (Uexküll, 1957) of successful action are missing – are something they don't care to be reminded of and which they view as untypical exceptions.

## Action explanations and the dilemma of the ethnographer

The typical and total dissipation of doubt with the final attainment of the solution to the problem shows that even the practices of natural scientists are based on an implicitly accepted, normally unquestioned connection between subjectively perceived signs and the intended effects. Other ethnographic studies on scientific practice have come to much the same results (see Latour, 1987).

If the observers in the field are – as in this case – not native to it, they are unable to judge the soundness of the explicit and verbalized theories and explanations from their own experience. If they take a critical view of the field in question, they will even tend to impute to the natives mythological thinking and the "fabrication of knowledge" (Knorr-Cetina, 1990) in a derogatory sense. In the case of the natural sciences, this calls for a certain degree of courage. However,

Table 1.    Complementary perspectives of actor and observer

| Course of action of an actor | Perceived features of the situation | Actual approach adopted |
| --- | --- | --- |
| From the actor's perspective | Familiar, self-evident | Not conscious, without reflection |
| From the observer's perspective | Unfamiliar, merely assumed | At variance with actor's explanation |

when investigating so-called primitive cultures or even ordinary industrial work-places, the field workers frequently have difficulty in not dismissing as superstitions or practical myths the discrepancies that strike them between explanations and practices. Table 1 shows the complementary strengths (bold outlines) and weaknesses of the actor's and the observer's perspective.

The dilemma of the qualitative method (Hammersley, 1989) is that the ethnographer wishes to record the subjective perspective, but it is precisely this that prevents him from approximating to his ideal of clarifying objective relations. This is because he is forced to recognize that the actor's perspective, while offering useful practical results, fails, in his judgment, to provide an adequate explanation of them. It is obvious that actor and observer both have their own privileged access to different aspects of the course of action but also their complementary blindness: the observer is unable to see the situation as the actor does, and the actor, for his part, remains unaware of certain important aspects of his own action. The gap that becomes evident here can, it is true, be bridged to some extent by a dialogue between "aliens" and "natives," but the ethnographer is left with the gnawing doubt that he may have been taken in by bogus explanations.

Such dialogues about the "correct" explanation of an approach to a particular task may, of course, also take place between the natives in the field itself. This is the case in the next example. It is a step more complex than observing a single actor, and concerns the possibility and necessity of a global explanation for practices in general.

## A navigation team logs the ship's position during an emergency situation at sea

> Knowledge may reside in the mind, but minds reside in communities of minds, and the fate of knowledge in a mind is in part shaped by interaction with other minds in the community. (Hutchins, 1988, p. 40)

The field that the ethnologist and cognitive scientist Edwin Hutchins has chosen for his observations differs in more than one respect from the previous example of scientific research: it is concerned with the work of navigators on a U.S. Navy vessel – work characterized by the constant repetition of routine actions in accordance with a strict set of regulations. At intervals, which may be long or short depending on their proximity to the coast, the team must determine, chart, and log the ship's current position. This work is event-driven and strictly time-governed, especially in difficult navigational situations (fog, shallows, etc.). The correctness of the result is absolutely vital for the ship and, therefore, the prescribed procedure allows the degree of error to be read from the result itself: since three bearings are used to determine the position, the charted result invariably takes the form of a triangle, the area of which is proportional to the degree of uncertainty with respect to the position. Of course, the ultimate test for freedom from error is always the successful physical movement of the ship without its sustaining any damage. The work of the ship's navigators is, however, of a purely semiotic nature, supporting at an absolutely vital point the self-regulation of the community formed for the duration of the ship's voyage.

In this case, the ethnologist is himself an expert on the theories and methods of navigation (see also Hutchins & Hinton, 1984). He observes over a period of days the smooth routine teamwork, which is only occasionally marred by beginners' errors on the part of some of the younger team members. But he is then lucky enough to witness an exceptional situation: there is a sudden total failure in the main turbines; for a lengthy period no electricity is available for making headway or stopping, and even the large rudder can at first only be moved by hand. The ship is currently travelling at a speed of 10 knots in a narrow channel and is already within sight of port. A number of sailing boats are cruising in front of the ship – a situation in which an accident might be expected at any moment. In cases such as this, the only thing to do is to keep the ship more or less on course until it has lost enough speed to enable the anchor to be dropped.

The captain hands over the helm to the navigator, instructing him to make for the nearest anchorage. The navigation team must work with great precision now, for, if the ship were to be involved in an accident or lost altogether, the ship's log would become a crucial piece of evidence in the subsequent inquiry before a naval tribunal. But their job is suddenly made a great deal more difficult by a further instance of damage ensuring from the loss of power, an eventuality for which no provision is made in the U.S. Navy's big book of regulations: the gyrocompass no longer works because the emergency power generator has failed to start, and the reserve compass is currently on shore being repaired. And so the team now has to work with the magnetic compass, and this means that, in order to determine the ship's real course or that of a bearing-line, the local magnetic declination must be taken into account as well as the specific deflections caused by the magnetic fields and the steel mass of the ship. Such deviations vary for each point of the compass; they are determined at intervals empirically and entered in a table attached to the compass.

None of the team is properly prepared for this. Even the experienced navigator can only vaguely recall the relevant formulas and, to begin with, he completely forgets about the deviation table. Doing the necessary calculations mentally proves no easy matter, and even the "new-fangled" pocket calculator needs to be operated properly. The ship's position is subsequently taken 30 times, and in the course of this, by a joint team effort involving numerous errors and corrections, a new cooperative pattern of action gradually emerges.

In the above-cited study, Hutchins confines himself to analyzing the microstructure of the interactions involved in calculating and charting the ship's position. From the transcript of the videotapes, he is able to demonstrate precisely that, while no individual member of the team is totally in the picture or totally in control of what is going on, each actor gradually acquires an increasing degree of control and self-assurance in his own local field of action. The cognitive scientist shows us here a perfect example of *socially distributed cognition* within a group:

> In this system, how an actor organized knowledge to deal with a task may depend not only upon what he "knows," but upon his location within the task-performing group. The organization of knowledge then affects the social organization for the task, which in turn influences the properties of locations of individual actors within the system. Thus, rather than thinking of it as a linear machine, the system of socially distributed cognition is better thought of as a set of mutually interdependent processes that mutually constrain each other. The solution arrived at represents a minimization of computational stress at the system level rather than individual level. (Hutchins, 1988, p. 21)

The individual subtasks performed by such a team are not, then, originally, linear steps; they are rather generated and transformed in the course of continuous task accomplishment. Opportunities for action are seized by one actor, observed by another, and adopted with slight modifications. They gradually become recognizable parts, distributable individual tasks, whose solution is briefly discussed at critical junctures and which may even be given proper names. Specific intermediate products are selected to be made public, and are regularly announced or noted down. During the distributed application of all these new means, the actors gradually come to form a well-functioning team. An observer arriving after this process of self-organization had been completed would probably see only another piece of routine work, unless the typically buoyant mood that characterizes any successful new pattern of action were to give some indication to the contrary.

### Self-organization of socially distributed patterns of action

All ethnographic studies of teamwork show that the internal semiotic coordination between the team members is strongly reliant on situative factors and defies formulation in terms of explicit rules. Suchman (1987) derived from this insight a theory of "situated action." If we refer to the chapters of this volume (Engeström, Goodwin & Goodwin, Heath & Luff, Hutchins, Suchman), we may piece together the following general picture of semiotic self-regulation in professional teams (navigators, air crews, dispatchers, etc.) who are working together in a common transactional space. It is meaningfully structured for the members, and may occasionally be extended via mediating links like intercom or radio to include actors at other physical locations.

The semiotic objects distributed throughout the work room (memoranda, charts, blackboards, monitor screens, etc.) are used by the actors in a wide variety of ways. Many people have a special tone of voice or intonation for important messages that is familiar to the others and an indispensable element here. Each team develops its own customs, special names, and vocal or dramatic signals for the most important types of problems in its own specific field of work. For most messages concerning the status of task accomplishment, there are several independent "channels," because the actors also listen in for others in order to be able to help out if needed. A global view of the work is verbalized only in extremely rare cases; but the actors are always *locally aware* of the important events and the necessary operations in their field of action.

The positive phrasing of this last fact: "Local awareness is sufficient" (Hutchins) is of considerable significance in terms of methodology, too. Let us recall the dilemma of the qualitative method from the previous section. What we diagnosed there were the complementary strengths and weaknesses of the actor's and the observer's perspective and the lack of criteria for judging the soundness of the actor's explanations of the way he or she acts.

In a team, the actors generally take turns in being native observers of the other actors, too. They are equipped with jointly produced explanations for the correct procedure that only need to be locally and interactionally "sound" – a scientific enquiry or engineering analysis might still find fault with them. In most cases, members know the work tasks of the others from their own experience as well, having lived through a typical developmental path from "apprentice" to "master," from peripheral to central subtasks (Lave & Wagner, 1989). By constant exchange and trial application of their local insights and operative improvements by means of dialogue, they arrive at a global and cooperative work style which, to some extent, is represented semiotically in group-specific "shared knowledge."

This active, self-organized coordination of the locally optimized operations by experienced actors is something which cannot be set down once and for all times in writing a book of rules. But it is pragmatically justified by the cooperating group's constant success in self-organization, which may ultimately be known in terms of the attainment of the desired result.[2]

The consensus about what it is that is desired, and how well the group has succeeded in producing it, may very well undergo drastic change during this development. However, at any one time, there is some set of action results or consequences that the actors jointly expect from their different angles of attack at the common production problem. And this set is only partly "mental," in the sense of consciously, but also nonperceptually and privately held signs of the future.[3] The set of consequences is also public and perceptual as the shared possibility structure of the work environment, which includes possibilities to grasp and realize physical things (Gibson's "affordances"), and interactive possibilities for engagement in public and private thought: reasoning, evaluation, or planning.

The clearest and most productive formulation of a method to understand the socially distributed possibility spaces emerging from this process, is still, in my view, Peirce's pragmatic maxim, published in 1878:

> Consider what effects, that might conceivably have practical bearings, we conceive the object of our conception to have. Then, our conception of these effects is the whole of our conception of the object. (Peirce 1968, p. 62; CP, 5, 402; Houser & Kloesel, 1992, p. 132)

The view that the group's common knowledge about their world of work includes the logical and the operational, the possible and the actual, consequences, too – even as the most important part of its meaning – is still very little understood outside the traditions of American pragmatism (see Leigh Star, this volume). There is, however, no other way for the result to appear than as a more or less familiar configuration in the "perceptual world" of the individual actors, and this means that the result is essentially a semiotic structure for the working group. This includes the symbolic products of the measuring and protocol devices [a perceptual class of "artifacts"[3] (Wartofsky, 1979), or "actants" (Latour, 1987)]. In this way, the result can be "written down" well before it is reattained – in gestural and mimetic sketches,[4] in discursive goal formulations, or in precise diagrammatic "blueprints," as the "objectives" of the whole enterprise.

Objective knowledge as a Platonic or even Cartesian ideal may very well be unattainable, as both postmodernists (Lemke, 1992) and radical constructivists (von Glasersfeld, 1987) keep reminding the scientific community these days, but *knowledge of objectives,* in the sense of working with and on a *symbolic presentation of the possible and the actual consequences of our conceptions,* is surely badly needed, and it can be gained, while reflecting on daily practice as well as in careful scientific research. As Peirce stressed many times, the skeptical attitude is highly needed and valuable in cases of real, actual doubt. But as a generalized outlook and metaphysical grounding of our practice, the antiobjectivism seems to be more of a sign of chaotic times, of social illness, and of the need for full-scale societal change than it could be a base on which such changes will actually be worked out.

Table 2, which aims to capture some essential elements necessary for distributed-action patterns to emerge and sustain themselves, follows from Table 1 by introducing an additional, third row in which the opposition of actor and observer is held in balance and argumentation during a dialogical exchange among the members of the community of practice who are, as we have seen, normally taking turns at being observers and actors.

What have been the blind regions of the actor and the observer (cells 2 and 4) may, as a result of recentering dialogue, be filled out in the course of time. The easier problem is for the observer to remember her or his own perceptual world when being busy at the task (1), and compare this with what he or she now sees from a horizontal distance in a detached perception of familiar or new distinctions (2). By noting differences between the sequence of operations, as remem-

Table 2.    Recentering as mediating moment of socially distributed action

| Socially distributed action pattern | Perceptual world: declarative, situated knowledge | Effectual world: operational knowledge, know-how |
| --- | --- | --- |
| Seen from the centered perspective of the actors | (1) Natural, intuitive grasping of the situation and task | (4) Knowing-how refined by observing oneself and others |
| Seen from the decentered perspective of the observers | (2) Detached perception of familiar or new distinctions | (3) "Writing down"/recalling sequences of operations and their results |
| Recentering perspective gained in dialogue | Contentious perception of institutionalized distinctions | Modifying or corroborating the traditional/usual approaches |

bered and seen anew at the same time, with the sequence that the observed actor deploys, the observer is able to "write them down" in some kind of memory (3), and then use this record for her- or himself when again being the actor of the same task (4). The record of things done serves as a target figure to aim for during the actor's own next try at working out one good way of doing it (not necessarily the "one best way," although this might be found, too).

Thus, the "effectual world" (Uexküll, 1957) of how the consequences are being physically brought about – which, as we have seen, is in itself partly unaccessible for the single actor – may be brought into the perceptual world as a written record in the big book of rules that helps to refine one's knowing of how to do it right first time, swiftly and intuitively, like a "real expert," "master," or "guru" (see Dreyfus & Dreyfus, 1986 and the expert research following this seminal book).

### Exchange, power structures, and shared knowledge

It is important to note that the incompatibility of the views of actor and observer is not overcome for good by recentering. This is no Hegelian synthesis from which another step of development to ever higher planes of the Spirit could start. On the contrary, the *complementarity* of centered and decentered stances means that the gulf between them cannot ever be bridged except for moments or phases. The discontinuous happening of new and nonanticipated events is the rule, and not the exception (see Wehner, 1992). Therefore, the third possible stance with regard to a socially distributed action pattern emerges in opposition to both the centered and the decentered one, and only for the phases and moments of true dialogue and cooperation (see Engeström, 1992 for a more penetrating analysis of three levels of collaboration). A decade ago, I have called this stance "recentering practice" (Raeithel, 1983), and am now striving to make clear how researchers may find this pattern, as the rare event that it must be, in empirical studies of collaborative work.

The main hindrance that has to be removed to get a clear sight is the illusion that cell (4) of table 2 – the personal knowledge about the way oneself is realizing one's aims – could ever become completely expressed. Until this point I have refrained from even mentioning the physical means used by the actors: Besides their own embodied skills there are trusted media, well-known instruments and tools, all kinds of machines, computer tools, and automata (see Budde & Züllighoven, 1992 for the latter distinction). All of these "operational means" are employed by the actors to make appear the consequences they are anticipating (Raeithel, 1992), without necessarily knowing how the result of their work is produced by these artifacts. All they must know are the effectual signs of successful operation with the artifacts, in terms of their own goals and rules.

It is always the central task of other groups, and not the one in the focus of research, to design, evaluate and rework most of the operational means used by the actors in the focal group. Thus, a more complete picture of socially distributed knowledge must also include the exchange relations between different communities of work (Engeström, 1987), because the know-how is not only distributed within any one group, it is spread out between groups, too.

As soon as we take the organizational and societal relations between communities of practice into account, we cannot but also see the economic and political distinctions within any one working group or community. The picture painted of teamwork at the beginning of the last section has also left out intentionally the relations of power, command, and authority, which make it normal for most actors to subject themselves to powerfully upheld demands, and for others to keep those signs publicly "readable" throughout the working time, be it just by marching around in the workspace, mimetically producing a reminder of their control over all the results, or by using a wealth of other semiotic means discovered in industrial sociology, or in recent studies of talk in school classes and clinical groups (see, e.g., Lemke, 1990; Drew & Heritage, 1993).

Thus, the layout and text of Table 2 is quite romantic, in a sense. In the majority of existing working groups the three different possible stances, which each member could take or leave in principle, are quite rigidly distributed between subgroups of different authority rank. There is a split, more or less deep, depending on tradition and "management philosophy," between workers doing the task, observer–controllers who look over states and results of the process, and those whose legitimate job is to lead and steer the dialogue of recentering practice, if it occurs publicly at all, and not completely outside the focal community of practice.

The hallmark of "hierarchy," i.e., literally, the "holy rule" of ancient times, is that the result of recentering is imported into the working groups from above and outside. Of course, this important event must be staged as a social drama, be put into discursive rationale, and also be visible in new blueprints, to be known henceforth as the new order to follow.

There is much talk presently of "the second revolution" of automated automobile production (Womack, Jones, & Roos, 1991). In Marxist terms, it seems to be "just again" a generalized production crisis. However, Margit Osterloh has recently shown that the movement towards "lean production" and "virtual corporations" is a deeply contradictory strategy. Many more flexible and self-organizing units are needed, but at the same time they must also be more accountable ones, in order to be pitted against each other as competing profit centers in some phases, then again being forced into close coordination, even full-blown cooperation, to ensure overall product quality (Osterloh, 1993).

It may, therefore, be more realistic to present the stratified self-organization of relatively autonomous working groups (communities of practice) as in Table 3. The additional column added in comparison with Table 2 is intended to capture the need for and endurance of a stance-specific mediation between perceptual and effectual world: Experience, generalized rules, and sense-making endeavors are both preconditions and products of the dialectic going on between situational anticipations and the actual courses taken for the production of results. I should perhaps add that this table is to be understood more as a conceptual tool for future research than a summary of already ascertained facts about working life.

In closing this section, a philosophical remark: The shared or common knowledge encompasses neither just what is formally possible nor simply what has "really" happened. Rather it contains points of contact to future possibilities in the strong sense – something that is not there but may be worked out by collective strain of body and mind. Please note that this sense of "possible" is totally different from what it used to mean in the Newtonian worldview. In this classically

Table 3.   The tripartite structure of shared knowledge in a community of practice

| Socially distributed action pattern | Perceptual world: declarative, situated knowledge | Effectual world: operational means and know-how | Shared knowledge: episodic, normative, contested or consensual |
|---|---|---|---|
| Realized from the centered stance of workers | Natural, intuitive grasping and defined measures of situation and task | Trusted and well-known skills, media, instruments, tools, machines, etc. | Experience: global/ local orientation and prototypal episodes |
| Prescribed from the decentered stance of observer-controllers | Detached analysis of familiar or new distinctions and data | "Writing down"/checking sequences of operations and their results | General rules: (situation operation) as symbolic objectives |
| Recentering stance of legitimate self-regulators of a group | Contentious/ consensual dispute of the central distinctions (of effects) | Modifying or corroborating the traditional/usual rules and approaches | Sense-making: disputing metaphors or using them as guides |

modern scheme, the possible is some point or linear stretch along a mechanically determined trajectory that is "really" far off in time, yet already present as the assured destiny of the system laid down by its "eternal natural laws." In the pragmatic and semiotic perspectives, however, the possibilities are just within reach of the actors. They are signs lying around, reverberating in the air, or being staged just at this moment of time inside the community. They may be taken up at will, and then taken further as pointers to attainable consequences, either in a logically disciplined theory, or in chaotic daily practice, or in the precarious coordination of both.

## Epilogue

What all this means in terms of the ethnographic research strategy is that the criterion for the correctness of explanations is determined, and constantly redetermined, in the field itself. If the actors have great confidence in a particular explanation, then it is based on socially distributed shared knowledge and the special know-how of the individuals concerned. Such explanations are *connectable to future actions in the field* ("anschlußfähig im Feld," Luhmann, see, e.g., 1986). They "quite naturally" indicate to the natives what is to be done next, what risks are to be expected, and so on. Thus, the ethnographer has no need for independent criteria, but can – and here again the systematic variation of the sampling is crucial – observe different work groups engaged in the "same" task. From the differences between the "sociosyncratic" explanations of each team, we are able to derive indications as to their respective generalizability.

According to the topological model outlined earlier, the explanations circulating in a work group constitute the shared *semiotic interior space* of the coacting group, i.e., the autoregulative nuclear structure of their specific and differently significant world of work that is constantly being regenerated from the stable or changing array of semiotic objects. The ethnographic strategy aims at producing an optimal written record and vivid description of such action-relevant meaningful spaces, leaving the criticism and correction of the explanations specific to a particular work area either totally to the experts in the field or handing over its own results to a subsequent phase of theoretical or design-related analysis.

However, the detached ethnography of possibly bizarre and dysfunctional systems of meaning of single groups can hardly be the last word when dealing with the evaluation or redesign of important work areas. After all, the field workers always have an important role to play, too, as mediators between the various cooperating groups and the other institutional and societal contexts of the work under investigation, and they have to take their own stand here (for example, see the research of Gerson & Star, 1986 or Zuboff, 1988).

There is a general strategy for work research that takes the institutional relations between working teams, their managers, and the researchers into account. This is "developmental work research," as developed in Finland (Toikka, Engeström, & Norros, 1985; see also chapters by Engeström and Norros, this volume). In this tradition, one principal instrument of organizing the multitude of research questions and results obtained is a generic triangular diagram (see Figs. 5 and 6 in Engeström's chapter). This semiotic tool was designed to capture Vygotsky's insight of the essential similarity of tools and signs (at the apex of the triangle called "instruments"). Furthermore, by being a representation of a working community, the whole diagram orients towards the joint activity of the members, their different task prescriptions, and the agreed-on (or presently contested) rules of "working in the right way," represented at the base of the triangle. Several such diagrams may be combined by asking where the work results go to in the exchange between groups, or what other groups' results are needed at the six nodes around the diagram (e.g., some group produces the instruments used by the focal group; the managerial group installs a certain division of labor).

What is important in the context of the ethnographic approach, however, is not the detailed makeup of these diagrams. Rather I want to point to the mediating power and regulative function of this kind of semiotic means, both in the sense of mediating between the researchers and the natives, i.e., the members of the focal group, and in the sense of regulating the transition between a present problematic and a future solution, instantiated in the emerging and stabilizing pattern of collaborative work after an expansion of the respective activity system. This developmental process as a whole might be steerable by the heuristic rules contained in the "cycle of expansion" (Engeström, 1987, Chapter 5), as further research will show.

The spatial metaphor of the semiotic interior of a group now can be shown to be helpful even for the transactions between research groups, field groups, and the teams of managers, in the following way: Every semiotic exchange between actors may be seen as happening on a stage internal to this differentiated and fluid community-in-the-making-or-breaking, which has several distinct regions and also private spaces. Everywhere, real symbolic tokens are accumulating like any other type of physical object would, as parts of the results of the actions being realized with them. Understanding a message (a complex dramatic, discursive, or object symbol) means to work with these signs in a similar way to the one that the publisher of the message anticipated. Personal and social sense is made – as we may read Peirce's semiotic philosophy – deploying a certain habit grown out of experience, reconstructing or inventing a certain argument and set of rules, or, most importantly, conceiving of a sensible future state of general affairs as if it was already present, thus making real and presently effective as a sign what remains possible and not yet fully attained.

One major task of a broadly conceived psychology of work thus seems to be to

develop basic types of semiotic means that prove useful in the productive practice of collaboration. The ethnographic approach then turns out as a gathering of
such instruments for self-regulation from the various fields, in order to generalize them by discovering their experiential base, their precise functions, and their
sense-making qualities.

## Acknowledgments

The chapter is the expanded English version of an earlier text (Raeithel, 1991)
written for a German audience. Phil Bacon has done a marvelous job in producing an English translation I could work with. Rewriting was easy using commentary by David Middleton, Edwin Hutchins, Michael Cole, and many others who
took part in the exchange over the electronic discussion group XACT, based at
UCSD's Laboratory of Comparative Human Cognition. And last, but not least,
the discussion in my Hamburg seminar on the Ethnographic Approach to Cooperative Work (Winter Semester 1991/1992) was very helpful in getting a clearer
picture. Thanks go to Uschi Carus, Christoph Clases, Egon Endres, Horst
Oberquelle, Uli Piepenburg, Martin Resch, Hartmut Schulze, and Theo Wehner.
For the remaining lack of clarity I am alone responsible, of course.

## Notes

1  Vygotsky's cultural psychology is, through the different ways it is connected to Hegel and to
   semiotics or linguistics, also closely related to George Herbert Mead's "Social Behaviourism."
   Both share with the (later) Wittgenstein the central conviction that the meanings of signs can only
   be produced and reproduced in social intercourse, and that the foundational class of signs is phys-
   iognomic or gestural (see Hintikka & Hintikka, 1986; also Fig. 8.4-1 in Raeithel 1992 and note 4
   below).
2  Any useful result functions as the central system-building factor; Anochin (1978) based his general theory of functional systems, i.e., self-optimizing organs of the animal body, on this insight.
   Communities, however, are not functional systems at all (see Luhmann, 1986; Lemke, 1992), yet
   there is a strict analogy as regards the importance of results for the developmental course of the
   system.
3  Michael Cole (1992, p. 21f) has given a beautiful example taken from Macfarlane (1977), which
   shows how signs of the future and of the past work together to form linkages between the different historical strands and timespans: A mother sees her baby for the first time, and exclaims,
   noticing the pink diapers: "I shall be worried to death when she's eighteen!" A minor drawback
   of the example is that, except for the color of the baby's clothes, no "external," public sign is being taken up by the mother to link biological characteristics of the child to her own sociocultural
   past and the possible future of the baby.
4  Three categories of semiotic exchange between actors are being distinguished here: mimetic, discursive, and object-symbolic (see Donald, 1991 and Raeithel, 1994). The important move is the
   distinction between two radically different classes of so-called nonverbal exchange: mimetic
   communication on the one hand, hypothesized to be much older than full-blown discursive language, and "external memory devices" (Donald), i.e., public object-symbolic knowledge (derived from drawing, reckoning with clay tokens, writing, and so on), which is the late achievement.

## References

Anochin, P. K. (1978). *Beiträge zur allgemeinen Theorie des funktionellen Systems.* Jena: G. Fischer.

Bartlett, F. C. (1932). *Remembering.* A study in experimental and social psychology. Cambridge: Cambridge University Press.

Berger, P. L. & Luckmann, T. (1963). A treatise in the sociology of knowledge. *The Social Construction of Reality.* New York: Doubleday.

Blumer, H. (1969). *Symbolic Interactionism.* Perspective and method. Englewood Cliffs: Prentice-Hall.

Budde, R. & Züllighoven, H. (1992). Software tools in a programming workshop. In C. Floyd, H. Züllighoven, R. Budde, & R. Keil-Slawik (Eds.), *Software Development and Reality Construction,* pp. 252–268. Berlin: Springer.

Busse, S. & Lampe, R. (1987). Ein Strukturmodell zur individuellen Handlungsfähigkeit. *Person, Handlung, Umwelt.* Leipzig: Karl-Marx-Universität, Probleme und Ergebnisse psychologischer Forschung.

Csikszentmihalyi, M. & Rochberg-Halton, E. (1981). Domestic symbols and the self. *The Meaning of Things.* Cambridge: Cambridge University Press.

Cole, M. (1978). Ethnographic psychology – so far. In G. S. Spindler (Ed.), *The Making of Psychological Anthropology.* Berkeley: University of California Press.

Cole, M. (1990). Cultural psychology. A once and future discipline? In J. Berman (Ed.), *Nebraska Symposium on Motivation,* Vol. 37. Cross-Cultural Perspectives. Lincoln: University of Nebraska Press, pp. 279–335.

Cole, M. (1992). Context, Modularity, and the Cultural Constitution of Development. In L. T. Winegar & J. Valsiner (Eds.). Research and methodology. *Children's Development within Social Context,* pp. 5–31. Hillsdale, NJ: Erlbaum.

Collins, H. M. (1985). Replication and induction in scientific practice. *Changing Order.* London: Sage.

Donald, M. (1991). Three stages in the evolution of culture and cognition. *Origins of the Modern Mind.* Cambridge, MA: Harvard University Press.

Drew, P. & Heritage, J. (Eds.) (1992). Interaction in institutional settings. *Talk at Work.* Cambridge: Cambridge University Press.

Dreyfus, H. L. & Dreyfus, S. E. (1986). The power of human intuition and expertise in the era of the computer. *Mind over Machine.* New York: Free Press.

Eco, U. (1990). Die Mitarbeit der Interpretation in erzählenden Texten. *Lector in fabula.* München: dtv.

Engeström, Y. (1987). An activity-theoretical approach to developmental research. *Learning by Expanding.* Helsinki: Orienta-Konsultit.

Engeström, Y. (1992). Studies in distributed working intelligence. *Interactive Expertise.* Research Bulletin 83, Dept. of Education, University of Helsinki.

Geertz, C. (1973). Selected Essays. *The Interpretation of Cultures.* New York: Basic Books.

Gerson, E. M. & Star, S. L. (1986). Analyzing due process in the workplace. *ACM Transactions on Office Information Systems, 4,* 257–270.

Glaser, B. G. & Strauss, A. L. (1967). *The Discovery of Grounded Theory.* Chicago: Aldine.

Habermas, J. (1984). *The Theory of Communicative Action.* Vol. 2. London: Heinemann.

Haug, F. et al. (Projektgruppe Automation und Qualifikation (1987). *Widersprüche der Automationsarbeit.* Berlin: Argument-Verlag.

Hammersley, M. (1989). *The Dilemma of the Qualitative Method.* Herbert Blumer and the Chicago tradition. London: Routledge.

Hinkle, D. N. (1970). The game of personal constructs. In D. Bannister (Ed.), *Perspectives in Personal Construct Theory,* pp. 91–110. London: Academic Press.

Hintikka, M. B. & Hintikka, J. (1986). *Investigating Wittgenstein.* Oxford: Blackwell.

Holzkamp, K. (1991). Experience of self and scientific objectivity. In C. W. Tolman & W. Maiers

(Eds.), *Critical Psychology,* pp. 65–80. Contributions to an Historical Science of the Subject. Cambridge: Cambridge University Press.

Houser, N. & Kloesel, C. (1992). Selected philosophical writings. *The Essential Peirce.* Vol. 1 (1867–1893). Bloomington: Indiana University Press.

Hutchins, E. (1988). Organizing work by evolution and by design. Paper presented at the Conference on Work and Communication, University of California, San Diego, July 1988.

Hutchins, E. & Hinton, G. E. (1984). Why the islands move. *Perception, 13,* 629–632.

Knorr-Cetina, K. (1990). *Die Fabrikation von Erkenntnis.* Frankfurt: Suhrkamp.

Krüger, P. (1990). *Kritik der Kommunikativen Vernunft.* Kommunikationsorientierte Wissenschafts-for-schung im Streit mit Sohn-Rethel, Toulmin und Habermas. Berlin: Akademie Verlag.

Lang, A. (1991). On the knowledge in things and places. In M. von Cranach, W. Doise, & G. Mugny (Eds.), *Social Representations and the Social Basis of Knowledge.* Proceedings of the 1st Congress of the Swiss Society of Psychology, Bern September 1989. Bern: Huber, pp. 76–83.

Lang, A. & Fuhrer, U. (1993). What place for culture in psychology? – An introduction. *Schweizerische Zeitschrift für Psychologie, 52,* 65–69.

Latour, B. (1987). *Science in Action.* Cambridge: Harvard University Press.

Lave, J. & Wenger, E. (1989). Situated learning. Legitimate peripheral participation. Palo Alto: Institute for Research on Learning, Report No. IRL 89-0013.

Leman, G. (1970). Words and worlds. In D. Bannister (Ed.), *Perspectives in Personal Construct Theory,* pp. 133–156. London: Academic Press.

Lemke, J. (1990). Language, learning, and values. *Talking Science.* Norwood, NJ: Ablex.

Lemke, J. (1992). Discourse, dynamics, and social change. To appear in *Language as Cultural Dynamic*; special issue of *Cultural Dynamics,* M. A. K. Halliday, Issue Editor.

Lofland, J. & Lofland, L. H. (1984). A guide to qualitative observation and analysis. *Analyzing Social Settings.* Belmont: Wadsworth.

Luhmann, N. (1986). The autopoiesis of social systems. In F. Geyer & J. van der Zouwen (Eds.), *Sociocybernetic Paradoxes,* pp. 172–192. Observation, control and evolution of self-steering systems. London: Sage.

Newell, A. (1980). Physical Symbol Systems. *Cognitive Science, 4,* 135–183.

Oesterreich, R. & Volpert, W. (1983). Ein Plädoyer für die Untersuchung der Prozestruktur bei der Erforschung über, Sozialisation durch Arbeit´. *Zeitschrift für Sozialisationsforschung und Erzieh-ungssoziologie, 3,* 59–71.

Osterloh, M. (1993). Arbeitsorganisation und Management – neue betriebswirtschaftliche Ansätze. Invited lecture, 8. Zürcher Symposium Arbeitspsychologie, University of Zurich, September 27–29, 1993.

Peirce, C. S. (1931–1935). *Collected Papers.* Vols. I–VI. (Vols. VII–VIII: 1958). Cambridge, MA: Harvard University Press.

Polanyi, M. (1967). *The tacit dimension.* New York: Anchor.

Raeithel, A. (1983). *Tätigkeit, Arbeit und Praxis.* Grundbegriffe für eine praktische Psychologie. Frankfurt am Main: Campus.

Raeithel, A. (1989). Kommunikation als gegenständliche Tätigkeit. Zu einigen philosophischen Problemen der kulturhistorischen Psychologie. In C. Knobloch (Hrsg.), *Kommunikation und Kognition.* Studien zur Psychologie der Zeichenverwendung. Münster: Nodus Publikationen 29–70.

Raeithel, A. (1991). Zur Ethnographie der kooperativen Arbeit. In H. Oberquelle (Ed.), *Kooperative Arbeit und Computerunterstützung.* Stand und Perspektiven. Stuttgart: Verlag für Angewandte Psychologie 99–111.

Raeithel, A. (1992). Activity theory as a foundation for design. In C. Floyd, H. Züllighoven, R. Budde, & R. Keil-Slawik (Eds.), *Software Development and Reality Construction.* Berlin: Springer 391–415.

Raeithel, A. (1994). Symbolic Production of Social Coherence. The evolution of dramatic, discursive, and objectified meaning systems. *Mind, Culture, and Activity, 1,* 69–101.

Sahlins, M. (1976). *Culture and Practical Reason.* Chicago: Chicago University Press.

Senghaas-Knobloch, E. & Volmerg, B. (1990). *Technischer Fortschritt und Verantwortungsbewußtsein.* Opladen: Westdeutscher Verlag.

Shotter, J. (1970). Men, the man-makers. George Kelly and the Psychology of Personal Constructs. In D. Bannister (Ed.), *Perspectives in Personal Construct Theory,* pp. 223–253. London: Academic Press.

Strauss, A. (1987). *Qualitative Analysis for Social Scientists.* Cambridge: Cambridge University Press.

Suchman, L. (1987). *Plans and Situated Actions.* The problem of human-machine communication. Cambridge: Cambridge University Press.

Toikka, K., Engeström, Y. & Norros, L. (1985). Entwickelnde Arbeitsforschung. Theoretische und methodologische Elemente. *Forum Kritische Psychologie, 15,* 5–41.

Uexküll, J. V. (1957). A stroll through the worlds of animals and men. In C. H. Schiller (Ed.), *Institive Behavior,* pp. 5–80. New York: International University Press.

von Glasersfeld, E. (1987). Contributions to conceptual semantics. *The Construction of Knowledge.* Seaside, CA: Intersystems Publications.

Vygotsky, L. S. (1978). The development of higher psychological processes. *Mind in Society.* Cambridge, MA: Harvard University Press.

Wartofsky, M. (1979). Representation and scientific understanding. *Models.* Dordrecht: Reidel.

Wehner, T. (Ed.) (1992). Sicherheit als Fehlerfreundlichkeit. Arbeits- und sozialpsychologische Befunde für eine kritische Technikbewertung. Opladen: Westdeutscher Verlag.

Womack, J. P., Jones, D. T., & Roos, D. (1991). Die zweite Revolution in der Automobilindustrie. (German translation of The Machine that Changed the World). Frankfurt am Main: Campus.

Zuboff, S. (1988). The future of work and power. *In the Age of the Smart Machine.* New York: Basic Books.

# Index